DATE DUE

Demco, Inc. 38-293

Learning to Learn

Making the Transition from Student to Life-Long Learner

Kenneth A. Kiewra
University of Nebraska, Lincoln

Nelson F. DuBois
State University of New York, Oneonta

Allyn and Bacon

Boston   London   Toronto   Sydney   Tokyo   Singapore

Dedication

To my parents and life-long teachers, Francis and Winifred Kiewra, who taught me firsthand that the pathway to success winds past dreams through hard work and persistence.

KAK

To my loving wife, Gail, whose untiring support and patience served as the inspiration for my continued pursuit of knowledge about learning strategies. I could not have achieved this work without her caring and support.

NFD

Publisher: Nancy Forsyth
Editorial Assistant: Cheryl Ouellette
Marketing Manager: Patricia Fossi
Production Administrator: Susan Brown
Editorial-Production Service: DMC & Company
Text Designer: Donna Merrell Chernin

Photo Researcher: Susan Duane
Composition Buyer: Linda Cox
Cover Administrator: Linda Knowles
Cover Designer: Susan Paradise
Manufacturing Buyer: Suzanne Lareau

Copyright © 1998 Allyn & Bacon
A Viacom Company
160 Gould Street
Needham Heights, MA 02194
www.abacon.com

Library of Congress Cataloging-in-Publication Data

Kiewra, Kenneth A.
     Learning to learn: making the transition from student to lifelong learner / Kenneth A. Kiewra,
       Nelson F. Dubois.
         p.   cm.
     Includes index.
     ISBN 0-205-26319-4
     1. Learning.   2. Learning strategies.   3. Study skills.   4. Self-culture.   I. Dubois, Nelson F.
     II. Title.
LB1060.K47   1997
370.15'23—dc21
                                                                 97-37766
                                                                  CIP

Photo Credits

Bob Kramer/Stock Boston: p. 27; Robert Harbison: p. 54; Brian Smith: p.59; North Wind Picture Archives: p. 70; Tony Neste: p. 86; Robert Harbison: p. 96; Courtesy of NASA: p. 190; Steve Margskjold/The Image Works: p. 203; Rhoda Sidney/Stock Boston: p. 216; Brian Smith: p. 243; John Elk II/Stock Boston: p. 269; Will Hart: p. 277; Kevin Horan/Stock Boston: p. 291; Robert Harbison: p. 293; Mark Antman/The Image Works: p. 318; Brian Smith: p. 339; Brian Smith: p. 341; Tony Neste: p. 379; Beringer/Dratch/The Image Works: p. 381; Robert Harbison: p. 386; Stephen Marks: p. 393; Will Hart: p. 395.

Credits

Preface: p. viii, This material first appeared in *Higher Education: Handbook of Theory and Research*, Vol. X, Copyright © 1994 by Agatha Press, New York, NY. Reprinted with permission.

Chapter 2: p. 49, Shel Silverstein, "Sick," *Where the Sidewalk Ends.* Copyright © 1974 by Evil Eye Music, Inc. Used by permission of HarperCollins Publishers; p. 63, Shel Silverstein, "The Search," *Where the Sidewalk Ends.* Copyright © 1974 by Evil Eye Music, Inc. Used by permission of HarperCollins Publishers.

Chapter 3: p. 79–80, Reprinted with permission from *Structured Exercises in Stress Management*, Vol. 2, copyright © 1984, 1994. Donald A. Tubesing. Published by Whole Person Associates, Inc., 210 West Michigan, Duluth, MN 55802-1908, 218-727-0500.

Chapter 4: p. 118, Steve Becker, "Bridge." Reprinted with special permission of King Features Syndicate; p. 122, J.D. Bransford, and N.S. McCarrell, W. Weimer and D.S. Dalermo (eds.), "A Sketch of a Cognitive Approach to Comprehension," *Cognition and the Symbolic Processes*, 1974. Hillsdale, N.J.: Lawrence Erlbaum Associates. Reprinted with permission.

Chapter 5: p. 140, This material first appeared in *Higher Education: Handbook of Theory and Research*, Vol. X, © 1994 by Agatha Press, New York, NY. Reprinted with permission.

Chapter 7: p. 242, Goetz/Alexander/Ash, "Educational Psychology: A Classroom Perspective," © 1995. Adapted by permission of Prentice-Hall, Inc., Upper Saddle River, N.J.

Chapter 9: p. 301, James M. Henslin, *Sociology*, 2nd edition. Copyright © 1995 by Allyn and Bacon. Reprinted/adapted by permission.

Chapter 10: p. 359, Rebecca J. Donatelle, and Lorraine G. Davis, *Access to Health*, 4th edition. Copyright © 1996 by Allyn and Bacon. Reprinted/adapted by permission.

Printed in the United States of America
10 9 8 7 6 5 4 3 2 1   01 00 99 98 97

Contents

Preface   **vi**

INTRODUCTION

Chapter 1
Changing How You Learn   **2**

Focus Questions   3
Introduction   4
Learning Beliefs and Activities that You Need
     to Change   6
   People Are Naturally Good Learners   6
   Effective Instruction Results in Successful
     Course Performance   8
   The Amount of Time You Spend Studying
     Is Not Important   9
   Repetition Is Crucial for Learning   10
   Constructing an Outline Is Effective   13
   Highlighting Aids Learning   15
   Record Few Lecture Notes   19
   Memorize Information for Tests   20
   The Key to Essay Writing Is Including a Lot
     of Information   22
   Strategies Have Minimal Value and Application
     in the Real-World   23
Make a Commitment to Change   26
   Reasons Why People Do Not Change   26
   Reasons to Change   32
Summary   39
Answers to Focus Questions   40

SELF-MANAGEMENT

Chapter 2
Getting Motivated   **42**

Focus Questions   43
Introduction   44

How Personal Attributions Become Barriers
     to Success   46
   "I Lack Ability"   46
   "I'm Not Sure About My Future Goals"   48
   "I Don't Feel Well"   48
   "I'm Not in the Mood to Study"   50
   "I Don't Like the Subject"   52
   "I'm Not Good at Tests"   53
   "I Was Careless"   53
   "I Have a Personal Problem"   54
How Environmental Attributions Become Barriers
     to Success   55
   "The Class Is Too Large"   55
   "The Class Is Too Early"   55
   "The Class Is Boring"   56
   "The Lecture/Readings Are Disorganized"   57
   "Things Happen to Make Me Miss Class"   57
   "Things Distract Me When I'm Studying"   59
   "The Test Was Unfair"   59
   "There's Not Enough Time to Study"   60
Enhance Your Motivation to Learn by
     Using DIFS   61
   Increase Your Desire   61
   Strengthen Your Intention   65
   Improve Your Focus   69
   Sustain Your Effort   71
Summary   72
Answers to Focus Questions   72

Chapter 3
Time Management   **74**

Focus Questions   75
Introduction   76
Time Management Principles You Should Follow   79
   Invest Time   79
   Invest in Time   85
   Invest Early   86
   Invest Daily   88

Invest Wisely   93
Monitor Your Investment   94
Enjoy Your Investment   96
Summary   97
Answers to Focus Questions   98

FOUNDATIONS OF LEARNING

Chapter 4
Principles of Learning and Memory   100

Focus Questions   101
Introduction   102
Focus Your Attention   105
Attend to Physical Properties   106
Attend to Personally Relevant Ideas   107
Attend to Objectives   108
Don't Rely on Rehearsal for Long-Term
Learning   109
Build Connections   111
Build Internal Connections   113
Build External Connections   118
Monitor Your Learning   122
Summary   126
Answers to Focus Questions   126

Chapter 5
Representations for Learning   128

Focus Questions   129
Introduction   131
Advantages of Representations   135
Similar Information Is Localized   137
Clutter Is Reduced   137
Missing Details Are Apparent   138
The "Big Picture" Is Developed   138
Re-examining the Advantages   138
Types of Representations and Their Relations   139
Hierarchies   141
Sequences   145
Matrices   148
Diagrams   152
Summary   158
Answers to Focus Questions   159

Chapter 6
Constructing Representations   160

Focus Questions   161
Introduction   164
Identifying and Using Alert Words   166
Identifying and Developing Repeatable
Categories   175
Learn to Recognize the Structure
of the Field   176
Learn to Recognize Repeatable Categories
Served on a Platter   177
Learn to Recognize Repeatable Categories
Embedded in the Material   179
Applying Principles of Representation   182
Group Information   185
Order Information   187
Develop Multiple Representations   188
Summary   190
Answers to Focus Questions   192

KNOWLEDGE ACQUISITION

Chapter 7
Learning from Texts   194

Focus Questions   195
Introduction   197
What to Do Before You Read   201
Set the Mood for Reading   201
Survey the Chapter   202
Focus Attention   210
Develop (Drop) an Anchor   213
Budget Time and Effort   215
What to Do While You Read   218
Mark the Text   218
Deploy Comprehension Strategies   227
How to Mark and Comprehend a
Sample Passage   239
What to Do After You Read   243
Generate Representations   243
Generate a Final Summary   244
Compile Questions   246
Summary   249
Answers to Focus Questions   249

Chapter 8
Learning from Lectures   252

Focus Questions   253
Introduction   254
What to Do Before the Lecture   256
    How to Prepare Emotionally   256
    How to Prepare Physically   257
    How to Prepare Mentally   260
What to Do During the Lecture   261
    How to Record Complete Notes   262
    How to Record Organized Notes   270
    How to Record Elaborate Notes   274
What To Do After the Lecture   277
    Make Your Notes More Complete   277
    Make Your Notes More Organized   278
    Make Your Notes More Elaborate   280
Summary   282
Answers to Focus Questions   283

Chapter 9
How to Review for Exams   286

Focus Questions   287
Introduction   288
Why You Should Review   289
Where You Should Review   290
When You Should Review   292
With Whom You Should Review   293
What You Should Review   297
How You Should Review   297
    Prepare the Content   298
    Build Internal Connections   299
    Build External Connections   303
    Conduct Test-Appropriate Practice   304
Summary   320
Answers to Focus Questions   320

    How to Prepare Mentally   326
    How to Prepare Physically   328
    How to Prepare Emotionally   330
Use General Test Strategies   334
Use Specific Item Strategies   342
    Use Item-Type Strategies   343
    Use Item-Form Strategies   348
How to Analyze Test Errors (Error Analysis)   366
Summary   371
Answers to Focus Questions   371

Chapter 11
Real-World Strategy Applications   374

Focus Questions   375
Introduction   376
Using DIFS to Get Fit   378
    Desire   378
    Intention   379
    Focus   379
    Sustain   380
Using Representations to Earn
    Financial Wealth   381
Using Strategies to Become a Chess Master   385
    The Will to Learn   386
    The Skills to Learn   387
Teaching My Child How to Learn   393
    Teaching Reading Comprehension   393
    Teaching Representations   394
    Teaching Studying   395
    Teaching Self-Control   397
Summary   398
Answers to Focus Questions   399

Index   I–1

PERFORMANCE

Chapter 10
Taking Tests   322

Focus Questions   323
Introduction   324
How to Prepare for Tests   326

Preface

A Note to Students

Welcome!

It's about time you got here! Can you believe that you've attended school for over a dozen years and you haven't been taught how to learn?

Schools teach content like math and science, but rarely how to learn such content. Have you ever been taught how to increase your motivation, manage your time, mark a textbook, record lecture notes, review for various types of tests, take tests, and analyze test errors? Probably not. Most schools bypass formal classes in learning strategies, and teachers rarely include strategy instruction in their courses.

Why don't schools teach you how to learn? There may be two reasons. First, because most teachers aren't qualified to teach learning strategies. After all, as students, they weren't taught learning strategies, either.

Second, because many schools and colleges believe that strategy instruction is remedial, something for *correcting* faulty study habits. But we wonder: How can strategy instruction be remedial if strategy instruction never occurred in the first place?

Maybe educators assume that students acquire strategies as naturally as they acquire height and weight. They don't. You learn learning strategies the same way Tiger Woods learned a fluid golf swing: through instruction and practice. Without strategy instruction, most students pick up weak, sloppy strategies like rereading, outlining, highlighting, and reciting, just like an untrained golfer develops an awkward swing.

Learning strategy instruction isn't for correcting, it's for enriching. Powerful learning strategies can transform even so-so students into great learners.

What strategies would you use to learn about fish in the passage below?

Characteristics of Fish

Fish fall into one of three social groupings: solitary, small, or school. Solitary fish generally don't socialize with other fish. Examples of solitary fish are the Hat and the Arch. Although the Hat and Arch are both solitary fish, they differ in several ways. The Hat swims at a depth of approximately 200 feet, whereas the Arch swims at approximately 400 feet. The Arch is 300 centimeters in size; the Hat is 150 centimeters. The Hat is a brown color and eats algae. The Arch is blue and eats minnows.

Fish in small groups are also varied. They can swim at a depth of 200 feet, like the Lup, or at 600 feet, like the Tin. The Lup is black, 150 centimeters, and eats algae. The Tin is tan, 500 centimeters, and eats Flounders.

Fish in schools also vary along several dimensions. The Bone, for example, is 300 centimeters and swims at a depth of 400 feet. In contrast, the Scale is 500 centimeters and swims at 600 feet. The Bone is orange and eats Minnows, whereas the Scale is yellow and eats Flounders.

Most students use weak strategies like rereading or outlining to learn this information. But both strategies present ideas sequentially, so they obscure the relationships among the fish. Neither rereading nor outlining reveals the relationship between a fish's swimming depth and its size, diet, color, and social grouping.

Now examine the representation in Figure P-1 and note the following relationships: As fish swim at greater depths, they increase in size, consume larger prey, grow lighter in color, and socialize in larger groups.

Figure P–1. *Representation Showing Relationships Among Fish*

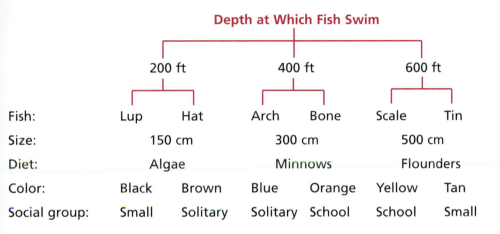

Depth at Which Fish Swim					
200 ft		400 ft		600 ft	
Fish: Lup	Hat	Arch	Bone	Scale	Tin
Size: 150 cm		300 cm		500 cm	
Diet: Algae		Minnows		Flounders	
Color: Black	Brown	Blue	Orange	Yellow	Tan
Social group: Small	Solitary	Solitary	School	School	Small

The representation is helpful in organizing facts and highlighting the relationships among those facts. Representation is just one of many powerful, enriching strategies that you haven't been taught.

When students—you—finally do learn and apply good learning strategies, three things are apt to occur:

First, you'll achieve higher grades in school.

Second, you become an autonomous learner—that is, a learner who learns without assistance. As an autonomous learner, you can learn regardless of whether college instruction is outstanding or poor. After college, as an autonomous learner, you'll be a lifelong learner who can learn things in the real world that make you healthy, wealthy, and wise. You'll be able to learn independently about vitamin supplements, arthritis, mutual funds, tax laws, Renaissance paintings, and child development.

Third, you'll enjoy learning. It's fun to learn when you know how. You can enjoy both the learning process and the knowledge you gain.

This book teaches you how to learn. It covers motivation, time management, learning principles, representation, text learning, lecture learning, test review, test-taking, and real-world strategy applications. It also addresses important concerns such as test anxiety, note-taking, writing, error analysis, and study groups.

This book stresses skill acquisition. It's not supposed to replace books and courses that help you adjust to college life. Alternatively, programs that promote college adjustment are no substitute for acquiring learning strategies. A troubled freshman with a 2.0 grade point average will probably become a contented senior with a 2.0 grade point average unless he or she is taught an arsenal of powerful learning strategies.

This book contains several unique features that help you learn. First, and most important, the book revolves around a single principle. The principle is that information is learned better and more easily when it's connected to related information. When individual puzzle pieces are connected, they form a meaningful picture. When information is connected, it, too, forms a meaningful picture. This book introduces four simple patterns for organizing or connecting ideas so you can see meaningful pictures. These patterns are the book's cornerstones, because they influence all aspects of learning. They help you to select ideas from texts and lectures, represent these ideas in notes, identify relationships during test review, organize essays, formulate test responses, analyze test errors, and succeed in the real world. Learning these four simple patterns pays dividends across your entire learning process now, and across your whole life later.

A second unique feature is that we describe review methods for different types of tests. You probably aren't aware that tests assess facts, concepts, and skills, and that you need different learning strategies for each of these.

A third feature is a section on error analysis. You probably haven't been taught how to analyze your test errors. But error analysis can show you the content you missed (for example, information about positive reinforcement), the type of item you missed (for example, concept), and the error's source (for instance, faulty note-taking). Once you know how to analyze errors, you stop being afraid of making mistakes, because you know you can learn from them and you know exactly how to improve your performance.

A fourth feature is a chapter on real-world applications. You see first-hand how academic strategies can make you healthy, wealthy, and wise outside the classroom.

Last, the book introduces two standard topics, time management and motivation, in fresh, new ways. We show you that time management is really a set of investment principles—the same principles that govern money investments govern time investments, too. And we look at motivation from the standpoint of barriers that can get in the way of your success. You'll see that often, you erect barriers, and that you can overcome any obstacle if you choose to do so.

This book also includes several design features that help you learn. Each chapter contains focus questions, headings, a summary, answers to focus questions, and practice exercises. Before you read a chapter, examine everything in it *except* the answers to focus questions. Doing so increases your attention and reading comprehension. Complete the questions and exercises while or after you read the chapter to check your understanding and promote your skill development.

Each chapter also includes an opening scenario that describes college students like you, who either use effective or ineffective strategies. Keep these folks in mind, because you'll be revisiting some at a class reunion in Chapter 11.

Another helpful feature is the figures appearing throughout the text. These demonstrate how to use the strategies you're learning in that chapter. Pay close attention to them when you see them mentioned in the text.

Last, the book is written in what we believe is a simple, straightforward, entertaining manner. We've left out theoretical arguments and research data in favor of simple principles, powerful strategies, and plenty of practical examples. We even made some occasional stabs at humor to make the book more fun.

Writing this book was a natural extension of our work as educational psychologists who conduct research on learning strategies and who teach courses in learning. As instructors, and now as authors, we're excited about lending a hand to students who want to learn more about learning. There's an old saying that "If you give a man a fish, you feed him for a day, but if you teach him how to fish, you feed him for a lifetime." Let's skip math and science for awhile and go fishin'.

A Note to Instructors

There are two effective and complementary ways to use this book to help students learn. The first is by direct teaching of the ideas and skills in this book. For instance, you present lessons on lecture note-taking and on test review. As you do, we recommend that you have students apply the ideas and skills to at least one target course they are presently taking, such as history or chemistry, so they can practice learning strategies in a natural and meaningful context outside your classroom.

The second way to help students learn involves embedding the ideas and skills in your lessons. Do this as the need for them arises. In this way, your course also becomes a target course, and your classroom a natural and meaningful context for acquiring learning strategies.

Here's how the "embedded" approach works. When students who have skipped class return, the stage is set to discuss the hazards of missing lectures and the compensatory strategies for recouping missed information. It may also be an ideal time to tear down "barriers" that "cause" absenteeism, such as illness, oversleeping, and working for a friend. When students neglect lecture note-taking, the time is ripe for stressing the importance of copious note-taking and for teaching note-taking strategies. While lecturing about time management schedules, you can also teach representation skills by showing students how to construct matrix notes that compare the time schedules. Following your first exam, teach error analysis by showing students how to analyze their errors.

The embedded approach to strategy instruction is identical to the approach that tradespeople use to teach an apprentice. You model the strategy, speak about its advantages and how it's employed, create opportunities for students to practice the strategy, and provide feedback on their strategy use. Through this process, the fishing pole is gradually transferred from your hands to theirs.

Acknowledgments

Writing *Learning to Learn: Making the Transition from Student to Life-Long Learner* was a dream that began many years ago. Many people made important contributions that enabled our dream to come true. Our thanks go out to those people.

We thank our students. You encouraged us to write this book. We appreciate your encouragement and the helpful suggestions you made while reading early versions of this text.

Next, we recognize three dear colleagues and friends whose influence appears throughout our book. Thank you, Dr. Stephen Benton (Kansas State University), Dr. Harold Fletcher (Florida State University), and Dr. Richard Staley (SUNY Oneonta) for all that you've taught us and for your unending support.

This work was also strengthened by the guidance offered by reviewers and consultants. We thank Mary K. Bixby, University of Missouri at Columbia; Stanley Coberly, West Virginia University at Parkersburg; Deborah Daiek, Wayne State University; Judith Lynch, Kansas State University; Charles Martin, California State University, San Bernadino; Ellen Oppenberg, Glendale Community College; Darlene Pabis, Wester-Moreland County Community College; and Monica Zeigler, Pace University, who reviewed early versions of the text and made insightful and helpful comments. We owe special thanks to Dr. David Christian (University of Idaho) who consulted on the topics of motivation and test anxiety and to Dr. Thomas O'Connor (University of Nebraska-Lincoln) whom we consulted on chess.

This book could not have been produced were it not for the many people who shared in its production. We thank the Instructional Design Center staff at the University of Nebraska-Lincoln. Thank you, Ken Jensen and Orville Friesen for designing many of our graphics. Thank you, Christy Hardin and Cindy DeRyke for transforming our stacks of handwritten pages into a professionally typed manuscript.

We also thank the outstanding Allyn and Bacon production staff who made our ideas come to life. Special thanks go to Nancy Forsyth, Senior Vice President and Publisher, who diligently oversaw our book's publication, offered bright ideas, and gently led us through the publication process. Thanks also to Cheryl Ouellette, Editorial Assistant; Susan Brown, Editorial Production Administrator; Linda Knowles, Cover Administrator; Susan Paradise, Cover Designer; Susan Duane, Photo Researcher; Suzanne Lareau, Manufacturing Buyer; and Donna Chernin and Sandra Sizer Moore of DMC & Company, whose design and editorial assistance was remarkable.

Most of all, we thank our families. Our wives, Christine Kiewra and Gail DuBois lent moral support but were also among our toughest and most helpful critics. This book is much better because of their contributions.

Last, we thank our children, Keaton Kiewra, Anna Kiewra, Kurt DuBois, and Jody DuBois for their inspiration. We hope this book helps you in becoming life-long learners.

Learning to Learn

Making the Transition from Student to Life-Long Learner

chapter 1

Changing How You Learn

OVERVIEW

Focus Questions

Introduction

Learning Beliefs and Activities that You Need to Change
    People Are Naturally Good Learners
    Effective Instruction Results in Successful Course Performance
    The Amount of Time You Spend Studying Is Not Important
    Repetition Is Crucial for Learning
    Constructing an Outline Is Effective
    Highlighting Aids Learning
    Record Few Lecture Notes
    Memorize Information for Tests
    The Key to Essay Writing Is Including a Lot of Information
    Strategies Have Minimal Value and Application in the Real World

Make a Commitment to Change
    Reasons Why People Do Not Change
        Lack of Self-Awareness
        Lack of Self-Control
        Lack of Strategies
        Lack of Motivation
    Reasons to Change
        Increase Achievement
        Increase Enjoyment
        Reduce Learning Time
        Take Control

Summary

Answers to Focus Questions

focus *questions*

1. Why are many students ineffective learners?
2. What are the differences among nonperformers, performers, and learners?
3. Can students learn even when instruction is poor?
4. Approximately how long does it take to become a chess Grandmaster? How is time spent becoming a Grandmaster related to studying?
5. How does people's inability to recall all the numbers, letters, and symbols associated with the calling pad of a push button telephone suggest that rehearsal is a weak learning strategy?
6. Why is a matrix superior to an outline?
7. Why is a highlighter a poor tool for marking a textbook?
8. What are your chances of recalling a lecture idea that you didn't record in notes?
9. What are three effective things you can do when studying?
10. What can you do to improve your essay writing?
11. What four obstacles get in the way of changing into a more effective learner?
12. How does lack of self-awareness get in the way of change?
13. How does lack of self-control get in the way of change?
14. How does lack of strategies get in the way of change?
15. How does lack of motivation get in the way of change?
16. What are four reasons to change your learning beliefs and activities?
17. How do strategies place you in control?

Pinball Wizard

During Joel's freshman year in college his grade point average was barely divisible by one. His scholastic future was about as promising as that of a piano player who wears mittens. Joel hated studying because it had as noticeable an effect on his test scores as vitamins have on general health. After a while Joel dispensed with studying and played pinball almost constantly.

Eventually, eye to eye with academic probation, Joel saw his way into an educational psychology course that taught students learning strategies. For Joel and the others in his classroom those strategies were about as familiar as the dark side of the moon. Joel wondered why he hadn't been told about these strategies earlier in his academic career. Were they maybe something that had been introduced that day in second grade when he faked a bellyache to stay home and watch the World Series? Had that lie doomed him all this time?

Joel first put the new learning strategies to the test about midway through a chemistry course during his second year. Up to that point he had attended all the lectures (even though they began really early—10:30 in the morning), and filled his notebooks with formulas for carbon compounds and hydrogen bonds, but he hadn't studied his notes, leaving him as lost as most $20 pens.

For two weeks prior to the midterm exam Joel used the new learning strategies each day. Having given up on studying for quite some time, Joel was at first as rusty as an old swingset. He was also very doubtful that his newly learned strategies could finally supply the lubrication needed to swing smoothly through chemical formulas longer than December shadows. During that two-week period, however, Joel's chemistry knowledge grew and his confidence as a learner rose. When he strode into the test room, Joel was as certain that he could make an A as he could ring up the day's high score on any pinball machine in the Student Union.

During the next class the chemistry professor looked sour when he announced that the test scores ranged from 37 to 98, and that the class average was an abysmal 72. He inquired where the party had been.

But Joel had scored a 98! When he learned that, he wasn't really surprised. He knew he had mastered the material by working hard and using effective strategies.

After that, Joel's pinball scores leveled off but his grade point average came up quicker than a diver with a broken air hose. His 98 in chemistry was quickly followed by many more high scores in other courses, including a string of 100s in Developmental Psychology. Joel enjoyed the high grades and his new-found interest in learning, and he was relieved at being set free from the frustration of trying to study when he didn't know how.

Today, Joel is a college professor helping students become better learners. On occasion, he is still spotted at the Student Union wielding some pretty mean pinball flippers.

This book is for those of you who, like Joel, have not yet been taught how to learn. Strategy instruction can make the difference for you as it did for Joel.

How could Joel get all the way to college without acquiring effective learning strategies? That seems impossible. How about you? Let's examine your learning beliefs and activities. Answer true or false to the following learning statements.

1. People are naturally good learners, or are taught to learn in school.
2. Successful course performance is largely the result of effective instruction.
3. The amount of time spent studying is not important; it is the quality of time spent studying that matters most.
4. Repetition is crucial for learning.
5. Constructing outlines is an effective learning technique.
6. Highlighting your textbook helps you learn.
7. It is best to record few lecture notes by jotting down only those things that you do not understand.
8. You are ready for a test when you have memorized all the relevant information.
9. The key to answering essay questions is including as much relevant information as possible.
10. Learning strategies have minimal value and application in the real world.

Learning Beliefs and Activities that You Need to Change

Many students have misguided beliefs about learning and use weak learning activities. Consequently, they perform below par in school. Here, we uncover why the list of learning beliefs and activities above shows misguided and weak ways to learn.

People Are Naturally Good Learners

> Learning skills must be taught to you and learned by you.

Some people believe that learning ability develops as naturally as height and weight: As you grow older, you naturally learn how to learn. Not so. As you get older, do you naturally learn how to solve quadratic equations, recite the Preamble to the Constitution, change the oil in a car, or play *Flight of the Bumble Bee* on the violin? Of course not. These things must be taught and learned.

The same is true with learning skills. Learning skills must be taught to you and learned by you. Do our schools teach learning skills? Most do not. Our schools teach subjects like math and history, but rarely how to learn such content.

Think about your own education. Did anyone teach you how to motivate yourself, manage time, mark a text, study for various types of tests, analyze test errors, or write an organized essay? Probably not. Teachers don't spend much time teaching learning strategies. Teachers largely teach subjects, not how to learn. It is odd that you are not expected to play *Flight of the Bumble Bee* without musical training, but you are expected to learn without being taught *how* to learn.

If learning is not taught, then how do some students perform so well in school?

Consider that there are three types of students: nonperformers, performers, and learners. Nonperformers know little about how to learn and have low motivation. They spend almost no time on school work and so they perform poorly in school.

Performers don't know much about learning, either. However, they work hard trying to memorize facts for tests. So they perform well on tests . . . but memorized learning is usually short-lived, and it's useless in nontest settings. For instance, the performers might be able to give the definitions of "genotype" and "phenotype" for a test, but later they won't be able to predict what their own kids will be like. Learners know how to learn—how to motivate themselves, manage time, record lecture notes, mark a text, study for various types of tests, analyze test errors, and write an organized essay. Using effective strategies, learners perform well on tests, remember ideas, and apply them in future settings.

Only a handful of students are learners. They somehow acquired learning skills in an education system limited to content instruction and emphasizing performance over learning.

If you are not yet a learner, then this text can help you become one. It is never too late to learn how to learn. If you are a learner, then this text can help you develop into an even better learner. Even seasoned musicians can improve their renditions of *Flight of the Bumble Bee*.

Exercise

Think about your own school career. Write down everything you can remember being taught in school about text learning, lecture learning, time management, motivation, studying, and test-taking.

Effective Instruction Results in Successful Course Performance

> *It is mostly what you do that determines what and how much you learn.*

Imagine two classrooms. In one, Teacher A tells students the objectives of what they are going to learn; presents the lecture in an enthusiastic and organized fashion; inserts questions throughout the lecture; and provides a complete set of lecture notes, a set of study notes, and questions for review. In the other classroom, Teacher B reads from lecture notes in a monotone fashion and offers no help. In which class would you learn more?

You can expect better learning with Instructor A, since the way she teaches helps students learn. But what if Instructor A's students just sit there without taking notes or answering questions, and don't study the notes Instructor A gives them. Meanwhile, what if Instructor B's students take extensive notes, ask meaningful questions, and study effectively. In this case, you expect Instructor B's students to learn more.

Suppose you are a student in Instructor B's class and Instructor B assigns you to learn the midwestern states and their capitals. Instructor B gives you a list of the states and their capitals. What do you do? Use good learning strategies.

A state and its capital can be learned by developing mental pictures relating the state and capital. Columbus, Ohio, for example, might be learned by imagining Christopher Columbus arriving at the New World and encountering several Native Americans waving and saying "Oh! Hi-ooo!" You might remember Topeka, Kansas by imagining a toe peeking from a can.

Learning is only partly based on your instructor's effectiveness and the instructional materials provided. Learning activities are more important. It is mostly what *you* do that determines what and how much you learn. An effective student succeeds in any class even when instruction is poor, but an ineffective student struggles in any class even when instruction is outstanding.

Many students don't believe this. They think their success is because of good instruction and their failure is due to poor instruction. Students who think this way are not motivated to learn because they think they have no control over their success or failure. You need to know that success is due to effective effort (that is, using effective strategies while studying for a sufficient time period), and that failure is due to ineffective effort (that is, using weak strategies while studying for an insufficient time period). Knowing that you control your learning increases your motivation, which, in turn, increases your learning. Motivation is discussed in Chapter 2, "Get Motivated."

Exercise

If possible, describe examples of times you learned a lot even though instruction was poor, and times you learned very little even though instruction was good. Describe specific things you did or did not do in each case that affected how much you learned.

The Amount of Time You Spend Studying Is Not Important

Suppose your dream is becoming a chess Grandmaster. Suppose too that you have available to you the best chess instruction in the world. You have computer programs, books, and a team of Grandmasters helping you eight hours a day to learn to play chess. With such high-quality instruction, how long do you think it would take you to attain Grandmaster status? The answer might surprise you. It probably will take you nearly twenty years. It is a long road from novice to Grandmaster, and there are no short-cuts. Unfortunately, you can't just pour the vast knowledge of a Grandmaster from his head into yours. You must learn it slowly, move by move, in your own mind.

It's the same with studying. Quality studying takes a long time. Mastering a single chapter, for example, requires you to use several hours for reading, text marking, note taking, and studying. There are no quick fixes or shortcuts.

College success requires a major time commitment. In fact, being a college student is a full-time job. How to find and plan time to excel in college (or in chess or music or even playing pinball . . .) is the topic of Chapter 3, "How to Manage Time."

Repetition Is Crucial for Learning

Most students believe that repetition is the key to learning. Let's find out. How many times in your life have you used a push-button telephone? Conservatively, you have probably made 7,000 telephone calls. This is based on an average of two calls per day over just a ten-year period. This does not even include the calls you got from telemarketers while you were eating dinner or taking a shower. And yet, has your repeated use of the telephone resulted in your learning about its appearance? Could you, without looking at a telephone, reproduce the calling pad of a push-button telephone? The framework in Figure 1-1 should help you. Put your cellular aside and try now to complete Figure 1-1 from memory.

Exercise

How much time each week do you spend learning outside of class? You should be spending roughly two hours learning outside of class for each hour spent in class. If you are taking fifteen hours, then you should be working on your courses about thirty hours per week outside of class. School is a full-time job!

Note how you might arrange your schedule to ensure sufficient learning time.

Figure 1-1. *Incomplete Calling Pad for a Push-Button Telephone*

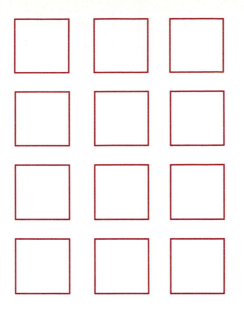

Check your response against the correct one in Figure 1-2. How did you do? Did you remember where all the numbers, letters, and other symbols belonged? Did you know that the letters begin on the second button and that letters *q* and *z* are missing (much like the thirteenth floors in hotels)? Probably not. Most people can't remember the telephone calling pad despite the many times they have used or seen a telephone.

In Chapter 4, "Principles of Learning and Memory," you learn that repetition or rehearsal is a weak strategy for learning, yet many students use a whole arsenal of repetitive strategies—rereading, reciting, recopying, repeating . . . *re-diculous*—while studying. You learn that the key to effective learning is building relationships or connections. Effective students connect new ideas to each other and to their past knowledge in the same way that a puzzler assembles the puzzle pieces to see what the completed puzzle looks like. When they are learning about birds of prey, for example, effective students compare hawks, eagles, and falcons in terms of their size and habitat, and then compare birds of prey to the songbirds studied previously. Learning each bird fact separately makes about as much sense as examining each puzzle piece separately to try to understand the completed puzzle.

Figure 1-2. *Calling Pad for a Push-Button Telephone*

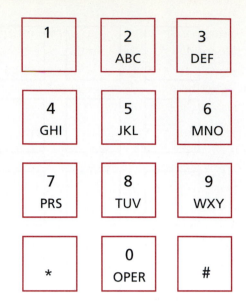

Exercise

Have you played cards a lot? Have you played card games such as "War," "Black Jack," "Old Maid," "Go Fish," "Poker," "Rummy," and "Solitaire"? Try now to sketch what the eight of spades looks like. Get a deck of cards and check your answer. No bluffing!

Constructing an Outline Is Effective

You probably learned to develop an outline to organize lecture or text ideas. A good outline is effective for two reasons: It contains the most important information, and it organizes the information so that various ideas can be related. As an example, read the passage below and the outline that follows. It's about schedules of reinforcement, a topic in psychology.

Schedules of Reinforcement   Suppose you have a pigeon and you want to train it to peck a key. To train the pigeon you give it food pellets for pecking the correct keys. There are four main schedules you can use to deliver the reinforcement. The type of schedule used determines several things about the animal's behavior.

Fixed-interval schedules deliver reinforcement following the first response after a fixed time interval. The pigeon, for example, might receive food for its first peck after a ten-second interval. Fixed-interval schedules produce slow response rates that contain pauses in responding. The animal tends to pause after it's reinforced and then increase responding as the interval ends, because reinforcement is again anticipated. It is relatively easy to extinguish (eliminate) behaviors learned on this schedule.

Variable-interval schedules deliver reinforcement following the first response after a predetermined but variable time interval. The pigeon, for example, might receive food following intervals of 5, 15, 2, and 18 seconds for an average interval of ten seconds. Variable-interval schedules produce slow but steady response rates. It is difficult to extinguish behaviors learned on this schedule.

Fixed-ratio schedules deliver reinforcement following a fixed number of responses. The pigeon, for example, might receive food following every ten key pecks. Fixed-ratio schedules produce rapid responding, although the animal pauses briefly following reinforcement. It is relatively easy to extinguish behaviors learned on this schedule.

Variable-ratio schedules deliver reinforcement after a predetermined, but variable, number of responses. The pigeon, for example, might receive food after making 5, 15, 2, and 18 pecks for an average ratio of ten pecks. Variable-ratio schedules produce rapid and steady responding. It is difficult to extinguish behaviors learned on this schedule.

Schedules of Reinforcement

I. Fixed Interval
   A. Definition: Reinforce first response after a fixed time interval
   B. Example: Food for first key peck after 10 seconds
   C. Response Rate: Slow, pauses
   D. Extinction: Relatively easy
II. Variable Interval
   A. Definition: Reinforce first response after predetermined but variable time interval

B. Example: Food for first key peck after 5, 15, 2, and 18 seconds
C. Response Rate: Slow, steady
D. Extinction: Difficult

III. Fixed Ratio
A. Definition: Reinforce after fixed number of responses
B. Example: Food after every 10 key pecks
C. Response Rate: Rapid, pauses
D. Extinction: Relatively easy

IV. Variable Ratio
A. Definition: Reinforce after a predetermined but variable number of responses
B. Example: Food after 5, 15, 2, and 18 key pecks
C. Response Rate: Rapid, steady
D. Extinction: Difficult

This outline is effective because it contains the most important ideas in an organized form. For example, you can easily see the most important ideas about fixed-interval or fixed-ratio schedules.

What you cannot see at a glance, however, are the ways these four schedules are similar and different. The outline structure, because it reads from top to bottom, actually obscures the similarities and differences. For example, it is not easy to see how the response rates compare across the schedules. A reader must "jump over" other information to determine these relationships. This problem increases for larger outlines covering several pages.

An outline helps you see relationships within a topic (such as fixed-interval) but not across topics (such as fixed-interval versus fixed-ratio). This is why an outline is generally not a good strategy to use.

A more effective way to represent information is the matrix shown in Figure 1-3. Relationships within a topic (for example, fixed-interval schedules have slow response rates with pauses and make behavior easier to extinguish) are easy to see and understand when you read vertically. More important, relationships across topics (the four schedules of reinforcement) are apparent by reading horizontally. Reading across the matrix, you can see that interval schedules cause slow responding but ratio schedules cause rapid responding. You can also see that fixed schedules cause pauses in responding and make behavior easy to extinguish, whereas variable schedules cause steady responding and make behavior difficult to extinguish. Although the same information appears in the outline, you have to get it from many different parts of the outline and then manipulate it to notice the important relationships just mentioned. The matrix puts information about response rates or extinction within the same row so comparisons are easily drawn. The matrix is a more powerful tool than an outline, because it organizes information so that you can easily see relationships

Figure 1-3. *Matrix Representation Shows Relationships Within and Across Topics*

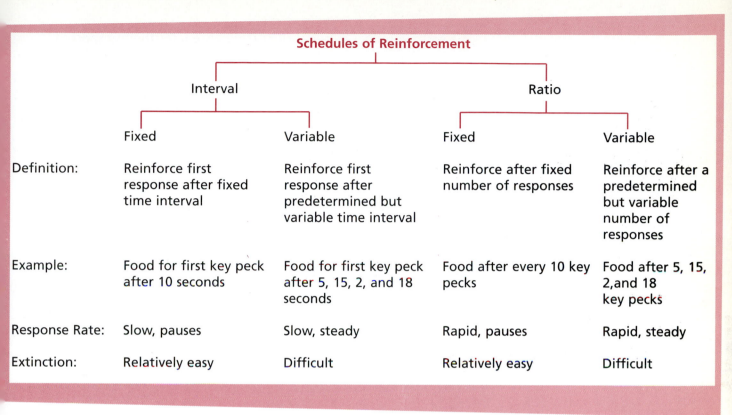

	Interval		**Ratio**	
	Fixed	**Variable**	**Fixed**	**Variable**
Definition:	Reinforce first response after fixed time interval	Reinforce first response after predetermined but variable time interval	Reinforce after fixed number of responses	Reinforce after a predetermined but variable number of responses
Example:	Food for first key peck after 10 seconds	Food for first key peck after 5, 15, 2, and 18 seconds	Food after every 10 key pecks	Food after 5, 15, 2, and 18 key pecks
Response Rate:	Slow, pauses	Slow, steady	Rapid, pauses	Rapid, steady
Extinction:	Relatively easy	Difficult	Relatively easy	Difficult

across topics. The matrix and other forms of representation are formally introduced in Chapters 5, "Representations for Learning," and 6, "Constructing Representations." These representations are the foundation for much of what is taught in this book.

Highlighting Aids Learning

We have thumbed through dozens of used textbooks at our university bookstores and have been nearly blinded by the bright yellow streaks covering nearly every line on every page. See, for example, some sample highlighting in Figure 1-4. In some cases, a rainbow of colors from fuchsia to chartreuse, bleeds from every page. Why? Students believe that highlighting equals understanding. The more and brighter they highlight, the more and better they understand.

Figure 1-4. *Sample Over-Highlighting of a Text Passage*

The earthworm has a special circulatory system for the transport of materials. It is a closed circulatory system, which means that the blood is transported within a closed system of tubes. In the open circulatory system, by contrast, the blood leaves the tubes and passes into large open spaces. Grasshoppers have an open circulatory system.

The highlighter industry might begrudge us, but we urge you to toss aside those highlighters in favor of a dependable pen and some paper. Learning from a text is not a passive process that involves reading and highlighting important ideas. As you read, use a marking system to distinguish topics, subtopics, common categories, and details. Sketch simple lists and frameworks in the margin and construct more sophisticated and complete representations (such as matrices and diagrams) on paper to capture the text's organization. Add your own comments to the text by writing your ideas and questions in the margins. Comment on the author's perspective and argue with her views. Examine Figure 1-5 to see how the same text passage might be marked with a pen.

Reading is an active, even aggressive, process beyond the capabilities of a crude highlighter. Using a highlighter to read is like using a spray can to paint the *Mona Lisa*. We explore methods for text learning in Chapter 7, "Learning from Texts."

Exercise

Try converting the following outline into a matrix to help you see relationships between the sympathetic and parasympathetic systems.

Autonomic Nervous System

   I. Sympathetic System

       A. Dilates pupil of eye

       B. Inhibits salivary gland

       C. Relaxes bronchi producing more rapid breathing

       D. Accelerates pacemaker heart

       E. Inhibits digestion

       F. Relaxes bladder

       G. Inhibits sex organ

  II. Parasympathetic System

       A. Constricts pupil of eye

       B. Stimulates salivary gland

       C. Constricts bronchi producing slower breathing

       D. Slows pacemaker heart

       E. Stimulates digestion

       F. Contracts bladder

       G. Stimulates sex organ

Figure 1-5. *Sample Marking of a Text Passage with a Pen Rather Than a Highlighter*

The earthworm has a special circulatory system for the transport of materials. It is a closed circulatory system, which means that the blood is transported within a closed system of tubes. In the open circulatory system, by contrast, the blood leaves the tubes and passes into large open spaces. Grasshoppers have an open circulatory system.

Is the worm the only one?

Circulatory System

Closed   Open

Transport: Tubes   Open spaces
Example: Earthworm   Grasshopper

Does open system circulate in a particular direction?

How are O_2 and CO_2 transported?

Open transport of gases does not seem feasible.

Exercise

There is no time like the present. Toss your highlighter aside and begin marking this text with a pen.

Use boxes, circles, and underlining to mark important ideas. Draw arrows connecting related ideas. Write your thoughts and organize ideas in the text's margins. Be an aggressive reader.

Record Few Lecture Notes

We applaud our environmentally sensitive students who do not waste paper, but we shudder at the thought of those who conserve this precious natural resource by recording sketchy lecture notes. Some students restrict their note-taking to those occasional lists instructors scribble on the chalkboard or to the unfamiliar terms instructors use. As a result, these students produce incomplete notes that are useless for review. For instance, how would you like to be studying the sketchy notes from health class recorded weeks before and found in Figure 1-6? Good luck!

Figure 1-6. *Incomplete Lecture Notes are Useless for Review*

Cardiovascular Diseases
1. Atherosclerosis
    plaque buildup because endothelium is damaged
    smoking
    cholesterol
2. Myocardial Infarction
    collateral circulation helps
3. Angina Pectoris
    due to atherosclerosis
    ischemia–O_2 is reduced
    nitroglycerin
4. Arrhythmias
    not serious by self
    electrical stimulation
5. Congestive Heart Failure
    pooling blood
    diuretics
6. Heart Disease
    congenital or rheumatic
7. Stroke
    cerbrovascular accident
    thrombus
    embolus
    aneurysm

A lecture goes by quickly, so you need to take **good** notes.

A lecture goes by quickly. You need to take good notes to capture in full the instructor's points and the relationships among those points, or you'll lose them. Believing that simply hearing a lecture means you'll remember it later is folly. In fact, most students can remember only about five percent of any lecture information they didn't write down in notes. During a lecture, pretend that a dying person is revealing the location of a treasure or the cure for cancer. Although you'll need time to plan and carry out your treasure hunt or concoct the remedy, for now, set down all relevant information before it's too late. Strategies for lecture note-taking appear in Chapter 8, "Learning from Lectures."

Exercise

Examine lecture notes that you made earlier this semester. Count the number of words you wrote for each lecture. Work hard to increase the completeness of your notes by writing down more lecture ideas and by recording them more fully so you can understand them better later. Do not write down exactly what the lecturer says. Use your own words to express the lecturer's ideas. Count how many words there are in your new notes. Most likely you will double or triple the completeness of your notes.

Memorize Information for Tests

Suppose you had to learn the following figures of speech for an English test. Could you memorize the definitions and supply them on a test? Probably. Most college students are good at memorizing a series of facts.

Figures of Speech

Alliteration	Repetition of the same initial consonant sound.
Hyperbole	Exaggerated statement.
Metaphor	Term that originally designates an object or idea is used to designate a dissimilar object or idea to suggest comparison.
Onomatopoeia	Formation or use of words that imitate what they denote.
Oxymoron	Incongruous or contradictory terms are combined.
Simile	Two essentially unlike things are compared, often in a phrase introduced by like or as.

But how well could you do answering the following application test questions that do not depend upon memorization?

Name the figure of speech exemplified in items 1 through 5, below.
1. I must have warned him a million times to wear his seat belt.
2. Jumbo shrimp
3. Dine at Daisy's Delicious Diner.
4. The crowd was buzzing.
5. He was in the twilight of his career.
6. Compose a paragraph below, about two people dining at a restaurant, that contains a novel example of metaphor, simile, oxymoron, and onomatopoeia. Label each example.

Techniques used to memorize definitions don't work for identifying new examples, as in items 1 through 5, or for creating your own, as in item 6. Review for these test items by creating a representation that includes definitions, examples, and nonexamples, as shown in Figure 1-7. Then think up and answer practice questions like those in items 1 through 6. Review these with a study group so that each member can complete several practice tests that fellow members have created.

Figure 1-7. *Representation Developed for Reviewing for Application Test Items*

Figures of Speech

	Alliteration	Onomatopoeia	Oxymoron	Hyperbole	Metaphor	Simile
Definition:	Repetition of the same initial consonant sound	Formation or use of words that imitate what they denote	Incongruous or contradictory terms are combined	Exaggerated statement	Term that originally designates an object or idea is used to designate a dissimilar object or idea to suggest comparison	Two essentially unlike things are compared, often in a phrase introduced by *like* or *as*
Examples:	• Big Bad Billy • Sally sells sea shells	• Cuckoo clock • The noisy car putted along.	• Deafening silence • Friendly adversary	• He ate all day long. • He never says a kind word.	• His grace rained down even upon his enemies. • "Let's kick off this staff meeting" he said.	• Her nerves were like steel. • She swayed like a daisy in the wind.
Nonexample:	• Magical mnemonics	• He putted the ball.	• Loud bang	• She is the smartest in the class.	• It rained cats and dogs.	• He had strong nerves.

You must be able to recognize and anticipate different types of tests, and master the review methods associated with each. Review is the topic of Chapter 9, "How to Review for Exams."

The Key to Essay Writing Is Including a Lot of Information

One particular type of test is the essay test. Some students prefer an essay test to a multiple-choice test because they think the essay test is a dumping ground for any or all of their knowledge about a particular topic. In dumping this knowledge, however, students often fail to answer the question adequately, so they fail the test.

Suppose you were asked to write an essay comparing three types of creativity (expressive, adaptive, and emergent) with respect to their motivation, time demands, and impact. Would you write a separate and complete paragraph about each creativity type? Such an essay fails to answer the question of how they compare. A more effective essay is organized by their common topics (motivation, time demands, and impact) and explains how the three creativity types compare along each common topic.

Writing a complete and well-organized comparative essay is easier if you first put the information into a matrix. As mentioned earlier, the matrix structure encourages the learner/writer to see and report relationships across topics. The writer, working from the matrix in Figure 1-8, for example, might report that "the motivation to create is external for expressive and adapative creativity, but internal for emergent creativity. Internal motivation is a must, given that the emergent creative product requires many years to develop. In contrast, expressive and adaptive products require but a few seconds or few weeks, respectively . . . ." Writing from representations and other effective test-taking techniques are addressed in Chapter 10.

Writing a complete and well-organized essay is easier if you first put the information into a matrix.

Figure 1-8. *Matrix for Writing an Essay About Creativity*

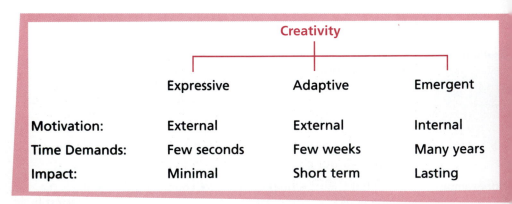

	Creativity		
	Expressive	Adaptive	Emergent
Motivation:	External	External	Internal
Time Demands:	Few seconds	Few weeks	Many years
Impact:	Minimal	Short term	Lasting

Exercise

Return to Figure 1–3, the matrix representation for "Schedules of Reinforcement." Using that matrix, write an essay that compares interval and ratio schedules. Be sure to report comparative relationships, not each fact separately.

--- --- --- --- --- --- --- --- --- --- --- --- --- --- --- --- --- --- --- ---

Strategies Have Minimal Value and Application in the Real World

You might think that learning ends when you graduate from college, law school, medical school, or trade school, but that's when it really just begins. You must continue learning at your job to stay with the times or ahead of them. Attorneys build case knowledge by poring over law books. Medical doctors stay up on medical procedures and drug treatments by carefully reading medical journals and attending seminars. Auto mechanics study repair manuals that go into detail on the parts and processes of a new braking system or an antiquated transmission.

Outside work, learning continues. Pursuing a hobby like chess or photography requires a lot of study. Consider that more books have been written about chess than all other games combined. Should you choose to remodel your kitchen or bathroom, then you must learn about construction, plumbing, city codes, and building permits.

Sometimes learning is not by choice, but by necessity. Perhaps a relative develops multiple sclerosis, bears a child with Down syndrome, or is stricken by Alzheimer's disease. Now you must learn about these afflictions and how to cope with them. The better you learn, the better you work, play, and survive.

The remainder of this section shows how one strategy (representation) helps solve one real-world problem: renting an apartment. Chapter 11, "Real-World Strategy Applications," presents other real-world strategy applications.

You're looking around for a new apartment. You've looked at a lot, and you've decided against the ones that look run down or are way too small.

You pare the list of candidates further by eliminating all apartment houses constructed of sticks or straw and those seen on the television program "Unsolved Mysteries." Finally, you've short-listed four apartments that merit further consideration. How do you choose? Develop a matrix representation like that in Figure 1-9. The matrix helps you compare the apartments along important factors such as square footage and price. The flat on Colt has the most square feet and, not surprisingly, is the highest priced. Calculate and compare "square foot price" (by dividing price by square feet), however, and you note in the matrix's bottom row that the apartment on Colt Street provides the most bang for your buck because you pay only sixty-three cents per month per square foot. Consider too that it has a deck and healthclub, and it's evident that this apartment provides the best value.

Figure 1-9. *Matrix Comparing Apartments Helps You Choose the One Best for You*

	Husker Road	Seminole Avenue	Knick Court	Colt Street
Bedrooms:	1	1	1	1
Square Feet:	460	580	600	800
Proximity to College:	.5 mile	1.5 miles	2.5 miles	4 miles
Proximity to Work:	2 miles	4 miles	6 miles	8 miles
Neighborhood:	+	+++	+++	++
Extras:		Fireplace	Fireplace, deck	Deck, healthclub
Monthly Price:	375	400	475	500
Square Foot Price:	**.82**	**.69**	**.79**	**.63**

Speaking of values, your personal values play a significant role in studying the matrix and choosing an apartment. Perhaps you hate the idea of a long commute to college and work, and you tremble at the sight of a stairmaster. Then this apartment far from college and work is not for you. Perhaps what you really want is an apartment that is affordable, in a good neighborhood, and close to work and college. If so, maybe the flat on Seminole Avenue is for you.

The matrix representation plays another role in apartment renting: determining a fair rental price. Is the Seminole Avenue place fairly priced? To find out, gather public information about comparable apartments in the area. Find out their square footage and what they rent for. Assemble the information in a matrix as shown in Figure 1-10. Next, calculate the square foot price for the comparable apartments by dividing the rental price per month by square feet. Looking across the matrix, it is evident that the average monthly square foot rental price for the comparable apartments is eighty-one cents. This means that the apartment on Seminole Avenue is a steal at only $400 per month. Gathering and organizing information in the real world can really pay off.

Figure 1-10. *Matrix Showing that Seminole Avenue Apartment is a Relatively Good Value*

	Seminole Avenue	Bowden Boulevard	Ward Parkway	Dunn Drive
Square Feet:	600	700	640	860
Rental Price:	475	600	525	650
Square Feet Price:	.69	.86	.82	.76

Explain and demonstrate how you could use a matrix to make decisions about purchasing a new sound system or mountain bike. Also, explain how a matrix might eventually help you select a graduate school.

Make a Commitment to Change

We hope you've learned two things thus far from this chapter. One, you learned what is ahead in this book. You now know there are chapters about motivation, time management, learning principles, representations, text and lecture learning, review, test-taking, and strategy applications. Two, you found out that many of your learning beliefs and activities are wrong. You now know that time-honored strategies such as highlighting and outlining are less effective than marking text and constructing representations. You also know that people are not naturally good learners and must be taught how to learn.

This book intends to do just that: teach you how to learn. Make no mistake about it: this book aims to change your learning activities and beliefs. It's going to change how you manage time, listen, record notes, read, review, and take tests, and it's going to change damaging beliefs such as "I can't learn because I haven't got the ability or because I have a boring teacher."

Change won't come easily, however. For example, consider all the people unable to change damaging or annoying behavior such as smoking cigarettes, not wearing seat belts, regularly eating fatty foods, spending too much money, arriving late for appointments, and leaving the cap off the toothpaste. Changing learning activities and beliefs is no easier.

Reasons Why People Do Not Change

There are at least four major obstacles that get in the way of change. Here, we describe those four obstacles and how this book can help you overcome those obstacles so that you can change your learning beliefs and activities.

Lack of Self-Awareness

Some people don't change because they don't recognize that a problem exists.

Some people don't change because they don't recognize that a problem exists. An alcoholic, for example, might not recognize alcohol's damaging physical, social, emotional, and financial effects.

Students are often unaware that their learning activities can cause problems for them. For example, if you're sitting in the classroom's back rows, you probably don't realize that your seating choice hurts your ability to learn. It is harder for you to see the board, hear the lecturer, and maintain attention from the back rows than it would be if you were seated toward the front.

Some students don't realize that they choose study times and locations that can be an obstacle to learning. Most students study between 7:00 P.M. and 10:00 P.M. in their residence hall room or study lounge—a time when their minds are tired and residence halls are buzzing.

Students sometimes pull all-nighters just before a big test. They're up all night before an exam rereading lecture notes and highlighted chapter portions. These students are unaware that review is best done over many days and weeks, and that it involves sophisticated activities such as creating representations and constructing and answering practice exams.

Some students look at their test grade and then just file the test paper away, unaware that the graded test holds important information about error types and sources, or that such information can increase future test achievement. Students who do not recognize these situations as problems certainly won't make changes.

This book directly raises your self-awareness in two ways. First, this chapter includes a very important Self-Awareness Questionnaire. Complete this questionnaire so you can see how you learn now. As you read, compare your current learning practices to those that we show you in this book. Second, each chapter in the book begins with a scenario describing ineffective (and sometimes effective) learning. Increase your self-awareness by determining whether you share some of the ineffective behaviors demonstrated by people described in the scenarios. To change ineffective behaviors, you must first become aware of what you actually do.

Students are often unaware of ineffective behaviors

Exercise

Self-Awareness Questionnaire

Respond to the following statements honestly by indicating the degree to which each statement describes your beliefs or activities. There are five possible responses:

1. *Very frequently*—The statement refers to you almost all the time.
2. *Frequently*—The statement refers to you most of the time.
3. *Sometimes*—The statement refers to you about one-half the time.
4. *Infrequently*—The statement refers to you only occasionally.
5. *Very infrequently*—The statement rarely or never refers to you.

Motivation

1. I believe ability determines my performance.
2. I believe poor teachers, unfair tests, and personal problems cause bad grades.
3. I develop challenging goals.
4. I develop plans to meet my goals.
5. I work hard to meet my goals.
6. I find ways to get around learning obstacles.
7. I sustain effort over a long period of time.

Time Management

8. I invest about forty hours per week going to class and studying.
9. I use written schedules to plan my time.
10. I plan ways to find additional time for school work.
11. I begin long-term projects and test preparation long before due dates and test dates.
12. I study for tests and complete projects over several weeks rather than in the final days.
13. I use pockets of time wisely.
14. I monitor my use of time.

Learning and Memory

15. I guide my attention by focusing on objectives and questions.
16. I eliminate or ignore distractions in the classroom and while studying.
17. I use rehearsal strategies for long-term learning.
18. I relate ideas being learned with one another.
19. I relate ideas being learned to previously learned ideas.
20. I ask questions of myself as I learn.
21. I anticipate what questions will appear on the test.

Representations

22. I learn information one idea at a time.
23. I construct outlines when I learn.
24. I construct representations when I learn.
25. I identify "alert" (key) words when I read or listen.
26. I look for the structure of the topic or field under study.

27. I search for topics, repeatable categories, and details when I read.

28. When creating representations, I group and order information.

Text Learning

29. I survey the table of contents, chapter headings, overviews and summaries, representations, highlighted material, objectives, and questions before reading.

30. I highlight text material.

31. I mark the text's topics, repeatable categories, and details.

32. I use comprehension strategies while reading, which means I raise questions, make predictions, and create summaries.

33. I record notes in the text's margins.

34. I generate representations after I read.

35. I generate a final summary after reading.

Lecture Learning

36. When I attend lectures, I am excited to learn and record notes.

37. I attend all classes and arrive on time.

38. I review past lecture notes and text readings in advance of lectures.

39. I write few lecture notes.

40. I slow the lecturer down when he/she speaks too quickly.

41. I organize notes during and after the lecture.

42. I elaborate on lecture notes by adding my personal comments.

Review

43. I review only so I can do well on exams.

44. I review in places that are free from distractions.

45. I am prepared for a test three days ahead of the test.

46. I form and participate in study groups.

47. I review by rereading notes and text highlights.

48. I relate ideas when I review.

49. I develop and answer practice tests when I review.

Test-taking

50. Before I take a test, I am confident that I will earn a high mark on the test.

51. When I get anxious during a test, I can reduce anxiety.

52. I establish a time plan for completing the test.

53. I read instructions carefully.

54. I make notes on the test while I work.

55. I retake the test when finished to best check my answers.

56. I use the allotted time for the test.

Real-World Applications

57. I use desire, intention, focus, and sustainment (DIFS) to increase motivation when I'm addressing real-world issues.

58. I apply the time management investment principles such as "investing early" and "investing daily" when I'm addressing real-world issues.

59. I monitor my thoughts and actions in real-world settings.

60. I develop representations when addressing real-world issues.

61. I use text-comprehension strategies when reading material in the real world.

62. I relate ideas when I learn in real-world settings.

Lack of Self-Control

Ask a smoker why he smokes cigarettes and he probably answers, "I can't quit" or "It's hard to stop because my friends (or family or coworkers) smoke." Both replies suggest that the smoker has no control over his own smoking. The smoker believes that his willpower cannot be strengthened and that social pressures cannot be curbed. Is that really true? Of course not. If he were offered a million dollars to successfully quit smoking, our smoker's willpower would soar and social pressures deflate faster than a bicycle tire in a glass recycling bin.

In school, students blame poor academic performance on factors such as low ability, a boring instructor, a disorganized textbook, or physical illness. And they say that such factors are beyond their control. You cannot possibly overcome low ability, a boring teacher, a disorganized text, and illness, can you? Of course you can. Remember that $1,000,000?

Many students doubt they can learn because they think they lack ability. They figure that ability is a fixed thing determined by their parents' genes. Not so. Ability is a rubber band, not a shackle. You can stretch that rubber band a long way through hard work. Top engineers, artists, musicians, athletes, and research scientists stretched their way to the top. Hard work propelled them, not innate ability. Consider that as youngsters, these top performers were sometimes less talented than their own brothers and sisters. It was desire and hard work that got them to the top. Talent or innate ability are worthless if they aren't developed. Remember the story about the tortoise and the hare? The hare had outstanding ability, but

squandered it snoozing under a tree. As a student, you can be absolutely sure that your ability can be stretched.

What about overcoming the other factors? Hard work and effective strategies are all that is needed. If your instructor is boring, then make class more interesting by offering comments and questions. Reduce boredom by taking a lot of notes. If you take complete notes, you can't get bored. If your textbook is disorganized, then use effective reading and representation strategies to organize the content and build relations among ideas. If you're sick, then have a classmate tape-record or videotape missed lectures. Or you can call your classmates to get assignments, and to ask the instructor for additional time to catch up if necessary.

A point made in all chapters, and primarily in Chapter 2, is that you control your learning through hard work and effective strategies. And with control comes change.

Lack of Strategies

Some people don't change because they haven't got the strategies that enable change. Fortunately, strategies are learnable. Someone afraid to fly in an airplane, for example, can learn strategies for overcoming the fear of flying.

Changes in academic performance are made by using an arsenal of learning strategies. For example, you can improve your reading comprehension by employing strategies such as questioning, predicting, organizing, elaborating, and summarizing. You can improve how you review for tests by using strategies such as mnemonics (memory tricks) and self-testing. Throughout this book, there are strategies to help you become a more effective learner.

Lack of Motivation

Perhaps the chief reason people don't change is because they don't want to change. Consider smokers who are aware of smoking's link to cancer, heart disease, and emphysema. They've learned smoking cessation strategies, and they believe they are capable of quitting. Why don't they quit? They lack motivation. They don't want to quit.

The same is now true regarding learning. If you don't want to change, then no one and nothing can make you change. Drop this course. Return this book. You will *not* change. Perhaps you are required to take this course or read this book because you are on academic probation, but you really don't want to change—someone has told you to change. Forget it. You won't change unless you want to.

Can your motivation to change be fueled? Maybe it can. We point out that you have already displayed motivation to change: You have nearly completed this book's first chapter. We hope maybe you've found your personal reason for changing and improving your learning skills. But if you're not sure about your motivation to change, we offer you the following "menu" of reasons to change the way you learn. Maybe a spark will ignite and we can fan the flames of change in forthcoming chapters.

> Perhaps the chief reason people don't change is because they don't **want** to change.

Menu

Exercise

Before considering our menu of reasons to change your learning beliefs and activities, consider your own reasons. What motivates you to learn about learning and improve learning activities? Describe your personal motivations.

Reasons to Change

In this section, four reasons to change learning beliefs and activities are offered: increase achievement, increase enjoyment, reduce learning time, and take control.

Increase Achievement

Would you like to earn high grades and learn more about marine biology, meteorology, American literature, and Impressionist art? The strategies presented in this text help you learn more and achieve higher grades. Strategies such as predicting, questioning, and elaborating help you understand your texts. Representation strategies help you organize text and lecture ideas. Mnemonic and self-testing strategies help you review for exams. Test-taking strategies help you perform at your absolute best. Error analysis strategies help you pinpoint error sources and raise achievement on subsequent exams.

There is considerable research evidence indicating that students who learn powerful strategies, like those presented in this book, increase their academic achievement. Even top students benefit. Consider that students at the University of California at Berkeley were performing below expectations in a physics class and were using weak strategies. When they were taught powerful strategies for organizing ideas and representing problems, their achievement increased markedly.

How important is high achievement? Consider what happens when you apply for employment or to graduate school. An employer or graduate admissions director will not seriously consider an applicant with a 2.5 grade point average when dozens of applicants hold 3.5 grade point averages.

Increase Enjoyment

One author recalls his early years as a golfer. He played for a long time without improvement and without enjoyment. Hitting worm burners or slicing shots into the drink was not fun. When this lifelong duffer finally took lessons and learned some basic golf strategies (such as holding the club at the handle end), his performance and enjoyment rose tremendously. It's not much fun doing things poorly.

Many students hate school because they're not good at it. They use ineffective strategies like rehearsal, or they use no strategies at all and fail miserably. Failure is not fun.

Other students employ effective strategies that bolster achievement and enjoyment. The enjoyment stems from two sources, one of which is high achievement. It's fun to perform well and receive recognition and awards such as high grades or a place on the Dean's List. The enjoyment also stems from pursuing your own interests. Watch little kids who care nothing about tests and grades, but uncover knowledge for its own value. They just want to know more about bees, tsunamis, sandhill cranes, or chess. They enjoy learning.

In college, it's fun to learn about moray eels, gulf winds, *The Murders on the Rue Morgue*, and van Gogh's *Starry Night*—when you have the tools and the strategies for doing so. It's fun to use the strategies, because they mark your progress toward understanding. As you produce notes, representations, questions, predictions, and summaries, you mark your path toward understanding. You see the progress you've made and what's still ahead. It's satisfying and enjoyable to know more about cranes and eels, and improve in chess and golf. It's fun to progress from hitting worm burners to knocking down occasional pars and birdies.

It's hard to believe that some college students cut class, sleep through lectures, and never crack their textbooks. They are missing out on golden learning opportunities. Find your North Star, your bliss, and follow it. Effective strategies can guide you and help you enjoy the ride.

Reduce Learning Time

Students who use traditional strategies like highlighting, rereading, reciting, and outlining are wasting time. As you know now, these strategies are relatively ineffective. Highlighting does not equal understanding. A more

Exercise

What is your North Star? What is your bliss? Do you want to become a medical doctor, a writer, or a chess expert? Do you want to become a successful accountant or teacher? Do you want to be an outstanding parent? Record your hopes and dreams. Describe how effective learning activities will help you climb to the stars and make the climb more enjoyable.

---

effective reading strategy is note-taking. The long trails of yellow lines throughout textbooks should be replaced with notes marking topics, subtopics, common categories, and details. Notes should also raise questions, make predictions, organize ideas, elaborate on ideas, and summarize ideas.

Rereading and reciting are repetitive and time-consuming strategies with little payoff. In addition to the note-taking strategies mentioned above, prepare for exams by constructing representations and generating and answering practice tests.

Representations should replace outlines because outlines are organized linearly and therefore obscure relationships across topics. Recall the outline on "Schedules of Reinforcement," presented earlier in the chapter. The outline was slow to reveal how the schedules compare in terms of response rate and extinction. The slower response rates of interval schedules compared to ratio schedules and the steady responding associated with variable schedules versus fixed schedules, for example, were immediately evident when reviewing the matrix representation, but they were obscured in the outline. Students studying representations locate information more rapidly and can learn facts and relations better than students who are studying outlines or text.

Learning to use representations is a real time-saver because representations are useful for all aspects of learning. They help you search for important ideas while reading texts or listening to lectures, represent ideas in notes, review for various types of tests, answer test questions, analyze test errors, write effectively, and solve real-world problems. If they can do all that, you need to use them!

Strategies not only reduce learning time, they help locate and manage time for learning. In Chapter 3, where we talk about time management, you learn to locate time by developing a block schedule that shows commitments, chores, leisure periods, and study times, and by purchasing time with money or trade. For example, the student who can't use a keyboard and pays a typist to type a term paper is purchasing time for other endeavors.

You learn to manage time by developing and following semester, weekly, and daily schedules. These schedules help you make smart time investments. You learn to invest early, daily, and wisely. Time-wise students plan and begin long-range projects and test preparation immediately. They make frequent investments in long-range tests and projects by working on them almost daily. They use pockets of time wisely between classes, when driving, or waiting for appointments. They organize lecture notes, listen to recorded lecture tapes, and make cards with definitions and examples for easy review.

> *Strategies not only reduce learning time, they help locate and manage time for learning.*

Take Control

Too often, students feel like pawns in the game of college learning. They feel powerless against fast-talking instructors, fat textbooks, and comprehensive final exams. Students must realize that an army of powerful strategies stands behind them ready to fight for them, and help them advance, grow more powerful, and win at college learning.

College is a scary place for students who feel they have no control over what's happening.

Consider these settings:

- The lecturer is speaking at about 860 words per minute and sparks shoot from your pencil as you scribble notes trying to keep pace.
- A disturbing personal problem occupies your mind, leaving no room for you to think about philosophy or algebra.
- You're bored during lectures. Your mind drifts like a bottle on the ocean.
- There is too much material to learn in preparation for the final test. You feel like your brain might explode.

- You have no idea what the test will be like. You've known more about blind dates. You worry whether you're ready for it.
- Looking at the test, your brain turns to mush and your fingers to stone.

Lacking control or being out of control is an unfortunate choice you make for yourself. You can instead choose to control what occurs as you learn and perform. Control, though, has a price. Control is secured through the use of effective strategies.

When a lecture is presented too rapidly, choose to slow it down or compensate so that you can still take good notes. The most obvious slow-down strategy is asking the lecturer to speak more slowly. Just as you wouldn't allow someone reading the winning number at a raffle to speak too fast, don't allow your instructor to race ahead. You can rein in a galloping instructor by asking a question or offering a comment. Other ways to harness the lecture ideas for later review include using abbreviations and notations, tape recording the lecture, questioning the instructor after class, and comparing notes later with fellow students. These strategies help you overcome a rapid lecture by securing complete notes.

Personal problems such as breaking up with a significant other are difficult to handle. You've lost control, though, when the problem seeps into other important aspects of your life and interferes with sleep and school. Regain control by isolating the problem. An effective strategy for dealing with this is to set aside adequate time each day to deal with the problem. Perhaps talk with counselors or friends for a couple hours each day until the problem is resolved. By focusing your attention on the problem during designated periods, you work constructively toward resolving it, and you prevent the problem from spilling into other important activities.

Boredom is also a choice. You can control or prevent boredom with effective learning strategies such as sitting in the front row at lectures, asking and answering questions, thinking about the material, and taking plenty of notes. It's hard to be bored if you're taking complete notes. If the material seems drier than a sauna, then try talking with graduate students and the instructor to learn what they find refreshing about the content. Find ways to apply that material to your own interests. In philosophy class, for example, use philosophical arguments to prove that your roommate does not exist.

Preparing for a final exam can be overwhelming. How can you possibly digest the tons of lecture notes and readings from throughout the semester? Time management and learning strategies help you gain control. Effective time management means you invest early and invest daily. Invest early by beginning the long ascent toward the final exam immediately, at the very beginning of the term. Remember that the best time to plant a tree is twenty years ago; the second best time is today. Beginning on the first day of class is not too soon.

Think of time management as climbing a mountain. Invest daily by moving closer to the crest each day so that in the final days, you can just enjoy the charge to the top. The unsteady climber, in the final days, is deep in the mountain's shadow. No amount of climbing now will bring him closer to the summit. Prepare every day for the next exam and the final exam. Cramming cannot get you to the top of the mountain and it won't produce excellent test scores—only anxiety and failure.

Powerful learning strategies can tame the mountain of information. Strategies such as representation, summarization, and self-testing are the footholds to the top.

It's frightening to have no idea about how you'll be tested. Instructors should inform students about what content they're going to test, what type of items (fact, concept, or skill) are included, and what form the test will take (for example, multiple choice or essay). Telling students this is hardly revealing the answer to the $64,000 question. It's more like leading them to pan for gold in rivers instead of trees.

Fortunately, there are ways for you to gain control. Ask the instructor about the test. Perhaps explain to the instructor that your study methods depend, in part, on the nature of the test. Also consult students who have recently taken the class from this instructor. They can usually help you predict test item content, type, and form.

If you can't find out the answers to any of your questions, then you should prepare for the full range of item types by using strategies aimed at learning facts, concepts, and skills. Build your confidence by predicting, generating, and answering test questions. Answer your own items and those of study group partners.

Most test-anxious students chose to be anxious by not preparing adequately for the test. Underprepared students are nervous about tests—and rightly so. Control anxiety by preparing yourself three days in advance of the exam. Test yourself so thoroughly that there is nothing the instructor can ask you that you haven't already asked yourself. Have faith that your hard efforts as reader, note-taker, and reviewer will produce excellent test performance.

When your nerves become frayed during testing, glue them back together with stress reduction strategies such as deep breaths and imagining a peaceful sanctuary. Use test-taking strategies that reduce anxiety, too, such as answering simple items first and sketching a time plan for completing the exam.

At a broader level, exert control by recognizing that you are capable of learning in any situation—even when instruction is poor. Effective learning always overcomes poor instruction. When information is disorganized, organize it using representations. When information seems unrelated, anchor it to past knowledge. When study guides and practice questions are unavailable, generate your own. Effective learners learn in spite of poor instruction.

> Powerful learning strategies can tame the mountain of learning.

In the future, after you've graduated, strategies offer control as well. You'll want to become an expert at your job. You'll want to peruse personal interests like chess, photography, and music. You'll have to learn about ordinary and self-preserving interests such as carbon monoxide detectors, mutual funds, and sump pumps. And you'll be yanked toward unexpected and life-altering diseases and problems such as multiple sclerosis, autism, and Alzheimer's.

If you can't learn about such things, you'll be less knowledgeable, less secure financially, and forever at the mercy of salespeople, technicians, and medical personnel who will do your thinking for you. Do not relinquish control.

Finally, remember that when things get tough, the tough get going. For every problem there is a choice: Give up or keep going. None of the strategies for success will work unless you do. Use the motivation, time management, and learning strategies that help you keep going. March forward, and even if the steps are tiny ones, soon you'll be a pawn no longer. Make a change for the better.

Exercise

Have additional sparks been ignited in your mind as you've read this last section? Have you found other reasons to learn how to learn? If so, add them to the list compiled earlier on page 34.

Summary

This chapter has three purposes: It introduces forthcoming topics, identi-fies and challenges your current learning beliefs and activities, and helps you commit to changing current learning practices.

This book covers a wide range of learning topics. Chapters 2 and 3 address self-management issues: Chapter 2 addresses motivation; Chapter 3 addresses time management. Chapters 4 through 6 address foundations of learning: Chapter 4 covers learning principles; Chapters 5 and 6 discuss representations. Knowledge acquisition is the focus of Chapters 7 through 9. Text and lecture learning are addressed in Chapters 7 and 8, respectively, and review is discussed in Chapter 9. Performance is the focus of the last two chapters. Chapter 10 covers test-taking and Chapter 11 covers real-world applications.

We challenged many long-held beliefs and long-practiced activities in this chapter. We hope you now recognize the following as true:

- People are rarely taught how to learn. Schools largely teach subjects, not strategies.
- Effective learners learn under any conditions, even when instruction is poor.
- Meaningful learning takes a long time. There are no shortcuts.
- Repetition is less effective than meaningfully relating ideas. Puzzle pieces must be connected for the picture to emerge.
- Outlines obscure relations among topics. A matrix representation aids relational learning.
- Highlighting does not equal understanding. Mark text passages with pens and make margin notes.
- Lecture notes should be complete. Note completeness is related positively with test performance.
- Memorization strategies have limited usefulness. Creating represen-tations and developing practice tests are good review strategies.
- Essays should be well organized. Preparing and writing from repre-sentations, such as matrices, can aid essay organization.
- Academic strategies such as representations are useful in real-world settings.

The goal of this book is to change you into a learner or make you a more effective learner. Unfortunately, you will not change if you lack self-awareness, self-control, strategies, or motivation. This chapter begins building self-awareness, advocates self-control, foreshadows the strategies taught, and offers a menu of motivators. Hopefully, you are poised for change.

1. Many students are ineffective learners because they were never taught how to learn. Schools commonly teach content such as math and science, but rarely teach strategies for how to learn.

2. Nonperformers know little about how to learn, have low motivation, and perform poorly in school. Performers are motivated, know little about how to learn, but perform well on tests because they memorize. Performers, however, have difficulty applying their knowledge in nontest settings. Learners are motivated and know how to learn. They perform well on tests and apply their knowledge in nontest settings as well. This information about types of students is summarized in Figure 1-11.

Figure 1-11. *Representation Summarizing Types of Students*

	Nonperformers	**Performers**	**Learners**
Learning:	Know little about learning	Know little about learning	Know how to learn
Motivation:	Low	High	High
Performance:	Poor	Good on tests but low in nontest settings	Good in test and nontest settings

3. Effective students learn whether instruction is good or bad. Effective learners use strategies to teach themselves the material.

4. It takes approximately twenty years for a chess player, given the best chess training, to ascend to Grandmaster level. There is much to learn. Similarly, effective test preparation takes considerable time. Mastering chess or studying for a test both require large time investments. There are no shortcuts.

5. Asked to place all numbers, letters, and symbols on a blank telephone calling pad, most people are unable to do so, despite having used the calling pad thousands of times. The repetition or rehearsal involved in making and receiving calls is not enough for learning the calling pad.

6. A matrix is superior to an outline because it helps students recognize relationships across topics. Outlines obscure across-topic relations.

7. A highlighter is not a good tool for marking textbooks because it discourages readers from using active reading strategies, such as marking topics, subtopics, and details; sketching lists and frameworks; and writing comments, questions, summaries, and arguments.

8. The probability of recalling a nonnoted lecture idea is five percent. This low percentage suggests that lecture notes must be complete.

9. Three effective study activities include studying with a group, creating representations, and constructing and answering practice tests. Standard memorization techniques like rehearsal are ineffective for answering certain types of test questions.

10. Essay writing is improved by writing from a matrix that organizes essay content.

11. Four things might prevent you from changing into a more effective learner: lack of self-awareness, lack of self-control, lack of strategies, and lack of motivation.

12. Someone who is unaware that a problem even exists is not likely to change. For example, a student unaware that studying in a noisy study lounge is a problem is unlikely to study elsewhere.

13. Some people believe they are not in control of their own destiny. They believe that innate ability, luck, or external factors control them, so they make no attempt to change, because they think change is outside their control. This is not true. People succeed because they work hard. "Ability" as a scientist or musician is not inborn, but acquired through hard work. Success in school is not due to luck or having outstanding teachers, but rather how hard and effectively you work. You control your destiny.

14. Strategies are the tools for change. A student who wants to improve his or her reading behavior, for example, cannot make this change without learning effective reading strategies.

15. Lack of motivation is the biggest obstacle to change. Someone who doesn't want to change won't change, even if they're aware that a controllable problem exists and that strategies for handling the problem are at hand. Some students lack motivation to learn.

16. Changing learning beliefs and activities can increase your level of achievement, increase your enjoyment of college and the learning process, reduce your learning time, and provide you with greater control.

17. Strategies place you in control. For example, when a lecturer speaks too quickly, there are strategies you can use to slow her down or handle the rapid presentation. When you're preparing for a test, strategies help you plan and manage study time and do the best preparation. Even personal problems, such as broken relationships and raising an autistic child, are manageable when you use effective strategies.

chapter 2
Getting Motivated

Overview

Focus Questions

Introduction

How Personal Attributions Become Barriers to Success
  "I Lack Ability"
  "I'm Not Sure About My Future Goals"
  "I Don't Feel Well"
  "I'm Not in the Mood to Study"
  "I Don't Like the Subject"
  "I'm Not Good at Tests"
  "I Was Careless"
  "I Have a Personal Problem"

How Environmental Attributions Become Barriers to Success
  "The Class Is Too Large"
  "The Class Is Too Early"
  "The Class Is Boring"
  "The Lectures/Readings Are Disorganized"
  "Things Happen to Make Me Miss Class"
  "Things Distract Me When I'm Studying"
  "The Test Was Unfair"
  "There's Not Enough Time to Study"

Enhance Your Motivation to Learn by Using DIFS
  Increase Your Desire
    Develop Challenging Goals
    Identify Enjoyable Goals
    Establish Behavioral Goals
    Make Goal Statements
  Strengthen Your Intention
    Use Mental Imagery
  Improve Your Focus
  Sustain Your Effort

Summary

Answers to Focus Questions

focus
questions

1. Why is it a bad idea for you to believe that success depends on ability?

2. How can your uncertainty about future goals become a barrier to success?

3. How can you control factors, such as illness or not finding a parking space on campus, that lead to you missing or being late to classes?

4. How can you create a good or bad mood for studying?

5. How can you do well in a course you dislike?

6. Why is it a problem if you attribute poor test performance to carelessness?

7. How can you prevent a personal problem from interfering with your success?

8. How can you succeed in large classes?

9. How can you deal with a boring professor or text?

10. How can you overcome disorganized texts or lectures?

11. What are the four components of motivation?

12. What are the three characteristics of good goals?

13. How can mental imagery improve your motivation?

14. Can you make an argument that talent is developed and not inborn?

"It's over. I'm dead. Make the funeral arrangements,"
George remarked solemnly to his roommate after
attending his first sociology class of the new semester.
"No way I'm going to even pass this course,"
George lamented. "The deck is stacked against me."
"What's wrong with the course?" George's roommate
asked sympathetically.
"What's wrong?" George echoed.
"Well, let me tell you.

"First, the class meets at 7:30 in the morning. I'm no morning person," George admitted wearily. "Classes should never begin before street lights are turned off," George proclaimed, as if citing an official ordinance.

"Second, the class meets in the Hawkins Building clear across campus. I believe that's a toll call from here," George quipped. "By the time I trudge over there, I'm late for class.

"Third, the class is huge: There are three hundred students. The class outdraws our basketball team," George admitted ruefully. "I sit way in the back and I can barely see or hear the instructor.

"Fourth, the instructor is BORRR-ING," George said. "He talks like a dentist with a mask on. I've seen statues move more than he does.

"Fifth, the lectures are hard to follow. One minute the instructor's talking about socialization, and the next minute he's talking about sororities and fraternities," George said, rolling his eyes.

"Sixth, the book is as thick as the New York City Telephone Directory and not nearly as interesting.

"Seventh, I heard the instructor gives true-false tests. I think they're tricky," George said. "I'm so gullible that I believe everything I read is true.

"Eighth, I really don't know how I'm going to find the time to study for this class. I have to work forty-plus hours a week to pay for school and cover my auto insurance payments—which just keep climbing," George added somberly.

"Ninth, I know I'll have trouble concentrating when I do study, having recently broken up with Debbie and Angie," George said dejectedly. "I can't get them out of my mind.

"Last, I just don't like sociology. I mean, what relevance does sociology have for me?" George asked. "When I'm designing buildings with other architects and engineers, we're not exactly going to discuss so and so's theory of group dynamics."

"Phew. You're right," George's roommate lamented. "You don't have a prayer. I'll round up the pallbearers."

Is George dead (figuratively speaking)? Or, to paraphrase Mark Twain, are reports of his death greatly exaggerated?

George cites several reasons for his impending doom, such as a large class, personal problems, and a dislike for the subject matter. But are these reasons for poor performance, or are they excuses? We believe they are excuses.

E ffective performance is a result of your skill and your will. Skill is the collection of strategies that you use. Much of this book describes strategies that can make you a skilled learner. Will is motivation. Motivation is a conscious choice to succeed. However, many students like George make conscious choices to fail or to perform poorly. They do so by attributing their poor performance to personal judgments such as, "I'm having personal problems," or external factors such as, "The class is too large." In reality, factors such as these are either irrelevant or controllable.

Return to George for a moment, and his reasons for failing sociology. Suppose George's rich aunt offers to pay him $10,000 if he earns an A in sociology. What do you think would happen then? Would a large class stop George? No. He would probably sit near the front where he could pay closer attention. Would his personal problems derail him? No, he would use strategies such as note-taking to improve his concentration during lectures and while studying, and he would deal with his personal problems at another time. Would George's disdain for sociology prevent him from earning the money? No way. George can hate sociology and still exhibit the skills and muster the will he needs to succeed. The fact that George dislikes sociology has nothing to do with his performance in the course.

We begin this chapter by presenting and then challenging many of the attributions or excuses made by students like George. We divide these faulty attributions into two categories: Those dealing with personal factors (personal attributions) and those stemming from the environment (environmental attributions).

Excuses are the nails used to build a house of failure.
Don Wilder and Bill Rotten, *North America Syndicate*

How Personal Attributions Become Barriers to Success

"I Lack Ability"

One of the greatest receivers in the history of the National Football League was Raymond Berry of the Baltimore Colts. His teammates probably joked, "He is small, but he's slow." Berry didn't fit the mold of typical wide receivers, who are usually tall and fast. Yet Berry was one of the greatest. He had a knack for getting into the open and catching the ball. Berry honed these skills during countless hours of practice with the Colt's quarterback, Johnny Unitas.

The point of this story is that Berry made up for his lack of natural ability by spending considerable time practicing and honing important skills.

Effective performance is a result of your skill and your will.

Another example in which low ability has proven unimportant is in special education. Students who are learning-disabled or who have below-average intelligence can learn memory strategies that markedly improve their memory performance.

Believing that you lack ability is dangerous, because it can rule out how you can use strategies and how you can spend time. A person who believes "I do poorly because I lack ability" is also likely to believe that strategies will not help, nor will spending more time. But effective strategies improve the memory performance of special students, and spending time practicing made Raymond Berry a great receiver.

Attributing good performance to high ability is almost as dangerous as attributing poor performance to low ability. There are three reasons for this: First, if you believe that your good performance is due to high ability, you might not try very hard. For example, you might not take notes during a lecture because you think that your strong memory will capture and keep all the key points. Or you might not study much, believing that your memory will serve you well when you take your exams. After all, why should you work hard if you believe that ability, rather than hard work, leads to success?

Second, if you equate success with high ability, you might later attribute any poor performance to low ability. For example, many students perform successfully in high school, where the workload is relatively light and exams test mostly simple facts. In college, however, many students who were successful in high school perform poorly because of the increased workload and the more difficult exams. Students who originally explained their high school success in terms of high ability now compare themselves to their more successful classmates, and attribute their college failures to low ability. Because they think their problem is lack of ability, these students resist learning strategies for success or spending more time learning.

Third, if you attribute good performance to high ability, you probably won't change your present strategies. Your reasoning is, "I have plenty of ability, and I'm performing well. Therefore, I don't need to learn new strategies." Unfortunately, this conclusion is false. Even in college, top students often use ineffective strategies, and they can benefit from learning strategies.

For example, the University of California in Berkeley conducted a classic study with students in the freshman class. University of California at Berkeley has very competitive entrance requirements, so most of its entering students have very high ability. Still, the study showed that these students were using ineffective strategies in physics and thus were performing poorly. When the students were taught strategies for classifying and representing physics problems, their physics performance increased markedly. So you see, even among high-ability students, strategies make a difference.

Remember, you perform effectively because of your skill and will, not because of your ability.

"I'm Not Sure About My Future Goals"

I recently received a phone call from John, a former undergraduate student. He is now interested in attending graduate school in psychology and was seeking information about the programs and expectations of certain schools. I didn't remember John very well. Before discussing the graduate schools, I asked John about his undergraduate GPA. John remembered that he had a 2.4, but that he was capable of performing much better. He reasoned that he didn't know what he wanted to do back then, but that now his goals were clear. I told John as gently as possible, "Although you want to attend graduate school, the graduate schools are not going to want you." It was too late to discuss his grades. John had already made choices in college that resulted in low grades. John put little time into his studying, choosing instead to work full time and socialize downtown most evenings.

Many college students are uncertain about their future goals. There is nothing wrong with that. Attending college provides a wonderful opportunity to sample many areas and ideas, and to determine interests and goals. However, not having clear goals during college is all the more reason to perform well, so that poor performance now doesn't block the paths and goals you may want to pursue later. For John, it may be too late to get into a quality graduate program, because he didn't consider that achieving his future goals depended on academic success as an undergraduate. You should cover your bases and perform at your best now so that you don't get shut out tomorrow.

"I Don't Feel Well"

Some students allow an illness to stand in the way of reaching their goals, and others do not. Consider the cases of Anna and Jennifer. One night, Anna arrived, early as usual, for her three-hour night class. Speaking with her, it was evident that she had a miserable cold and a hacking cough. Anna completed the test administered during the first hour of class and remained for the two-hour lecture. The other student, Jennifer, left immediately after the test. She complained that she was catching a cold and wasn't feeling very well. Their test scores reflected their outlooks more than their illnesses. Anna scored a 97 and Jennifer a 75.

By all standards, Anna was very sick and should have stayed home, but she wasn't going to allow her sickness to block her commitment to class and learning. Jennifer, who was not very sick, let her illness become an obstacle.

SICK

by Shel Silverstein

"I cannot go to school today,"
Said little Peggy Ann McKay.
"I have the measles and the mumps,
A gash, a rash and purple bumps.
My mouth is wet, my throat is dry,
I'm going blind in my right eye.
My tonsils are as big as rocks,
I've counted sixteen chicken pox
And there's one more—that's seventeen,
And don't you think my face looks green?
My leg is cut, my eyes are blue—
It might be instamatic flu.
I cough and sneeze and gasp and choke,
I'm sure that my left leg is broke—
My hip hurts when I move my chin,
My belly button's caving in,
My back is wrenched, my ankle's sprained,
My 'pendix pains each time it rains.
My nose is cold, my toes are numb,
I have a sliver in my thumb.
My neck is stiff, my voice is weak,
I hardly whisper when I speak.
My tongue is filling up my mouth,
I think my hair is falling out.
My elbow's bent, my spine ain't straight,
My temperature is one-o-eight.
My brain is shrunk, I cannot hear,
There is a hole inside my ear.
I have a hangnail, and my heart is—what?
What's that? What's that you say?
You say today is . . . Saturday?
G'bye, I'm going out to play!

Motivated students and instructors don't let illness prevent them from doing their jobs. Students who are sick can arrange for another student to tape-record or videotape a lecture. An instructor who is ill can videotape a lecture for students. Years ago, one of this book's authors videotaped lectures from a hospital bed following the removal of his appendix. His students were heard to remark that this was cutting-edge material.

Do you remember the news reports about the third grader in Lincoln, Nebraska, the one who competed in and won citywide swimming tournaments in spite of the fact that he was receiving radiation therapy and other treatments to combat brain cancer? For this brave child, illness was not an obstacle.

Next time you're feeling sick, consider whether your illness is really bad enough to knock you out of the game and keep you on the academic sidelines.

"I'm Not in the Mood to Study"

A professional is someone who can do his best work when he doesn't feel like it.

Alistair Cooke

Many students believe that their moods are outside of their control. Actually, students put themselves in the mood for not studying. They actually develop plans for doing so. Do you want some proof? Record five plans that you use for not being in the mood to study in the exercise below.

Perhaps you recorded some of the following plans for creating a bad mood:

- Studying where it is noisy
- Studying when friends are going out for the night
- Having to read six chapters at one time
- Studying alone
- Studying when a favorite television program is on
- Studying so you could get a high (or passing) grade

Exercise

Record five plans that you use for not being in the mood for studying. We'll get you started by providing the first two plans.

1. Studying late at night

2. Got a hot date

3.

4.

5.

All of these plans are conscious choices. You could just as easily make choices that create a positive mood for studying, such as:

- Studying in the morning or between classes when you're more alert
- Studying before your date arrives or studying with your date
- Studying in a quiet location, such as a study carrel in the library
- Studying before friends go out for the night
- Studying a chapter a week, rather than six at once
- Studying in a group, rather than alone
- Studying now and watching a favorite program on videotape later
- Studying to learn, rather than to get a grade

Perhaps the main reason for students not being in the mood to study is that they're not sure *how* to study. And without instruction in how to study, many students use ineffective and passive strategies such as *re*reading, *re*copying, and *re*citing. Such strategies are "*re*diculous."

Studying is more satisfying when you use active strategies that result in tangible study products, for instance, a marked text, visual representations, study questions and answers, and summaries. This book explains these and other active strategies that should teach you how to study, which will put you in a better mood for studying.

Remember that mood is something *you* create. You can choose to create a positive or a negative mood for studying.

Exercise

What works for you? Identify five choices you could make to put yourself in the best possible mood for studying. (We did the first one for you.)

1. I want to learn more about this subject

2.

3.

4.

5.

"I Don't Like the Subject"

A common complaint heard from students is that they dislike the subject matter. Consequently, they expect—or allow themselves—to do poorly in the course. (For example, a student will say, "I'll aim for a C in this class.")

Students who have expectations like these should first consider the plight of my former student John, mentioned earlier. Poor performance now can hurt you later. If you think of it this way, then not liking a course is irrelevant. Whether you like the course or not, it is important to perform well. In life, you may not enjoy driving to work, cutting the lawn, making dinner, or completing your income tax forms. So what. These and other distasteful activities have to be done.

More to the point here, it is possible for you to learn to like a course. Suppose that you dislike biology. We offer two suggestions: First, find out more about biology. Read articles, attend lectures, talk to graduate students and professors in biology. Find out why they have chosen biology as a field of intensive study. As you learn more about biology, your interest is likely to increase. Second, try to apply biological ideas to things that are important and familiar to you. For example, biology can answer many questions you might have about yourself and others, such as:

- Why do I get sick?
- Why do I recover from sickness?
- Why do I need so much sleep?
- How can I train for a sport most effectively and efficiently?
- Are hair loss and wrinkles imminent?
- What cancers are preventable and curable?

As you learn about biology, consider its ideas and implications as they relate to your own life and interests.

Exercise

Remember George at the start of the chapter? He didn't like sociology. On your own sheet of paper, explain to George why his dislike for sociology is irrelevant.

"I'm Not Good at Tests"

Some students attribute their poor performance to the format of the test, for example, multiple-choice or essay. When they say that the test format was hard, our conversation with them might go like this:

Student: I'm lousy at multiple-choice tests.

Instructor: Who was the first president of the United States: a) Lincoln, b) Jefferson, c) Washington, or d) Johnson?

Student: Washington, of course.

Instructor: I thought you were poor at answering multiple-choice questions?

Student: Well, that question was easy.

Instructor: That's the point. If you know the answer, multiple-choice questions are not difficult.

Most test-taking problems are really study problems. Students who study effectively are prepared for all forms of questions covering all types of learning. This book shows you how to study for and take various types of tests.

Exercise

Convince George from the example at the beginning of the chapter that his perceived difficulty with true-false tests is an excuse.

"I Was Careless"

Occasionally, you really do make careless errors while taking tests. More often, you might say your test errors happened because of carelessness, rather than the real reason: ineffective studying. This reasoning explains how students might miss three different multiple-choice questions about a concept such as reinforcement and still attribute their errors to carelessness.

The problem with this reasoning is that if you believe that carelessness really was the cause of your error instead of poor test preparation, then you are not likely to study any differently next time. At best, you might be more careful while taking the next test.

Isolate personal problems and deal with them at appropriate times, and in appropriate ways

But what if you analyze why you made certain errors? Were the errors the result of incomplete note-taking, lack of comprehension, failure to study appropriately, or some other reason? You need to find the real source of your errors and repair them, rather than blaming poor performance on unrelated factors, such as carelessness.

"I Have a Personal Problem"

As a college student, you will probably experience personal problems that range from being physically challenged to having an ailing family member to a wrenching breakup with a partner. You might find yourself thinking about that problem while you're sitting in English class, or maybe reading a history textbook, or trying to study for a biology exam. The problem distracts you, and you might begin to think that the problem is the direct cause for ineffective study behaviors and poor academic performance. However, letting a personal problem distract you is a choice *you* make.

We are not suggesting that personal problems are unimportant. Not true. They are very important. However, effective students have strategies for isolating the problem and dealing with it at appropriate times. For example, you might put aside time to meet with a counselor or talk with a partner at a time when doing so does not interfere with class attendance or studying. You might record thoughts and feelings in a journal as they occur and think about them later that evening. History is filled with people who had awesome personal problems but nevertheless achieved great success. For example, President Roosevelt was badly crippled by polio and was confined to a wheelchair—but that didn't stop him from becoming one of the greatest presidents we've ever had. The point is, people like Roosevelt don't allow personal problems to interrupt their work.

Exercise

On your own sheet of paper, list personal problems that occupy your attention when they should not. Develop a plan for addressing the problems when time permits.

How Environmental Attributions Become Barriers to Success

"The Class Is Too Large"

Some college classes enroll more people than are in an entire high school graduating class or in some students' hometowns. Large classes can be intimidating and impersonal, but they don't need to be "too large" for you. You can do several things to make a huge class seem more personal and comfortable. First, sit toward the front, where there are fewer distractions between you and the instructor. Sitting toward the front, you can make eye contact with the instructor and get the impression that he or she is speaking directly to you.

Second, ask questions and offer comments. Most instructors welcome student questions and comments—even when the class is big. Comments and questions show instructors that you are interested. Remember, too, that this is your education and you're paying for it. Don't be afraid to speak up if you have something to contribute.

Finally, be mentally active. In your mind, try to answer the instructor's questions, raise your own questions, and think about what the instructor says. Look for relationships among presented ideas or how the ideas relate to your background knowledge. Evaluate the merit of the ideas the instructor presents. Mental activities like these keep you tuned to the lecture despite the large class size.

"The Class Is Too Early"

If you were out in the real world and you tried telling your boss or your drill sergeant that you weren't a morning person, it is very, very doubtful that either would be sympathetic.

Avoid blaming poor performance on scheduling factors that are controllable. If you prefer sleeping in, try to arrange to take classes later in the day. When you must take classes earlier, then adapt your schedule. Going to bed earlier at night is one good way to overcome the early class problem. Getting up early to exercise and eat a healthy breakfast (think of this as brain food—because that's what it is!) before your first class might also put you in a positive frame of mind. B. F. Skinner, the noted behavioral psychologist, got up at 4:00 A.M. each day and wrote until 7:00 A.M., a time when most people are just rising. This early morning period was the most productive part of Skinner's day. Perhaps it can be yours.

Exercise

Explain to George why it's true that a class that is both early and large is not a real barrier to success in his sociology class.

"The Class Is Boring"

Classes are not boring. Boredom is a choice you make. If you find that a lecture isn't stimulating, there are several choices you can make to combat boredom. During the lecture you can record a set of quality notes—notes that are complete, well organized, and elaborated. Elaborations, perhaps made with a different colored pen, are notations that go beyond the lecture content. For example, you might jot down references to related knowledge, criticisms, evaluations, and questions and answers. Recording high-quality lecture notes is incompatible with boredom.

As we mentioned previously, lectures can become more interesting if you make comments and ask questions of the instructor throughout the

CLASSES ARE NOT BORING FOR STUDENTS WHO RECORD QUALITY NOTES, WHO MAKE COMMENTS, AND WHO ASK QUESTIONS.

lecture. Reading more about the topic, particularly in advance of the lecture, also makes the lecture seem more interesting. After the lecture, you can speak with the instructor or fellow students to learn more about the topic.

Texts aren't boring, either. You can choose to become bored while reading them. Some of the strategies you can use to aid your text comprehension and thereby reduce boredom include marking the text, constructing a quality set of notes, generating and answering questions, and writing summaries. When you listen and read aggressively, you cannot be bored.

"The Lectures/Readings Are Disorganized"

Sometimes lectures or texts seem to be disorganized, or scattered like puzzle pieces dumped from a box, making it difficult to understand how ideas relate to one another. When information appears disorganized, ask the instructor how the pieces fit together. Remember, you are the consumer. If you are dissatisfied with the product (the text or lecture), then ask for help.

You can also assemble the puzzle and uncover the text's or lecture's organization. One important method involves searching for "alert words" that reveal how information is organized. Words like *types* or *parts*, for example, alert you that information is organized hierarchically. The phrase *parts of an atom*, for example, alerts you to the idea that atom is the general, or superordinate, term and that its parts (neutrons, protons, and electrons) are the subordinate, or more specific, terms. This hierarchical relation is shown in Figure 2-1. Methods for identifying alert words and organizing and representing information graphically are covered in Chapters 5 ("Representations for Learning") and 6 ("Constructing Representations").

Figure 2–1. *Representation for Parts of an Atom*

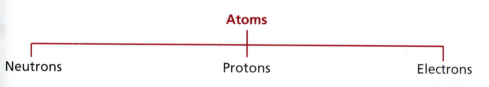

"Things Happen to Make Me Miss Classes"

Students have posed hundreds of excuses for missing class, and every time, they blame their absence on some "uncontrollable" force. A sample of excuses and our solutions and reactions are presented in Figure 2-2.

Also, don't expect your instructors to pardon you from your sins. Often, students ask instructors if it is okay if they miss class due to illness or a touring grandmother. Even if the instructor does provide absolution, ask yourself whether it is really okay to miss vital lecture content that cannot be fully recaptured in textbooks, course handouts, borrowed notes, or conversations with classmates. Can you miss class? Of course you can. It's your choice.

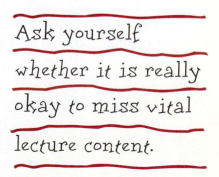

Ask yourself whether it is really okay to miss vital lecture content.

Figure 2–2. *Sample Excuses and Solutions*

Excuses	Solutions
"My ride didn't show up."	Find more dependable friends. Call a taxi. Run. Would you leave your fiancée at the altar because your ride to the church didn't show up?
"I couldn't find a parking place."	There were probably several spaces available at 7:00 A.M. Park early in the day when spaces are available. Park off campus and walk. Use public transportation. Ride your bicycle. Would you miss a concert that you paid for because you couldn't find parking nearby?
"I had to work for a friend."	Did the friend force you to do so? Tell your friend that you have a prior commitment to attend class. Would you work for your friend when you have expensive tickets to a play?
"I had to pick up my grandmother at the airport."	Ask your grandmother to wait until your classes are finished. Arrange for a friend to chauffeur her. Order a taxi, bus, or limousine for her. Grandmother will respect your commitment to school and probably slip you a few bucks in support of it.
"I overslept."	Use multiple irritating alarm clocks, placing one across the room. Arrange for a wake-up call. How long would you remain employed if you overslept while working in a large corporation or as a teacher?

Quick Tips if You *Must* Miss Class

- Arrange for a friend to videotape the class.
- Arrange for a friend to audiotape the class.
- Arrange for friends to record detailed notes for you to borrow.
- Ask fellow students questions about the class.
- Ask the instructor for reading materials related to the class.

Exercise

List five more excuses students make for missing classes. On another sheet of paper, challenge each excuse and provide a solution.

1.

2.

3.

4.

5.

"Things Distract Me When I'm Studying"

From time to time you probably complain about environmental distractions while studying, such as the telephone ringing all the time or a roommate who plays the stereo, bounces tennis balls off the wall, or snores too loudly. Again, you choose these distractions when you study in places where they're most likely to happen. Students who study in a residence hall lounge where people come and go, talk, giggle, munch on snacks, sneeze, cough, and sniff make this choice more for social reasons than academic ones.

Find a quiet, private location to study. This could be in your room, the library, or under a tree in the park. Sometimes, like vacation oases, effective study spots must be discovered. Be creative. You might study in vacant campus classrooms at night, in a part of the library undergoing renovation (when the carpenters are through their work), or in the stands lining the soccer field (when games are not in progress). Studying early in the morning is also an ideal way to beat distractions. Morning is one of the quietest times on college campuses.

Find a quiet, private location to study

"The Test Was Unfair"

Have you ever attributed a bad grade to an unfair test? Tests often do contain poor items that are too hard, fail to discriminate between those who know and do not know the content, or fail to correspond to course objectives. Instructors should ignore these items when they evaluate student performance. However, students who blame their poor performance on the nature of the test or the scoring method probably won't improve their test preparation for the next test.

Students who perform poorly on tests often blame the instructor and display hostility toward the instructor. This is evident when the student publicly challenges every test answer that was marked wrong. The student becomes offensive and repeatedly asks questions like, "Why did I get this wrong?" or "Why wasn't my answer right?" This student isn't interested in understanding why an answer was wrong, only in challenging the instructor.

Brooding over poor test performance, which they attribute to teacher unfairness, leads some students to cut class, retreat to the back of the room, sit sideways in their chairs with arms folded, and stop listening and taking notes. These behaviors are counterproductive. There is no way that acting like this can lead to better performance on the next exam. Even if a test is unfair, don't make choices likely to result in even lower test performance on the next exam. Most importantly, analyze your test errors, deter-

I DESERVED A HIGHER SCORE ON LAST MONTH'S TEST!

mine their source, and take productive steps toward correcting them.

Blaming poor course performance on the instructor's grading policies is also futile. For example, a student who has a 69 average and receives a D in the course might contend that the grade should be a C, since it was only one point shy of a C average. The student blames the instructor for giving a low grade. Students must realize that instructors do not give grades, they assign them based on a student's academic performance. Instructors don't choose grades, students do. Students can choose to earn an A or an F. The student who received a D chose to earn test and assignment scores that averaged less than 70%.

The tendency to blame somebody or something else for poor performance is often seen in sports. When a team loses, the officials get blamed. Consider the following situation: With five minutes left in the game, a basketball official calls a fifth and final foul on the team's star player. The player leaves the game with her team trailing by one. A videotape of the call indicates that the player did not foul, and that the call was wrong. The team goes on to lose by three points. Afterward, the coach is livid and berates the official who made the bad call. The coach blames the official for the loss.

Now examine the "stats" for the losing team: Twenty-one turnovers, 32% shooting from the field, eight for fifteen from the free-throw line, and outrebounded 48 to 62. You decide whether the bad call was the reason for the loss. Don't forget that the star player had four previous fouls and the team was trailing at the time the fifth foul was called.

This is not to say that instructors are always right and students are always wrong. Our point is that students need to identify the real source of their poor test or course performance. They need to take steps toward improving performance next time, usually through better study methods.

When you do believe that you have been evaluated unfairly, then you should discuss the matter privately and politely with your instructor. Explain why you think a test item was unfair, perhaps because it was unclear or didn't touch on course objectives. Provide evidence why your answers or assignments were worth more than the assigned value. If your instructor's responses are unconvincing, you can take your grievance to the department chairperson, who might refer you to a grievance committee within the instructor's department.

"There's Not Enough Time to Study"

Do you have enough time to study? Many students claim they do not. They cite other commitments like work, sports, and family. College success depends on spending a lot of time studying—roughly two hours outside of class for every hour in class. Carrying a full course load, a student should study about thirty hours per week. How can you find thirty hours per week for studying? As you will learn in the next chapter, you must make sacrifices, such as reducing the number of hours you work or play each week, and you must learn to invest time more wisely. Reducing lunch hours to twenty minutes and studying while waiting for appointments or between classes are examples of wise time investments. Rather than blame poor academic performance on a lack of time, it is possible to manage time more effectively so that school work, employment, and play are accomplished.

Exercise

George contends that he has little time for studying because of the full-time job he needs to pay his tuition and car insurance. How might you now interpret George's situation and what advice might you offer him?

Enhance Your Motivation to Learn by Using DIFS

The personal and environmental attributions examined in this chapter are not reasons for poor academic performance; they are excuses. There are only two reasons that account for student success or failure: skill and will.

Skill is strategy use. Effective students use effective strategies. Ability alone is not sufficient. To benefit from this book, you must believe that strategies make a difference and that strategies can be learned. For instance, you must believe that writing summaries is effective and learn to do so.

Will is motivation. Motivation to learn means choosing to succeed rather than to fail in academic performance. Motivated students do not erect barriers such as the ones described in this chapter. Motivated students display the four factors that characterize motivation: **D**esire, **I**ntention, **F**ocus, and **S**ustainment (**DIFS**). Remember, DIFS makes a difference.

Increase Your Desire

In 1993, a New York Yankees pitcher realized his lifetime dream of throwing a no-hitter in the major leagues. A remarkable feat, this was made more remarkable because the pitcher, Jim Abbot, has only one arm. Abbot throws, catches, and occasionally bats with his single arm. As a youngster, Abbot's missing limb didn't squelch his dream or minimize his desire. Abbot is proof that desire is the engine that turns the wheels of fate.

Desire means wanting to accomplish some goal. Successful students are high in desire. They develop goals that are challenging and enjoyable. They state their goals and identify specific behaviors that help them achieve those goals.

Develop Challenging Goals

What are the goals of American youth? Based upon what appears in the national media, it seems that society wants its youth to "say no to drugs" and "stay in school." Is this the best our society can do? Are these the goals that dreams are made of? Do you believe these were Einstein's goals as a youth? There is nothing challenging about these goals. "Stay in school?" That's kid stuff. Replace that goal with mastering courses and graduating with honors. "Say no to drugs?" You can do better than that. Say "yes" to developing a healthy lifestyle that includes nutritious foods, regular exercise, plenty of sleep, and a clear mind.

Speaking of Einstein, he admonished his fellow scientists for their meager research goals. He said, "I have no patience with scientists who take a board of wood, look for its thinnest part, and drill a great number of holes where drilling is easy."

As a student, apply this to yourself: Never back down from a challenge. Strive for mastering and earning an A+ in every course. We're always shocked when we ask students to write down at the start of a semester what grade they expect to earn. More than half report they expect to earn a grade less than A. Set challenging goals and go after them. No one ever rises to low expectations.

Exercise

Turn the meager goals listed on the left into challenging goals. The first few were done to get you started.

Meager Goals	**Challenging Goals**
1. Read Chapter 4.	1. Comprehend Chapter 4.
2. Pass Spanish.	2. Ace Spanish.
3. Study history for an hour.	3. Generate a time line, a summary, and study questions for history.
4. Complete student teaching.	4.
5. Get a job.	5.
6. Take fifteen credit hours.	6.
7. Attend all lectures.	7.
8. Make a time management schedule.	8.

Identify Enjoyable Goals

Success is a journey, not a destination.

Consider Kiewra's experience: I have been a runner for nearly twenty years. During that time I have set and met many training and racing goals. One goal I have never accomplished, however, is breaking two hours and thirty minutes in a marathon (roughly 5:45 per mile pace for twenty-six miles). The fact that I have never reached this goal is inconsequential. The point is that I have striven to reach it, and I have enjoyed the years of planning and training that have gone into the attempt. In fact, there was never much celebration after a goal was met. The real fun came in setting the next goal and setting out after it.

When Jim Thorpe, arguably the greatest athlete of all time, was stripped of his Olympic medals for having played professional baseball, he was unflappable. His reaction was that the officials could take away the medals, but could never rob him of the enjoyment that came in attaining them.

Our point is that it is the process—not the product—that is most enjoyable. Competing or working at your highest level is what's fun. Pursue, for the most part, goals whose paths wind through enjoyment. Don't spend too much time on pursuits that bring you little pleasure. Avoid the trap of chasing a dream that is not your own. We all know people who go to college (although they hate doing so) to land a job (that they hate) that leads to a more prestigious and higher-paying job (that isn't much fun and which requires long hours and living somewhere they don't want to live).

Enjoy college and the academic goals you set. Do this by choosing a major and courses that interest you. Whenever possible create and pursue projects you enjoy. Participate in activities that are fulfilling.

Remember how you spend your days is how you spend your life.

THE SEARCH

by Shel Silverstein

I went to find the pot of gold
That's waiting where the rainbow ends.
I searched and searched and searched and searched
And searched and searched, and then—
There it was, deep in the grass,
Under an old and twisty bough.
It's mine, it's mine, it's mine at last. . . .
What do I search for now?

Establish Behavioral Goals

When you're setting your goals, do so by defining the behaviors you'll need to accomplish your goals. For example, don't say that you want to be a good writer. This goal is too vague. It doesn't specify the behaviors you demonstrate when the goal is met. A better goal might be "I will write essays that include topic sentences, more active verbs, better transitions, and correct grammar." These are behaviors that are observable and measurable.

Behavioral goals are specific. Goals such as studying for one hour are too vague. Instead, identify your activities and the products you'll produce. For instance, you might say that you will read Chapter 7 aggressively and produce a marked text, representations of the relationships among text ideas, and several questions and answers to share with your study group.

Make Goal Statements

Whether you're setting broad long-term goals, such as graduating with honors, or specific short-term goals, such as recording quality notes from your history text, you should jot down brief goal statements on index cards. These statements should reflect your desires. Post the goal statements on your notebooks or above your desk to remind you about your goals. Kiewra posted the goal statement "sub-three-hour marathon" on the refrigerator to discourage snacking and on his nightstand to boost training motivation on cold or rainy mornings. As one final reminder of their dreams, many football teams post goal statements in the tunnels heading out to the field.

One of the most dangerous forms of human error is forgetting what one is trying to achieve.

Paul Nietze

Exercise

Try turning these vague goals into behavioral goals.

Vague Goals	Behavioral Goals
1. Learn history.	1.
2. Study math for two hours.	2.
3. Improve my time management.	3.
4. Work harder.	4.
5. Be a better student.	5.

Exercise

Below are sample short-term and long-term goal statements related to college and career. List your own short-term and long-term goal statements related to college and your career. Be sure your statements reflect goals that are challenging, enjoyable, and behavioral.

Goal Statements

College

Short term

1. Earn A's in core courses in education.
2. Volunteer in elementary classroom one day per week.
3. Be elected to student senate.
4. Land part in school play.
5. Make Dean's List.

Long term

1. Graduate with honors.
2. Have successful and rewarding student teaching experience.
3. Complete two courses toward masters degree.
4. Develop a reading program to help nonreaders.

Career

Short term

1. Get elementary school teaching job.
2. Coach tennis.
3. Teach drama club.

Long term

1. Attain doctoral degree in education.
2. Become reading specialist for school district.

Strengthen Your Intention

"Intention" means planning to meet the goal.

A runner who wants to run a marathon in less than three hours has to develop and follow a plan that results in a sub-three-hour marathon. For example, the runner plans to run a minimum of fifty miles per week for eight weeks preceding the marathon. Included in that weekly fifty-mile total are planned workouts involving a twenty-mile run, a hill workout, a run of ten miles at a 6:30/mile pace, and a run of five miles at 6:00/mile pace.

Academic success depends on intention, too. You need to have a detailed plan for achieving academic success. For example, your plan for achieving an A on a history test might be as follows:

- Attend all lectures and make lots of notes.
- Revise and supplement notes immediately following each class.
- Study lecture notes for three hours every Wednesday evening.

> "Intention" means planning to meet the goal.

- Organize notes and identify relationships.
- Read and study one chapter each Thursday. Mark text, create organized notes, and identify relationships among text ideas.
- In the two weeks prior to the test, integrate text and lecture notes, generate and answer practice questions, and study with study partners.
- Three days before the exam, commit information to memory and conduct general review.

The marathon runner and the student must both turn their plans into action if they are going to reach their goals. Before they do, however, they should capitalize on the benefits of mental imagery.

Use Mental Imagery

Imagine the following basketball demonstration, which has been played out in gymnasiums across America: A player is asked to jump as high as possible and try to touch the rim of the basket. The player jumps four or five times but misses the rim by three or four inches each time. In fact, the player has never touched the rim. The coach asks the player to sit down and relax. Next, the coach tells the player to visualize himself jumping up and touching the rim. The player visualizes the speedy approach, the firmly planted left foot, the powerful leap, the extended right arm, and the straining fingers curled around the metal rim. The player revisualizes this scene many times, takes a few deep breaths, and tries once more. Bingo! He gets the rim.

Motivation involves more than desire; a motivated person plans to succeed and visualizes that success. The would-be marathon runner visualizes the grueling training—the hills, long runs, and speed work—and the digital clock showing 2:55 at the finish line. The would-be A student visualizes the intense study sessions—marking text and generating notes—and the semester grade report listing the A in History.

Having a plan and using mental imagery help you in four ways:

1. You become a believer.
2. You get worthwhile practice.
3. You hurdle prospective barriers.
4. You assume a new role.

Exercise

Return to the goal statements you listed previously. Spend some time each day before you go to bed, while walking to class, or while driving, imagining that you're making your goals come true. Imagine the effort. Imagine the payoff.

You Become a Believer. You cannot accomplish what you believe you cannot accomplish. You often can accomplish what you believe you can accomplish. In the 1950s, no runner had ever broken the four-minute mile. Roger Bannister finally broke that barrier. His record-setting performance was quickly duplicated by several other runners who finally believed and imagined that they too could break the barrier.

You must believe that you can work hard, apply strategies, and achieve academic success. Visualizing these things helps make them a reality.

You Get Worthwhile Practice. Mental imagery is an effective form of practice. Studies show that people who mentally practice free-throw shooting in basketball improve more than those who do not practice mentally. The mental practicers improve almost as much as those who physically practice free-throw shooting. In some ways, your body can't tell the difference between real and imagined events.

For example, imagine biting into a lemon. Notice how your face puckers and your mouth salivates as if you had actually taken a bite. Or hold both arms in front of you parallel to the ground and close your eyes. Imagine that you are holding the handles of shopping bags in each hand. Imagine that the bag in your left hand contains a box of laundry detergent, a gallon of milk, and a dozen apples. Imagine that the bag in your right hand is stuffed with inflated helium balloons. Try it now and then open your eyes. Notice that your left arm points downward and your right arm points upward? Your body again interpreted the visual images as if they were real.

Spend some time each day imagining yourself being an effective student. See yourself taking detailed lecture notes and answering the instructor's questions. See yourself reorganizing lecture notes, writing summaries, and preparing practice questions. See yourself receiving a high test grade. Soon your imaginings will become reality.

> Mental imagery is an effective form of practice.

Exercise

Imagine what you might do when the following occurs:

1. You feel too tired to study.
2. Friends call on you when you are studying.
3. The instructor is speaking too quietly and too fast.
4. The lecture seems disorganized.
5. You are assigned a science project, and it's due in one month.

You Hurdle Prospective Barriers in a Single Bound. Although your mental images should generally be positive and successful ones, don't dismiss the negative images that occasionally interrupt and distract. Those occasions are perfect times to imagine how you might hurdle these imagined barriers.

Suppose you are mentally rehearsing studying for a chemistry test. You see yourself working conscientiously at your desk solving chemistry problems. Imagine a friend dropping by to chat when you're in the middle of solving a problem. Continue visualizing, thinking how you might confront this interruption by announcing assertively that you must continue studying until your studying goals are met, and that you can meet your friend later.

This sort of mental exercise helps in hurdling real barriers when they arise.

You Assume a New Role. All people play one or more roles. You might on occasion play the role of friendly roommate, star athlete, busy mom, or jealous sibling.

In classrooms, students play the role of "disinterested student" or "interested student" or a role somewhere in between. The role of disinterested student is played by those who often sit in the classroom's back row, toothpicks hanging from their mouths, hats worn backwards, and feet propped on the chairs or students in front of them. Notebooks, if they have them, are closed. Their arms are folded across their chests as a last shield against learning. Obviously, this is a caricature of the disinterested student, but we want to make the point that this is a student who in reality is anyone who is uninvolved in learning.

The role of interested student is played by those who commonly occupy front row seats. They sit forward in their chairs and visually track the lecturer as attentively as if he were an uncaged bear. They record copious notes and frequently make insightful comments and questions.

Transforming your role from disinterested to interested student is not simple. The disinterested student first has to recognize the role he or she is playing, and its inherent dangers. The problem is that people playing dysfunctional roles might not know they are doing so. For instance, a substance abuser rarely recognizes the destruction being wrought on him- or herself, family, and friends. And, disinterested students might not recognize their poor school performance or that they are not well respected or appreciated by most students and faculty.

A disinterested student is first helped by caring teachers and friends who point out that he or she is playing a dysfunctional role. If the student has the desire to change, then teachers and friends can explain and model more functional roles. As instructors, we did this by including advanced graduate students in our undergraduate study skills courses. The graduate students modeled the role of interested student by asking probing questions, making insightful comments, recording lots of notes, and forming study groups. The undergraduate students were encouraged to model these behaviors by practicing them visually and in the classroom, thus establishing a new, better-functioning role.

You must dare to visualize and assume the role of the expert student. Don't be afraid that doing so makes you a nerd, a doofus, or a dweeb (whatever those are). Medical schools, law colleges, doctoral programs, science laboratories, powerful corporations, successful one-person enterprises, and happy households are replete with nerds, doofuses, and dweebs. Remember, if it's okay to "be like Mike," then it's fine to be like Einstein. Imagine what it's like to be Einstein or Mozart or Gandhi or someone else you respect. Try on the role. You might like the fit.

Exercise

Describe as honestly as possible the academic role you now play. Describe specific changes you would like to make to that role. Explain what you will do to facilitate the change to a more functional role. Imagine making those changes and playing that more functional role.

Improve Your Focus

The vision must be followed by the venture: It is not enough to start up the steps—we must step up the stairs.

Vance Havner, in *Vance Havner: Journey from Jugtown*

Gardening requires lots of water—most of it in the form of perspiration.

Lou Erickson, in *Atlanta Journal and Constitution*

Focus or hard work is necessary for carrying out your plan.

The runner who strives to complete the marathon in under three hours must maintain focus. There are days when the temperature drops below zero, when work or school keep her busy from morning until night, when business or vacation plans throw regular routines into a turmoil. On these days, running becomes inconvenient or nearly impossible. The focused runner runs nonetheless. On cold days, the runner runs indoors or wears

Mme Curie

Marie Curie's two Nobel Prizes in science were the result of hard work

appropriate outdoor clothing. On busy days, the runner wakes up earlier to run, runs over the lunch hour, or at night. While traveling or on vacation, the runner creates the opportunity to run—even if running is done in place in a hotel room, or inside an airport. On other days, a twenty-mile run seems too long or a hill workout too hard. The focused runner completes the workout anyway. The focused runner does not stray from the plan because of minor inconveniences or occasional laziness. The focused runner "just does it."

The student striving for an A in history maintains focus. Occasional late-night parties or midnight blankets of snow do not stop the focused student from attending early morning classes. The five hundred pages of text to be marked, noted, and evaluated are attacked five days a week. Even in the months when there is no test in sight, the focused student hoards knowledge like the squirrel storing acorns for the winter. The focused student keeps working on major projects until they represent the very best work he or she can do. In spite of the semester's downers—illnesses and personal crises and "others"—the focused student "just does it."

Focused individuals work hard to follow their plans and reach their goals. Many students don't realize this. They look at outstanding individuals such as Mozart, Marie Curie, Picasso, Freud, Martha Graham, Einstein, or former chess champion Bobby Fischer, and they believe that those people possess God-given talent that springs forth in a shower of inspiration. Freud scoffs at that notion. He says that "when inspiration does not come, I must go halfway to meet it." Talented people are made, not born.

Harvard psychologist John Gardner examined a group of talented individuals and showed that creative ideas or products are the result of hard work over a long period of time—usually ten to twenty years. Ralph Waldo Emerson said "Every artist is first an amateur." Chess champions, for example, practice a minimum of fifty thousand hours to reach Grandmaster status. Do the math yourself. That's roughly seventeen years of playing chess, eight hours a day, every day. Einstein toiled in physics for more than ten years before offering his breakthrough contribution on relativity. Even the prodigious Mozart, who began his musical career at age four, did not create a significant composition until he was fourteen—ten years later. Success as a scientist, artist, composer, or student requires hard work. Consider what Sarah Brown said, "The only thing that ever sat its way to success was a hen."

Exercise

Keep a journal for the next two weeks. List all your activities in the quest of your goals. Also indicate how much time you spend meeting your goals. Are you working hard enough to reach your goals?

Sustain Your Effort

Let me tell you the secret that led to my goal. My strength lies solely in my tenacity.

Louis Pasteur

Motivation must be sustained. How many people do you know who quit smoking—five times? Or who go on and off diets on a monthly basis? These people have trouble sustaining their motivation and performance.

Sustaining motivation produces remarkable results. Remember that the Tortoise defeated the Hare by sustaining motivation, and that a steady trickle of water moves mountains while intense earthquakes and hurricanes produce little effect. Consider too, baseball pitcher Nolan Ryan, the career strike-out leader, who pitched in the major leagues for more than twenty-five years. While his contemporaries participated in "Old Timers" games, Ryan threw his eighth no-hitter at age forty-four. Ryan attributed his longevity and success to keeping in top shape throughout his career. He trained hard every day to sustain his remarkable physical conditioning.

Consider what another world-class athlete says, former American miler Jim Ryun: "Motivation is what gets you started. Habit is what keeps you going."

Similarly, a student who plugs away—registering perhaps only small gains—throughout the semester and throughout college is likely to accomplish a great deal. We know a graduate advisor who offered a single piece of advice each time he met with a student: "Stay with it now," he would invariably say before he and the student parted. "Stay with it now." What a great piece of advice! It means that no matter how difficult or impossible things become, you just stay with it. You keep plugging away and never, never give up.

Of course it's easier to stay with something if you enjoy doing what you are doing. Consider our friend who works as a guide in the Rocky Mountain National Park, leading long hikes six days a week. On her day off, you might think she sleeps in, soaks her bunions, and puts her feet up. Nope. She hikes. It's what she loves to do.

Hopefully, it is the joy of learning that sustains you throughout college, not just the desire to achieve high grades or receive awards and diplomas. College is tremendous fun for those who know how to learn and are willing to sustain the effort.

Exercise

On your own sheet of paper, make a list of the things that you enjoy about college—the things that help you sustain your effort.

Summary

Poor academic performance is due to using ineffective strategies (poor skill) and having insufficient motivation (poor will). It is not the result of personal factors, such as boredom and problems with a boyfriend or girl-friend, nor is it the result of external factors, such as large classes and a disorganized text. These are excuses. Effective students overcome personal and environmental barriers to learning by controlling their personal situation and their environment. They use effective strategies and they maintain motivation. Motivation is the result of Desire (setting goals), Intention (planning), Focus (working hard), and Sustaining effort. DIFS makes the difference. It's up to you to control these factors. "Just do it!"

Answers to focus questions

1. Believing that success depends on ability is dangerous because if you think you have either low or high ability, you're not likely to use strategies or spend more time trying to improve your academic performance.

2. Uncertainty about your future goals becomes a barrier to success if you fail to recognize that good performance in college now is crucial for attaining goals that develop later. Cover your bases by performing well in college now so that you don't deny yourself the opportunity to attain goals later.

3. The parking problem is handled by coming to school early in the day when parking spaces are empty. Or you can walk to school, ride your bike, take the bus, or drive with a friend. If you're ill, ask a fellow student to record the lecture or lend you his or her notes. Most factors that you think might cause you to miss class or be late can be overcome.

4. You create a bad mood for studying by studying when you prefer doing other things like sleeping, visiting with friends, or watching television. You also create a bad mood by studying under difficult conditions, such as in a noisy lounge. You create a good mood for studying by studying when your mind is fresh, when you are rewarded, and when you use study strategies that work.

5. You can do well in a course you dislike by finding out more about the subject, applying course ideas to your own life, and using effective strategies.

6. The problem with attributing poor test performance to carelessness is that carelessness is rarely the cause of poor performance. If you believe that carelessness is the problem, you're likely to engage in the same ineffective learning strategies that actually caused the problem.

Being more careful next time doesn't help much if the problem is really in your note-taking or review strategies.

7. Personal problems don't have to interfere with your success. Isolate personal problems by setting time aside, outside your study hours, to deal with them.

8. Succeed in large classes by sitting in the front and interacting with the instructor both verbally and in your mind.

9. Professors and text aren't boring. Students choose to be bored. Combat boredom in class by sitting up front, asking questions, making comments, and making lots of notes. After class, learn more about the subject and your professor's interests. Deal with "boring" texts by taking notes, writing summaries, etc.

10. Overcome disorganized texts and lectures by organizing ideas yourself. Do this by identifying alert words and constructing representations. Listen for words that alert you to the information's organization, such as *parts* and *types*. These words signal that the information should be represented hierarchically. Also, ask your instructor how ideas are organized and relate to one another.

11. The four components of motivation are desire, intention, focus, and sustainment (DIFS). Desire is wanting to accomplish a goal. Intention is the plan for reaching the goal. Focus is the hard work that goes toward accomplishing the goal. Sustainment is continuing to work toward the goal over a long period of time despite any barriers.

12. The three characteristics of good goals are that the goals should be challenging, enjoyable, and behavioral.

13. Mental imagery improves your motivation and performance by helping you a) become a believer, b) get worthwhile practice, c) hurdle prospective barriers, and d) assume a new role.

14. Individuals like Mozart, Einstein, and Fischer developed their talents and reached their goals through years of hard work. Chess Grandmasters, for example, practice for a minimum of fifty thousand hours before reaching that level.

chapter 3
How to Manage Time

Overview

Focus Questions

Introduction

Time Management Principles You Should Follow
    Invest Time
        How to Develop a Block Schedule
    Invest in Time
    Invest Early
    Invest Daily
        How to Develop a Semester Planner
        How to Develop a Weekly Planner
        How to Develop a Daily Planner
    Invest Wisely
    Monitor Your Investment
    Enjoy Your Investment

Summary

Answers to Focus Questions

focus questions

1. Give two reasons why college students fail to recognize the importance of time.
2. Approximately how many hours per week should you spend studying?
3. Name the four components of a block schedule.
4. What should be done when a leisure activity conflicts with studying?
5. How can students who have full-time jobs, and perhaps families or other major outside commitments, find enough time to study?
6. What is meant by the principle, "invest in time"?
7. Is reducing work commitments a smart investment?
8. How should you plan to read seven chapters in preparation for a midterm exam?
9. What is a semester planner?
10. What is a weekly planner?
11. What is a daily planner?
12. What are some ways that you can invest time wisely?
13. How can you monitor your time investment?
14. How should you enjoy your time investment?

Tammy: Marsha, can you believe someone in our class got a 100 on the physics test? That nerd must be president of the Albert Einstein fan club.

Marsha: No, just the treasurer. I got the 100.

Tammy: Wow! I got a lousy 67 and I studied for four hours last night! How long did you study last night, ten hours?

Marsha: No, I didn't study at all last night. I went to my son's concert. He had a trombone solo.

Tammy: Well, when *did* you study?

Marsha: I've studied over the past five weeks— about ten hours a week.

Tammy: My goodness! I didn't think I'd have to study that much over four years of college! How do you find the time, carrying a full course load, working a part-time job, and caring for your family? Are your husband and children going to file charges against you for neglect?

Marsha: Not at all. I miss very few chances to be with my family. I start studying about five o'clock each morning when they're all still asleep and the house is peaceful—and most of all, when my mind is clear.

Tammy: No way! My mind is still mostly cloudy when I get up around nine.

Marsha: After we eat breakfast together, I drive my kids to school and head right over to campus, and on my way, I usually listen to lectures I've tape recorded.

Tammy: Talk about your moldy oldies!

Marsha: I get to campus about 8 A.M., so I have no trouble parking.

Tammy: I usually do about twenty laps around campus before I find a space. That's why I'm often late for physics.

Marsha: Then I head straight for the library where I read text assignments until my first class.

Tammy: If I have time, I usually hit the Fitzelle Coffee Shop for a bagel with cream cheese. Have you tried the blueberry bagel?

Marsha: No—I guess I've missed out there. When I get to my classes, I spend time going over the notes from the last class meeting before the instructor begins.

Tammy: If I'm early I take a fast look at the *Campus Times*. I just love reading the personals.

Marsha: After my 11:30 class I grab a quick bite at the cafeteria before work. I lunch with all the bigwigs, like B. F. Skinner and William Shakespeare, and even Albert Einstein.

Tammy: You study while you eat? I read somewhere that's bad for your digestion. I usually cruise across town with some other students to the Hamburger Hut. I love their iced tea. It's really murder finding another parking space though when we come back.

Marsha: After lunch, I go over to the Psychology Department. I'm a research assistant there. It's fun work and I'm learning tons of things. I might go on to graduate school in psychology.

Tammy: I get back to campus for my 2:30 class, and then it's back across town to work at the Holiday Hotel. My title is "Resort Steward," which is a fancy way of saying I make beds and clean toilets. It's gross.

Marsha: "Gross" is watching my son blow spit through the spit valve on his trombone! Anyway, after I get through at the Psych Department, I pick up my kids from school at 3:30, and we go play tennis, or ride our bikes, or jog with our dog.

Tammy: I'm too busy to exercise.

Marsha: My husband gets home around five. He and the kids make dinner while I study for another hour. After dinner, it's family time. We usually read stories, or talk about what's happened that day, or sometimes we play games together.

Tammy: I watch the *Star Trek* reruns. Spock is adorable. I also play computer games, or find people to talk with in the study lounge.

Marsha: I usually read or study for another hour or two before bed.

Tammy: I'm too beat at night to get work done then.

Marsha: On the weekends, we all do chores on Saturday morning. It's more fun doing it all together.

Tammy: I can't face cleaning my room after cleaning up after slobs all week.

Marsha: The rest of Saturday, we play. Saturday night, my husband and I have a late supper together after the kids are in bed. Sunday morning, I'm up early doing schoolwork before church. Sunday afternoons I can usually find another four hours to study and to plan my week's schedule while my kids are out playing with their friends and my husband's out with his friends, doing whatever they do.

Tammy: I avoid studying on Sundays. I want to be sure I'm fresh for the new week. And— I never plan. I like to study when the mood strikes.

*B*ased on the conversation between Marsha and Tammy, answer the following questions:

1. Which student do you suppose is going to earn a higher college GPA?
2. Which student would you invite to join your study group?
3. Which student would you ask to complete a survey (requiring about two hours) for your advertising class?
4. Which student do you believe leads a more fulfilling life?

You probably answered "Marsha" for each question, because Marsha has control over her time and her life, and Tammy doesn't. Marsha spends a great deal of time on her school work; as a result, she is likely to earn a high GPA and to make important contributions to a study group. Marsha is busy. But when you want something done, such as the completion of a survey, it's better to ask a busy person, because a busy person always finds the time to get a job done. Marsha seems more fulfilled than Tammy, because she has identified a few things of importance—family, school, work, and exercise—and spends her time pursuing these interests.

In contrast, Tammy has no clear direction and fritters her time away. Fortunately for Tammy and other students, effective time management principles, like those used by Marsha, can be learned and practiced. This chapter describes seven effective time management principles.

Exercise

Generate two lists. In one, list the ways that Tammy wastes time. In the other, list the ways that Marsha uses time effectively.

Time Management Principles You Should Follow

"Time is money." You have heard that expression over and over again—but is it true? Both time and money are certainly valued. You want money and "free" time because both can be redeemed for things you enjoy. You can spend your money on a new car or a Florida vacation, and then spend your time driving the car or visiting Florida. And both time and money have to be earned. You have to spend time to earn money at your job and, conversely, spend money to earn time (such as when you pay someone to fix your car or type your term paper).

Another similarity is that both money and time can be wasted. Many people go bankrupt investing their money unwisely. Similarly, many fail to excel in jobs or school because they invest their time unwisely.

Because money and time are so intertwined, many of the principles that govern the investment of money can be applied to the investment of time. What follows are seven investment principles for managing your time more effectively.

1. Invest time
2. Invest *in* time
3. Invest early
4. Invest daily
5. Invest wisely
6. Monitor investment
7. Enjoy investment

Becoming an effective student takes time.

Invest Time

EACH DAY IS A NEW ACCOUNT

If you had a bank that credited your account each morning with 86,400…

That carried over no balance from day to day…

Allowed you to keep no cash in your accounts…

And every evening canceled whatever part of the amount you had failed to use during the day…

What would you do?

Draw out every cent, of course, and use it to your advantage!

Well, you have such a bank…

and its name is "TIME."

Every morning, it credits you with 86,400 seconds.

Every night, it writes off as lost whatever of this you have failed to invest to good purpose.

It carries over no balances.

It allows no overdrafts.

Each day, it opens a new account with you.

Each night, it burns the records of the day.
If you fail to use the day's deposits, the loss is yours.
There is no going back.
There is no "Tomorrow."
It is up to each of us to invest this precious fund of hours, minutes and seconds in order to get from it the utmost in health, happiness, and success![1]

What do world class track athlete Jackie Joyner Kersey, composer Ludwig Van Beethoven, chess expert Bobby Fischer, dancer and choreographer Martha Graham, and golfer Tiger Woods have in common? All of them were or are fiercely dedicated to their endeavors, and each person invested incredible amounts of time in their specialties, spending large portions of their life practicing and honing their skills. Another famous golfer, Gary Player, having often heard appreciative fans call out "Gary, I'd do anything to hit the ball like you," one time shot back, "No, you wouldn't." Player was thinking about his years of practicing in all sorts of weather from morning till night, until his hands could barely grasp the club. That level of dedication is necessary to excel. Though you may not have realized it till now, becoming an effective student also takes considerable time.

An informal survey of freshman students indicated that most were studying less than ten hours a week, and some were studying only two to three hours per week. This is not nearly enough study time to excel in school.

Many students don't think learning takes much time. One reason is their belief that expertise occurs naturally, that it's due to innate ability. Looking at this book, for example, you might think that our words "just wrote themselves." In fact, writing this book took years. Furthermore, the knowledge base for this book, and the prerequisite writing and research skills, took more than ten years to develop. Experts like Jackie Joyner Kersey, Bobby Fischer, and Tiger Woods are built, not born. Remember what Emerson said: "Every artist is first an amateur."

A second reason why you might not recognize the importance of time is that learning in high school probably didn't take much time. Unfortunately, many high school courses require that students do only a minimal amount of reading, and answer only very simple, factual test questions. In college, the reading load is generally heavier, and exams test more sophisticated learning outcomes, such as recognizing concepts and applying skills.

How much should you study? Whatever amount of time you need to master the course material. At a minimum, you should follow the long-held rule of thumb and spend about two hours studying for every hour in class. This means that if you carry fifteen hours of class work, you would study about thirty hours per week. Altogether, you'd make a total investment of forty or fifty hours each week in your education.

[1]Reprinted with permission from *Structured Exercises in Stress Management*, Volume 2, copyright © 1984, 1994. Donald A. Tubesing. Published by Whole Person Associates, Inc., 210 West Michigan, Duluth, MN 55802-1908, 218-727-0500.

That sounds like a full-time job. It is. And that is how you should consider school—as a full-time job. But in this time of escalating college costs, many students treat college like a second, part-time job. They work forty hours a week to support their education, but then they don't study enough and so short-change the very thing they're working for.

We have some suggestions for those students who are carrying a full class load and who work, or who are considering working:

1. If possible, don't work during the academic year. Earn money in the summers. Spend your *time* now, earning a good education that will pay dividends the rest of your life.
2. If you must work, try to reduce your work to ten or twenty hours per week. Full-time employment is negatively associated with academic performance. Remember that your number one job now is college.
3. If you work, get a job on campus if you can. Students who work on campus outperform those who work off campus. They are more deeply involved in their college environment and enjoy college more.

> Remember that your number one job now is college.

Whatever time you have, you can make the most of it by completing a block schedule like that shown in Figure 3-1. A very strict, detailed schedule isn't a good idea, because change happens. You might have to deviate from, and ultimately abandon, such a schedule. Most students do best when they plan a general schedule like the completed block schedule presented in Figure 3-2. This schedule shows a) classes and commitments, b) chores, c) study times, and d) leisure activities.

How to Develop a Block Schedule

Record Classes and Commitments   First, fill in all class times. Next, include ongoing commitments. For example, work, track practice, and church meetings. Whenever possible, schedule commitments outside your nine-to-five work day.

Record Chores   Before they get to college, many students are shielded from dreaded chores like washing clothes, cleaning house, preparing meals, maintaining the car, cutting the grass, and shopping. But as a college student, you take on many more responsibilities. Therefore, when you're planning a schedule, be certain to block out time for laundry, eating, vacuuming, etc. These chores must be done, and they require time. Whenever possible, try to minimize the time needed for these things. For example, exercise first thing in the morning rather than in the afternoon. You need only one shower instead of two. Fold laundry or do your ironing while you're watching your favorite television program. Reduce your "lunch hour" to twenty minutes, or consider meeting with a study group over lunch. Once again, try to accomplish chores outside the nine-to-five work period whenever possible. Don't forget that weekends are a great time to catch up on these chores.

Figure 3–1. *Block Schedule*

BLOCK SCHEDULE

	Sunday	Monday	Tuesday	Wednesday	Thursday	Friday	Saturday
6:00–7:30							
7:30–8:30							
8:30–9:30							
9:30–10:30							
10:30–11:30							
11:30–12:30							
12:30–1:30							
1:30–2:30							
2:30–3:30							
3:30–4:30							
4:30–5:30							
5:30–6:30							
6:30–7:30							
7:30–8:30							
8:30–9:30							
9:30–10:30							
10:30–11:30							

Figure 3–2 *Completed Block Schedule*

BLOCK SCHEDULE

	Sunday	Monday	Tuesday	Wednesday	Thursday	Friday	Saturday
6:00–7:30		Exercise Breakfast	Exercise Breakfast	Exercise Breakfast	Exercise Breakfast	Exercise Breakfast	
7:30–8:30		Study	Study	Study	Study	Study	
8:30–9:30	Breakfast	History	Study	History	Study	History	Exercise
9:30-10:30	Church	Study	Psych	Campus Errands	Psych	Psych	Breakfast
10:30–11:30	Church	French	Study	French	Study	French	Chores
11:30–12:30	Chores	Lunch	Lunch	Lunch	Lunch	Lunch	Chores
12:30–1:30	Chores	Study	Chem	Study	Chem	Teacher Aid	Chores
1:30–2:30	Lunch	Study	Chem	Study	Chem	Teacher Aid	Lunch
2:30–3:30	Leisure	Study	Study	Study	Study	Study	Study
3:30–4:30	Leisure	Tennis	Tennis	Tennis	Tennis	Tennis	Study
4:30–5:30	Leisure	Tennis	Tennis	Tennis	Tennis	Tennis	Work
5:30–6:30	Supper	Supper	Supper	Supper	Supper	Supper	Work
6:30–7:30	Study	Algebra	Work	Study	Work	Study	Work
7:30–8:30	Study	Algebra	Work	Study	Work	Study	Work
8:30–9:30	Study	Algebra	Work	Church Mtg.	Work	Leisure	Supper
9:30–10:30	Study	Leisure	Work	Leisure	Work	Leisure	Leisure
10:30–11:30	Bed	Bed	Bed	Bed	Bed	Leisure	Leisure

Record Study Times   Next, fill in a sufficient number of study hours. Do not indicate the subject of studying, however, since this will change from week to week. Remember to schedule about two hours of studying for every class hour. Most people's minds are fresher in the morning, so try to schedule the bulk of your study time for the morning. Morning is usually a quieter time to study, as well. In between classes is also a good time to study, and a particularly good time for reviewing notes from your previous class or before your next class.

You will probably need to schedule some study time on weekends, depending on what your other commitments and priorities are. Ideally, weekend time is used mostly for fun. Many top students, however, like to study on Sunday afternoon or evening to consolidate information learned throughout the week.

When you plan your study times, try to make them one to four hours in length. If you study longer than four hours, you'll get tired and your studying will be less effective. Breaks, of course, should occur throughout longer study sessions.

Caution: With shorter study times, be careful: Many students spend too much time "warming up." This was taken to extreme by one residence hall student who would shower, fix a snack, make a couple of phone calls, and straighten his desk before beginning the little studying he managed to complete each night.

Record Leisure Time   A college student on semester break went with his roommate for supper at a restaurant near the college. While there, the student met his favorite professor, who asked him how vacation was going. The student commented on the school work he was accomplishing. The professor nodded approvingly, but then he asked, "What are you doing for fun?" The student answered that he had been skiing twice, played some pinball, and won a fair share of fussball games at the Copper Fox in the evenings. With that the professor nodded and said, "Good, good, good, that's what college should be all about." From that point on, the student and his roommate echoed those words. Whenever one of them was headed out to play basketball, attend a party, or socialize at the Copper Fox, the other would say, "Good, good, good, that's what college should be all about."

And, in many ways it should. College should provide a balance of intellectual and learning experiences. College offers you a smorgasbord of ideas and activities to sample. Take advantage of these opportunities. Although excelling in the classroom is your primary objective in college, you should attend concerts, films, and lectures; join groups and clubs; and simply have fun. Those students who don't find time for fun will surely find time for fatigue and illness. Therefore, leisure time should be incorporated into your block schedule. But be sure to schedule it outside your nine-to-five work period.

Here's another caution: If something special comes up, such as an impromptu party in honor of Ground Hog Day, and you choose to toast Punxatawnee Phil rather than study calculus, then remember to "pay back"

> College should provide a balance of intellectual and learning experiences.

that time by taking other time you've set aside for leisure activities and spending it on studying. Remember to borrow time, rather than to steal it.

Most college students can schedule their classes and commitments, chores, study times, and leisure activities comfortably within the block schedule. However, some cannot. The number of nontraditional college students with families and full-time jobs is rising. For them, study time is at a premium and leisure time might be spent by taking a shower. Can these students succeed? They can if they use time wisely (like Marsha, who you met at the start of the chapter) and use powerful study strategies like those described in this book. Using powerful strategies can reduce learning time and increase performance.

However, if you're a nontraditional student, you might want to reconsider your definition of success. If you spend fifty hours a week in school, get straight A's, but neglect your spouse, children, and job, then are you successful? Perhaps, if you're one of those students who have pressing responsibilities outside of school, you should reevaluate your goals and priorities. Maybe attending college is more feasible when your youngest child starts school. Maybe achieving A's in all classes is not a realistic (or important) goal. Nontraditional students need to face and address difficult issues such as these. And they, too, must remember that succeeding in school requires investing considerable time. Without that investment there is little payoff.

Invest in Time

When you work, you sell your time in exchange for money, which, in turn, purchases life's necessities and pleasures. Usually, the deal is a good one. Sometimes, however, it is necessary to buy time rather than sell it. Many people, for example, hire someone to prepare their taxes or cut their lawns. The time saved is then spent on other activities, such as working or socializing with family or friends. Investing in time is particularly valuable for college students who require considerable study time.

Consider Phil. Phil is a sophomore business major carrying a 2.8 grade point average. He's taking fifteen credit hours and he plays varsity tennis. He

Exercise

Complete the blank block schedule in Figure 3–1 by including a) classes and commitments, b) chores, c) study times, and d) leisure activities. (You may want to make several copies of the blank schedule so that you have extras on hand for those inevitable changes.)

How can you buy time for studying and leisure activities?

also works twenty hours a week at minimum wage slinging burgers at the Hungry Heifer. Phil has to work to help pay his tuition, room, and board. He receives minimal financial assistance from his parents and he hasn't got any scholarships, so he's taken out several bank loans. He crams his studying into about ten hours each week. Tennis, which he loves, is becoming more like a chore, because he is constantly tired.

Phil realizes that he has a time management problem. He decides to drop tennis so he can spend more time studying. At first glance, Phil's choice seems a wise one. After all, school should come first, and Phil needs the money from work to support himself. Or does he?

Phil makes roughly $75 a week, which works out to $300 per month. At his current rate of pay, Phil will make about $7,500 while he's completing college. This is not a negligible amount of money—but is it enough to make up for low grades and taking away the pleasure and experience associated with playing scholastic tennis, a one-time opportunity? Perhaps Phil should invest in time by quitting his job and taking out more loans. Then he could not only enjoy college more, but also perform more effectively. Consequently, he might land a better (and higher-paying) job after college than he would have otherwise. In which case, paying back additional loans is relatively painless.

There are other ways in which you can invest in time. If you live on campus, either in a residence hall or in other student housing, you save time commuting to and from campus. Furthermore, you might not have to spend time cleaning the kitchen or bathroom or hanging around a laundromat. Campus life also minimizes the need for a car and its maintenance costs, which saves both time and money.

Working in study groups also is an investment in time. Each group member focuses on a particular topic and supplies fellow study-group members with detailed study aids covering that topic. This reduces the overall workload for each member.

Last, you can pay others for services that are time-consuming and outside your area of expertise. For example, it's nonsense to spend four hours typing a paper if an experienced typist can type it in thirty minutes for a few dollars. If repairing your car's transmission is going to take you several days, you might do better paying an expert to fix it and spending your extra time studying or having fun.

Invest Early

The cost of a college education is high now, and the projected costs are unbelievable. If your child were born today, how much money do you think you would have to save each month to finance your child's college education eighteen years from now? Maybe $10 to $25 a month, depending on the type of college? How about $150 to $300 per month! The point is that

Exercise

Develop a plan for how you can "invest in time."

---

the best (and perhaps the only) way to afford a future college education is by investing early.

The early-investment principle is also understandable relative to a new car. Should you wait four or five years after buying a new car before you polish the finish or service the engine? Keeping a new car new requires early investments.

The point in both these questions is, if you miss the opportunity to invest early, then invest now! The best time to plant a tree was 20 years ago; the second best time is now.

Early investments in time also aid learning. You should begin assignments and study activities early. If you're assigned twelve chapters to read for the midterm in seven weeks, you need to make an early investment. You should break the task into parts and master two chapters each week, beginning the first week. Reviewing lecture notes deserves an early start as well. Do not try to grasp and integrate eight weeks worth of notes just prior to the exam. Begin reviewing notes early in the semester and review them daily.

The "invest-early" principle also means that you should get a fast start at the beginning of the semester. For example, one student, Ron, missed the first day of class, believing that not much important happens that first day. By doing this, Ron lost points for being

absent, received a zero on a homework assignment given that day, and a zero on the quiz administered the next class period. Ron never overcame his slow start. Although he achieved an 88 average and a B+ in the course, the attendance, assignment, and quiz points he forfeited that first day cost him an A in the course.

Invest Daily

Each day that we awake is a new start, another chance. Why waste it on self pity, sloth and selfishness?

Roll that day around on your tongue, relish the taste of its freedom. Breathe deeply of the morning air, savor the fragrance of opportunity. Run your hands along the spine of those precious 24 hours and feel the strength in that sinew and bone.

Life is raw material. We are artisans. We can sculpt our existence into something beautiful, or debase it into ugliness. It's in our hands.

Cathy Better, in the Reisterstown, MD, *Community Times*

Do you like to read? How would you like to read fifteen or twenty novels every year in addition to your textbooks? It sounds impossible, doesn't it? But in order to read that many books in a year, all you need to do is read for fifteen minutes before bed each night. In a year, you will have read about fifteen or twenty books.

Many of our colleagues complain that they don't have time to stay current in their field by reading professional journals. But if they read one journal article each night (requiring about twenty minutes), five days a week, they would complete 250 articles per year. In four years, they would read a thousand more articles than the person who believes there isn't enough time to stay current.

Investing daily not only produces more learning, it produces *better* learning. Consider the cases of John and Jan. John studies his lecture notes for twenty minutes after each class. Each week, he spends an hour integrating his class notes for that week. During the week before his midterm exam, he studies an extra hour every day. In total, John studies about twenty hours for the exam.

Jan, however, does not begin to study until two days before the exam. She studies ten hours each day, and she, too, has a total of twenty hours studying.

What are the likely outcomes for John and Jan? Before you answer, consider John and Jan's approaches relative to another area. Suppose that both want to improve their cardiovascular fitness by running. They set as their goals running ninety miles per month. John runs three miles every day for a month. Jan doesn't get started until the last three days of the month. Even

Investing daily not only produces more learning, it produces better learning.

if she were to run thirty miles each day over the next three days (very unlikely, even for a seasoned runner), would she benefit as much as John?

The answer is no. Each day, a little at a time, John builds a higher level of muscular and cardiovascular fitness. Thus, his running improves throughout the month, because each day he is capable of running more effectively. Jan, on the other hand, cannot possibly attain the same fitness level with three days of running, regardless of the number of miles she runs. In fact, her attempt to run thirty miles in one day is likely to do nothing more than leave her sore and tired.

The same is true regarding their study behaviors. By studying each day, John "stays up" with the instructor. He can understand new lecture material better than Jan. Even studying for forty hours before the test might not help Jan if she cannot understand her lecture notes, which she never reviewed. By not studying regularly, Jan simply cannot bring a sufficient depth of knowledge to her late studying efforts. Furthermore, Jan's marathon study sessions are likely to leave her tired and poorly motivated.

To help with the early and daily investment of time, you should develop three planners, in addition to your block schedule: a semester planner, a weekly planner, and a daily planner.

How to Develop a Semester Planner

A semester planner highlights the dates of all tests and assignments in all subjects throughout the semester. These are written in the spaces of a monthly calendar for the months spanning the semester.

For example, suppose your psychology instructor announced that the midterm and final exams were going to be on October 22nd and December 19th, respectively, and that a term paper was due on November 15th. These important dates are noted on the semester planner, as shown in Figure 3-4.

In addition to important dates like exams and term papers and such, you should also divide long-term assignments and test preparations into segments and record these self-imposed deadlines or due dates on the semester planner. In other words, establish a time line that specifies what should be completed when. Plan to complete a major assignment at least one week in advance to relieve anxiety (procrastination's partner) and to offset unforeseen problems that might occur during the week that the assignment is due (such as illness or a broken computer). A sample time line appears on the following page in Figure 3-3, and as part of the semester planner in Figure 3-4.

For example, you should begin the term paper, due in two and a half months, immediately (the invest-early principle) and work on it regularly (the invest-daily principle).

You can also create a time line to help divide your preparations for major tests. For example, suppose that the psychology midterm in Week 8

Figure 3–3. *Psychology Term Paper*

Psychology Term Paper

Date:	Sept. 10	Sept. 25	Oct. 1	Oct. 25	Oct. 30	Nov. 8	Nov. 15
Task:	Choose Topic	Review Literature	Represent Paper's Structure	Write 1st Draft	Produce 2nd Draft	Complete Polished Draft	Paper Due

Figure 3–4. *Semester Planner*

September

Sun	Mon	Tues	Wed	Thurs	Fri	Sat
1	2	3	4	*Psych. Ch. 1* 5	6	7
8	9	*Psych. Choose Topic* 10	11	*Psych. Ch. 2* 12	13	14
15	16	17	18	*Psych. Ch. 3* 19	20	21
22	23	24	*Psych. Review Lit* 25	*Psych. Ch. 4* 26	27	28
29	30					

November

Sun	Mon	Tues	Wed	Thurs	Fri	Sat
					1	2
3	4	5	6	*Psych. Ch. 10* 7	*Complete Polished Draft* 8	9
10	11	12	13	*Psych. Ch. 11* 14	*Term Paper Due* 15	16
17	18	19	20	*Psych. Ch. 12* 21	22	23
24	25	26	27	*Psych. Ch. 13* 28	29	30

October

Sun	Mon	Tues	Wed	Thurs	Fri	Sat
		Psych. Create Structure 1	2	*Psych. Ch. 5* 3	4	5
6	7	8	9	*Psych. Ch. 6* 10	11	12
13	14	15	16	*Psych. Ch. 7* 17	18	19
20	21	*Psych. MidTerm* 22	23	*Psych. Ch. 8* 24	*Psych. Write 1st Draft* 25	26
27	28	*Psych. Write 2nd Draft* 29	*Psych. Ch. 9* 30	31		

December

Sun	Mon	Tues	Wed	Thurs	Fri	Sat
1	2	3	4	*Psych. Ch. 14* 5	6	7
8	9	10	11	*Psych. Ch. 15* 12	13	14
15	16	17	18	*Psych. FINAL* 19	20	21
22	23	24	25	26	27	28
29	30	31				

covers Chapters 1 through 7 and the final covers Chapters 1 through 15. You should study one chapter per week, rather than study many chapters just prior to the tests. This plan is recorded in the semester planner in Figure 3-4. Once again, to relieve anxiety and to offset unforeseen problems, you want to be prepared for a major test at least three days in advance.

It is very important to stick to your long-range semester plan even when the instructor falls behind the instructional plan. Often, instructors cover a lot of content at the end of the semester to compensate for falling behind early on. This frustrates students whose studying objective is to "stay up" with the instructor. Although falling behind is not good teaching, following an instructor's faltering pace is not good learning. A motivated student who understands the principle of investing daily works at a uniform rate throughout the semester. If you have more work to complete in December than October, perhaps your work load was inadequate in October.

How to Develop a Weekly Planner

The weekly planner illustrates the week's tests, assignments, and activities. The activities might apply to tests and assignments occurring this week or in future weeks. Examine the weekly planner in Figure 3-5. It schedules study time for three history chapters on Monday, Tuesday, and Wednesday for a future test. French study is scheduled for Sunday, Monday, and Tuesday for a test on Friday. A final review for an algebra test on Tuesday is scheduled for completion on Sunday. Algebra assignment #3 should be completed on Friday. In chemistry, a lab report due Thursday is completed Monday and Tuesday. And Chapter 3 in psychology is scheduled for study on Wednesday and Thursday in preparation for a future test.

When you generate the weekly planner, consult both your semester planner and block schedule. Check your semester planner to determine what tests, assignments, and activities are scheduled for that week. Check your block schedule to determine the best time to complete activities. For example, on Tuesday you want to study French, complete the chemistry lab report, and study history. Consulting your block schedule tells you when you can complete those activities.

The weekly planner's matrix structure helps you to clearly and rapidly understand your week's activities by day and by subject. Read vertically the planner illustrates activities by day; read horizontally it illustrates activities by subject.

Generate a weekly planner at the start of each week and review your previous week's planner to monitor how well you're managing time.

Figure 3–5. *Weekly Planner*

WEEK 3

	Sun	Mon	Tues	Wed	Thurs	Fri	Sat
History		Study Ch. 4	Study Ch. 5	Study Ch. 6			
French	Study French	Study French	Study French			French Test	
Algebra	Review For Test		Test			Complete Assignment 3	
Chemistry		Write Lab Report	Write Lab Report		Lab Report		
Psychology				Study CHapter 3	Study CHapter 3		

How to Develop a Daily Planner

The daily planner is a prioritized list of tasks that must be accomplished that day or the next. Priority tasks must be completed that day; secondary tasks can hopefully be completed that day before they become priorities another day.

Record your daily plans in product-oriented terms. That is, specify the product you will produce. Rather than write that you will "Read Chapter 2," for example, you might write that you will "Read and mark the text and produce text representations." Some people recommend that each task be given a special time slot. Doing so helps you to see exactly what your job is throughout the day. Figure 3-6 shows a sample daily planner.

Figure 3–6. *Daily Planner*

Monday's Tasks

Priorities:
- Use Mnemonics to Learn French Vocabulary in Chapter 2 (7:30–8:30)
- Write First 3 Sections of Chemistry Lab Report (9:30–10:30)
- Read, Mark, and Represent Chapter 4 in History (12:30–2:30)

Secondary:
- Write Remainder of Chemistry Lab Report (2:30–3:30)
- Computer Search for Psychology (if time permits)

Exercise

Using Figures 3–4, 3–5 and 3–6 as guides, develop a semester planner, a weekly planner, and a daily planner. Continue to develop weekly and daily planners throughout the semester.

Invest Wisely

Have you noticed that everybody seems to be in a rush? People can barely wait forty-five seconds for something to warm in the microwave. They get restless when a cashier is too slow counting out change or bagging purchases. People drive dangerously fast, as if their lives depended on arriving home for supper at 5:30 instead of 5:32. And what do these people do with all the time they save? Probably waste it.

The idea of investing time wisely reminds us of the story about a dog who is home alone each day. He spends the whole day napping. When his master comes back each evening, the dog is fed for the only time that day. His master fills his dish with food and within thirty seconds the dog gobbles it up. As the dog turns from the bowl, the master asks "Hey! Are you late for a nap?" Like the dog, most people rush to waste time.

Instead, you can invest time wisely by spending your spare time judiciously. For example, you can use the few minutes before class to review notes or anticipate the direction of the day's lecture. You can do some studying just before bed or first thing in the morning. You can study while waiting for appointments or a bus. If you're waiting for a medical appointment, you can probably read the complete works of Charles Dickens.

When you have shorter waits, such as when you're waiting in line at the bank or a bus stop, review study cards on which you've written important terms. While you're driving, think about a topic or listen to an audiocassette of a lecture. (Please don't try to read a textbook!) Of course, the time between classes is ideal for studying and consistent with what we said earlier about being a nine-to-five, full-time student.

Also, try to accomplish chores more efficiently. Beat the crowds. Shop for groceries in the morning or evening, but never on Saturdays. Stay away from banks on Friday afternoons. Have your paycheck or other regular income deposited directly into your bank account. Drive to and from campus when traffic is light. There are peak times for everything. Try to avoid those peaks.

Exercise

Explain how Marsha, the woman at the start of the chapter, used time wisely. Explain how her friend Tammy did not.

Monitor Your Investment

You probably wouldn't invest your money in various stocks and bonds and then not monitor the performance of those investments. The same is true for your time. Your investment of time must be monitored.

Begin by monitoring how you spend time *now*. For a week or two, keep track of how you spend time by charting your time expenditures on a daily basis, using a copy of the blank block schedule. Most students who do this are amazed how much time they waste and how much time is actually available for studying.

Once you construct a block schedule, monitor its use. Be sure that it is a workable schedule, and that you are doing reasonably well in holding to it. Do the same for your weekly schedules. Determine whether you are accomplishing things as planned. As you actually study, monitor your use of time. Are you concentrating on your work? Are you taking study breaks that are longer than the study segments? Are you spending an appropriate amount of time on all subjects? At a broader level, consider setting an alarm for 11:00 P.M. each night. When it sounds, ask yourself one question, "If I were the president of a corporation and a worker accomplished what I did today, would I fire that worker or give her a raise?"

Exercise

Here is a check list you can use for monitoring your time investment. Complete it at least once a week throughout the semester.

Yes No

☐ ☐ 1. I spend about two hours studying outside of class for each hour in class.

☐ ☐ 2. I generally follow my block schedule.

☐ ☐ 3. I use morning hours for studying.

☐ ☐ 4. I get exercise and leisure time each day.

☐ ☐ 5. I accomplish necessary chores.

☐ ☐ 6. I take short breaks during extended study sessions.

☐ ☐ 7. When I want to change my schedule, I borrow time rather than steal it.

☐ ☐ 8. I spend sufficient time studying for all my subjects.

☐ ☐ 9. I look for ways to invest in time.

☐ ☐ 10. I begin assignments and test preparations without delays.

☐ ☐ 11. I break large assignments into parts and make plans for completing each part.

☐ ☐ 12. I complete my assignments and test preparations well in advance of due dates.

☐ ☐ 13. I use a semester planner.

☐ ☐ 14. I use weekly planners.

☐ ☐ 15. I use daily planners.

☐ ☐ 16. I waste little time.

☐ ☐ 17. When I can I do things during "off-peak" hours.

☐ ☐ 18. I monitor my use of time.

☐ ☐ 19. I enjoy how I spend my time.

☐ ☐ 20. If I were the president of a corporation, I would give myself a raise.

Enjoy your investment

Enjoy Your Investment

Students who study effectively should enjoy their investment. First, they should learn a great deal and earn high grades. Second, they should reward themselves throughout and following the studying process.

Reward successful study sessions by engaging in some fun activity. For example, study for a few hours each evening, and then socialize with friends. It is critical, however, that studying precede the fun activity.

While you're studying, five-minute breaks every thirty to sixty minutes are rewarding and refreshing.

Consider the story of two men who chopped wood all day long. The first chopped straight through without a break. The second would stop every fifty minutes and rest for ten minutes. At the end of the day both had a sizable pile of logs, but the second man's was larger. The first man wondered at this and asked the second man how this was possible. The second man answered, "Each time I stopped to rest, I also sharpened my ax."

Summary

Time is a valuable resource that you control. You can save it by investing it wisely or you can waste it. Developing time schedules helps you invest time wisely.

Develop a block schedule that includes your classes and commitments, chores, study times, and leisure activities. Remember to schedule about thirty study hours per week if you're carrying a full course load. You may need to schedule even small pockets of time between classes to find time for all you must do.

Develop a semester planner that highlights the semester's tests, assignments, and your plans for completing them.

Develop weekly planners that show your academic commitments and activities for each subject each day.

And develop daily planners that highlight the day's tasks. These schedules should help you to invest early, daily, wisely, and monitor your investment.

You might need to "buy" time for your scholastic and personal activities by trading money or goods for additional time, such as when you pay someone to type a paper that would otherwise take you hours to type. Finally, enjoy the time you saved by spending it on fun activities.

> Time is a valuable resource that you can control.

Exercise

Now that you've completed this chapter, go back to the beginning and reread the conversation between Marsha and Tammy. Play the role of a caring friend and give Tammy some advice on how she can better manage her time.

Answers to focus *questions*

1. College students fail to recognize the importance of time because they believe that expertise occurs naturally (without hard work), and because the time they needed to spend on learning in high school was minimal.

2. You should study about two hours outside of class for every hour in class. If you are carrying fifteen credit hours and attending class fifteen hours per week, you should study about thirty hours per week. Combining study time and class time means that you should spend about forty-five hours each week on learning activities—the same time you'd spend working a full-time job.

3. A block schedule includes classes and commitments, chores, study times, and leisure activities.

4. It's okay to enjoy a leisure activity during a scheduled study period as long as the study period is "made up" during a scheduled leisure period. Remember to borrow, not steal, time.

5. Combining powerful learning strategies and sound time management strategies should help most students get the most from their time. When time is still not sufficient, consider reducing or eliminating other "commitments," such as employment, or reducing your scholastic responsibilities. Instead of taking five classes and holding down a full-time job, take one or two classes or find a part-time job.

6. "Invest in time" means that you "buy" time. This is done by making an investment that results in more time. For example, buying a washing machine saves time traveling to a laundromat. Paying someone to type a paper provides more time for studying or other activities.

7. Reducing work commitments is a smart investment. Students should remember that college is a full-time job. Working many hours per week is likely to hinder learning and make college less enjoyable. Whenever possible, students should minimize work, excel in school, and pay for college with scholarships, summer employment, and loans.

8. If you're assigned seven chapters for a midterm exam, you should invest early and daily. Plan to read about one chapter each week, beginning this week.

9. A semester planner is a series of monthly calendars showing all major assignments, tests, and plans for completing assignments and preparing for tests.

10. A weekly planner is a grid showing the days of the week across the top and the student's academic subjects down the left side. The grid is completed with assignments, tests, and study activities for that week.

11. A daily planner is a list of priorities and secondary tasks to be completed that day. It's a "to-do" list drawn from the weekly schedule.

12. Invest wisely by using periods of time, such as between classes or while you're waiting for appointments, to study, complete a chore, or have fun.

13. Monitor time investments by recording all your activities in a block schedule for two weeks. Then analyze the block schedule to see if time is being squandered or used productively.

14. Enjoy the time you save by spending it on things you enjoy, such as recreation or outings with friends or family.

chapter 4
Principles of Learning and Memory

OVERVIEW

Focus Questions

Introduction

Focus Your Attention
  Attend to Physical Properties
  Attend to Personally Relevant Ideas
  Attend to Objectives

Don't Rely on Rehearsal for Long-Term Learning

Build Connections
  Build Internal Connections
  Build External Connections

Monitor Your Learning

Summary

Answers to Focus Questions

1. How do instructors vary the physical properties of their lectures to grab your attention?
2. How can you offset distractions while learning?
3. What are the cues that tell you where to focus attention?
4. Is rehearsal an effective strategy for long-term remembering?
5. What are internal and external connections?
6. What are the benefits of building internal connections?
7. What must you already have if you are to build external connections?
8. What are some ways that external connections are formed?
9. What are mnemonics?
10. How do you know when you are ready for a test?
11. When should you self-monitor?

Carlos: Hey Gabe, how did you do on the first biology quiz?

Gabe: Let's put it this way. I doubt I'll include this score in my applications to medical schools. I had no idea what to study.

Carlos: Really? Professor Ruck included a list of objectives on the course syllabus.

Gabe: Oh really? I never look at that stuff. I just read over all my notes.

Carlos: The objectives told us to focus our attention on cell parts and functions.

Gabe: Yeah, I read that material over and over, but I had trouble memorizing all that stuff.

Carlos: Probably because you didn't connect it to something meaningful. I related each cell part to a part of a city that shares the same function.

Gabe: What? Were you drinking?

Carlos: No, listen. The cell wall defines the cell's boundary and protects the cell the same way a wall might surround a city and protect it from intruders.

Gabe: I guess if they can build a wall around China you can have one around your city.

Carlos: The cell membrane allows material to be transferred in and out of the cell just like border guards and gatekeepers let people and things in and out of the city.

Gabe: The gatekeepers might allow something healthy to come in like food but not something destructive like guns.

Carlos: Exactly! The cytoplasm is the watery environment where cell functions occur. This is the city itself.

Gabe: Sounds like Venice.

Carlos: The cell nucleus is the information center. In a real city, this might be the mayor's office.

Gabe: Or the city college.

Carlos: You're catching on. The mitochondria produce energy like a . . .

Gabe: . . . power plant?

Carlos: Exactly!

Gabe: Wasn't there a plastic rectangle or something?

Carlos: You're warm—it's called the endoplasmic reticulum. These are the transport channels within the cells. I likened them to city streets.

Gabe: I can just hear you giving directions. "Go to the end of Plasmic and make a right on Ticulum."

Carlos: Hey, that's helpful! The golgi apparatus is where secretions are packaged for discharge. What do you think I related them to in my city?

Gabe: To our cafeteria. Just kidding! Maybe a waste treatment plant.

Carlos: You betcha.

Gabe: So that's it?

Carlos: Not quite. After connecting the cell and city parts, I tested myself several times making sure I could recall this information easily. I knew going into the quiz that I'd ace it.

Gabe: You city guys are so smart.

Carlos learned and remembered biology not because he's smart, but because he did smart things. In line with the course objectives, he focused his studying on cell parts and their functions. He related cell parts to parts of a city that share common functions. And he tested himself prior to the quiz to ensure that he was fully prepared.

Carlos' learning activities (or strategies) illustrate several general principles that are listed below and described in this chapter.

1. Focus your attention
2. Don't rely on rehearsal for long-term learning
3. Build internal and external connections to aid learning
4. Monitor your learning

These general principles are important because they support many of the more specific strategies taught throughout this book.

In Carlos' case, the first principle, "focus your attention," supports his selection of which information to study based on objectives. The second principle, "don't rely on rehearsal for long-term learning," supports his not using rehearsal activities, such as reading things over and over—a strategy used by Gabe, who performed poorly. The third principle, "build connections," supports Carlos' relating cell parts and city parts by function. And the fourth principle, "monitor your learning," supports his self-testing strategy.

Principles not only support strategies, they suggest strategies. This is critically important for you to know, because it means that you can develop effective strategies for situations where there aren't any. For example, suppose that you cut your leg. You are likely to use the common medical strategy of applying a bandage. This strategy is usually effective in stopping the bleeding. But suppose the cut continues to bleed, and you don't know what to do now—you have no other strategy. Are there general principles that might guide you and suggest another strategy? If you know the principle that blood flows in greater quantities to active muscles, and you couple that knowledge with the principle of gravity, it would suggest that an effective strategy might be to rest and elevate the wounded leg. General principles can help you develop an effective strategy when none is known.

We tell you this because many study skills books provide students with specific strategies such as sitting toward the front of the classroom, but these books don't supply the general principles that support those strategies and suggest others. Our belief is that general principles are more important than specific strategies, because people who understand the principle can often develop their own strategies for dealing with situations, such as biology quizzes or unrestricted bleeding. People who know only strategies and not principles might not prepare adequately for tests, and they might never get past the Band-Aid® stage in medical treatment.

We hope that you acquire many specific strategies from reading this book. More than that, we hope you acquire a handful of general principles that support and suggest specific strategies. We believe that the following four principles are crucial for helping you adopt or develop effective learning and memory strategies.

General principles can help you develop an effective strategy when none is known.

Focus Your Attention

In any learning situation, hundreds of stimuli (events or messages) could be competing for your attention. In the classroom, for example, the instructor's voice, the information written on the chalkboard, the hum of the overhead projector, the turning of notebook pages, whispers, pens tapping, and legs swinging—all these compete for attention. Your brain, however, handles only a single message or incident at a time. So, since your attention is limited (by nature) to one selected stimulus at one time, if you attend to the swinging leg you cannot pay attention to the instructor's voice or any other stimulus. Therefore, you want to use strategies that help you focus on the most important stimulus and ignore the less important ones.

To better understand the limited and selective nature of attention, imagine, for a minute, going to a party. Imagine that you are trapped talking with a not-at-all interesting person. As he explains the great gas mileage his Chevy Vega got when he traveled to Okachoochoo, you find that your attention wanders around the room selecting more interesting stimuli to process. You notice some "nut" with a lampshade on his head. You see someone accidentally drop a potato chip, look around, and then quite deliberately step on it so that no one will notice it. You smell the host's dog, which needs bathing. You hear that Bob is splitting from Carol; Ted is leaving Alice; Bob is now interested in Alice; Carol is intrigued by Ted; and Ted is interested in Bob. There are, however, many other conversations and observable incidents that you do not notice at this party, including the fantastic gas mileage the Vega once got on a trip to Shreveport.

Whether you're at a party, a ball game, in a classroom, or at home, you are confronted by many stimuli. You focus attention on some of them, such as the "nut" with the lampshade. You perhaps remember this selected information. The information you don't focus on, such as the message about the Vega and the trip to Shreveport, is never learned. Similarly, you have to focus on the information presented in a lecture, rather than the coughs and whispers, or that information will be forever lost.

Knowing that you need to focus your attention is not sufficient, however. It is important to know the types of things that are likely to grab your attention. Researchers have conducted experiments in which students listen to two different messages simultaneously via headphones. One message is played in each ear. Students are asked to shadow or repeat the message in a designated ear as it plays. This is a very demanding task, requiring practically all of the student's attention. As a result, the student hears and remembers very little of the message in the other, nonshadowed, ear.

It is interesting to note, however, what types of messages *are* heard in the nonshadowed ear. Students can recall hearing physical changes, such as a change in volume or pitch. They can also respond to personally relevant information, such as their own name. Finally, students can process information relevant to the shadowed message, which suggests that information that relates to the student's objective is captured. There are countless other examples of how physical properties, personal relevance, and

Exercise

Create two lists. In the first, list all the things that can or do distract you in classroom settings. In the second, list all the things that can or do distract you while you read or study. Later, you will be asked to develop strategies for handling these distractions.

objectives influence attention in academic and nonacademic settings. Some examples are provided below, along with a few strategies for focusing attention.

Attend to Physical Properties

Why do you think that television commercials are louder than the programs they interrupt? Why is it more expensive to place a boldface advertisement in the newspaper? Why do you notice a bird flying past your window when you are intently reading a book? In each case, the answer has to do with physical properties of the stimulus grabbing your attention. Stimuli that are suddenly loud, bold, or moving command your attention.

In academic settings, the same principle applies. Textbooks put some information in bold letters, underline it, italicize it, or print it in an unusual color. Heed these attention-getting signals.

Focus your attention on signaled ideas. For example, a teacher gains attention by varying the physical properties of the stimulus. He varies the volume, pitch, or rate of his words as he lectures. Occasionally, he speaks very loudly or very softly, or speaks slowly, enunciating certain words or syllables differently for effect. Pay attention to these signs. They're like trail markers in the mountains: They signal you which way to go. The instructor also commands attention by using movement. Walking about the room and incorporating subtle hand and facial gestures commands your attention.

Movement, however, can force you to attend to irrelevant stimuli. If a student sitting in front of you in class frequently swings his leg, your attention will shift from the instructor to the swinging leg. The solution to this distraction is to sit in the front row of all classes so that fidgeting students can't distract you.

While studying, minimize the number of stimuli that might distract you. Study in quiet areas. Most residence hall study lounges are filled with distractions, and thus are not suited for serious studying. It's much better to study in your room and to use "white noise," such as a fan or earphones playing instrumental background music, to drown out potential distractions. Never study with the radio or television on, both of which are certain to grab your attention with stimuli such as deafening commercials, screeching commentators, and songs with alluring lyrics. The messages might also have personal relevance, and grab your attention with something such as an old song that takes you back to another time, or advertisements for a product you're in the market for.

CERTAIN STIMULI
COMMAND ATTENTION

Attend to Personally Relevant Ideas

A second type of stimulus likely to receive your attention is one that is familiar. For instance, have you ever sat down in a crowded cafeteria where dozens of conversations were occurring? Very often your ears "perk up" when you hear something familiar or interesting being discussed. If someone mentions East Northport, your hometown, you are much more likely to tune in than if they mention Frost Bite Falls, Minnesota (unless, of course, you are a fan of the *Rocky and Bullwinkle* show). If someone mentions a movie that you saw two nights ago, again, you are likely to attend selectively.

One of this book's authors remembers going to a basketball game on the campus of Kansas State University. During this particular game, several large pieces of paper were being passed around for signing. Each was a get-well card for the coach, who had become ill. (The author thought the illness was understandable, given the Wildcat's poor offensive showings.) When a card with perhaps seventy-five signatures reached the author, he quickly signed it without reading it. As he began to pass it along, however, he noticed a familiar name that seemed to just jump right off the list. He could have sworn that he hadn't looked at a single name on the list, and yet that one familiar name caught his attention. Why? Because humans have a tremendous capacity to automatically scan all available information and then select only the most relevant.

Take advantage of this tendency by making new information personally relevant. For example, when you're practicing problems in math, you could relate them to the purchase and maintenance costs of a new car if you're interested in cars. When you learn about a present-day war that's occurring abroad, or if you're studying the War of 1812, imagine how you'd feel if you were there. Consider the personal implications of that war.

Caution! Be careful not to limit your attention to just those ideas that are personally relevant. An entomology student interested primarily in wasps must maintain attention when discussions turn to other bugs, such as bees and ants. Using the course objectives to guide your attention is one helpful way around this potential problem.

Attend to Objectives

Stimuli that you look for also tend to gain your attention. There is an old adage, "When a thief meets a saint, all the thief sees are the saint's pockets." People often notice what they are looking for, to the exclusion of other stimuli. Dentists notice teeth, not hands; mechanics notice fuel pumps, not car mats.

Often, you may try hard to learn but fail to select the most important ideas. You can do several things to focus on relevant stimuli. The six important suggestions below describe strategies for focusing your attention:

1. *Be alert for objectives provided by an instructor or textbook.* An instructor, for example, might say that students should be able to compare and contrast the three types of creativity—expressive, adaptive, and innovative—with respect to products, motivation, and myths. Using the instructor's guidelines, try to select information about the products, motivation, and myths associated with each type of creativity. Remember that paying attention to objectives helped Carlos focus his study behaviors and excel on his biology quiz.

2. *Be alert for focus or other questions embedded throughout instruction.* These questions, in turn, help you focus your attention on the information necessary to answer them. The Focus Questions throughout this text are provided to direct your attention while you read.

3. *Pay special attention to overviews that your instructor provides prior to instruction, and to summaries provided throughout or following instruction.* These contain crucial information. Overviews are particularly helpful because, like objectives or focus questions, they direct your attention to important information. Summaries do the same. This textbook, for example, provides an overview and introductions at the beginning of chapters, and summaries at the conclusion of each chapter to focus your attention on relevant information.

4. *Pay special attention to important signals that appear during written and oral instruction.* In text, pay attention to certain physical cues, such as those described previously, including underlining, italics, and bold print. In addition, titles and headings also signal upcoming information of importance. In lecture contexts, be aware of cues such as information written on the board or verbal cues such as "This is critical."

5. *Increase your attention and learning by re-presenting information.* Do this by tape-recording hard-to-follow lectures and taking notes from the recorded lecture more than once. Repeated presentations allow you to home in on details ordinarily missed from a single presentation. When you first hear a lecture, listen for and note the main ideas. For subsequent, re-presentations, shift your attention and note-taking from the main ideas to the subordinate details that support the main ideas. Adding to an already existing set of notes also produces a more detailed record of the lecture for studying.

6. *Identify the "alert words" that signal the structure of the information.* Alert words key you to the relations among ideas. Words like types, parts, aspects, and kinds indicate hierarchical relations. Words like next, first, later, and before signal sequential relations. Words like whereas and however signal comparative relations. The following chapters, "Representations for Learning," and "Constructing Representations" explain how to identify and represent relations among ideas.

Don't Rely on Rehearsal for Long-Term Learning

Once you have selected information, you need to do something with it to make sure it's retained permanently in your memory. Most students believe that the appropriate strategy for long-term learning is rehearsal (that is, repeating the information over and over). Rehearsal is actually an ineffective strategy for long-term learning.

To demonstrate, study the two trigrams[1] below for about five seconds. Then cover them with a piece of paper, wait about ten seconds, and then try to recall them.

SGR   TCN

Now check your answers. Did you get them both correct? How were you able to retain that information? Most of you probably used the rehearsal strategy of repeating them in your mind.

Now try the same task again. Examine the two trigrams below for about five seconds, cover them with a piece of paper, wait about ten seconds, then read the instructions below before attempting to recall them.

VSL   BTR

[1]Adapted from Peterson, L. R., and Peterson, M. J. (1959). Short-term retention of individual verbal items. *Journal of Experimental Psychology*, 58, 193–198.

Exercise

Return to the lists you made earlier. Identify a strategy for reducing or eliminating each distraction on your list. You might compile your distractions and strategies in a table like the one shown below.

Classroom		Studying	
Distractions	**Strategies**	**Distractions**	**Strategies**
1. Movement	1. Sit toward front	1. Noise	1. Instrumental music or fan
2. Daydreaming	2. Take complete notes	2. Telephone ringing	2. Unplug phone
3. Noise	3. Ask instructor to repeat information—sit toward front	3. Hunger pangs	3. Eat

Before recalling the trigrams, count out loud, backwards, from sixty to zero, by threes. Sixty, fifty-seven, fifty-four . . . zero. Now try to recall the trigrams. You probably didn't remember them correctly this time. That's because the counting task prevented you from rehearsing further, and without continuous rehearsal, the information was lost from memory. Now try to remember the initial trigrams. You probably couldn't this time, although you tried only moments after having both rehearsed and recalled them.

Rehearsal is an effective strategy for holding information for a short time, such as when you hold a new phone number in memory while dialing it, but it's a poor strategy for long-term learning. You know this is true because if the line is busy you will probably not remember the phone number a moment later when you try to place the call again. The key to long-term learning is building internal and external connections.

For further proof that rehearsal techniques are ineffective, try the exercise on page 112 with a friend.

Build Connections

When students ask us, "What is the key to learning and memory?" without hesitation we answer, "Building connections." This is the most important learning principle.

Connections are relationships among ideas. For example, suppose you are asked to learn the three ideas below:

1. White rhinos live in grasslands.
2. White rhinos eat grass.
3. White rhinos have square lips.

Of course, you could memorize each idea separately, as many students do, or you could make connections among the ideas. For instance, you can connect the first and second ideas, since it is logical that rhinos who live in grasslands eat grass. You can also connect the second and third ideas since square lips are well suited for scooping up and eating grass.

Another type of connection is possible if you relate this new information about white rhinos to past knowledge about cows. You know that white rhinos are like cows, because both have square lips for scooping up and eating grass.

There are two types of connections you can build when learning: internal and external. Internal connections are those built within the material being learned. External connections extend outside the material being learned. External connections are built between the new material being learned and past knowledge already stored in memory.

Exercise

Tell your friend that you are going to read a long list of words, and that his/her task is to remember the *last* word that begins with the letter "*p*."[2] Notice that in the list we've provided, varying numbers of non-*p* words occur between *p* words. We did this to control the number of rehearsals each *p* word receives. It is likely that your friend will rehearse a *p* word when it's presented, and continue to rehearse it each time a non-*p* word is presented until another *p* word comes along. Thus, the word *pliers* in the list below receives three rehearsals, whereas the word *pebble* receives six rehearsals.

If amount of rehearsal really does affect long-term learning, then words that receive more rehearsals should be better recalled than those receiving fewer rehearsals when you unexpectedly ask your friend to later recall all the *p* words. Do just that. After presenting the list below, wait a few minutes and then ask him/her to recall all the *p* words from the list. We think you'll see there is no relation between the number of rehearsals a word receives and its recall.

1. Table	11. Lamp	21. Park (9)	31. Wall
2. Ball	12. Dog	22. Scissors	32. Pepperoni (1)
3. Cat	13. Pebble (6)	23. Tire	33. Pocket (5)
4. Peach (4)	14. Office	24. Table	34. Flower
5. Window	15. Book	25. Magnet	35. Sky
6. Lake	16. Curtain	26. Shovel	36. Letter
7. Floor	17. Shirt	27. Arrow	37. Milk
8. Puck (2)	18. Cup	28. Shoe	38. Pool (3)
9. Rope	19. Parchment (2)	29. Temple	39. Tree
10. Pliers (3)	20. Canal	30. Pizza (2)	40. Glass

The numbers in parentheses equal the number of rehearsals a *p* word probably received.

[2]Adapted from Craik, F. I. M., and Watkins, M. J. (1973). The role of rehearsal in short-term memory, *Journal of Verbal Learning and Verbal Behavior*, 12, 599–607.

To help you remember that internal connections pertain to connections made within the learning material and external connections pertain to connections made between the learning material and past knowledge, look at the diagram in Figure 4-1, which shows a student learning from a page of text. The Xs represent text ideas selected by the student. The broken lines represent the internal connections built among selected ideas. For example, the student reading about white rhinos connects facts about their habitat, food, and lips. These are internal connections because they are built within the learning material. The solid lines represent external connections built between the new material (the Xs) and past knowledge stored in memory (the triangles). For example, the student might be relating the food and lips of white rhinos to those of cows. These are called external connections because the connections are made outside the learning material.

The next two sections describe internal and external connections in greater detail.

Build Internal Connections

One important way to learn new information is by building internal connections among the ideas to be learned. Building internal connections helps you learn relationships among presented ideas and see how ideas are organized. Building internal connections is like putting together a puzzle. At first, the pieces lie scattered and unconnected. The puzzler connects two pieces that relate in color, shape, or size. Eventually, several related pieces are organized to form a picture that can be seen only when the pieces are properly arranged.

Figure 4–1. *Internal and External Connections*

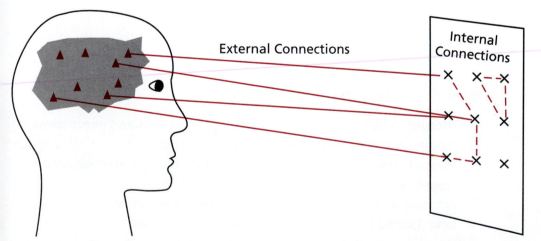

Consider the task of having to memorize the sixteen foods listed in Figure 4-2. Many students attempt to learn this list as sixteen different foods by rehearsing the list. That's like constructing a line of puzzle pieces and repeatedly scanning the line, hoping to realize what picture they might form.

Using the principle of internal connections, the appropriate strategy involves arranging the foods into a few logical categories by following the familiar sequence of a meal. For instance, chocolate cake and strawberry shortcake are placed in the dessert category. Iced tea and club soda are placed in the drinks category. Figure 4-3 shows how the sixteen foods can be organized.

These groupings make it possible for you to learn better than you would by memorizing the list. There are several reasons for this. First, in one sense, there is less to learn. You learn four categories, each with natural subcategories and members, rather than sixteen discrete terms. This is like learning the fifty states by region (for example, midwest, northeast, southwest) instead of using a long alphabetized list. By connecting adjoining states and grouping regional states, you learn a few groups of affiliated states.

Second, information that is well organized is easier to retrieve from your memory. This is because there are many pathways for retrieving the information. For example, the french fries in Figure 4-3 are retrievable by recalling the category "main course," the subcategory "potatoes," or by recalling the other item in that category "potatoes au gratin." Even remembering a main course such as "filet mignon" can help in retrieving an accompanying potato dish.

Similarly, you can remember the state of Nebraska by recalling its midwest region or any one of its surrounding states such as Iowa, Kansas, and South Dakota.

One more example involves a book stored in a library. You can access it by title, author, and subject. Any or all of these connections lead to the book's retrieval.

Figure 4–2. *Sixteen Foods to Memorize*

1. chocolate cake
2. asparagus with cream sauce
3. filet mignon
4. tossed salad
5. potatoes au gratin
6. baked salmon
7. strawberry shortcake
8. iced tea
9. string beans and mushrooms
10. club soda
11. fresh baked cinnamon rolls
12. french fries
13. french onion soup
14. spinach salad
15. cream of mushroom soup
16. crackers and cheese dip

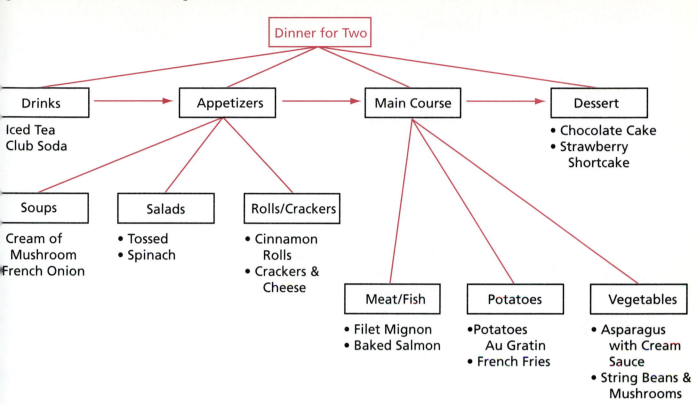

Last, you can understand organized information better than unorga-
ized information. In this case, you can easily understand how these six-
een foods provide a dinner for two.

This easy comprehension of organized ideas is also illustrated in the
xample below. Read the following passage about moths and butterflies.

Moths and Butterflies

A moth has two sets of wings. It folds the wings down over its
body like a roof when it rests. The moth has feathery antennae
and spins a fuzzy cocoon. It has a gray or white color and usually
flies at night. The moth goes through four stages of development:
egg, caterpillar, pupa, and adult.

A butterfly goes through four stages of development (egg,
caterpillar, pupa, and adult) and has two sets of wings. Its antennae are long and thin with knobs at the ends. When a butterfly
rests, its wings are straight up like outstretched hands. A butterfly
is brightly colored and flies during the day.

What did you notice about this passage? It described moths and then
utterflies, but it did not connect them by explaining how they are alike or
ifferent. The passage read as if these two insects had nothing in common.
s a result, most students learn this information as if it were a list of dis-
rete facts, as shown in Figure 4-4. They memorize moth facts and then go
n to memorize butterfly facts without connecting their similarities and dif-
erences.

Moths
- Wings—two sets
- Rest—wings folded down
- Antennae—feathery
- Cocoon—fuzzy
- Color—gray or white
- Flight—night
- Stages of Development—egg, caterpillar, pupa, adult

Butterflies
- Stages of Development—egg, caterpillar, pupa, adult
- Wings—two sets
- Antennae—long and thin with knobs
- Rest—wings outstretched
- Color—bright
- Flight—day

Now examine the same information represented in a matrix form in Figure 4-5. By reading across the matrix, you can see in a glance that moth and butterflies are alike in two ways: Each has two sets of wings and progresses through four stages of development. Now examine their difference by reading across the matrix. The moth folds its wings down, but the butterfly's wings are outstretched. The moth's antennae are feathery, and the butterfly's antennae are long and thin with knobs. The moth has drab colors and flies at night, whereas the butterfly has bright colors and flies during the day.

Figure 4–5. *Matrix Representation of Moths and Butterflies Passage*

	Moths	Butterflies
Moths and Butterflies		
Development:	Egg → Caterpillar → Pupa →	Adult
Wings:	Two sets	Two sets
Rest:	Wings folded down	Wings outstretched
Antennae:	Feathery	Long with knobs
Color:	Gray or white	Bright
Flight:	Night	Day
Cocoon:	Fuzzy	

By making these internal connections, it is easier to understand how these insects relate. They are similar in terms of development and number of wings, and different along all other dimensions.

What is particularly intriguing, though, is that all of these peripheral differences really amount to one central difference: In all cases the moth is drab, inconspicuous, or subdued, whereas the butterfly is vibrant, conspicuous, or pronounced. Understanding this central difference is crucial in understanding the differences between moths and butterflies.

Note, however, that none of these connections were stated in the passage or apparent in the list. Seek to build internal connections whether authors or instructors present them or not. Sadly, in many cases, the responsibility for building internal and external connections falls upon you, the student. But building connections is the single most important principle guiding effective learning.

Seek to build internal connections whether authors or instructors present them or not.

Exercise

Below is a brief passage about the nervous system and the endocrine system. Build internal connections to help you understand their similarities and differences.

The nervous system is composed of nerves that secrete neurohumors. Nerves also secrete noradrenaline. The nervous system helps to maintain homeostasis. Nerve responses are rapid and of short duration. Nerves transmit impulses via neurons.

The endocrine system is composed of glands that secrete hormones. The adrenal gland also secretes noradrenaline. The endocrine system helps to maintain homeostasis. Endocrine responses are slow but last for a long time. Hormones are carried by the blood plasma.

Build External Connections

Learning and memory are also improved by building external connections. You do this by relating new to-be-learned information to past knowledge already in your memory. As you learn about the unfamiliar game of cricket, for example, you might relate new information about cricket (it involves a ball and bat) to past knowledge about baseball (it, too, involves a ball and bat).

External connections make the new information more meaningful, make its storage in memory more economical, and aid retrieval. For example, if you're learning about insulin shock in a health class, you might relate this new information to past knowledge about diabetic coma. You remember that too little insulin is the cause of diabetic coma, and you recognize that too much insulin is the cause of insulin shock. Thus, you can store the new information about insulin shock in memory along with information about diabetic coma. Recalling information about one of these is now likely to trigger recall about the other.

From the discussion of external connections, it's obvious that you must have past knowledge to build external connections. Without past knowledge, you can't make external connections and you can't learn information meaningfully.

For an example, consider the following portion of a newspaper column written by Steve Becker about the card game, Bridge. We authors didn't have the past knowledge necessary to understand it. Do you?

> Eventually, declarer decided that his best shot for the contract was to lead the heart queen at trick two. On top of the possibility that the queen might be ducked, this also allowed him to keep in reserve a follow-up play that virtually guaranteed making five diamonds.
>
> East took the queen of hearts with the ace and returned the jack of clubs at trick three. South won with the ace and thereupon made the key play of leading the five of diamonds to dummy's six!
>
> This unusual move—deliberately losing a trump trick he did not have to lose—had the desired effect.

Not understanding the terms declarer, contract, trick, ducked, dummy, and trump, it is impossible for us to connect this new information to past knowledge and understand it.

Can you do any better understanding the following passage?

> After checking the log it was obvious that I had been doing far too much LSD. As a result, my max VO_2 was bound to suffer. It was obviously a time to attempt some fartleking.

Although you had no difficulty reading this second passage, chances are that you didn't know what it was about. If you were asked to remember it, you might memorize it word-for-word—but you'd still not be able to

External connections make the new information more meaningful, make its storage in memory more economical, and aid retrieval.

recall it in a meaningful fashion. For example, you wouldn't know why it's time to attempt some fartleking.

If you have difficulty learning and remembering this passage, which is about running, it's because you didn't have the prior knowledge in memory necessary to form meaningful external connections.

To explain briefly, a log is a journal in which workout records are kept. LSD is not the acronym you think it is—it stands for long, slow distance. Max VO$_2$ is not a hair conditioner but maximum oxygen intake, which represents ability to transform oxygen into energy. "Fartleking" is a Swedish word. It means "speed play" and involves running fast for portions of your run.

The passage above means that this particular runner was aware that she had been running too slowly, and that she was perhaps losing physical efficiency. A fartlek workout with occasional hard running was a possible solution for regaining some fitness. If you yourself are a runner, then you can make many more external connections, relating this passage to your personal running experiences—such as the time you were ill and could not run, and lost conditioning.

Even if you're not a runner, now that you understand what the words mean, you have the knowledge necessary to make external connections and thus learn the passage. You might, for example, relate the passage to a sputtering car engine that reduces speed to a maximum of fifty miles per hour. A tune-up (like a fartlek workout) is necessary to revitalize the engine so it can perform at its best.

Another example of the importance of prior knowledge for making external connections comes in having to learn that the Native Americans of the Northwest Coast lived in homes with high-pitched roofs made with wood planks. This information about roof pitch and wood planks appears arbitrary to most learners—unless they can make an external connection between this new information and past knowledge about the timber resources and yearly rainfall of the Pacific Northwest. Knowing that this region is famous for its plentiful rain and timber, it's easy to remember that Native Americans built high-pitched wood roofs to deflect heavy rains.

There are several additional ways you can develop external connections. One is to think about how new information fits with past knowledge. If you're learning about the causes of World War II, for example, you can relate its causes to the causes and/or the outcomes of World War I, if you have previously learned about World War I. The causes of World War II can also be related to the causes of more recent world conflicts. And if you were learning about a new bird, such as the redbilled hornbill, you could relate it to more familiar birds with respect to origin, habitat, appearance, and mating rituals.

Another strategy you can use is generating examples or analogies for new concepts. In Psychology, for example, if you're learning about the defense mechanism of repression, which means that memories of a traumatic event are covered up and not easily retrievable, generate an example like the following: John rarely thinks of his old girlfriend, Samantha, and especially the events that caused their breakup. An analogy for repression might be a box of old love letters that lies forgotten in the attic. Carlos, earlier in the chapter, used the analogy of a city to understand and remember cell part functions.

The examples of external connections presented thus far have all involved making natural connections between the new information and prior knowledge. It is natural, for example, to relate new information about World War II to previous knowledge about World War I, or to relate information about the structure of homes to the environmental conditions surrounding those homes. However, if you haven't got the knowledge to make natural associations, then contrived (made up) associations should be developed.

Perhaps you have used contrived associations to remember your school locker combinations. As a long-time New York Yankees fan, one author remembered a locker combination by relating it to the jersey numbers of Yankees players. He imagined ace left-hander Ron Guidry (19) pitching to slugger Reggie Jackson (44) and volatile manager Billy Martin (1) arguing with Jackson about whether to bunt or swing away. This seems like a better way to remember than that used by movie boxing champion Rocky Balboa, who for years remembered his locker combination by pulling it from a slip of paper tucked under his hat.

Perhaps you've used contrived associations to remember phone numbers. While he was in college, the same author and his roommate visited friends at the start of school who announced that their new phone number was "Columbus minus two." They explained that Columbus sailed the ocean blue in 1492 and that their new number was 432-1490.

The roommate never liked to be outdone, and since he was a history major, this association challenged him all the more. He thought for several minutes, and then proudly reported that his new phone number was "Magellan plus five." "Simply add five to the year Magellan sailed around the world and that's our phone number," he boasted.

Unfortunately the story does not end there. That evening, in the middle of a driving rainstorm, the author was downtown late at night (probably studying) and needed a ride back to campus. He decided to call his roommate and ask (beg) for a ride. (After all, what are roommates for?) Unfortunately, he had not yet learned his new telephone number and could only remember the roommate's clever connection, "Magellan plus five." In desperation, he pleaded for help from nearby strangers, who could only return confused expressions when asked when Magellan sailed the globe. It was a long and soggy trek back to campus.

The moral of the story is that even a contrived connection must be understood to some degree.

Contrived connections like those just described are called mnemonic techniques (which is another way of saying "memory tricks"). Mnemonic techniques are useful for helping you remember academic content, as well as locker combinations. Perhaps you are already familiar with the mnemonic for remembering the nine planets. The sentence "My very educated mother just served us nine pizzas" is used to remember the planet names in order from the sun. The first letter of each word in the sentence corresponds to a planet: My = Mercury, very = Venus, educated = Earth, and so on out to Pluto. We revisit mnemonics in greater detail in Chapter 9, "How to Review for Exams."

Exercise

Generate an external connection for the following definitions by relating each to a familiar example.

Reflex   An inborn, unlearned response.

Instinct A complex, innate act performed without training.

Habit   A learned response which has become completely automatic.

Can you make an external connection that relates the information below about memory to your past knowledge about computers?

Humans are thought to have a short-term memory (STM) and a long-term memory (LTM). The STM holds incoming information briefly. It can only hold a limited amount of information at one time. It is sometimes called "working memory," because it works or operates on information currently being processed. Long-term memory is where permanent storage takes place. The capacity of LTM is thought to be limitless.

Monitor Your Learning

The real goal of education should be to produce autonomous learners, that is, students capable of learning on their own. An autonomous learner does not depend on an instructor to guide or monitor her learning. She does it herself. Most students, however, fail in this regard.

Read the following passage.

> The man was worried. His car came to a halt and he was all alone. It was extremely dark and cold. The man took off his overcoat, rolled down the window, and got out of the car as quickly as possible. Then he used all his strength to move as fast as he could. He was relieved when he finally saw the lights of the city, even though they were far away.

Did you understand the passage? Most people say they understood it. It is only when they are asked particular questions, like the following, that they realize that they did not understand: "Why did the man take off his overcoat? Why did he roll down his window?" People finally gain complete understanding only when they're told that the passage is about a man escaping from a submerged car.

The problem is that students usually don't ask themselves whether or not they know what's being said. When they're reading a textbook, they continue to turn pages without asking whether they really understood what they read. As a result, they often have no understanding of what it was they read.

If they're preparing for an exam, they don't test their own understanding, so they don't know that they don't know the material until the instructor tests them. Then, of course, it's too late.

What should you do? You should self-monitor your progress and performance. When you're reading, never turn a page until you summarize what's on that page. When you're studying, test yourself so thoroughly that there is nothing the instructor can ask you that they haven't already asked yourself. Walk confidently into your classroom on test day knowing you can correctly answer any question asked. A smart skydiver doesn't wait until she jumps to find out if her chute is packed correctly. Similarly, an effective student never waits for the instructor's test to learn whether she knows the material.

Sometimes students self-monitor and still perform poorly. This perhaps occurs because students aren't checking their knowledge in a manner that matches the way they will be tested. For example, students can probably correctly assess their ability to answer a fact item about the concept of negative reinforcement, such as "Define negative reinforcement," but fail to assess their ability to answer a concept item involving the recognition of a novel example, such as "A rat repeatedly presses a lever to avoid a shock." As a result, students often perform poorly on higher-order items that involve recognizing concepts or demonstrating skills.

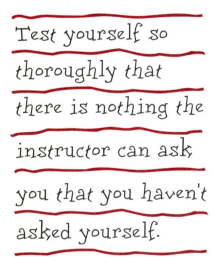

Test yourself so thoroughly that there is nothing the instructor can ask you that you haven't asked yourself.

Why do students fail to prepare adequately for different types of tests? One reason is that instructors often shroud the criteria in secrecy; they simply do not tell students what type of test to expect and prepare for. This tendency to hide the criteria is one of the oddest and most enduring aspects of education.

HOW SHOULD I KNOW WHICH PART OF THE CELL IS LIKE CITY MAYOR? I STUDIED CELL FUNCTIONS, NOT CITY GOVERNMENT.

We cannot think of another area in our society where people are kept ignorant about the task for which they are preparing. Where else but in schools do individuals prepare for the unknown? Do football teams prepare for a game against an unknown opponent? Do vacationers prepare for a trip to an unknown destination? Of course not! Students, however, are often clueless about how they will be tested. Instructors should tell students whether the test assesses the recall of facts, the recognition of novel examples, or the demonstration of skills. However, when students lack criteria knowledge, they should prepare for all of these potential test types.

But there is another problem. Students armed with knowledge of the criteria might still not study and monitor their performance effectively, because they have not been taught how to prepare differently for different types of tests. As a result, they prepare and monitor as if every test assesses only factual recall.

It is important that you learn how to study for different types of tests so that you can monitor your progress and performance accurately in advance of the test. This is a topic addressed in Chapter 9, "How to Review for Exams."

Self-monitoring occurs not only while you're studying for a test, but throughout the entire academic process. Effective students monitor their motivation. They monitor their desire, intention, focus, and sustainment, and they monitor their attributions. They don't allow themselves to falsely attribute lack of success to barriers (such as a boring instructor) that they can control. Effective students also monitor their time. They check to see that they're investing time, investing daily, investing early and wisely, and enjoying their investment.

Effective students monitor their use of strategies. They check to ensure that the strategies they use are based on powerful learning principles, such as building internal and external connections, rather than on weak learning principles, such as rehearsal. They continually monitor their attention to be sure they're focusing on important stimuli from the lecture or text instead of focusing on irrelevant stimuli (such as noises) or daydreaming. Overall, effective students talk to themselves throughout the learning process, holding a dialogue with the "little teacher inside the brain," who is continually asking questions of them, such as, "Are you understanding this?" and "Are you using your time wisely?" and "What external connection can be made here?" As they learn more about learning, their little teacher will ask better and better questions to guide their academic progress and performance.

Self-monitoring is not just an academic skill, it is a life skill. Successful workers monitor their performance. Before the day even begins, they think about their meetings with supervisors and clients, and they anticipate what they might be asked and how they might respond. They employ visual imagery and imagine in detail being successful in these situations. While the meetings are actually in process, they monitor their performance. They ask themselves whether they are being understood and making a favorable impression. They adjust accordingly and continue to monitor.

Perhaps another excellent reason to learn effective monitoring is that it is extremely important in our personal lives: Self-monitoring can save lives. We recently read about three horrific events that occurred in the same weekend. In one instance, several boys and counselors were killed in a cave when a flash flood struck. In another instance, several children were killed when their boat capsized on a lake. In the last event, several young children were killed when a fire raged through their house. All of these "accidents" could have been avoided if the adults involved had used self-monitoring.

The counselors saw signs warning about flash floods that had occurred only the week before. Had the counselors considered the potential dangers, they either would have not entered the cave, or at least they would've developed a warning system for alerting those in the cave of danger.

Nine people were on board the boat designed for a maximum of three people, and not one of them wore a life vest. The supervising adults failed to consider the potential dangers of overloading a boat and not issuing life vests.

The house fire broke out while the supervising parent was walking a friend home. The supervising parent didn't anticipate that the children might play with matches and that they could start a fire in only a short time.

As students, workers, and family members, we must learn to effectively monitor our own performance and learn to anticipate what lies around the next bend. Doing so can boost your grades now and accelerate your career advancement later. In your personal life, it can raise your family's happiness and sense of well being. Failing to monitor performance might produce just the opposite.

Exercise

List three questions you might ask yourself while you're reading.

List three questions you might ask yourself while you're attending a lecture.

List three questions you might ask yourself while you're studying with a study group.

List three questions you might ask yourself while you're driving.

List three questions you might ask yourself while you're tending to a child.

Summary

General learning principles are important because they produce the strategies that you should use. Four principles were presented in this chapter: Focus your attention, don't rely on rehearsal for long-term learning, build your internal and external connections, and monitor your learning.

Focus your attention on important stimuli. Certain lecture and text aids such as objectives and headings direct your attention to important ideas.

Once information is selected, you must store it in memory. Contrary to popular belief, rehearsal is not effective for long-term learning. Eliminate rehearsal strategies such as rereading, recopying, and reciting. Instead, build connections or relationships among presented ideas (internal connections) or between presented ideas and previously learned ideas (external connections).

Build internal connections by representing information spatially, such as in a matrix where the relationships among ideas are easy to see.

Build external connections by generating examples and analogies for the presented ideas, and by comparing the presented ideas to familiar ideas. Mnemonics, or memory tricks, are also useful ways to build connections when more meaningful connections are hard to build.

Finally, monitor your learning throughout the learning process. Engage in an ongoing dialogue with your brain as you take notes, read texts, and review for exams. Know when you're ready for an exam and never let the instructor be the first to test you.

Answers to focus *questions*

1. Instructors grab your attention in several ways. For example, voice variations, including speaking louder (or softer), higher (or lower), and faster (or slower), capture attention. So too do movements and gestures. Writing on the board in colored chalk or capital letters is also likely to command attention.

2. Offset potential distractions by studying in a quiet place and covering distractions with "white noise," such as the hum of a fan. In classrooms, avoid distractions by sitting in the front row.

3. There are many cues that can direct your attention to relevant information. Pay special attention to objectives, questions, overviews, summaries, headings, and verbal or printed signals that specify important information.

4. Rehearsal is a poor strategy for long-term remembering. Rehearsal only retains information in memory while it is being rehearsed. Long-term remembering depends on constructing internal and external connections.

5. Internal connections involve relating the ideas being learned to one another. External connections involve relating the ideas being learned to past knowledge. Internal and external connections are the keys to learning and long-term remembering.

6. The benefits of building internal connections are that there is "less" to learn and information is easier to understand and retrieve.

7. Because external connections are those built between new information and previously learned information, you must possess background knowledge to build these connections.

8. External connections are formed in several ways, such as developing examples and analogies for new information and comparing new information to related ideas.

9. Mnemonics are memory tricks. They are used to remember isolated facts that are hard to connect to more relevant ideas.

10. You know you are ready for a test when there is nothing the instructor can ask you that you haven't already asked yourself.

11. Self-monitor throughout the academic process. Monitor while note-taking, reading, reviewing, test-taking, writing, and analyzing errors. Monitor your motivation and time management.

chapter 5
Representations for Learning

OVERVIEW

Focus Questions

Introduction

Advantages of Representation
    Similar Information Is Localized
    Clutter Is Reduced
    Missing Details Are Apparent
    The "Big Picture" Is Developed

Re-examining the Advantages

Types of Representations and Their Relations
    Hierarchies
    Sequences
    Matrices
    Diagrams

Summary

Answers to Focus Questions

focus questions

1. What four advantages do representations have over outlines?
2. What is the benefit of localization in representations?
3. How do outlines obscure the "big picture"?
4. Can you match the pattern name on the left with the patterns on the right?

   1. Hierarchies

   A. ☐ → ☐ → ☐

   2. Sequences

   B.

   3. Matrices

   C.

   4. Diagrams

   The Brain

   D.
   ← Cerebrum
   ← Cerebellum
   ← Medulla
   ← Spinal Cord

5. In the hierarchy below, what is subordinate to C?

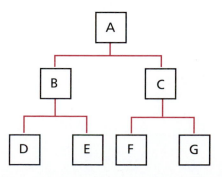

6. In the hierarchy above, what letter forms a group with B?

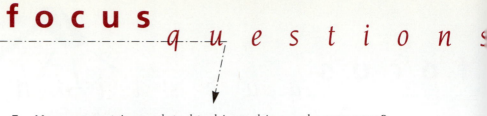

7. How are matrices related to hierarchies and sequences?
8. Below is a hierarchy for saws. Can you extend it into a matrix by adding potential repeatable categories?

9. In the matrix below, can you identify the topics, repeatable categories, and details?

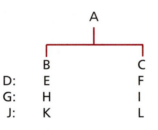

10. What are within-topic and across-topic relations?
11. What is the difference between a static and dynamic diagram?

Keth: Sandy, I studied for the psychology quiz.

I tried to memorize the definitions of operant

concepts but I couldn't keep them straight.

Operant Concepts

Positive reinforcement: A stimulus is presented following a behavior and the behavior increases.

Negative reinforcement: A stimulus is removed following a behavior and the behavior increases.

Positive punishment: A stimulus is presented following a behavior and the behavior decreases.

Negative punishment: A stimulus is removed following a behavior and the behavior decreases.

Keth: Can you help me?

Sandy: What's in it for me?

Keth: If you can teach me how to learn this stuff,

I'll treat you to a mushroom and garlic pie at

the Factory.

Sandy: Ah, the magic words! Throw in pepperoni, oh Swami, and you've
got a deal.

Keth: What choice do I have! I'm just a thin crust from failing.
Pepperoni it is. Now work your magic.

Sandy: The key, Keth, is learning the concepts all together.

Keth: Say what?

Sandy: These four concepts are related. To understand them, they have to
be tossed together like the vegetables in a salad.

Keth: No upping the ante, Sandy. I promised pizza, not salad.

Sandy: I was speaking figuratively. Lettuce continue, oh tomato head. Look
at the names of the first two concepts: positive reinforcement and
negative reinforcement. Do you think they are alike in some way?

Keth: I suppose. They're both a type of reinforcement.

Sandy: Right. Do you think they are different in some way?

Keth: I suppose.

Sandy: They must be, otherwise there would be just one concept called "reinforcement." Your job is to find out how they're alike and how they're different. Read the definitions and find out.

Keth: They're alike because they both *increase* behavior. They're different because positive reinforcement involves a *presented* stimulus and negative reinforcement involves a *removed* stimulus.

Sandy: Way to go! I can smell that pizza baking. Now, without reading the definitions, predict how punishment differs from reinforcement.

Keth: Well, if reinforcement involves an increase in behavior, I predict that punishment means a decrease.

Sandy: Okay. What is your prediction about positive and negative punishment, based on what you learned about reinforcement?

Keth: My hunch is that positive punishment involves a presented stimulus and that negative punishment involves a removed stimulus. Am I right?

Sandy: Exactamundo!

Keth: Wow! I knew the definitions before I even read them! This is magic!

Sandy: It gets better, oh pizza supplier.

Keth: Now do I have to kick in the salad?

Sandy: Save your croutons. I'll show you how to represent this information so you can see all the relationships at once and be able to remember the concepts easily. Look at this matrix I developed. When you read it vertically, it shows that when a behavior increases, reinforcement has occurred, and when a behavior decreases, punishment has occurred. When you read it horizontally, it shows that when a stimulus is presented, the technique is positive, and when a stimulus is removed, the technique is negative.

Operant Concepts

Behavior

		Increase	Decrease
	Presented	Positive Reinforcement	Positive Punishment
Stimulus	Removed	Negative Reinforcement	Negative Punishment

Keth: This matrix is awesome for seeing relationships. This operant concept stuff is easy.

Sandy: As easy as pie.

Suppose that your biology instructor wants to teach you about human bones. To help you learn, he places a replica of each bone in the human skeleton in a long line across the floor. You examine each bone in turn, and study it carefully. What is wrong with this approach?

Although this instructional approach might help you observe how bones vary somewhat in shape or size, it doesn't teach you how the bones join together to form a hand, ribcage, or a complete skeleton. Examining each bone separately is about as helpful as examining a jigsaw puzzle that's lying in separate pieces on the floor. The scattered pieces don't provide much hint of what the assembled puzzle will look like.

Unfortunately, information is usually presented to you in a linear form, one idea at a time, like the puzzle pieces strewn across the floor. This is true when an instructor speaks the information in a lecture, or you see it printed in a paragraph or converted into an outline or list. The fact is that schools have fed you a steady diet of linear information, which has made it difficult for you to learn relationships among those "pieces" of information.

You might protest that if that's true, then teachers and textbook authors should present information in nonlinear ways to aid learning. Your protest is right on. However, until they do, *you* must be able to convert linear presentations into representations that highlight, rather than obscure, relationships.

Remember that effective learners learn in spite of poor instruction. They do not excuse themselves from learning because information is poorly organized. Don't be content to examine each "bone" or "puzzle piece" separately when you can assemble the entire "skeleton," or "puzzle." The piecemeal approach to learning is the costliest educational mistake that you can make, because examining information one piece at a time results in less meaningful learning and requires more time than examining ideas collectively.

To demonstrate that the piecemeal approach is ineffective, consider the following example: Suppose you're studying whales in a marine biology course. Your instructor lectures about two small whale types: dolphins and porpoises. The instructor provides three important facts about dolphins: they are about twelve feet long, have beak-like snouts, and swim far from shore. Later, your instructor describes porpoises and explains that they are about six feet long; have short, blunt snouts; and swim near shore. Certainly, you can learn each of the six facts separately, but doing so causes problems.

One problem associated with the piecemeal approach is that it results in nonmeaningful learning. The pieces are never assembled to reveal the "big picture." The piecemeal approach obscures the "human skeleton" or the completed "puzzle." Examine Figure 5-1. The information about dolphins and porpoises is represented in a matrix. The matrix form was introduced in Chapter 1 and discussed again in Chapter 4.

Remember that effective learners learn in spite of poor instruction.

Figure 5–1. *Matrix Representation Comparing Dolphins and Porpoises*

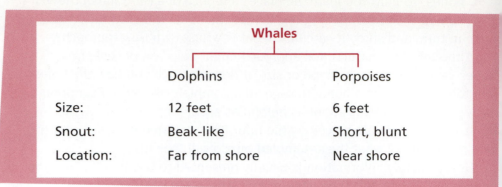

	Dolphins	**Porpoises**
Size:	12 feet	6 feet
Snout:	Beak-like	Short, blunt
Location:	Far from shore	Near shore

As you read down and across the matrix, notice that a revealing picture comes into focus—the dolphin is "greater" than the porpoise in all respects. The dolphin is longer, has a longer snout, and swims farther from shore. Recognizing this pattern makes learning more meaningful. It makes sense that a larger animal has a longer snout and lives in deeper, more remote waters. The individual ideas alone do not produce this meaningful revelation.

A second problem associated with the piecemeal approach is that because facts are learned one at a time, learning time is increased. Isn't it harder to figure out what the whole picture will be from looking at each puzzle piece instead of looking at the single picture emerging from the completed puzzle? Recognizing patterns reduces learning time because you learn facts collectively. Where dolphins and porpoises are concerned, the easy thing to remember is that everything about the dolphin is greater.

The following analogy shows very clearly that ideas are worth more when they're combined than when they're separated. Suppose that you have one hundred one-dollar bills. If you handled them separately, you could only purchase merchandise costing one dollar or less at any time. For one dollar, you could, for example, purchase a can of soda, a cheap pen, or a newspaper, but it's impossible for you to purchase items like sleeping bags, pizzas, jackets, textbooks, and compact discs. However, if you combine the bills, you can buy these other items. Although the number of bills is unchanged, they're worth more when they're combined.

In the same sense, ideas are more valuable when they're combined with other ideas to form relationships and patterns, such as those associated with dolphins and porpoises.

To summarize: Learning depends on combining ideas so that relationships and patterns are apparent. Collections of individual bones, puzzle pieces, and dollar bills reveal little about the human skeleton, the completed puzzle, or the buying power of a stack of bills. The piecemeal approach to learning must be replaced with the integrative approach, which emphasizes how ideas are combined. In this chapter we describe the advantages of representations and our own system for representing ideas and their relations.

Exercise

Try to solve this problem in two minutes. Hint: A piecemeal approach will not work.

The Mr. Young Problem

1. The man with asthma is in room 101.
2. Mr. Alex has cancer.
3. Mr. Osborne is in room 105.
4. Mr. Wilson has TB.
5. The man with mono is in room 104.
6. Mr. Thomas is in room 101.
7. Mr. Wilson is in room 102.
8. One of the men has epilepsy.
9. One of the patients is in room 103.

What disease does Mr. Young have?

The solution to the problem appears in Figure 5–2.

Advantages of Representations

Representations are the cornerstone of effective learning. Later in this book, you will see that representations are crucial for text and lecture learning, studying, test-taking, error analysis, writing, and success in the real world.

As we've already mentioned, in the academic sense you've grown up on a steady diet of linearly organized information. You've listened to linear presentations in lectures and read linear presentations in text. Often, you have been instructed to convert text or lecture information into an outline—but outlines are organized linearly, just like lectures and text paragraphs. Research on learning strategies has determined that outlines are no more effective than text and sometimes, compared to text, outlines actually make learning harder. Research also shows that outlines are less effective than representations for learning facts and relations.

Figure 5–2. *Matrix Representation Displaying Solution to the "Mr. Young" Problem*

Name	Disease	Room
Thomas	Asthma	101
Alex	Cancer	103
Osborne	Epilepsy	105
Wilson	TB	102
Young	Mono	104

There are four advantages of representations over outlines. These advantages, which we'll discuss in depth in a minute, are: similar information is localized, clutter is reduced, missing details are apparent, and the "big picture" is developed.

First, to demonstrate the advantages of representations over outlines, we're going to revisit the moths-and-butterflies material presented in Chapter 4. We compare the outline in Figure 5-3 to the representation in Figure 5-4 to see if the four advantages for representations hold true.

Figure 5–3. *Outline Representation of Moths-and-Butterflies Passage*

Moths

- Wings—two sets
- Rest—wings folded down
- Antennae—feathery
- Cocoon—fuzzy
- Color—gray or white
- Flight—night
- Stages of Development—egg, caterpillar, pupa, adult

Butterflies

- Stages of Development—egg, caterpillar, pupa, adult
- Wings—two sets
- Antennae—long and thin with knobs
- Rest—wings outstretched
- Color—bright
- Flight—day

Figure 5–4. *Matrix Representation of Moths-and-Butterflies Passage*

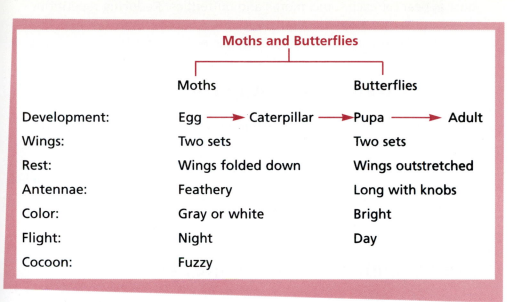

	Moths	Butterflies
Development:	Egg → Caterpillar →	Pupa → Adult
Wings:	Two sets	Two sets
Rest:	Wings folded down	Wings outstretched
Antennae:	Feathery	Long with knobs
Color:	Gray or white	Bright
Flight:	Night	Day
Cocoon:	Fuzzy	

Similar Information Is Localized

"Localization" is defined as the physical closeness—the proximity—of similar pieces of information.

An outline separates similar pieces of information, rather than localizing them. For example, the information about the moth's and butterfly's rest is separated by eight intervening facts.

In the matrix, that information is located in the same row. You need only look across a single row to compare how moths and butterflies rest.

The localization advantage is important, because it helps you to make connections quickly between topics (for example, how moths and butterflies rest). If you're studying outlines, you're not as likely to make connections between topics, because the information is separated. As a result, studying outlines often results in learning information in a piecemeal fashion, one idea at a time, without relating ideas between topics.

Clutter Is Reduced

The matrix format is less cluttered than the outline. The matrix lists the categories (for example, wings, development, and rest) one time, whereas the outline lists them twice, once for each insect. If six insects were considered, then the matrix would still contain only seven labels, but the outline would contain forty-two.

The matrix is less cluttered in another way: Because some details are common to moths and butterflies (that is, number of wings and the four stages of development), they need only appear once. In the outline, details must appear for each topic: moths and butterflies. Reducing repetitious labels and details from the matrix not only reduces clutter, but also emphasizes the shared characteristics and details between topics.

Missing Details Are Apparent

The matrix's two-dimensional structure makes it easy to spot a missing detail, because an empty matrix cell is immediately apparent. In contrast, the outline's structure can't emphasize the missing detail about the butterfly's cocoon. Recognizing that there is missing information is important. You can either look for this missing information, or you can simply acknowledge that there are certain details you don't need to know.

The "Big Picture" Is Developed

The "big picture," the information's structure and its overriding relations, can be developed more easily from the matrix than the outline. Using the two-dimensional matrix, the information's structure is apparent in a glance.

For example, with the moths and butterflies it is immediately evident that the two types of insects are being compared along the lines of seven characteristics. They are similar in two characteristics and different in four.

When you look closely at the matrix, an overriding pattern emerges. It is evident from reading across the matrix that butterflies have more pronounced characteristics than do moths. The big picture, which shows the information's structure and overriding relations, develops far more slowly, if at all, from the outline. The outline's linear, one-dimensional arrangement obscures this picture.

Re-examining the Advantages

Let's examine the four advantages once more, this time using an example about the characteristics of fish, introduced earlier in this book's Preface. An outline and matrix representation appear in Figures 5-5 and 5-6, respectively, for comparison.

Localization   As you can see, the outline separates related information, rather than localizing it. For example, concerning fish size, there are three intervening facts (diet, social group, and color) between each size designation. This is not true with the matrix, in which all fish sizes appear together in the same row. Because there is no intervening information in the matrix, comparing information across topics is easier and more likely.

Clutter   In the outline the labels for social group, color, size, and diet appear a total of 23 times, but only four times in the matrix. If you study more fish, then the number of labels increases for the outline, but not for the matrix. Because some information is identical for certain fish (for instance, size and diet), the matrix reports these details one time. Consequently, the matrix contains less information within its cells than the outline. In this case, six repeated details are eliminated from the matrix. Of course, reducing labels and details not only reduces clutter, but also emphasizes the shared characteristics among fish.

Missing details   In the matrix, missing details about the Tin fish's social group is immediately apparent because a certain cell is blank. Not so in the outline, where the missing information is easily overlooked.

The "big picture"   The fish matrix presents the big-picture patterns better than the outline. If you examine the matrix vertically, it's immediately clear that fish at two hundred feet eat algae, are 150 centimeters in length, and are dark colored. The outline gives you this information only if you use greater effort to search it out.

If you examine the matrix both vertically and horizontally, you see the major patterns: As fish swim deeper, they consume larger prey, increase in size, become lighter in color, and tend to swim in larger social groups. If you tried to pull this pattern out of the outline, you'd have to do an extensive reordering of information. The pieces are there, but they're scattered and unattached—like the bones lined up across the floor or the puzzle pieces scattered all over the place.

Figure 5-7 gives you a matrix that summarizes the advantages of a matrix over an outline.

Types of Representations and Their Relations

You've now seen the problems associated with information presented in a linear, piecemeal fashion, and you've seen that representations present information by using a spatial pattern, which helps you recognize and understand the relations among ideas that are usually obscured in linear presentations. Recognizing and understanding relations among ideas are the keys to effective learning.

Now you're going to meet four types of representations: hierarchies, sequences, matrices, and diagrams. You'll learn about their structures and the relationships they illustrate. You'll also learn how they are used in combination with one another. For instance, hierarchies and sequences can always be extended into matrices. It is important for you to get to know these four representations really well, since you will be revisiting them throughout the book and using them to gain effectiveness as a learner.

> Recognizing and understanding relations among ideas are _the_ keys to effective learning.

Figure 5–5. *Outline Representation for Fish Characteristics*

Depth at Which Fish Swim

I. 200 feet
   A. Lup Fish
      1. Social group: Small
      2. Color: Black
      3. Size: 150 cm
      4. Diet: Algae
   B. Hat Fish
      1. Social group: Solitary
      2. Color: Brown
      3. Size: 150 cm
      4. Diet: Algae

II. 400 feet
   A. Arch
      1. Social group: Solitary
      2. Color: Blue
      3. Size: 300 cm
      4. Diet: Minnows
   B. Bone
      1. Social group: School
      2. Color: Orange
      3. Size: 300 cm
      4. Diet: Minnows

III. 600 feet
   A. Scale
      1. Social group: School
      2. Color: Yellow
      3. Size: 500 cm
      4. Diet: Flounder
   B. Tin
      1. Color: Tan
      2. Size: 500 cm
      3. Diet: Flounder

Figure 5–6. *Matrix Representation for Fish Characteristics*

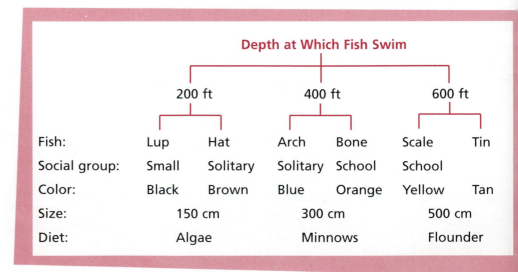

	Depth at Which Fish Swim					
	200 ft		400 ft		600 ft	
Fish:	Lup	Hat	Arch	Bone	Scale	Tin
Social group:	Small	Solitary	Solitary	School	School	
Color:	Black	Brown	Blue	Orange	Yellow	Tan
Size:	150 cm		300 cm		500 cm	
Diet:	Algae		Minnows		Flounder	

Figure 5–7. *Matrix Comparing Outlines and Matrices*

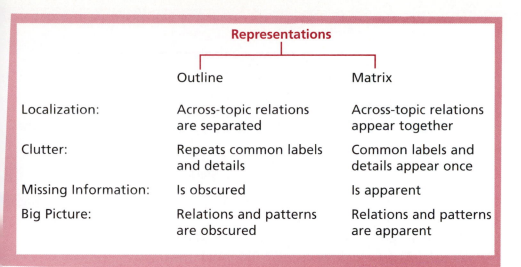

	Representations	
	Outline	Matrix
Localization:	Across-topic relations are separated	Across-topic relations appear together
Clutter:	Repeats common labels and details	Common labels and details appear once
Missing Information:	Is obscured	Is apparent
Big Picture:	Relations and patterns are obscured	Relations and patterns are apparent

Hierarchies

A hierarchy organizes ideas into levels and groups, as shown in Figure 5-8. It shows levels by positioning *superordinate* (general) ideas above *subordinate* (specific) ideas. In Figure 5-8, the Level 1 idea (A) is superordinate to the Level 2 ideas (B and C), each of which is superordinate to their respective Level 3 ideas connected to them. B is superordinate to D and E, and F, G, and H are subordinate to C.

   The hierarchy shows groups by positioning similar information together along the same level. In Figure 5-8, B and C form a group, as do D and E, and F, G, and H.

   Let's look at the example in Figure 5-9. The bird hierarchy shown here has four levels. "Birds," the superordinate concept, is the label at the top level of the hierarchy. Subordinate to "Birds" are three kinds of birds—raptors, waterbirds, and songbirds. Under these classifications are the general classes of birds, such as the songbirds—sparrows and thrushes. At the lowest level are the specific bird types (for example, trumpeter and black swans).

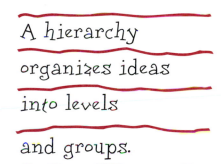

A hierarchy organizes ideas into levels and groups.

Figure 5–8. *Levels and Groups in a Hierarchy*

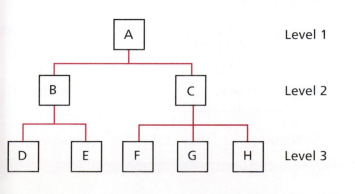

A	Level 1
B C	Level 2
D E F G H	Level 3

Figure 5–9. *Bird Hierarchy*

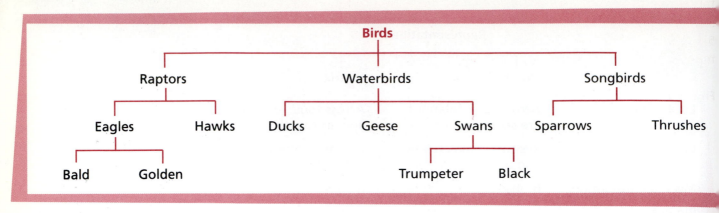

Several specific relationships are clear when you look at levels in the hierarchy: There are three classifications of birds (raptors, waterbirds, and songbirds), two types of raptors (eagles and hawks), and two types of eagles (bald and golden).

Groups show up when two or more ideas appear in the same row, and beneath the same idea, in a hierarchy. Several groups are apparent within the Figure 5-9 hierarchy. For instance, raptors, waterbirds, and songbirds comprise a group of birds. Ducks, geese, and swans comprise a group of waterbirds. Bald and golden comprise a group of eagles.

Hierarchies not only show types of something (such as birds or fish), they also show the parts or characteristics. The characteristics of insects are shown in the hierarchy in Figure 5-10. The parts of insects are shown in Figure 5-11.

Figure 5–10. *Hierarchy of Insect Characteristics*

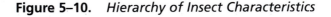
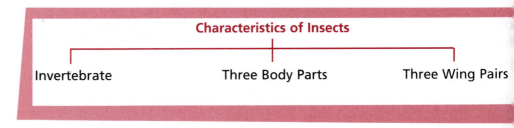

Figure 5–11. *Hierarchy of Insect Parts*

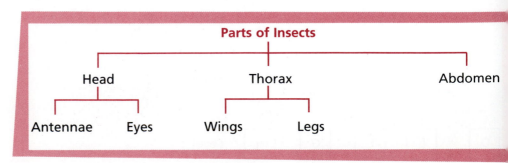

When you construct a hierarchy, make sure that it reflects all the important levels and groups. For instance, suppose you were learning about skunks, lions, snakes, dogs, cats, turtles, and cows. Is the hierarchy in Figure 5-12 the most functional? Probably not. The hierarchy in Figure 5-13 does a much better job of displaying the various levels and groups of animals.

Figure 5–12. *Nonfunctional Animal Hierarchy*

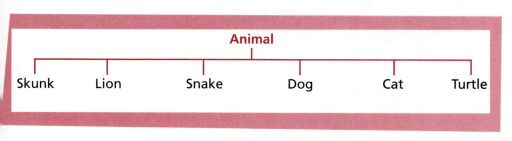

Figure 5–13. *Functional Animal Hierarchy*

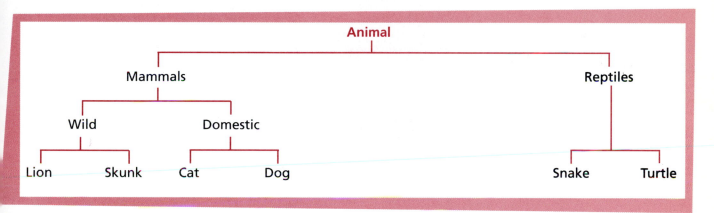

Another example of a hierarchy that doesn't work well is one that subordinates the nine planets under the superordinate topic, "Planets." A more functional hierarchy, shown in Figure 5-14, shows that the planets are grouped into those that are inner and outer planets.

A good rule of thumb is this: "If you've got more than seven things, you don't." In other words, long strings of information (many bits) can almost always be grouped (into a few bites).

Figure 5–14. *Hierarchy of Planets*

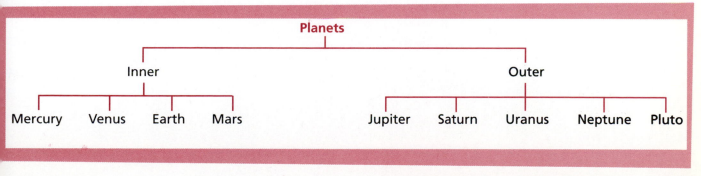

Exercise

Construct a hierarchy from the following list of punctuation terms:

colon   dash
period   exclamation point
comma   within-sentence punctuation
question mark   semicolon
end-of-sentence punctuation

Construct a hierarchy from the following biology terms:

liver   trachea
stomach   digestive system
esophagus   nostrils
respiratory system   excretory system
kidneys   skin
small intestine

Construct two hierarchies from a course in your major.

Sequences

Sequences order ideas chronologically. Sequences show the ordering of steps, events, stages, or phases. Sequences appear in a left-to-right pattern, with arrows between the steps. Sequences are illustrated in Figures 5-15 and 5-16.

Figure 5–15. *A Sequence*

Figure 5–16. *A Sequence Displaying Piaget's Stages of Cognitive Development*

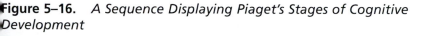

Sequences, like hierarchies, can be multilevel, as you can see in the scientific procedure for creating oxygen illustrated in Figure 5-17. Below the "prepare blue solution" step are the components of the solution. This information forms a subhierarchy. Below the step "ignite splint" is a sub-sequence showing how that is done. Thus, Figure 5-17 shows how sequences and hierarchies are sometimes combined to represent information.

Sequences are useful for learning mathematical procedures. Figure 5-18 shows the four main steps and substeps for adding mixed fractions. Displaying this information sequentially makes it easier to understand and apply.

Figure 5–17. *Sequence Representation That Includes Hierarchy and Sub-sequence*

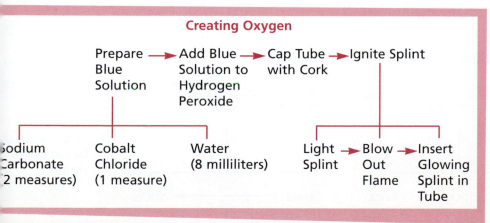

Figure 5–18. *Sequence and Sub-sequences for Adding Mixed Fractions*

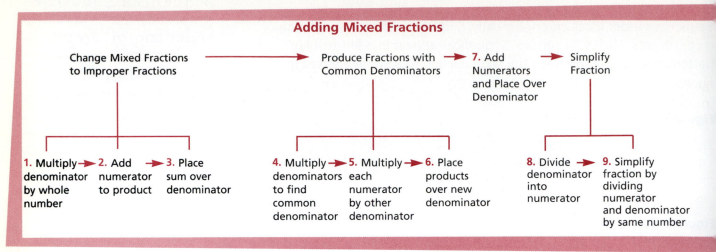

Adding Mixed Fractions

Change Mixed Fractions to Improper Fractions → Produce Fractions with Common Denominators → **7.** Add Numerators and Place Over Denominator → Simplify Fraction

1. Multiply denominator by whole number → **2.** Add numerator to product → **3.** Place sum over denominator

4. Multiply denominators to find common denominator → **5.** Multiply each numerator by other denominator → **6.** Place products over new denominator

8. Divide denominator into numerator → **9.** Simplify fraction by dividing numerator and denominator by same number

Although you'll find sequences in all content areas, two other areas in which they are especially useful are history and literature. Both subjects invariably involve a sequence of events. History is comprised of events and all events have antecedents (previous events) and consequences (post events)—and this makes it a natural for using sequences. For example, American wars can be studied sequentially (see Figure 5-19), as can the events leading up to the French Revolution.

Literature, too, is comprised of events. Remember the children's story "The Three Little Pigs"? Figure 5-20 shows how easily its events can be described by using a sequence representation. Note that this sequence also contains a subhierarchy and a subsequence.

Figure 5–19. *History Is a Sequence of Events*

Revolutionary War → Civil War → World War I → World War II

Figure 5–20. *Sequence of Events for the Story, "The Three Little Pigs"*

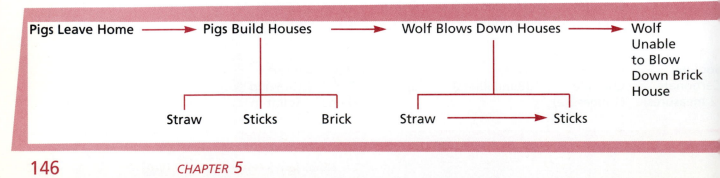

Pigs Leave Home → Pigs Build Houses → Wolf Blows Down Houses → Wolf Unable to Blow Down Brick House

Straw   Sticks   Brick

Straw → Sticks

Exercise

Construct a sequence representation for each of the following areas. Remember to create sub-sequences or subhierarchies where necessary.

1. The stages of digestion

2. The months of the year

3. Making pancakes

4. Registering for classes

5. A food chain ending with lions

6. Construct two sequences from a course in your major area

Matrices

A matrix is developed from a hierarchy or sequence. All hierarchies and sequences can be extended downward to form a matrix. For example, the "Planets" hierarchy in Figure 5-14 and the mixed fractions sequence in Figure 5-18 are extended in Figures 5-21 and 5-22, respectively, to form a matrix.

Figure 5–21. *Hierarchy Extended into a Matrix*

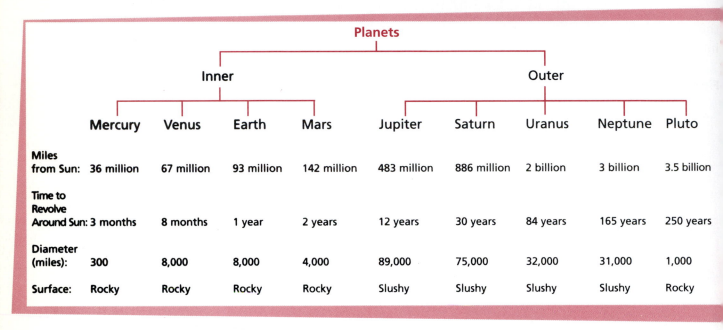

Figure 5–22. *Sequence Extended into a Matrix*

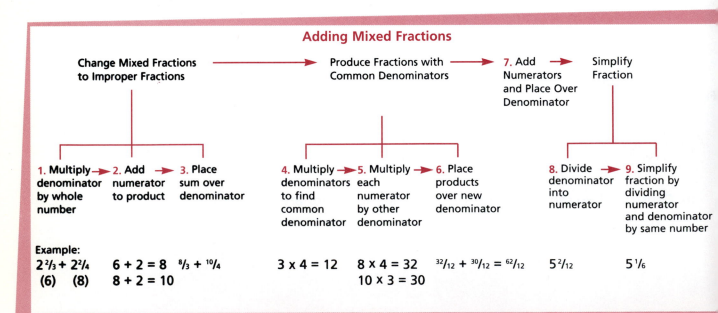

These aren't isolated examples of extending a hierarchy and sequence. Hierarchies and sequences can always be extended to form matrices.

Suppose that your chemistry instructor said that atoms are composed of protons, neutrons, and electrons. Would your instructor stop there, or would she describe several of their characteristics, such as size, valence, location, and number? These characteristics are represented in a hierarchy at the top of Figure 5-23 and then extended into a matrix framework.

Or suppose that your music instructor told you that there were three major periods of music: Baroque, Classical, and Romantic. Would your instructor stop there, or would he describe several of the periods' characteristics, such as rhythm, melody, harmony, and composers? In Figure 5-24, these musical periods are represented in a sequence and then extended into a matrix framework.

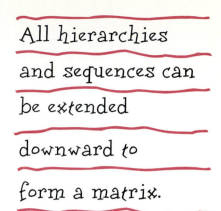

All hierarchies and sequences can be extended downward to form a matrix.

Figure 5–23. *Hierarchy Extended into a Matrix Framework*

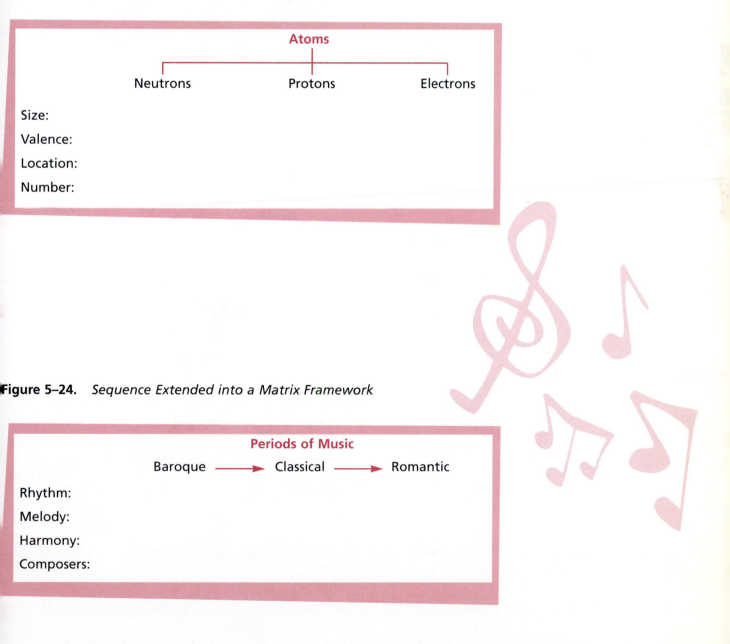

Atoms

Neutrons · Protons · Electrons

Size:
Valence:
Location:
Number:

Figure 5–24. *Sequence Extended into a Matrix Framework*

Periods of Music

Baroque ⟶ Classical ⟶ Romantic

Rhythm:
Melody:
Harmony:
Composers:

Lecturers and textbook authors always explain and describe the topics they present. At the very least, they will probably provide definitions and examples, and when they do, a matrix is the most appropriate representation for displaying these ideas.

Matrices have three parts: topics, repeatable categories, and details located inside the matrix's cells. These parts are shown in Figure 5-25 and summarized in the matrix representation in Figure 5-26.

Figure 5–25. *Parts of a Matrix*

	Topic	Topic	Topic	Topic
Repeatable category:	Detail	Detail	Detail	Detail
Repeatable category:	Detail	Detail	Detail	Detail
Repeatable category:	Detail	Detail	Detail	Detail

Figure 5–26. *Matrix Summarizing the Matrix Parts*

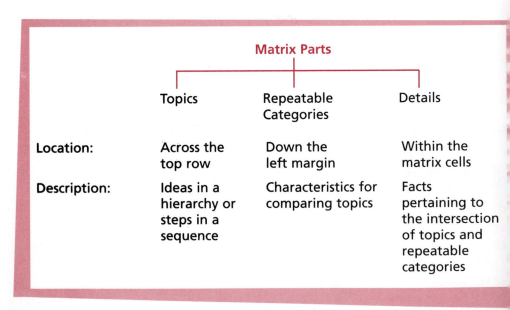

	Topics	**Repeatable Categories**	**Details**
Location:	Across the top row	Down the left margin	Within the matrix cells
Description:	Ideas in a hierarchy or steps in a sequence	Characteristics for comparing topics	Facts pertaining to the intersection of topics and repeatable categories

Topics appear across the top of the matrix. They are the superordinate or subordinate ideas in a hierarchy, or the steps in a sequence.

The repeatable categories appear down the left margin. They are the characteristics by which the topics are compared. They are called "repeatable categories" because each category is repeated for each topic. The details are the facts that pertain to the intersection of topics and repeatable categories.

Details appear inside the matrix in the cells or slots at the intersection of topics and repeatable categories.

Figure 5-27 gives an example of the matrix parts for the psychology topic, "Operant Conditioning." The topics appear across the top, repeatable categories appear down the left margin, and details are recorded in the matrix cells.

Figure 5–27. *Parts of a Matrix for Operant Conditioning*

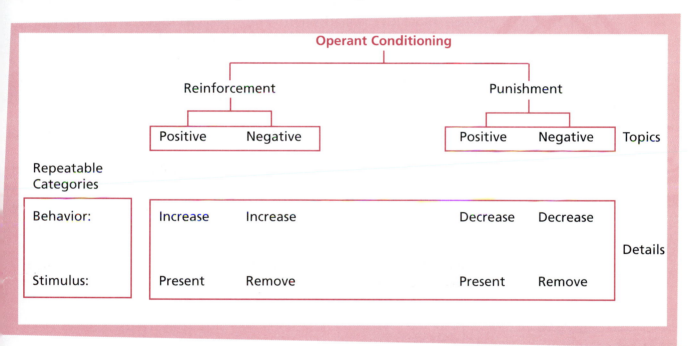

Because matrices are extensions of hierarchies and sequences, they display the levels, groups, and order relations found in hierarchies and sequences. They also display comparative relations both within and across topics.

Within-topic relations exist within a single topic. You find them by reading the matrix vertically. For instance, reading down the matrix on the topic of positive reinforcement in Figure 5-27, you can see that positive reinforcement involves both an increase in behavior and the presentation of a stimulus. These two ideas together define positive reinforcement.

Across-topic relations cross over between two or more topics. You find these by reading the matrix horizontally. For example, if you examine the matrix in Figure 5-27, you see two key across-topic relations: 1) reinforcement involves an increase in behavior, whereas punishment involves a decrease in behavior; and 2) positive techniques involve a presented stimulus, whereas negative techniques involve a removed stimulus.

Across-topic relations are the most important to construct. They specify how topics are similar and how they are different. This critical information is often overlooked in texts, lectures, and outlines that present information one idea at a time without giving you any idea about how these ideas compare. It's impossible to understand how operant concepts compare, how moths and butterflies compare, how whales compare, or how fish compare unless you can develop across-topic relations. The matrix representation is ideal for displaying across-topic relations.

As a final example, consider the "Planets" matrix shown in Figure 5-21 When you study the matrix horizontally, you can spot several important across-topic relations. First, the inner planets are closer to the sun than the outer planets. Second, the inner planets require less time to revolve around the sun than do the outer planets. In fact, you can see that there's a linear relation between miles from the sun and revolution time. The further the planet is from the sun, the longer it takes to revolve around the sun. Third, the inner planets are generally smaller than the outer planets, except for tiny, far-out Pluto. Last, inner planets are rocky, whereas outer planets are slushy—again with the exception of Pluto. If this information appeared in an outline it would appear like a bunch of unrelated astronomy facts. Presented in a matrix, the astronomy facts are easily related and important across-topic relations are learned. The matrix shows there is an order to the universe and to our solar system. In the same vein, *all* information has order. A matrix gives us a powerful representation for displaying the relationships that exist in space and in the world as we know it.

Diagrams

Just like hierarchies, sequences, and matrices, diagrams (which, for purposes here, include illustrations) organize information. Diagrams, when appropriate, are the most efficient type of representation. Although they may be worth a thousand words, they actually use very few.

Diagrams can serve two functions. They can show the appearance and location of parts of something (static relations) and how those parts operate (dynamic relations). Look at the diagram in Figure 5-28, which shows the parts of a braking system. This is a static diagram that shows what each part of the braking system looks like, where it's located, and its relative size. Figure 5-29 illustrates the dynamic relations among the parts. The figure also shows how the parts operate. You can imagine that a text describing a braking system's appearance and operation would be far less helpful.

> Diagrams, when appropriate, are the most efficient type of representation.

Exercise

1. Construct a matrix that compares, by format and function, the four time management schedules presented in Chapter 2.

2. Construct a matrix that compares, by appearance and purpose, hierarchy, sequence, and matrix representations.

3. Construct a matrix that compares, by location, food, atmosphere, price, and service, your three favorite restaurants.

4. Construct matrix representations by extending the course-related hierarchies and sequences you developed in the Exercises following the hierarchy section (p.144) and the sequence section (p.147).

5. Identify the topics, repeatable categories, and details in the matrices you constructed.

Figure 5–28. *Static Diagram of a Braking System[1]*

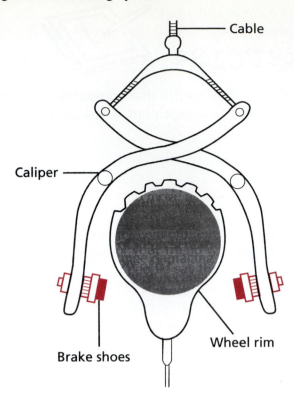

Cable

Caliper

Brake shoes

Wheel rim

Figure 5–29. *Dynamic Diagram of a Braking System*

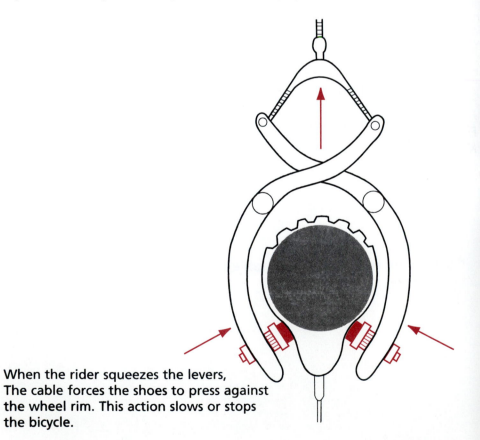

When the rider squeezes the levers,
The cable forces the shoes to press against
the wheel rim. This action slows or stops
the bicycle.

[1]Adapted from *World Book Encyclopedia* (1989). Scott Fetzer Co., New York, NY. Volume 2, pp. 570–572.

Figure 5-30 shows a diagram of a chess board and pieces, and the relative appearance and location for each chess piece. Although this same information could be displayed in a matrix, that would be a less powerful representation.

Figure 5-31 continues with chess, illustrating the dynamic relationship among chess pieces. In this diagram, the white knight is forking the black king and queen (a royal fork). The arrows show the two royal pieces being threatened by the white knight.

Figure 5-32 is a matrix comparing static and dynamic diagrams.

Figure 5–30. *Static Diagram Showing Chess Board and Pieces*

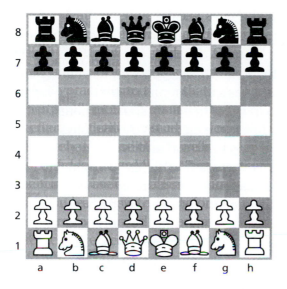

Figure 5–31. *Dynamic Diagram Showing the Movement of the White Knight, Which Is Forking the Black King and Queen*

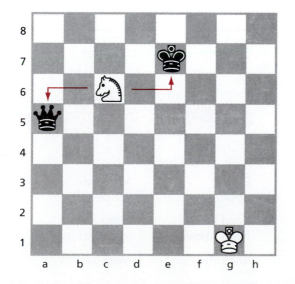

Figure 5–32. *Static and Dynamic Diagrams*

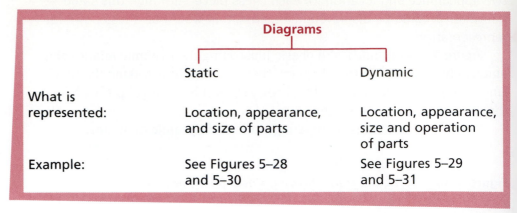

	Diagrams	
	Static	Dynamic
What is represented:	Location, appearance, and size of parts	Location, appearance, size and operation of parts
Example:	See Figures 5–28 and 5–30	See Figures 5–29 and 5–31

Diagrams are useful across almost every subject area. In science, diagrams showing the parts of a butterfly or a bee help you to learn their appearance. In geography, diagrams of peninsulas and isthmuses can help you in learning to identify these. Topographical maps are diagrams that certainly depict an area's topography better than a verbal description. In mathematics, diagrams of triangles, squares, perimeters, and areas are useful for understanding these elements. And in physical education, diagrams help athletes learn positions and tactics.

Diagrams aren't necessarily alternatives to hierarchies, sequences, and matrices. They can easily be incorporated in each. A sequence that names the eight phases of the moon can be strengthened by transforming it to a matrix that includes the repeatable category "appearance" and contains diagrams of moon phases within the matrix cells.

Consider Figure 5-33, which shows a new version of a fish matrix. It includes a diagram of each fish within the matrix's cells. The diagrams are helpful in understanding how a fish's appearance helps it to hide from its predators or prey within its habitat.

Figure 5–33. *Diagrams Included in a Matrix*

	Fish			
	Crappie	Catfish	Croaker	Albacore
Diagram:				
Appearance:	Mottled	Dark upper side	Vertical stripes	Light-colored belly
Purpose:	Hide in rocks or bottom	Hard to see from above	Hide in vegetation	Hard to see from below
Habitat:	Bottom	Bottom	Vegetation	Surface

Exercise

1. Construct simple diagrams of a leg and an arm that show the location of the calf, biceps, triceps, quadriceps, and hamstring muscles.

2. Construct a matrix representation that includes diagrams of geometric shapes.

3. Construct a dynamic diagram that shows how a pump operates.

4. Construct a diagram for a course in your major area.

Summary

Information from text and lectures is often presented linearly, one idea at a time. Linear information obscures the relationships among ideas, particularly those relationships that span two or more topics. Relationships are clearer when you use representations, such as hierarchies, sequences, matrices, and diagrams, to organize information. Representations are effective because they localize similar information, reduce clutter, highlight missing details, and develop the "big picture," the relationships and patterns hidden in paragraphs, lists, and outlines.

The four types of representation can be used independently or in combination with each other. Figure 5-34 summarizes each one's specialized function.

Hierarchies display the superordinate and subordinate relations that emphasize the level and grouping of ideas.

Sequences display temporal or chronological relations that emphasize the order among ideas.

Matrices display comparative relations. In particular, they emphasize the relations existing within topics and across topics.

Diagrams display the parts of something. Static diagrams show the relative appearance and location of the parts. Dynamic diagrams show both appearance and how the parts operate.

Figure 5–34. *A Matrix That Compares Representations*

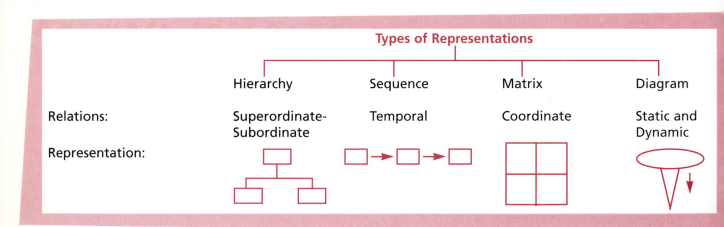

	Hierarchy	Sequence	Matrix	Diagram
Relations:	Superordinate-Subordinate	Temporal	Coordinate	Static and Dynamic
Representation:				

Types of Representations

1. Representations have four advantages over outlines. These are:
   1) Similar information is localized; 2) information is less cluttered;
   3) missing details are apparent; and 4) the "big picture" is developed.

2. When similar information is localized in representations, you are more likely to make connections between ideas and to learn important relationships.

3. Because outlines present information linearly, one idea at a time, they obscure the relationships across topics. Their linear structure makes it difficult to see how topics are similar or different.

4. 1. b, 2. a, 3. c, 4. d

5. F and G are subordinate to C.

6. C forms a group with B.

7. Matrices are downward extensions of hierarchies and sequences. All matrices begin as hierarchies or sequences.

8. Some potential categories for saw are shown along the left side of the matrix framework below.

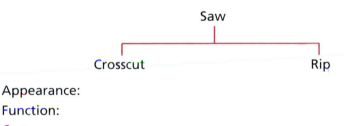

Appearance:

Function:

Cost:

9. The topics are B and C. The repeatable categories are D, G, and J. The details are E, F, H, I, K, and L.

10. Within-topic relations are those pertaining to a single topic. In a matrix about white and black rhinos, for instance, a white rhino (the topic) has square lips for grazing on grass. Across-topic relations are those pertaining to two or more topics. For instance, white rhinos (one topic) have square lips, whereas black rhinos (the other topic) have hooked lips.

11. A static diagram shows the relative appearance and location of parts. A dynamic diagram shows appearance, location, and how each part operates.

chapter 6
Constructing Representations

OVERVIEW

Focus Questions

Introduction

Identifying and Using Alert Words

Identifying and Developing Repeatable Categories
    Learn to Recognize the Structure of the Field
    Learn to Recognize Repeatable Categories Served on a Platter
    Learn to Recognize Repeatable Categories Embedded
      in the Material

Applying Principles of Representation
    Group Information
    Order Information
    Develop Multiple Representations

Summary

Answers to Focus Questions

1. Given the following phrases, can you identify the alert words and sketch an initial representation?

   A. Three types of cancer.

   B. Sunken Meadow is one of the top two cross-country courses in New York.

   C. The embryo next becomes a fetus.

   D. There are three characteristics of effective students.

2. Can you construct a representation for the passage below?

Java

Two different worlds exist side by side today beneath the great central mountains of Java, but the ancient rural way of life appears to be prevailing over the recently westernized cities. The bamboo tubes which carry water to the terraced rice fields of the countryside are more durable than the cracked pipes of the cities. The simple wooden huts of the villages are more enduring than the unpainted, cracking facades of the Western-style buildings in the city. The hammered copper utensils of the countryside are both handsomer and more durable than the cheap, patched tin-ware used by city dwellers. The colorful sarongs in the countryside are more attractive than the bunchy and poorly cut Western dress-es seen on the city streets. While the twentieth century seems to deteriorate before one's eyes, the ancient vigor of the Javanese peasant survives in its timeless way.

3. Can you tell what representation principle is being shown in the examples below?

A. Changing Representation 1 into Representation 2.

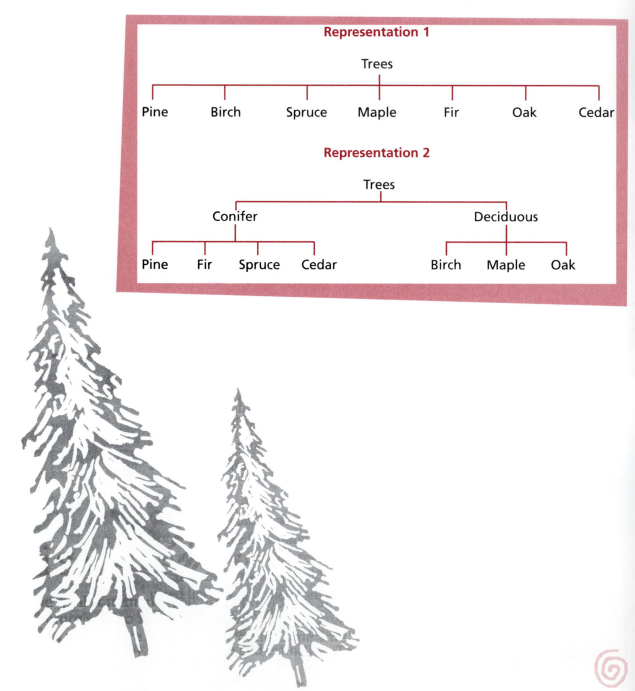

Representation 1

Trees

Pine   Birch   Spruce   Maple   Fir   Oak   Cedar

Representation 2

Trees

Conifer   Deciduous

Pine   Fir   Spruce   Cedar   Birch   Maple   Oak

B. Developing Representations 2 and 3 from Representation 1.

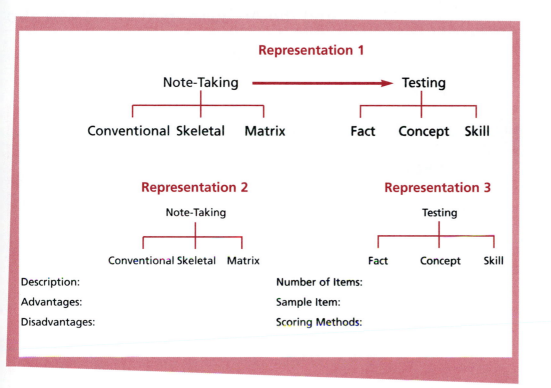

C. Changing Representation 1 into Representation 2.

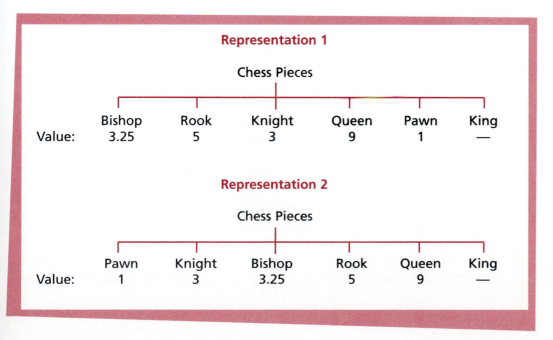

Keth: Sandy, I did it! I did it! I got a hundred on the psychology quiz! Should we dine on the celebration pepperoni pizza tonight?

Sandy: I'm booked solid. I've got meetings with the Sultan of Hither and the Archbishop of Yon. I was also going to change the oil in my car—but tomorrow's another day.

Keth: Hey great, and can you also teach me how to do that matrix stuff for the next quiz?

Sandy: What's—
Keth: . . . in it for you? You're as predictable as new shoes and blisters. How about double cheese?
Sandy: You think I can be bought so easily? Try tossing in a salad.
Keth: Side.
Sandy: Not chef?
Keth: Side!
Sandy: Side salad. Settled. Okay, so let's look at the next text assignment dealing with animal behavior. Maybe we can construct a matrix to help us.

Animal Behavior

Two branches of psychology are concerned with the investigation of animal behavior: ethology and comparative psychology. The two branches are compared along several factors.

Ethologists work largely in Europe and study many animal species. Comparative psychologists work in America and study very few species. Comparative psychologists approach animal behavior by seeking general laws that apply to any given species including man, whereas ethologists look to define species-specific behaviors. Comparative psychologists use diligent experimental methods in controlled laboratory settings. Ethologists, in contrast, observe their subjects freely in the animals' natural surroundings. The two camps' biggest contrast perhaps deals with behavior development. Ethologists believe that behavior is instinctive and due to nature whereas comparative psychologists believe that behavior is learned and due to nurture.

Keth: Boy, that's confusing. Can we use the matrix to straighten that out?

Sandy: Sure we can. First, we look for alert words. Remember to be alert. The world needs more "lerts."

Keth: I think your brain is ajar. But that's okay, the world needs more jars.

Sandy: Do you know what alert words are?

Keth: Are they words you're alert for, like "fire" and "class dismissed"?

Sandy: Close. Alert words tell you how information is organized. In the first sentence, the alert word "branches" tells you the information about animal behavior is organized hierarchically. There are two branches of investigation—ethology and comparative psychology. These topics appear beneath the superordinate term "animal behavior."

Keth: No matrix?

Sandy: Hold your horses. You construct matrices when you compare topics. Now, the second sentence tells you that the two branches of animal behavior are compared along several factors. Those factors become the repeatable categories in the matrix.

Keth: Is pepperoni a repeatable category? It repeats on me for hours.

Sandy: Maybe we should switch to Canadian Bacon. Now pay attention! Repeatable categories are the factors along which two or more topics are compared. Notice that the text first compares comparative psychologists and ethologists in where they work and what they study. Those repeatable categories are listed down the left side of the matrix.

Keth: It seems like the author next describes their approach. Is "approach" the next repeatable category?

Sandy: It is.

Keth: Are "methods" and "setting" next?

Sandy: You catch on faster than Velcro®! What's the last repeatable?

Keth: Behavior development.

Sandy: Bingo! After locating the repeatable categories, the details—all the nitty-gritties for all the topics and repeatable categories—are placed in the matrix cells like this:

Animal Behavior

	Ethology	Comparative Psychology
Where:	Europe	America
Study:	Many species	Very few species
Approach:	Define species-specific behavior	Seek general laws
Methods:	Observation	Experiments
Setting:	Natural surroundings	Laboratory
Behavior Development:	Instinctive/Nurture	Learned/Nature

Keth: Hey, this is great!

Sandy: Maybe I'll show you how to study a matrix some day.

Keth: That would be the day I change your oil?

Sandy: That would be the day. You're so . . . alert.

I t's easy to sit back and appreciate an exquisitely decorated home, but it's something else to master the principles of interior decorating necessary to beautifying a home. That takes practice.

The same is true with representations. It's time for you to become expert in constructing representations—and that means practice. Practice the techniques that follow and you'll be able to construct powerful representations while you learn and study.

Identifying and Using Alert Words

Alert words tell you how information is related and what representation (hierarchy, sequence, matrix, or diagram) to construct. Alert words are in lectures and texts but most students are not alert to them. Soon you will be. Suppose, for instance, that a text says, "There are four types of food groups." The alert word *types* signals a hierarchical relationship between food groups and its four types. This hierarchical relationship is shown in Figure 6-1.

Figure 6–1. *Hierarchy for the Phrase "Four* Types *of Food Groups"*

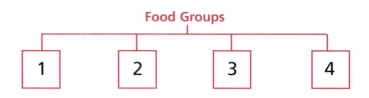

The lecture phrase "phases of the moon" contains the alert word *phases*, which signals the sequential relationship shown in Figure 6-2. In the sentence "The eastern meadowlark has a well defined song, whereas the song of the western meadowlark is more variable," the alert word *whereas* signals that two things are different. The best way to represent comparative information is in a matrix form, as shown in Figure 6-3.

Figure 6–2. *Sequence for the Phrase "Phases of the Moon"*

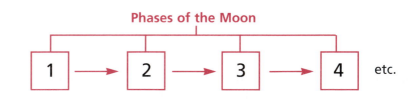

Figure 6–3. *Matrix Representation Based on the Alert Word* whereas

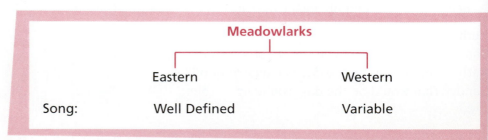

There are several different alert words that signal hierarchy, sequence, or matrix representations. Figure 6-4 shows some of the common ones.

Figure 6–4. *Common Alert Words*

Alert Words

Hierarchy	Sequence	Matrix
Parts	Steps	Whereas
Types	Stages	However
Characteristics	Phases	Often
Components	Next	But
Elements	Before	Occasionally
Properties	Then	Alternatively
Kinds	Second	Similar
Section	Develop	Contrast
Aspect	Cycle	Liberal
Levels	Sources	
Group	Period	

Alert words that signal you to use diagrams for representations can identify an object's parts (examples: shaft, arm, stem), appearance (examples: blue, large, triangular), relative position (examples: under, alongside, above), and movement (examples: slides, turns, oscillates). A simple diagram such as that in Figure 6-5 represents the following sentence: "The doohicky is a long rod with a round and triangular fitting on opposite ends. The round fitting can be moved anywhere along the rod's surface.

Figure 6–5. *Diagram of a Doohicky*

Below are more examples of sentences that contain alert words. The alert words are italicized, and a simple representation follows each.

1. Five *stages* of mitosis.

Mitosis

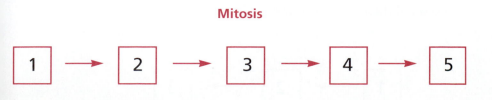

2. *Parts* of objectives.

3. Three *types* of rocks.

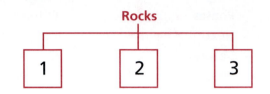

4. *Following* surgery.

5. Four theories *contrasted*.

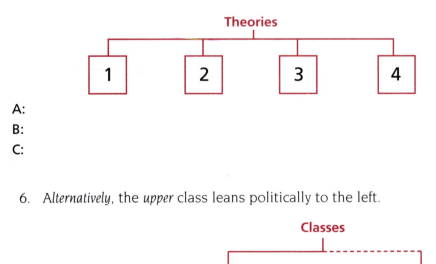

A:

B:

C:

6. *Alternatively*, the *upper* class leans politically to the left.

7. *Phases* of the immune system.

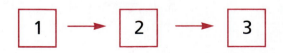

8. The American League *East has* five teams.

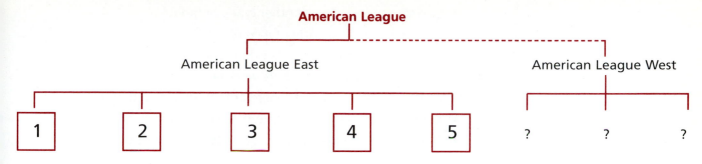

9. When the ball is *moved up* the *left side*, the *right wing* should be *positioned* at the *right post*.

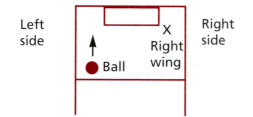

10. The *medulla* is located at the *top* of the *spinal cord*. Just *above* that is the *cerebellum*. The *cerebrum* is located *above* the cerebellum.

The Brain

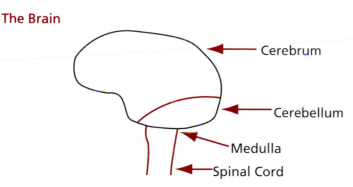

Most of these examples are self-explanatory. However, two of them do need some explanation: The alert word *alternatively* in conjunction with the adjective *upper* in example six suggests that the upper class is being compared to the *lower* class, which must stand *alternatively* to the political *right*. In much the same way, the phrase *American League East* in example 8 suggests that there must be an American League *West*, and probably an *American League* that includes both.

Alert words like *upper* or *east* are important, because they signal what information is coming in a lecture or text or what information has been left out. For instance, if you see the term *"beefsteak* tomato," then you know that there must be other types of tomatoes. Were there not other types of tomatoes, then there wouldn't be any reason to use the adjective *beefsteak*. Tomato alone would be adequate. Similarly, when you hear *white* pine, you realize there must be other types of pines. The phrase *"liberal* viewpoint" suggests that a *conservative* viewpoint exists. More examples are listed below:

- *trigger* finger—suggests other types of fingers
- *Scotch®* tape—suggests other types of tape
- *coffee* cup—suggests other types of cups
- *Oxford cloth* shirts—suggests other types of shirts
- *early* settlers—suggests there were late settlers
- *domestic* flights—suggests there are international flights
- *nearsightedness*—suggests there is farsightedness
- *expressive* creativity—suggests other types of creativity

Exercise

On a separate sheet of paper, construct an initial representation or representation framework for the following twelve phrases. Circle the alert words. We've completed the first two for you.

1. (Development) of the embryo . . .

2. The (Bitiok) method for repairing broken picture frames . . .

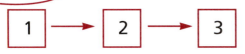

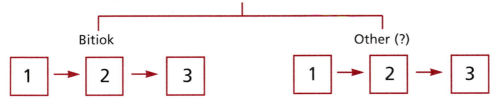

3. The characteristics of thyroxin hormone . . .

4. Layers of the atmosphere . . .

5. Benefits of zone defenses . . .

6. Direct current . . .

7. Beneath the attic . . .

8. Four types of plaster . . .

9. Advantages of RK surgery . . .

10. Investment trends . . .

11. Radical interpretation of the American Revolution . . .

12. After the food is chewed . . .

Identifying alert words is something you need to do while listening to lectures or reading. What follows are four short passages to demonstrate how alert words are identified and how corresponding representations are constructed. Try to identify alert words and represent the passages before reading our answers below.

Passage 1: Nervous System

The nervous system has two major parts: the central nervous system and the peripheral nervous system. The central nervous system includes the brain and the spinal cord.

The peripheral system, which carries information from and to the central nervous system, is comprised of the cranial and spinal nerves, afferent nerves, and efferent nerves. There are two kinds of efferent nerves. Sympathetic nerves mobilize the body's resources and parasympathetic nerves help to conserve the body's resources.

In the first sentence, the alert word is *parts*. You learn that the nervous system has two parts, the central nervous system and the peripheral nervous system. That information is represented in a hierarchy in which *nervous system* is the superordinate idea and *central* and *peripheral* are the subordinate ideas.

In sentence two, the alert word is *includes*. You learn that the central system includes the brain and spinal cord. These new terms are placed in the hierarchy subordinate to the central system.

In the first sentence of paragraph two, the alert word is *comprised*. You learn about the three major parts of the peripheral system. That arm of the hierarchy is extended downward to include the three categories of nerves.

In the next sentence, the alert word *kinds* refers to the two types of efferent nerves. The subordinate information about sympathetic and parasympathetic nerves is added to the superordinate concept of efferent nerves. The completed hierarchy appears in Figure 6-6.

Figure 6–6. *Nervous System Hierarchy Developed From Alert Words*

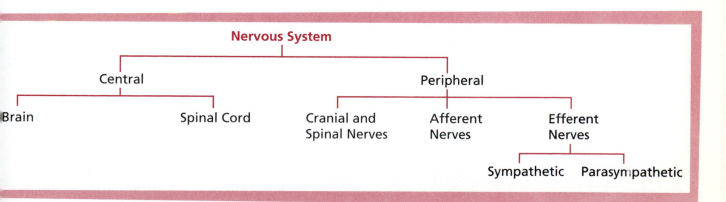

Passage 2: Experimental Procedure

Students first viewed the lecture either by taking notes in a conventional format, in a skeletal outline, or in a matrix framework. Following the lecture, students studied either by reviewing their notes or by writing an essay from their notes. Immediately following the study period, students were tested. The first test administered was the synthesis test. Next, students had to complete an application test. The last was a factual recognition test. One week later, all the students returned to complete the delayed test, which was a recall test.

The first alert word, *procedure*, appears in the title. This word suggests that information is organized in a sequence pattern. The alert word *first* in sentence one confirms that a sequence is being described. The first part of the procedure was viewing the lecture. The alert word *either* in sentence one signals that students did one of several things as they viewed the lecture. Reading on, it appears that students took notes using either a conventional format, a skeletal outline, or a matrix framework. These three types of note-taking are represented in a hierarchical form under the superordinate first step *viewed the lecture*, as shown in Figure 6-7.

Figure 6–7. *Experimental Procedure Sequence Developed From Alert Words*

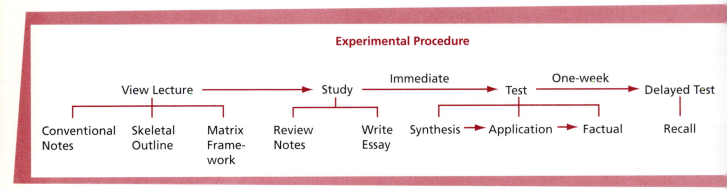

The alert word *following* in sentence two signals the second step, which is studying. Again, the alert word *either* signals the various ways that students might have studied (by reviewing or writing an essay). These study techniques are subordinate to *studying* and collectively they form the hierarchy shown in Figure 6-7.

The alert words *immediately following* in the third sentence signal the next step, which is testing. The fact that testing *immediately* followed review seems important, so it should be included in the representation. A convenient way to represent it is by indicating the time span (*immediate*) along the arrow, as you see it in Figure 6-7.

The next sentence is a bit confusing at first, given the alert words *first*, *next*, and *last*. Your initial reaction might be, "How can something else be first, next, or last when I've already identified the first three steps of the procedure (which were viewing, studying, and testing)?" But if you read it more carefully, you see that *first*, *next*, and *last* refer to the order of the *immediate* tests. This information is represented as a sub-sequence to the third step of the procedure in Figure 6-7.

In the next-to-last sentence the alert words *one week later* signal the time and nature of the final step. The phrase *one week* is placed along the arrow between the third and fourth steps to show the time span between them. The last sentence explains that the delayed test was a recall (*type*) test. The complete representation appears in Figure 6-7.

The next passage is made up of nonsense words. We included it to show you just how powerful alert words are. Even though you have no idea what the nonsense words mean, you can still represent their relationships.

Passage 3: Blixtwixing

Blixtwixing has been around for years in one form or another. It began as moshwoshing and then developed into pagwaging before it reached the popular form we know today.

Blixtwixing, though, is really made up of two central components: flobing and drobing. Flobing involves snafing, crafing, and blafing. Drobing involves whiming, then fliming, and finally, rhyming.

The alert words *began* and *developed* in sentence two reveal that the overriding structure is a sequence involving moshwoshing, pagwaging, and blixtwixing, respectively. The alert words *made up of* and *components* in the third sentence suggest a hierarchy among the superordinate term *blixtwixing* and the subordinate terms *flobing* and *drobing*. The alert word *involves* in the next sentence indicates that flobing is superordinate to *snafing*, *crafing*, and *blafing*. The alert words *involves*, *then*, and *finally* indicate that the terms *whiming*, *fliming*, and *rhyming* are a sub-sequence beneath the superordinate term *drobing*. Confused? Check out the complete representation in Figure 6-8.

Figure 6–8. *Blixtwixing Sequence Developed From Alert Words*

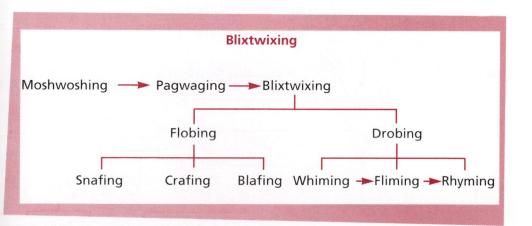

Sepals are small, green, leaflike structures found below the outermost whorl of petals. The petals are located above or inside the sepals. They are usually highly colored.

Stamens are the male reproductive parts of the flower. They usually number three or more, and each is composed of an anther and filament. The oval-shaped anther is located at the top of the filament. The filament is a long stalk, emanating from the receptacle, that supports the anther. There are special glands at the base of the stamens called nectaries.

The pistil is the female reproductive part of the flower. The pistil is composed of the stigma, style, and ovary. The stigma is an opening at the top of the pistil. The style is a tubelike structure connecting the stigma above to the ovary below. The ovary sits atop the receptacle.

The support structures are the receptacle and pedicel. The receptacle is located at the base of the flower. The trunklike part below the receptacle which supports the flower is called the pedicel.

The alert words in this passage contain the flower parts (*sepal, stamen, petals, anther, filament, nectaries, stigma, style, ovary, receptacle*, and *pedicel*), their appearance (*small, green, leaflike, highly colored, three or more, oval, long, stalk, opening, tubelike*, and *trunklike*), and their relative position (*below, above, inside, top, emanating from, at the base, connecting*, and *atop*). A diagram of the flower is shown in Figure 6-9. Ideally, the diagram would be colored to show the green sepals and highly colored petals.

Figure 6–9. *Diagram of a Flower*

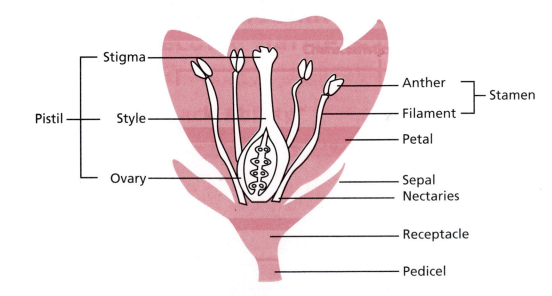

Exercise

Mark the alert words and construct a representation for the following passage:

Swimming

Swimming is a sport that offers many physical benefits. It increases aerobic capacity, exercises all major muscles, particularly strengthens the upper body, and increases flexibility. Because of the many physical benefits it offers, swimming is considered one of the best overall body conditioners.

Swimming can take place under many conditions. It can be done indoors when it is cold, or outdoors in a pool or lake when the weather is warm.

Equipment needs are minimal—a swim suit and goggles are all that's needed.

However, there are some disadvantages to swimming. One is that a person might not have access to water. Two, swimming doesn't control body weight like some other forms of aerobic exercise.

Identifying and Developing Repeatable Categories

You've now seen how alert words can reveal the representation's structure (hierarchy, sequence, matrix, or diagram). Because all hierarchical and sequential representations can be extended to form matrix representations, you need to know how to determine the matrix's repeatable categories. Without repeatable categories, you can't develop a matrix.

There are three ways that you can use to uncover repeatable categories:

- learn to recognize the structure of the field
- learn to recognize repeatable categories served on a platter, and
- learn to recognize repeatable categories embedded in the material

You need to know how to determine repeatable categories.

Learn to Recognize the Structure of the Field

Recognize a field's structure by studying it.

All fields, such as history, literature, and music, have structures. For example, history is always a sequence of events. Common to all historical events are facts about who was involved, what happened, when it happened, why it happened, and how it happened. Knowing this structure, you know the repeatable categories for learning historical events.

As you learn the events of several wars, for example, you should gather information about who, what, when, where, why, and how. Of course, your repeatable categories can be more specific than that. In learning information about the Civil War, for instance, you might want to ask *who* were the generals, *what* were the specific battles, *when* was the year or years the war was fought, in what states the war was fought (*where*), *why* the war was fought, and *how* the war affected the United States socially and politically. Figure 6-10 shows a generic structure for organizing information in history. The events form a sequence and the repeatable categories extend it into a matrix.

In literature, all stories have a plot, a setting, and characters. You can use these common characteristics for organizing information about any story and for comparing stories, as shown in Figure 6-11.

Other examples: In music, all compositions have melody, rhythm, and harmony. These are the basic repeatable categories for comparing musical compositions or musical periods. The field of psychology is full of theories, and all theories include theorists, research evidence, and applications. In biology, all living things have an appearance, habitat, food source, and mating patterns.

Recognize a field's structure by studying it or consulting with content experts. Then use that structure to help you learn about that field.

Figure 6–10. *Structure of History*

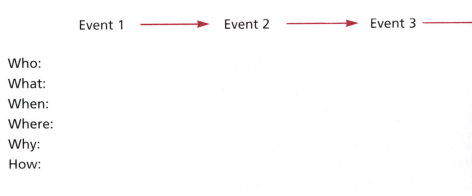

Who:
What:
When:
Where:
Why:
How:

Figure 6–11. *Structure of Stories*

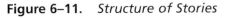

Plot:
Setting:
Characters:

Exercise

Given the following topics, identify three or four possible repeatable categories for each.

1. Clouds
2. Laws
3. Weather
4. Religions
5. Games
6. Geometric figures
7. Scientific elements
8. News stories
9. Architecture
10. Planets

Learn to Recognize Repeatable Categories Served on a Platter

Sometimes, textbook authors or lecturers make repeatable categories so obvious that we can say they really serve them up to you on a platter. Consider the lecturer who announces at the start of the lecture, "Today, we're going to discuss four types of creativity, and we're going to look at each type by its definition and characteristics, and we're going to look at examples and myths." The lecturer has provided the complete structure of the lecture. Now you know the topics: the four types of creativity. You also know the repeatable categories: definition, characteristics, examples, and myths.

Instructors can also signal the repeatable categories by providing the lecture's structure on the chalkboard or in handouts. The teacher can give you a matrix framework that shows the lecture topics (for example, moths and butterflies) across the top of the matrix and the repeatable categories down the left margin (for example, color, flight, wings, and development). You can see this in Figure 6-12. This framework is useful for guiding note-taking.

Figure 6–12. *Matrix Framework Presented to Guide Student Note-Taking During a Lecture*

Moths and Butterflies

	Moths	Butterflies
Color:		
Flight:		
Wings:		
Development:		

Texts often present the repeatable categories in much the same way. For instance, a statistics book that describes three different statistical procedures might designate each procedure as a chapter heading. Under each heading might be identical subheadings, such as purpose, formula, and restrictions. These subheadings are the repeatable categories for understanding the statistical procedures (or topics).

Exercise

Create a matrix framework that includes topics and repeatable categories given the following information.

1. Different birds use different directional cues, or different combinations of cues, when they migrate. The cues are the sun, stars, landmarks, and earth's magnetic field.
2. When investing in a mutual fund, be sure to know the fund's price, objective, and costs.
3. Clouds can be compared by their level, appearance, and associated weather pattern.
4. Automatic and manual cameras must be considered relative to their ease of use, quality of photographs, and price.
5. Normal and abnormal prostates can be categorized by size, shape, firmness, and composition.

Learn to Recognize Repeatable Categories Embedded in the Material

Unfortunately, most texts and lectures obscure the repeatable categories. Often, you have to really search long and hard to identify the repeatable categories that are embedded. But they are there, as you will see in the next three passages. Try to identify the repeatable categories and accompanying details yourself *before* you read the answers.

Passage 5: Types of Measurement

There are four types of measurement: nominal, ordinal, interval, and ratio.

The purpose of nominal measurement is to categorize items into sets. For example, on a form you might mark #1 if you are male and #2 if you are female. Other categories, such as learning disabled and attention deficit disorder, are examples of nominal categories. The limitation of nominal measurement is that no quantitative information is provided.

The purpose of ordinal measurement is to identify the order or rank of objects. For example, a chess player might be ranked third in a tournament. The limitation of ordinal measurement is that the distance between ranks is not known. The second- and third-ranked chess players could be very close or very different in ability.

The purpose of interval measurement is to show how much higher one score is compared to another. With interval measurements, for example, we learn whether the second-ranked chess player is rated 1 or 101 points better than the third-ranked player. The limitation of interval measurement is that there is no true zero point by which to anchor scores.

The purpose of ratio measurement is to see how much a score differs from zero. Height is an example of something that is measurable by using a ratio scale, because something can have zero height. The limitation of ratio measurement is that it is useful only in areas that have a true zero point.

The title of the passage and its first sentence include the alert word *types*. *Types* signals a hierarchical structure in which *measurement* is the superordinate term and the four measurement types are the subordinate terms or topics.

After establishing the topics, look for repeatable categories along which the four types of measurement are compared. The author makes these fairly evident in the passage by using the same category names throughout. The repeatable categories are *purpose*, *example*, and *limitation*. These are listed along the left margin.

Next, search for the details that correspond to the topics and repeatable categories. For instance, the *purpose* of nominal measurement is to categorize things into sets; the *limitation* of ordinal measurement is that the distance between ranks is unknown. Put the details in the matrix cells at the intersection of the topic and the repeatable category they describe. Figure 6-13 shows the completed matrix representation.

Figure 6–13. *Matrix Representation for Types of Measurement*

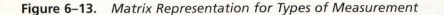

	Types of Measurement			
	Nominal	Ordinal	Interval	Ratio
Purpose:	Categorizing into sets	Ordering objects	Comparing scores	Comparing scores with zero
Example:	Male-female LD-ADD	Chess rankings	Rating points among chess players	Height
Limitation:	No quantitative information	Difference between ranks not known	No true zero point	Some areas have no true zero point

Passage 6: Personality Theories

There are two major personality theories, behaviorism and humanism. I discuss each of these in turn.

Behavioral theory was developed during the early 1900s in the United States. The founder of behavioral theory was J. B. Watson. The central idea of behavioral theory is that a person behaves in certain ways, either to receive a reward or to avoid a punishment. For example, a student will work hard on an assignment either to receive a high grade or to avoid a poor one. Behavioral therapists try to shape people's behavior by getting them to work for a reward or to avoid a punishment.

The main idea of humanism is that people behave in healthy ways when they are treated by others with dignity and respect. For example, someone who is a member of a supportive family is usually well adjusted. Therefore, therapy focuses on helping people to feel good about themselves and to treat themselves with dignity and respect. Humanism was founded by Carl Rogers in the United States during the mid-1900s.

The first paragraph indicates that two types of personality theories are covered. The two theories are represented in a hierarchy below the superordinate term, *personality theories.* The remainder of the text provides the repeatable categories and details.

The first sentence in paragraph two pertains to *where* and *when* the theory was developed. These become the first repeatable category. The next sentence names the next repeatable category, *founder. Central idea,* or *definition,* is the next repeatable category, and the following sentence gives an *example.* Last, the lecturer gives you the repeatable category, *therapy.* The repeatable categories and the accompanying details for behaviorism appear on the left-hand side of Figure 6-14.

Search for the same (and additional) repeatable categories for the next theory. In that paragraph, *main idea* is introduced first. This is another term for *central idea.* The paragraph follows with the repeatable categories *example,*

Figure 6–14. *Matrix Representation for Personality Theories*

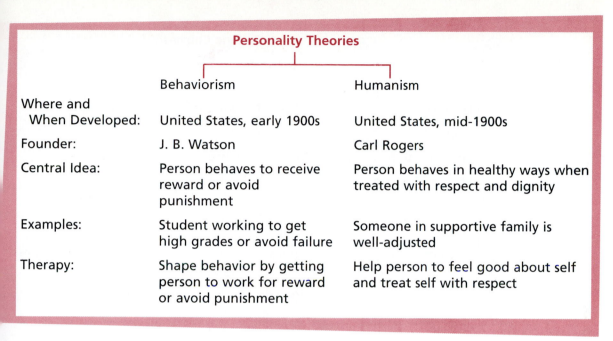

Personality Theories

	Behaviorism	Humanism
Where and When Developed:	United States, early 1900s	United States, mid-1900s
Founder:	J. B. Watson	Carl Rogers
Central Idea:	Person behaves to receive reward or avoid punishment	Person behaves in healthy ways when treated with respect and dignity
Examples:	Student working to get high grades or avoid failure	Someone in supportive family is well-adjusted
Therapy:	Shape behavior by getting person to work for reward or avoid punishment	Help person to feel good about self and treat self with respect

herapy, founder, and *where and when developed.* The fact that the repeatable categories appear in a different order for the two theories shouldn't be a problem for you. The matrix structure ensures that you represent them in the same order so you can see the across-topic relations easily by looking directly across the matrix. See the completed matrix in Figure 6-14.

In the next passage, the repeatable categories aren't so obvious, because the author doesn't always "name" the repeatable category directly, as in the previous passages. This means you have to invent an appropriate name for some repeatable categories.

Passage 7: College Choices

Students in the northern region of the state have the choice of enrolling in either of two very different schools, Stanton College or Burns College.

Stanton College is nestled in the Oakdale mountains. Stanton is a state-supported college specializing in math and science. Large oak trees fill the hilly campus, and several ponds and footbridges are located throughout the campus. Stanton's instructors are generally famous. Many have lectured at other prestigious colleges. Stanton charges a minimal registration fee and a small tuition fee.

Burns College, on the other hand, is a privately supported college. Its teachers are usually successful business people from the community. Burns is in the city of Burnsforth. Its few trees are shadowed by the neighboring skyscrapers of the city. Burns is largely a business school. Registration and tuition costs are therefore high.

A matrix representation for this passage is shown in Figure 6-15. everal of the repeatable categories are easily identified, such as *support* nd *fees*. Others are not so clear, such as *location*. Although this term is not

Figure 6–15. *Matrix Representation for College Choices*

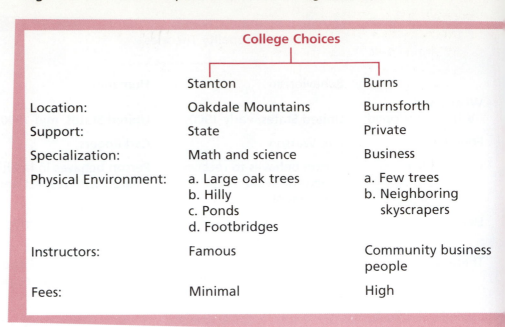

	College Choices	
	Stanton	**Burns**
Location:	Oakdale Mountains	Burnsforth
Support:	State	Private
Specialization:	Math and science	Business
Physical Environment:	a. Large oak trees b. Hilly c. Ponds d. Footbridges	a. Few trees b. Neighboring skyscrapers
Instructors:	Famous	Community business people
Fees:	Minimal	High

> *When you choose names for repeatable categories, select those that are the most accurate.*

specifically mentioned in the passage, the colleges' locations are given. The word *nestled* in sentence two means located. A later sentence states that "Burns is (located) in the city of Burnsforth."

Still less clear is the repeatable category *physical environment* which was chosen to describe the trees, hills, ponds, footbridges, and skyscrapers. *Atmosphere* was not chosen, because it can send a message describing a social environment, such as friendly. You could use the term *physical surroundings*, which would also be appropriate.

When you choose names for repeatable categories, select those that are the most accurate. Students often make the mistake of thinking up names that are too general (for example, *atmosphere* rather than *physical surroundings*, or *course offerings* rather than *specialization*) or too narrow (for example, *city* rather than *location*, given that Stanton's city is unknown).

Figure 6-16 summarizes the three ways you can identify repeatable categories.

Applying Principles of Representation

In Chapters 5 and 6, you have learned several principles for constructing representations. These include:

1. Construct hierarchies top to bottom, with superordinate ideas above subordinate ideas.
2. Construct sequences from left to right.
3. Combine hierarchies and sequences when appropriate.
4. Extend hierarchies and sequences to form matrices.

Figure 6–16. *Ways to Identify Repeatable Categories*

Repeatable Categories

	Structure of Field	On a Platter	Embedded
Meaning:	All fields or areas have a common set of repeatable categories.	Repeatable categories are often named at the start of a lesson.	Repeatable categories are obscured in lessons and must be defined.
Example:	All historical events share the repeatable categories: *who, what, when, where, why,* and *how.*	"Each type of creativity will be discussed with respect to *definition, example,* and *characteristic.*"	"Large oak trees and several ponds" pertain to an area's *physical environment.*

5. Use diagrams separately or in conjunction with hierarchies, sequences, and matrices.

6. Position topics across the top, repeatable categories down the left margin, and details within the matrix cells.

7. Select or invent repeatable category names that are neither too general nor too specific.

Now we give you three additional principles. These deal with grouping information, ordering information, and generating multiple representations. We illustrate these principles below:

Passage 8: Imaginative Literature

There are nine different forms of imaginative literature: novel, short story, novelette, narrative, dramatic, lyric, tragedy, comedy, and tragicomedy. The first three of these forms are prose.

A novel is a book-length work of fiction. Novels usually contain over 150 pages. The novel contains a number of characters, many incidents, and often subplots as well as the main plot. The short story usually centers around a single incident. It has a less complicated development of characters and situations than the novel. Most short stories are less than fifty pages. The novelette falls somewhere between the novel and the short story in length and complexity. Its typical length is between 50 and 150 pages.

The next three forms are types of poetry. Narrative poetry tells a story from the perspective of a narrator or third person. Dramatic poetry tells a story through the speech of its characters. Lyric poetry, the most common type, expresses a thought or feeling of the poet.

The last three forms are types of drama. Drama can be divided into tragedy—a serious story that ends in disaster, but attempts

Exercise

Represent the following passage, which includes embedded repeatable categories.

Cytoplasm of the Cell

Within the cytoplasm of the cell there are six important structures: 1) mitochondria, 2) centrosphere with its centrioles, 3) fibrils, 4) golgi apparatus, 5) vacuoles, and 6) inclusion bodies. The first four of these are known as "organelles" and are the integral parts of the cell. Organelles are specialized structures for carrying out cell functions.

The mitochondria are short, threadlike, granular structures scattered throughout the cytoplasm. The mitochondria appear to be associated with cell respiration.

The centrosphere is a small sphere of protoplasm that lies close to one of the poles of the nucleus. It contains two centrioles. The centrioles in a resting cell are related to cell division.

Fibrils are fine filaments and are found in most cells. They form a fine web throughout the cell, particularly in nerve and muscle cells.

In some tissues, they pass from cell to cell to form a bridge.

The golgi apparatus are a conglomerate of fibrils that are located close to the centrosphere. They are responsible for synthesizing and packaging material in the cell.

Some cells have round or oval empty spaces called "vacuoles." These often form a system of fine canals throughout the cell. The wall of the vacuole expands and contracts, absorbing fluid from the protoplasm and discharging it to the outside. In this situation, the vacuole acts as an excretory organ. In other cases, the vacuole stores and digests ingested food.

Finally, inclusion bodies are found in cytoplasm. They consist of granules of carbohydrates (that is, stored food), pigment (in the skin), and secretor granuoles.

to teach some kind of lesson; comedy, a light drama with a happy ending; and tragicomedy, a drama which tells about a serious situation but which ends happily.

Each of these classifications can be subdivided into more precise units, but these forms provide at least an overview of the forms of imaginative literature.

Group Information

Tuck this little axiom away for safekeeping. Use it whenever you are generating representations or considering the structure of any academic area: "Wherever you have more than about seven things, you don't." Seven is a magic number in our world. Aren't there seven continents, deadly sins, wonders of the world, years of bad luck, and dwarfs? Seven is also about the number of items our brains can deal with at any given time. Never try to deal with more than seven things. Regroup them.

There are twenty-eight teams in Major League baseball, but these are subgrouped into six, five, or four-team divisions. There are fifty states, but these are divided into a few regions (such as the Northeast), each including about seven states. (Hawaii and Alaska are the exceptions.) The many psychological theories that exist are narrowed down to five major categories: cognitive, behavioral, developmental, social, and personality. The human body's many organs are grouped by systems such as circulatory, digestive, and reproductive.

Let's go back to the imaginative literature material. You can see that it's inappropriate to consider the nine types of imaginative literature as nine distinct types, and to represent them as shown in Figure 6-17. Instead, the forms should be grouped according to whether they are forms of prose, poetry, or drama, and represented as shown in Figure 6-18.

"Wherever you have more than about seven things, you don't."

Figure 6–17. *Nongrouped Representation for Imaginative Literature*

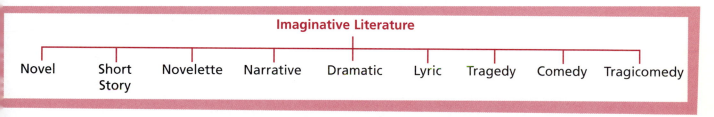

Figure 6–18. *Grouped Representation for Imaginative Literature*

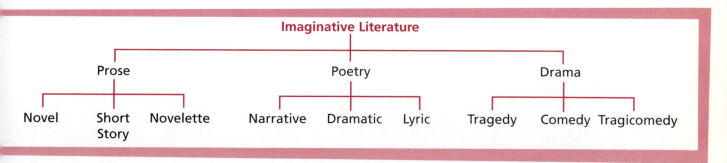

You also want to group the repeatable categories. Look at the representation in Figure 6-19, which describes prose. You can see that there are two primary repeatable categories, *length* and *complexity*. The repeatable category *page numbers* has been subgrouped under the repeatable category *length*, since it is a specific indication of length.

Figure 6–19. *Representation for Prose Showing Grouping of Repeatable Categories*

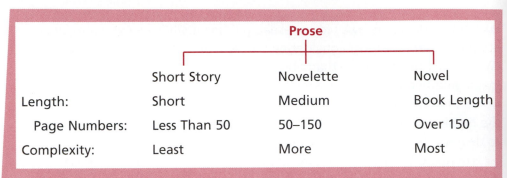

	Short Story	Novelette	Novel
Length:	Short	Medium	Book Length
Page Numbers:	Less Than 50	50–150	Over 150
Complexity:	Least	More	Most

Exercise

Do some grouping to improve the representation framework below.

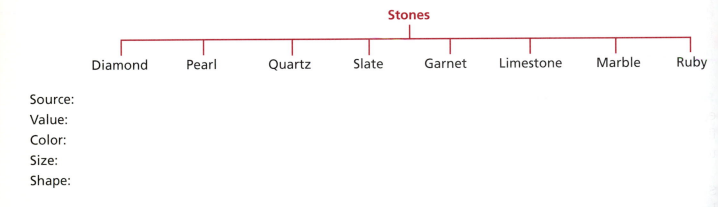

Stones

Diamond   Pearl   Quartz   Slate   Garnet   Limestone   Marble   Ruby

Source:
Value:
Color:
Size:
Shape:

Order Information

Notice that the ordering of the topics in Figure 6-19 is different from their order in the passage. The different ordering in the representation makes more sense because it reflects the increasing length and complexity of each form. For example, moving from the short story to novelette to novel, there is an increase in length and complexity. The reordered representation captures this pattern better than the text, which obscures it.

Notice that the drama forms have also been reordered in Figure 6-20. The represented dramas now progress from the happy and light *comedy* on the left to the serious and disastrous *tragedy* on the right. Again, when you reread the text, you can see that it completely failed to reveal this important pattern.

When you construct representations, approach it as you would a puzzle. Consider the order of the topics. Move the pieces about until you determine how they best fit together. Position them so that relationships across topics are revealed.

Order topics so that relationships across topics are revealed.

Figure 6–20. *Representation for Drama Showing Reordering of Topics*

	Comedy	Tragicomedy	Tragedy
Tone:	Light	Serious	Serious
Ending:	Happy	Happy	Disastrous

(centered above: Drama)

Make the same sort of judgment about the order of the repeatable categories. Two rules of thumb are 1) to place the most important categories first, and 2) to order the repeatable categories so that patterns within topics are apparent.

Let's go back to the college choices' representation in Figure 6-15. Suppose that you are using this representation to make a choice about colleges. How might you reorder these repeatable categories? Using the first rule, you put the important considerations first. If costs and finances are the most important elements, then position the repeatable categories *fees* and *support* at the top. If your chief consideration is *specialization*, then that's the repeatable category that goes first.

Using the second rule, reorder the repeatable categories so that within-topic relations are clearer. For instance, the college's location and physical environment are related, so you should consider those items jointly. The college located in the mountains has a pastoral environment that includes large trees and ponds. The college located in the city has skyscrapers and few trees in its environment. The revised matrix in Figure 6-21 positions these related, repeatable categories together.

Figure 6–21. *Revised College Choices Matrix With Reordering of Repeatable Categories*

College Choices

	Stanton	Burns
Location: Physical Environment:	Oakdale Mountains a. Large oak trees b. Hilly c. Ponds d. Footbridges	Burnsforth a. Few trees b. Neighboring skyscrapers
Support: Fees:	State Minimal	Private High
Specialization: Instructors:	Math and science Famous	Business Community business people

We've also reordered the repeatable categories *support* and *fees* to convey their relationship (see Figure 6-21). The state school naturally has minimal fees, whereas the private school has high fees.

Last, we've reordered and positioned together the repeatable categories *specialization* and *instructors*. We did this to show you the link between the schools' specialization and the faculty teaching in those areas.

Develop Multiple Representations

For many of the examples that you've looked at up to now, such as "College Choices," "Moths and Butterflies," "Whales," and "Depth at Which Fish Swim," a single representation was sufficient. But with the "Imaginative Literature" example, we presented four representations, including the one on poetry in Figure 6-22, below. Why are multiple representations needed?

When you first look at it, you would think that you could just add repeatable categories to the initial representation in Figure 6-18, showing

Figure 6–22. *Poetry Representation*

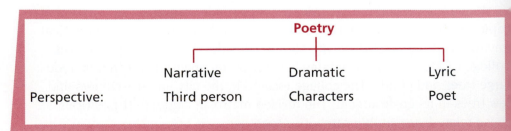

the nine forms of imaginative literature, and discard the subsequent representations (Figures 6-19, 6-20, and 6-22). That would work fine if the repeatable categories were the same, or potentially the same, for all forms. For example, if all nine forms could be compared with respect to length, perspective, and tone. In reality, however, the same repeatable categories aren't used because they're not appropriate for all forms. The repeatable categories vary among prose, poetry, and drama.

So it's necessary to construct one overriding hierarchical representation (Figure 6-18) that shows how all the forms interrelate, and then make three subsequent representations (Figures 6-19, 6-20, and 6-22) that develop and extend each arm of the original hierarchy.

Exercise

Reorder the representations below.

Digestive System

| | Stomach | Mouth | Small Intestine | Esophagus | Large Intestine |

Function:

Appearance:

Reproduction in Vertebrates

	Fish	Mammals	Reptiles	Birds	Amphibians
Development:	External	External	Internal	External	External
Fertilization:	External	Internal	Internal	Internal	External

Multiple representations, like an airplane ride, provide wide angle and close-up views

Think of this set of representations as being like a trip in an airplane. From high above the earth, you can see an entire city, complete with housing areas, a lake, and a stadium. While all of these are visible collectively, details about any of them are impossible to recognize. But as you swoop down toward the stadium, you can focus on its particular structure, size, and color—but the houses and lake are no longer visible. Later, flying over the houses, you can clearly see their roofs, backyard pools, and fences—but nothing of the stadium or lake. Still later, flying just above the lake, you notice waterfowl and marshes that had escaped your attention when you were flying higher up. Again, there is no sign of the stadium or houses located in opposite corners of the city.

The multiple representations are a lot like the plane ride, and they offer similar advantages. The hierarchy in Figure 6-18 reveals the big picture that is only visible from afar, like when you're flying high in an airplane. The subsequent representations (Figures 6-19, 6-20, and 6-22) provide the close-ups of different portions of that big picture, much the same as you get when your little plane swoops down to give you closer looks at the stadium, the lake, and the houses. When multiple representations are used together, they give you both a wide-angle and a close-up look at the ideas you want to learn.

Figure 6-23 gives you a summary of the three representation principles.

Summary

This chapter emphasizes how to construct representations. Certain alert words signal the type of representation you should construct. Words like *phases*, *stages*, and *next* signal sequential relations. Words like *types*, *parts*, and

Exercise

Construct multiple representation frameworks for the following lesson about chess. The first part of the lesson introduced the six chess pieces, and taught about how they move and their relative values. The second part introduced chess tactics (the pin, fork, and skewer), and provided descriptions and examples. The last part of the lesson introduced various king and queen pawn openings and explained their relative utility.

Figure 6–23. *Principles of Representations*

Principles of Representations

	Grouping	Order	Multiple Representations
Principle:	Group topics and repeatable categories logically so that there are fewer things in a group.	Order topics and repeatable categories logically, such as from smallest to largest.	Construct multiple representations when repeatable categories vary among topics.
Examples:	Group teams by divisions.	Order short story, novelette, and novel by increasing page numbers.	Prose and drama require different representations since the repeatable categories vary (see Figures 6–19 and 6–20).

components signal hierarchical relations. Words like *whereas, however,* and *similar* indicate comparative relations and signal a matrix representation. Words pertaining to an object's parts (for instance, *hand, feet, head*), appearance (for instance, *big, webbed, hairy*), relative position (for instance, *base, below, on*), or movement (for instance, *shake, walk, turn*) indicate a static (stationary) or dynamic (moving) relationship among the parts, and signal a diagrammatic representation.

Hierarchies and sequences are easily extended to form matrix representations. Matrix representations include repeatable categories (placed along the matrix's left side) for comparing the matrix's topics. Repeatable categories are sometimes made explicit at the start of a lecture or a text section (repeatable categories are served up on a platter), such as when an author writes "We will compare the types of trees according to their *size, foliage,* and *natural environment.*" Other times, repeatable categories are less obvious (embedded repeatable categories). They appear within lectures and text, but you have to identify them and sometimes invent names for them. At the start of the chapter, Keth and Sandy identified repeatable categories for comparing ethology and comparative psychology.

Last, repeatable categories might be evident from the structure of the field. Historic events, for example, can all be compared with respect to who, what, when, where, why, and how.

Effective representations are guided by several construction principles. The most important of these are grouping, order, and multiple representations. Topics and repeatable categories should be grouped wherever possible to uncover similarities and simplify learning. For instance, if you're learning about different kinds of saws, these might be grouped by type, such as hand saws and power saws.

Whenever possible, topics and repeatable categories should follow a logical order. For instance, if you're studying clouds, you might arrange these in ascending altitude order. Doing so highlights an important relationship among clouds.

Last, always use multiple representations when a single representation cannot adequately highlight relationships.

Answers to focus *questions*

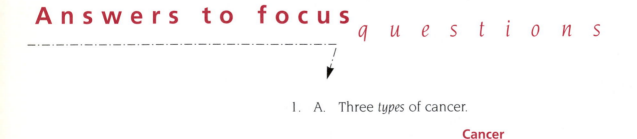

1. A. Three *types* of cancer.

Cancer

B. Sunken Meadow is *one* of the top *two* cross-country courses in New York.

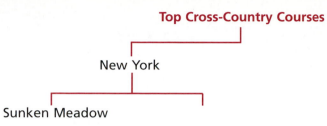

Top Cross-Country Courses

New York

Sunken Meadow

C. The embryo *next* becomes a fetus.

Embryo ⟶ Fetus

D. There are *three characteristics* of *effective* students.

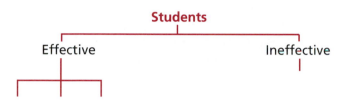

Students

Effective   Ineffective

2. Java

	Java	
	Ancient Rural Life	Westernized Cities
Irrigation:	Durable bamboo tubes	Cracked pipes
Buildings:	Enduring wooden huts	Unpainted, cracked Western-style buildings
Utensils:	Handsome and durable	Cheap, patched tinware
Clothing:	Colorful sarongs	Bunchy and poorly cut Western dresses
Overall Impression:	Timeless ancient vigor	Twentieth century deterioration

3. a) Group information

b) Develop multiple representations

c) Order information

chapter 7
Learning from Texts

OVERVIEW

Focus Questions

Introduction

What to Do Before You Read
  Set the Mood for Reading
  Survey the Chapter
    Determine the Text's Structure
    Survey the Table of Contents
    Survey Chapter Headings
    Survey Overviews and Summaries
    Survey Representations
  Focus Attention
    Survey Highlighted Material
    Survey Objectives and Questions
  Develop (Drop) an Anchor
  Budget Time and Effort

What to Do While You Read
  Mark the Text
  Deploy Comprehension Strategies
    Raise Questions
    Make Predictions
    Organize Ideas
    Generate Elaborations
    Create Summaries
    Monitor Your Comprehension and Strategy Deployment
  How to Mark and Comprehend a Sample Passage

What to Do After You Read
  Generate Representations
  Generate a Final Summary
  Compile Questions

Summary

Answers to Focus Questions

focus *questions*

1. What are the differences between how low- and high-achieving students read text?

2. What are the benefits of each of the following text aids: highlighting, overviews and summaries, headings, objectives and questions, representations, and examples?

3. What two things should you learn from surveying a chapter's structure?

4. Other than determining a chapter's structure, what should you do while surveying a chapter?

5. What three things are revealed by a marked text?

6. What symbols are recommended for marking a text?

7. Can you generate a repeatable category label for each of the following?

     A. The patient takes penicillin and sulfur.

     B. . . . in 1963.

     C. On the property were flowers, native grasses, and pear trees.

     D. They traveled by rail and by covered wagon.

8. How would you mark the following text passage so that your markings show topics, repeatable categories, and important details?

Comparative Psychologists versus Ethologists

Comparative psychologists can be compared with ethologists along several dimensions. Comparative psychologists study animal behavior in laboratory settings. They conduct diligent experiments on a few animal species trying to uncover general learning principles common to all animals. These American psychologists believe that behavior is learned. Ethologists, on the other hand, study animal behavior in the animal's natural surroundings. Their methods are less rigorous. They usually observe animals. The ethologists study many animals to learn how each behaves. These European psychologists believe that behavior is innate.

9. Can you generate a representation for the passage in item 8?

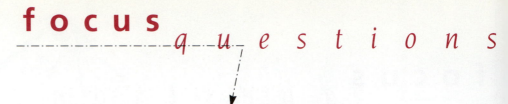

f o c u s
q u e s t i o n s

10. Can you match the strategy name in column 1 with an example of the strategy in column 2?

1. Questioning
2. Predicting
3. Organizing
4. Elaborating
5. Summarizing
6. Monitoring

a) "Short-term memory has a limited capacity, whereas long-term memory has an unlimited capacity."
b) "Short-term memory reminds me of a workbench. It can only hold a few things."
c) "Does long-term memory store information visually?"
d) "My hunch is that information is never really forgotten, just misplaced."
e) "I'm not sure I follow this explanation. I'll break it down sentence by sentence."
f) There are three memory systems: sensory, short term, and long term. The sensory memory is characterized by . . ."

11. How can you use both questions and predictions effectively while you're reading?
12. When you're reading, how can you show the organization of text ideas?
13. How can you note elaborations while you're reading?
14. What is the formula for writing effective summaries?
15. What aspects of your reading should you monitor?
16. What should you do following reading?

Josh: How 'bout we have a catch later and knock out a few flies?

Dennis: If I read the Student Handbook right, we'd be breaking a college rule if we didn't on a beautiful day like this. But first I've got to knock out Chapter 5.

Josh: Me too. Should we meet at the fields in an hour?

Dennis: An hour? No way. I'll probably need about three hours.

Josh: What you need is a speed-reading course. What takes so long?

Dennis: First I survey the chapter.

Josh: What a waste of time. That's like sorting your clothes before washing them. Good readers get right down to reading. I clear a couple of dirty dishes from my bed, lie down, and get busy reading.

Dennis: Surveying tells you the lay of the land. It tells you what the chapter is about, how the content is organized, and what you need to search for when you read.

Josh: Okay, so how do you survey?

Dennis: I read the table of contents, the chapter headings, the introduction, and the summary. Then I check out the charts and graphs— and I pay close attention to questions and objectives.

Josh: That's the stuff you're supposed to ignore, like a four-way stop sign.

Dennis: What if everyone was as "ignore-ant?"

Josh: Funny. Besides, I like to read a textbook like a good novel. I just let the story evolve.

Dennis: A novel is a winding path; a textbook's like exploring a new country.

Josh: So how do you explore it?

Dennis: When I read, I pay a lot of attention to the "countryside." I mark my text—I use boxes, circles, and underlining to highlight important ideas and show how they're organized.

Josh:	I just use a yellow marker to highlight important ideas.
Dennis:	I've seen your texts. They're a sea of yellow. It looks like you highlight with a can of spray paint.
Josh:	I figure if I highlight it I'll understand it.
Dennis:	I don't just mark the text. I use a pen to make notes in the margin and on paper. I jot down my predictions and questions while I'm reading. I also construct representations, write summaries, and relate text ideas to other things.
Josh:	What on earth for?
Dennis:	Writing questions and predictions forces me to think about the text and understand it better. Questions and predictions also focus my attention as I read so I can answer my questions and confirm my predictions. I construct representations to organize ideas and I generate summaries after every page to check my understanding. I relate material to other things to make the information more understandable and more useful.
Josh:	Wow! The author probably didn't spend that much time writing the chapter.
Dennis:	Sometimes it really seems that way!
Josh:	I just read. If I don't understand something, I read it again.
Dennis:	Does that help?
Josh:	Not really . . . Hey, can we read Chapter 5 together so I can see you in action?
Dennis:	Sure, if you don't mind pushing baseball back a few hours.
Josh:	I don't mind. You're aware, of course, that the Student Handbook also stipulates that any study session lasting three hours or more must also be followed by a milkshake?
Dennis:	It's been noted.

We asked students enrolled in an educational psychology class to describe how they read their educational psychology textbook. Below are two sets of comments. The first is from students who averaged below 70% on three course exams. The second is from students who averaged above 90% on the same exams. What conclusions can you draw about the reading activities of high and low achievers?

Students Below 70%:

1. I figure out key words in the paragraph. I try to understand what the author is trying to get across.

2. I look for boldface words and read the sentences before and after the boldface words. I read the last sentence in the paragraph and then the entire paragraph.

3. I read the paragraph once. I then reread the material and highlight what I feel is important.

4. I read through the paragraphs. I usually read the boldface or italicized words with their meanings. If possible, I sometimes read aloud.

5. I highlight the important information. I read straight through most of the time without going back.

6. When reading, I skim through the chapter and focus on italicized or boldface words. Then I read the whole paragraph completely.

7. As I read, I highlight important information like definitions or important sentences or paragraphs, if necessary. If I don't understand, I reread the paragraph.

Students Above 90%:

1. I look for the main idea and pay attention to any technical terms. Sometimes I stop and relate information to other information (that I read in previous paragraphs or somewhere else in the chapter) or just stop to assimilate what I've read.

2. I try to visualize an organization of the information, a sort of chart in my head. I try to think of examples for definitions that I can relate to better than those in the book. I try to pick out the important words or phrases. I try to connect the last idea with the next one.

3. When I read a chapter, I visualize myself in the examples that are given. I try to relate the words I don't know to words that I do know. When I use my own life experiences for examples, I understand the words and examples better.

4. When I read, I try to understand what the paragraph is about and try to relate it to what I already know about the subject. I also try to relate what's been said in class so I can make connections between the two.

5. When I read, I try to fit the new information to what I already know and try to create as complete a picture as possible of what I am reading. Doing this helps me organize my notes.

6. When I read, I underline parts I feel are important and are going to help me make connections when I note the chapter. I sometimes reread something to make it fit with what I'm learning.

7. I try to make connections with other stuff I've read beforehand or to class discussions. I try to organize my thoughts and predict what the next step might be. I remain active in my reading.

What conclusions did you come to? We concluded that the high achievers were more active readers. All of them used activities aimed at building connections. They "related," "connected" and "organized" ideas. In contrast, low achievers learned in a piecemeal fashion, one idea at a time. They focused on each highlighted term separately. They didn't organize the ideas or relate them to previous knowledge. Low achievers also employed other weak strategies, such as highlighting and rereading, in much the same way Josh did at the start of the chapter.

By reading this chapter and practicing the strategies it presents, you can become a high achiever. When you're asked to describe how you read your textbook, your answer could read something like this:

> Before I read, I survey the chapter. I examine the chapter headings, overviews, summaries, objectives, questions, highlighted terms, and representations so I can establish the chapter's organization and to activate previous knowledge related to the chapter's content. Doing so focuses my attention and helps me build connections while I'm reading.
>
> When I read, I mark the text. I use a few symbols to designate the topics, subtopics, repeatable categories, and details. The marked text illustrates the organization among ideas. While I'm reading, I also use comprehension strategies aimed at increasing attention, building connections, and monitoring learning. I generate questions and predictions to guide my attention. I build connections by organizing text ideas, evaluating text ideas, and relating text ideas to previous knowledge. I monitor my understanding by generating summaries throughout the chapter.
>
> After I read, I generate representations that capture the text's structure, important details, and relations. I answer questions from the text as well as the ones I generated myself. I also write a summary that captures the chapter's meaning.

This seems like a lot to do—and it is. But once you learn these activities, you can carry them out quite quickly. Our students report that they can use these strategies while they read a text chapter, and still take less time than they would if they read a chapter twice. What's more, they learn much more that they did doing it the old way.

On the other hand, we've spoken to many highly motivated students who read their text two or more times. However, their efforts are not rewarded to the extent they might be, because they use passive strategies like those of the students who scored below 70%.

Effective reading requires will and skill. If you are willing to spend a sufficient amount of time reading it, then this chapter can give you the skills to read successfully.

We've divided the reading process and its strategies into those that occur before, during, and after reading.

What to Do Before You Read

There is much to do before you read. The first thing you do is develop the proper mood or attitude for reading.

Set the Mood for Reading

How do you get yourself in the mood to exercise? You probably rely on the DIFS (Desire, Intention, Focus, and Sustain) model of motivation introduced in Chapter 2. Desire stems from having fitness goals such as lower body fat, increased stamina, or improved performance in a sport. You demonstrate your intentions by carefully planning workouts to achieve fitness goals. You maintain your focus by working hard to carry out your plan. You overcome barriers such as cold weather and sore muscles. You sustain your level of fitness as you continue your exercise regimen over a period of several months.

How do you get yourself in the mood to read? Do you have clear goals and detailed plans for your reading? Do you have a history of working hard and sustaining your effort? Maybe not. Many students begin with a nonproductive mood for reading. Their goal is simply to read a chapter for an upcoming test. Their plan is simple—just rereading highlighted material. Their focus is poor. They usually flop down on the bed and read the chapter—line by line, page by page—as if they were reading a novel. They make no attempt to mark the text or record notes that show the important ideas and the relations among them. When they begin to realize that they've learned little from what they read and that their ineffective reading has produced poor test performance, these students become frustrated, likely to abandon future reading altogether. They only thing they "sustain" is an attitude of defeat.

Create a productive mood for reading by using the DIFS model. Desire to set and reach challenging goals: Set the goal of mastering the chapter and earning an A on the chapter test. Why settle for anything less? Reach these goals by generating plans based on sound learning principles and strategies. For instance, plan to survey a chapter to determine its structure. Plan to mark the topics, repeatable categories, and details, and to create corresponding representations. Plan to use comprehension strategies, such as prediction, questioning, elaboration, and summarization. Establish your focus by visualizing yourself working hard to carry out the plan. Imagine producing a marked text, notes, representations, and a summary. Then turn this vision into reality. Imagine sustaining these efforts for all of your reading in all of your classes. Sense the satisfaction of having learned from text and of earning high grades because of your will and skill.

Overall, forget the idea that reading is just a leisurely stroll in the park. Instead, it's a cross-country race of marathon proportions. So "get psyched" for the race—realize its difficulty and plan for its completion. Imagine your hard work and the benefits of sustained effort. Prepare yourself for active—even aggressive—reading and for the rewards—thorough comprehension and high achievement—that follow.

Survey the Chapter

Suppose that you plan a trip to Disney World in Florida. Your travel agent books your air travel, hotel accommodations, and admission passes into the Disney theme parks such as Magic Kingdom, Epcot, Pleasure Island, MGM Studios, and Typhoon Lagoon. On your first vacation day, with no idea how big the Disney theme parks are, you stumble from your room into the Magic Kingdom. You enter Tomorrowland and begin your day by riding Space Mountain. Enthralled by this roller coaster ride, you repeat Space Mountain over and over throughout the morning. After a lunch that doesn't set too well, you visit two other attractions in Tomorrowland. Impressed by these as well, you revisit them throughout the afternoon. By day's end you've experienced only about one-tenth of the Magic Kingdom's attractions and a tiny fraction of what is available throughout Disney World. With two vacation days remaining, you'll probably miss the majority of Disney's attractions. How could this happen?

When you visit somewhere new, such as a city, school, or recreation facility, the best thing to do first is to get the "lay of the land," an overview of what is available. Without an overview you have no idea about how the place is organized, how it meets your interests, or how to spend your time. You can easily overview Disney World or a city by previewing maps, skimming brochures, and taking an initial tour to learn the lay of the land.

Exercise

Use the DIFS model (**D**esire, **I**ntention, **F**ocus, and **S**ustain) to set the mood for reading the remainder of this chapter.

This same strategy is crucial for acquiring text information. It makes as little sense to begin a book by reading the first chapter's first paragraph as it does to stumble into Disney's nearest attraction or the first restaurant you pass outside your hotel room in a new city. Just as you should overview Disney World or a new city, you should survey a new text chapter to get the lay of the land. More specifically, you should survey a text chapter to determine its structure, focus attention, develop an anchor, and budget time and effort.

Determine the Text's Structure

Before you visit Disney World, it's helpful to have a map that illustrates and briefly describes the major attractions. Understanding its structure in advance provides you with a rough sketch of Disney World that is easily colored in by personal experiences as you visit the various attractions. Similarly, it is important to recognize a text's structure in advance so you can easily place text details within that structure while you read. Without the text's structure in mind as you read, reading becomes very difficult. You encounter dozens of new facts and ideas, but you have no understanding of how these are organized. As a result, you're left with dozens of "loose bones" or tiny "puzzle pieces" rather than an intact skeleton or a completed puzzle that we talked about in Chapter 5.

Survey maps and text chapters to learn the "lay of the land"

When you look at text structure, there are two things you should determine when you survey the chapter: its organizational patterns (hierarchy, sequence, or matrix) and the "players" involved in those patterns (topics, subtopics, and repeatable categories).

How do you determine the organizational patterns and players before you begin reading? Examine text aids that reveal the text's structure. Four common aids include the table of contents, headings, overviews and summaries, and representations. Each aid is described below.

Survey the Table of Contents

First, consult the chapter's table of contents. Often, it will reveal the organizational patterns and players. For instance, the table of contents below for learning theories reveals a matrix structure, topics (the theories of learning), and repeatable categories (theory, evidence, strengths, weaknesses, and implications), which are illustrated in Figure 7-1.

Learning Theories
  I. Contiguity Theory
      A. Theory
      B. Evidence
      C. Strengths
      D. Weaknesses
      E. Implications

II. Reinforcement Theory
   A. Theory
   B. Evidence
   C. Strengths
   D. Weaknesses
   E. Implications
III. Cognitive Theory
   A. Theory
   B. Evidence
   C. Strengths
   D. Weaknesses
   E. Implications

Figure 7–1. *Text Structure Drawn from Chapter's Table of Contents*

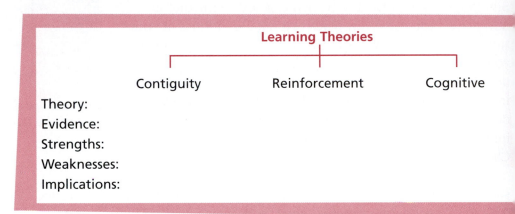

Below, you see another table of contents. This one is about Lutheranism. From this table of contents a sequential organization is evident, as shown in Figure 7-2. In addition, the table of contents suggests other possible ways to organize chapter content. These are shown in Figures 7-3, 7-4, and 7-5.

Martin Luther and the Protestant Reformation

I. The Church on the Eve of the Reformation
   A. Abuses and corruption
   B. Church reform before Luther
II. Luther's Thesis
   A. Luther's views versus the Church
   B. The dissemination of Luther's views
III. The Church's Response to Luther
   A. A demand for retraction
   B. Excommunication
IV. The Establishment of Lutheranism
   A. In Germany
   B. The spread of Lutheranism

Figure 7–2. *Chapter Organization Based on Table of Contents*

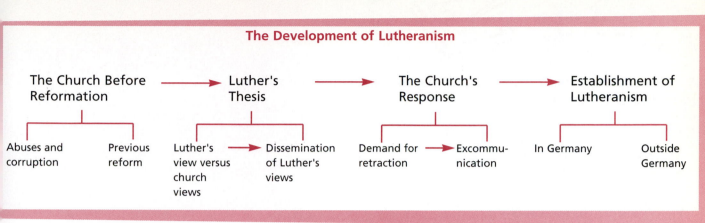

The Development of Lutheranism

The Church Before Reformation → Luther's Thesis → The Church's Response → Establishment of Lutheranism

Abuses and corruption — Previous reform

Luther's view versus church views → Dissemination of Luther's views

Demand for retraction → Excommunication

In Germany — Outside Germany

Figure 7–3. *Potential Organization Based on Table of Contents*

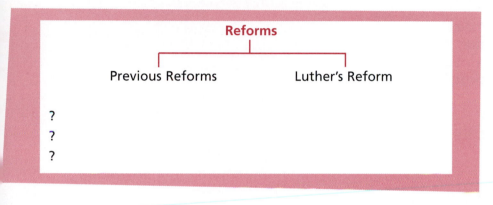

Reforms

Previous Reforms   Luther's Reform

?
?
?

Figure 7–4. *Potential Organization Based on Table of Contents*

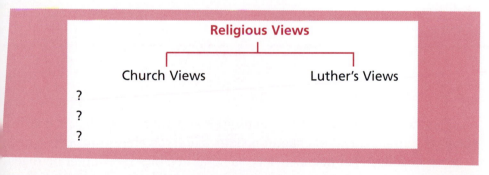

Religious Views

Church Views   Luther's Views

?
?
?

Figure 7–5. *Potential Organization Based on Table of Contents*

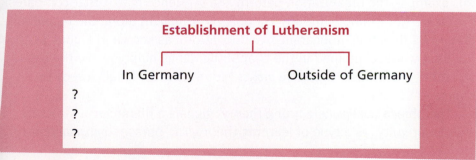

Establishment of Lutheranism

In Germany   Outside of Germany

?
?
?

Exercise

Develop an organization for the chapter containing the following table of contents.

The Plant Kingdom

I. Phylum—Bryophyta
    A. Class—Liverworts
    B. Class—Mosses
II. Phylum—Tracheophyta
    A. Subphylum—Lycopsida
    B. Subphylum—Sphenopsida
    C. Subphylum—Pteropsida
        1. Class—Filicineae
        2. Class—Gymnospermae
        3. Class—Angiospermae
            a) Subclass—dicotyledons
            b) Subclass—monocotyledons

Survey Chapter Headings

Alert words contained in the chapter headings help you see the text's structure.

A second way to determine the organizational patterns and players is to survey the arrangement of chapter headings and the alert words contained in those headings. For instance, let's say that in a biology chapter on digestion, each section heading names a part of the digestive process. Subheadings within each section are function, appearance, and location. In this example, the organization pattern is a sequence matrix that compares the topics (for example, mouth, esophagus, stomach) along the repeatable categories (function, appearance, and location), as shown in Figure 7-6.

Alert words contained in the chapter headings help you see the text's structure. The phrase "digestive *process*," for example, signals a sequential structure.

The phrase *"contiguity* learning theory" signals a hierarchical structure with "contiguity" as a type of learning theory. The phrase *"contiguity* theory" also suggests a potential matrix structure, because if there is one subtype of learning theory (contiguity), there must be others that are comparable. See Figure 7-7.

Here in Chapter 7, the headings indicate that there are three major topics: *Before*, *During*, and *After* reading. Under the *Before* heading are five subheadings including the subheadings *Set the Mood* and *Survey the Chapter*. Subsumed beneath the *Survey* heading are five subheadings. This structure continues for all the chapter's elements. Figure 7-8 shows a partial framework for Chapter 7's headings.

Figure 7–6. *Text Structure Drawn from Chapter Headings*

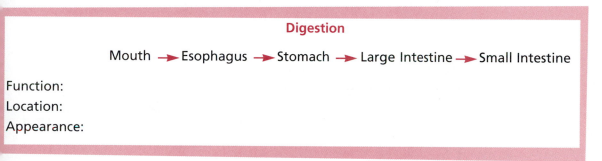

Figure 7–7. *Text Structure Drawn from Alert Words*

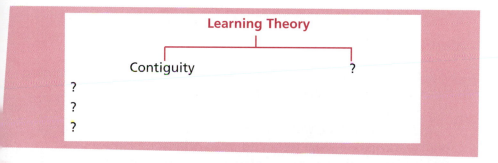

Create a chapter organizer based on the headings found in Chapter 8.

Survey Overviews and Summaries

Overviews are located at the beginning of a chapter or chapter section and summaries are located at the chapter's or section's end. Their purpose is to focus your attention on the main points that are either forthcoming or presented earlier, and to organize those points so that their relations are apparent. Read overviews and summaries prior to reading the text to provide you with a framework for selecting and organizing chapter content.

Figure 7–8. *Partial Framework for Chapter 7 Based on Chapter Headings*

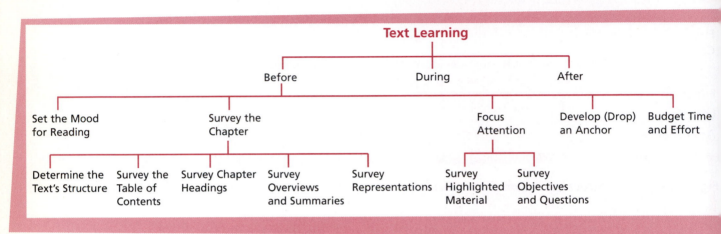

Read the following excerpt from an overview for a measurement chapter. Try to determine the chapter's framework(s).

> In this chapter, we will examine the fundamental measurement principles that underlie tests and other educational measurements. As we will see, measurement can be practiced at many different levels of sophistication: nominal, ordinal, interval, and ratio. Each provides increasingly more information and has fewer limitations. Next, we examine three measures of central tendency: mean, median, and mode. We show how to calculate each and describe their benefits and limitations. Last, we examine dispersion. We discuss three measures: range, variance, and standard deviation. Calculation methods, benefits, and limitations of each measure are discussed.

From this overview you should recognize the overriding structure, which you see displayed in Figure 7-9. The overriding structure is a hierarchy displaying the title measurement, the superordinate topics (levels of measurement, central tendency, and dispersion) and their respective subtopics. Figures 7-10, 7-11, and 7-12 display matrix frameworks for the three respective topics. Use these frameworks to fill in important details as you read. To capture the text's organization and provide an advance organizer to guide your reading, try generating representational frameworks like those in Figures 7-9 through 7-12.

Figure 7–9. *Overriding Structure of Measurement Chapter Based on Chapter Overview*

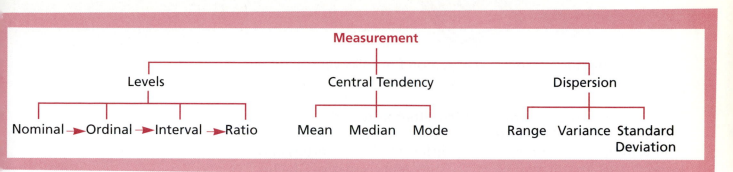

Figure 7–10. *Matrix Framework for Measurement Levels Based on Chapter Overview*

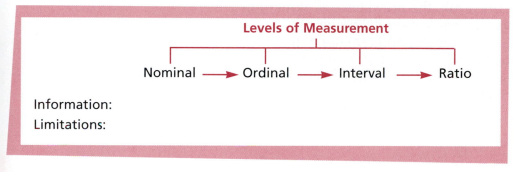

Figure 7–11. *Matrix Framework for Central Tendency Based on Chapter Overview*

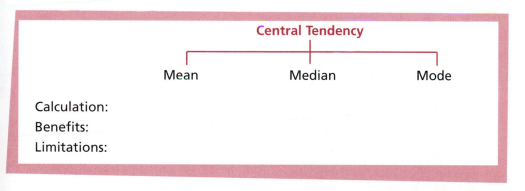

Figure 7–12. *Matrix Framework for Dispersion Based on Chapter Overview*

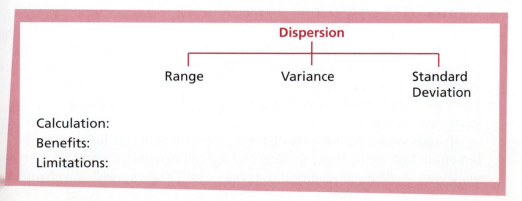

Exercise

Create a chapter organizer(s) based on the following chapter overview.

This chapter explores three problems that affect adolescents—drugs, alcohol, and delinquency. You'll read about current trends in drug use and about the different kinds of drugs adolescents use—marijuana, nicotine, stimulants, sedatives, hallucinogens, cocaine, and heroin. You'll learn to identify these drugs, recognize their dangers, and understand their prevalence. We then focus on the most widely used drug—alcohol. We'll discuss why adolescents drink, the prevalence of drinking, and the associated dangers. The section on delinquency describes the varying patterns for males and females with regard to completing school, criminal activities, and potential for adult criminality. We also describe intervention programs to combat drug, alcohol, and delinquency problems.

Survey Representations

Some texts make your job easier by including representations that display the chapter's structure. A chapter on skin cancer, for example, might present the matrix organizer you see in Figure 7-13, which helps you select and organize chapter information.

Focus Attention

The text aids just described, which promote organization (table of contents, headings, overviews and summaries, and representations), also focus your attention by telling you what text ideas to select. The heading "Focus Attention," for example, signals you to select information about how to focus your attention.

In addition to the text aids just described, three others help you select important text ideas. These include highlighted material, objectives, and questions. Pay special attention to these as well when surveying a chapter.

Figure 7–13. *Text-Provided Representation to Aid in the Selection and Organization of Text Information*

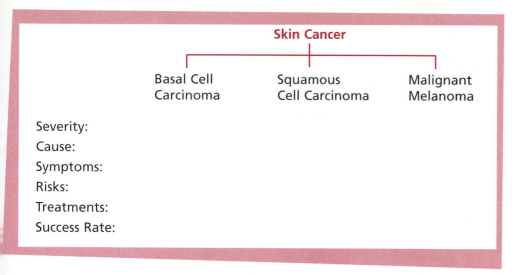

Survey Highlighted Material

When you're surveying a chapter, focus your attention on highlighted material—material that appears in boldface, italics, or capital letters. These text markings designate new or important information.

When reading about skin cancer, for example, the term **squamous cell carcinoma** may appear in boldface type and the terms *metastasize, cryosurgery, chemosurgery,* and *radiation therapy* may appear in italics. These text markings draw your attention to one form of skin cancer (squamous cell carcinoma), the fact that it may spread (metastasize), and forms of treatment (cryosurgery, chemosurgery, and radiation therapy). By noting these highlighted terms prior to reading, you gain awareness about the text's content and sharpen your focus as you strive to understand the highlighted terms.

Survey Objectives and Questions

Authors sometimes insert objectives and questions to guide attention. Ordinarily, objectives are inserted at the start of the chapter, and questions appear at the beginning, middle, or end of a chapter. If you examine objectives and questions before reading, they can guide your attention as you search for information pertinent to them. For example, if you were given the question "What are the limitations of interval scales?" you know that what you want to search for are *limitations*.

Although questions and objectives both guide your attention, objectives are usually more general than questions. In general, objectives indicate what you must know or do following reading, but they don't test you directly. For instance, an objective associated with measurement might be "Given a set of scores, calculate the mean, median, and mode." However, objectives can be transformed into corresponding test questions. For example, you can easily transform the presented objective into the test question "Calculate the mean, median, and mode for the following test scores: 8, 7, 3, 9, 7, 7, 6." Similarly, the objective, "State the benefits of ordi-

Exercise

Survey the paragraph below. What is it about? Record terms you will focus on when you read.

There are four major types of representations. The first is **hierarchy**. Hierarchies show *superordinate-subordinate* relations. One example is the American government. The president is superordinate to the Senate and the House of Representatives. The second type of representation is **sequence**. Sequences display *temporal* relations such as the steps involved in starting your car. The **matrix** is a third representation showing *coordinate* or *comparative* relations. An example is the relationship between tigers and lions which can be compared with regard to their size, habitat, and social behaviors. Last, there are **diagrams**. Diagrams show *static* and *dynamic* relations. Static relations pertain to something's appearance or location whereas dynamic relations deal with movement. A diagram showing the keys on a keyboard is static. A diagram showing how the planets revolve is dynamic.

nal scales over nominal scales," is easily transformed into the question "What benefits do ordinal scales have over nominal scales?"

When you find specific test questions that are presented without objectives, don't believe that your attention should be focused only on those questions, or that answering them indicates full comprehension of the material. To illustrate, suppose that after reading a text section on central tendency, you are presented with the following questions:

1. Define the median.
2. Calculate the mean for the following scores: 7, 3, 9, 1, 9.

You might be able to answer these questions, and if you can, you might believe you have mastered that section. But—realize that inserted questions only direct you to some of the important points and merely sample your knowledge. Rarely do the inserted questions cover all the important chapter information. The specific questions are a guide. If you're asked to define the median, assume that the mean and mode must also be defined. If you're asked to calculate the mean, assume that the median and mode must also be calculated. In other words, use inserted objectives and questions as springboards for generating many more questions to guide attention and check your understanding.

Develop (Drop) an Anchor

Remember from Chapter 4 that your learning depends on developing external connections between what you're learning now and your previous knowledge. Previous knowledge acts like an anchor for securing new information in your memory. If you're learning about cricket, for example, prior knowledge about baseball is the anchor for securing new information about cricket.

Returning to our Disney World example, using prior knowledge about other theme parks, movie studios, romantic resorts, and oceans can provide useful anchors for understanding the Disney experience. On another, subject-oriented level, one author recalls a government and law class in high school in which the students conducted a mock trial at the semester's beginning. The mock trial became the anchor for later learning more detailed information about jury selection, admissible and inadmissible evidence, Miranda rights, and the like.

Text chapters are usually weighted down by several anchors that you can uncover by surveying the chapter. Survey the overviews and summaries, the headings and subheadings, and any highlighted material in advance of reading. These provide a "taste" for the chapter's content. Once you recognize that the chapter is about learning theories, measurement, or skin cancer, for example, you can retrieve all of your existing knowledge about the topic and anchor the new information to it. Before reading about skin cancer, for example, recall all that you can about cancer in general, such as types of cancer and the experiences of people you know who developed cancer. The more information you bring to the text, the more meaningful and memorable your reading becomes.

Authors sometimes provide readers with anchors in the form of scenarios and application questions. Scenarios are stories that precede a chapter or chapter section, and they're easy to spot while you're surveying. Often, they're contained in boxes or appear at the beginning of a chapter or chapter section. So far, in this chapter, we have presented scenarios about Josh and Dennis, students' reading strategies and test performance, and about planning a trip to Disney World. You'll find scenarios at the beginning of each chapter in this book.

Survey scenarios to establish anchors for reading. Scenarios provide an interesting story or event to which you can apply chapter information while you read. For example: Do you remember the story about George in Chapter 2? George confronted many barriers on his first day in class (such

> Survey scenarios to establish anchors for reading.

Exercise

Turn the following objectives into questions.

1. The student will state three rules for dividing words into syllables.
2. The student will divide a variety of two-syllable words into syllables.
3. The student will identify nouns and verbs in a given sentence.

Suppose that in the Chapter 5 section about the four types of representations (hierarchy, sequence, matrix, and diagram), you were presented with the following questions. What other questions might you anticipate answering?

1. What is the function of hierarchies?
2. What alert words signal a sequence representation?
3. What types of relations are displayed in a diagram?
4. What principles guide the construction of matrices?

as early class, large class, boring instructor). We wrote this scenario to help you select and apply motivational ideas from Chapter 2 that would help George (and you) understand and surmount barriers.

Similarly, chapter questions that require application provide a stable anchor. For instance, a question inserted at the end of a chapter about skin cancer might challenge you to "develop plans for skin cancer avoidance and detection." If you had surveyed the chapter before reading the text, this application question would anchor the text information you collect about skin cancer.

Exercise

For each text topic below, list the anchors you might bring to the reading assignment to help you understand and learn the text content.

1. Trial law
2. Child development
3. Sports psychology
4. The Civil War
5. Group dynamics

An anchor can be dropped by your course instructor, too. Suppose that your statistics instructor assigns you to calculate the mean, mode, median, and variance for an upcoming test. This assignment becomes an anchor for selecting and evaluating text information.

Budget Time and Effort

You remember that not having an overview of Disney World led to poor planning on how to take advantage of all the theme park's attractions. An advance understanding of Disney's attractions would have aided planning.

Similarly, you can easily establish a plan for reading and understanding a chapter when you survey it. First, using this chapter's activities and strategies, estimate how long you need to read the chapter. Make an estimate by considering the chapter's length, instructional aids, and density. (See below for an explanation of density.) Measure length by page numbers and the number of words on a page. You need not count words, however. Just look! A page containing tiny type, narrow margins, scant headings, and few pictures takes longer to read than a page containing large type, wide

Reading a text is nothing like watching a movie—you never start at the beginning and read straight through

margins, several headings and pictures. Plan your time accordingly.

Texts that include several text aids, such as headings, examples, questions, and representations, should be faster to read than texts without such aids. Not, mind you, because these should be skipped over, but because text aids can reduce reading time. They reduce the need for some learner activities (for example, you need not make a diagram of a dicot flower if one is provided), and they present information more efficiently. A diagram, for example, can be worth a thousand words.

When you're estimating text reading time, you should also consider text density and text difficulty.

A dense text is one that presents a great deal of new information in a short space. Consider two texts: One introduces five terms and their definitions on every page; the other introduces one new term per page. The latter text is considered less dense, generally less difficult, and quicker to read.

Estimate a text's density by surveying the number of terms that are highlighted throughout the chapter. A text that highlights many new terms is relatively dense. Or survey two or three paragraphs from different parts of the chapter. Skimming a few paragraphs will give you an idea of how many new terms are introduced throughout the chapter. For a personal experience example, consider that one of this book's authors can now positively attest that his tenth-grade biology textbook was incredibly dense. Look how many unfamiliar terms there are in this one single paragraph.

> The bryophytes are small green plants that grow in moist places. They have simple leaves, but [either] lack a stem or have a very simple stem. In their reproductive cycle, bryophytes alternate from one generation to the next between two types of plants. One generation produces sexually (by gametes) and is called gametophyte. The next generation reproduces asexually (by spores) and is called sporophyte. In the bryophytes, the gametophyte generation is the larger of the two and the more easily seen. The bryophytes are divided into two classes, the liverworts and the mosses. Their name is derived from *bryon*, the Greek word for moss.[1]

High-density texts are difficult to understand. Without an arsenal of effective reading strategies back then, the author only remembered "liverworts," which became, henceforth and forevermore, his new name for liverwurst.

Survey texts to allocate reading time and energy. Not every text section requires an in-depth reading. Perhaps your biology instructor has emphasized learning about malignant melanoma instead of other forms of skin

[1]Adapted from *Concepts in Modern Biology*, by David Kraus. Published by Cambridge Book Company, Inc., A subsidiary of Cowles Communications, Inc., Bronxville, New York, 1969, p. 74.

cancer. In this case, spend more time studying malignant melanoma. Maybe your statistics instructor informed the class that recognizing the appropriate statistical test was crucial but that the mathematical formulas for conducting the tests was not. In this case, you pay the most attention to sections covering test selection.

Figure 7-14 organizes by their purpose the various text aids introduced in this section. Figure 7-15 presents a checklist for activities that should take place before you begin reading.

Figure 7–14. *Text Aids and Their Purposes*

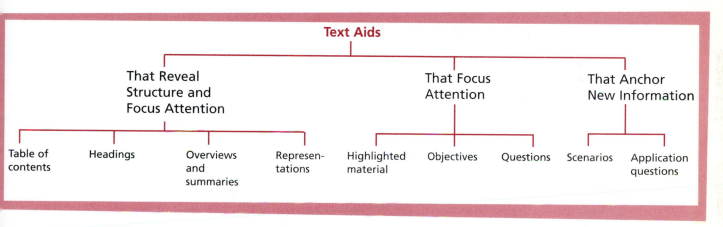

Figure 7–15. *A Checklist for "Pre-reading" Activities*

You'll know you're ready to read if you've answered "yes" to the following questions.

☐ 1. I'm in the mood to read. I'm "psyched" and I'm ready to work hard.

☐ 2. I've surveyed the chapter's table of contents, headings, overviews and summaries, and representations to determine the text's structure.

☐ 3. I've generated representation frameworks that display text structures.

☐ 4. I've surveyed questions, objectives, and highlighted terms to help focus my attention while reading.

☐ 5. I've surveyed the text and activated my prior knowledge related to the text content.

☐ 6. I've established the text's difficulty and have planned to spend more time on some sections than others.

What to Do While You Read

Many college readers are "passive" readers—they read textbooks as if they were thumbing through the daily newspaper, leisurely and without purpose. Over breakfast or while relaxing after supper, they leaf through textbooks as easily as if they were skimming through an editorial or a letter to "Dear Abby," and yet they believe they absorb and retain the information in the text. Their primary strategy is highlighting key words, just like the majority of students described earlier who scored below 70%. They, like those other students, mistakenly believe that highlighting equals understanding.

Effective students read aggressively and with purpose, as if they were scrutinizing a treasure map or a rich uncle's will. They mark important "landmarks" and "pathways" that reveal the text's structure. They use note-taking strategies that unearth the text's "treasures." This section focuses on text-marking methods and note-taking strategies that you can incorporate while you're reading.

Mark the Text

The purpose of marking your textbook is to determine and display the text's structure (hierarchy, sequence, or matrix); the players (topics, subtopics, and repeatable categories); and important details. A properly marked text can be transformed rapidly into representations that illustrate the text's structure, players, and details.

Before we show you how text is marked, we want to introduce you to the few symbols that comprise the marking system. These appear in Figure 7-16.

Learn our marking system. Try it out. You don't have to use the exact same marking system—feel free to make whatever changes you want, as long as you identify and note topics, repeatable categories, and details while you read. Following are five sample passages that illustrate our marking system.

Figure 7–16. *Marking System Symbols and Descriptions*

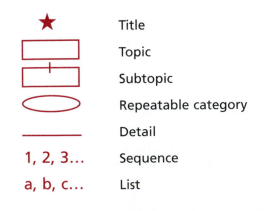

★	Title
▭	Topic
▭	Subtopic
⬭	Repeatable category
————	Detail
1, 2, 3…	Sequence
a, b, c…	List

★

Lepidoptera consist of moths and butterflies. A moth has two sets of wings. It folds the wings down over its body like a roof when it rests. The moth has feathery antennae and spins a fuzzy cocoon. It has a gray or white color and flies mostly at night. The moth goes through four stages of development: egg, caterpillar, pupa, and adult.

A butterfly goes through four stages of development and has two sets of wings. Its antennae are long and thin with knobs at the ends. When a butterfly rests, its wings are straight up like outstretched hands. A butterfly is brightly colored and flies during the day.

In the marked passage you'll notice that we drew a star on top of a potential title (Lepidoptera). Boxes were drawn around the two topics (moths and butterflies) and we circled the repeatable categories (wings, rest, antennae, cocoon, flight, and development). The details (such as fuzzy) associated with each repeatable category (such as cocoon) for each topic (such as moth) were underlined.

This marked passage is easily transformed into the representation in Figure 7-17. The title appears at the top. Topics are placed along the top row. Repeatable categories appear down the left margin and details are housed within the matrix cells.

Figure 7–17.   *Lepidoptera Representation Constructed from Marked Text*

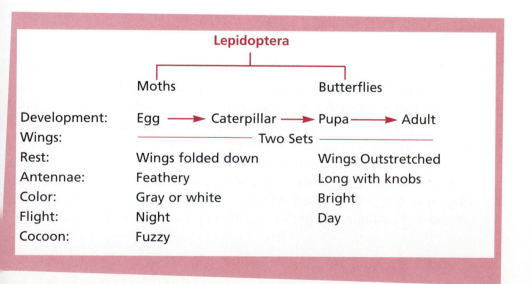

	Moths	Butterflies
Development:	Egg → Caterpillar → Pupa → Adult	
Wings:	Two Sets	
Rest:	Wings folded down	Wings Outstretched
Antennae:	Feathery	Long with knobs
Color:	Gray or white	Bright
Flight:	Night	Day
Cocoon:	Fuzzy	

$$\begin{bmatrix} \star \\ \text{college} \\ \text{choice} \end{bmatrix}$$

Students in the northern region of the state have the

of enrolling in either of two very different schools, Stanton College

(Location) or Burns College. Stanton College is nestled in the Oakdale

a.   b.

mountains. Large oak trees fill the hilly campus and

c.   d.

(Appearance) several ponds and footbridges are found throughout the

campus. Stanton is a state-supported type of college.

a.   b.

Therefore, it charges a minimal registration fee and a small

tuition fee. The school specializes in math and science. Its

instructors are generally famous. Many have lectured at other

prestigious colleges.

Burns College, on the other hand, is a privately supported

a.   b.

(Fees) type of college. Registration and tuition costs are therefore

(Specialty) high. Burns is largely a business school. Its teachers are

(Instructors) usually successful business people from the community. Burns is

a.

(Location) in the city of Burnsforth. Its few trees are shadowed by the

b.

(Appearance) neighboring skyscrapers of the city.

Marking this text was more involved because the repeatable categories were not always directly stated, repeatable category labels differed somewhat between topics, and multiple details were sometimes presented for a topic and repeatable category. However, all of these complications were easily handled by using the text-marking system.

When the author described the colleges' locations and appearances in paragraphs one and two, he didn't provide explicit labels. These had to be inferred. For example, the phrase "nestled in the Oakdale mountains" in paragraph one refers to the college's *location*. When repeatable categories are not explicitly labeled, it means you must generate a suitable repeatable category label, place it in the adjoining margin, and circle it like any repeatable category. As you can see, we also did this for the repeatable category *specialty* in paragraph two.

In two instances the author changed the terminology used to label repeatable categories. *Instructors* in paragraph one was changed to *teachers* in paragraph two. *Fees* in paragraph one was changed to *costs* in paragraph two. To maintain consistency and reduce confusion, we renamed the terms in paragraph two so they were consistent with their original names in paragraph one.

In some cases, we used letters to designate a list of points. In a list format, lettering the points shows that the points belong together. We didn't use numbers to distinguish the points because numbers, in this particular marking system, convey order. Because this passage was untitled, we developed a title and included it in the bracketed portion of the marked passage. All other text markings are consistent with those used in passage one. The representation corresponding to the marked passage appears in Figure 7-18.

Figure 7–18. *College Choices Representation Constructed from Marked Text*

	College Choices	
	Stanton	Burns
Location:	Oakdale Mountains	City of Burnsforth
Appearance:	a. Large oak trees b. Hilly c. Ponds d. Footbridges	a. Few trees b. Neighboring skyscrapers
Type:	State supported	Private
Fees:	a. Minimal registration b. Small tuition	a. High registration b. High tuition
Specialization:	Math and science	Business
Instructors:	Famous	Successful business people from community

Running and Swimming ★

Running is an excellent activity for increasing one's level of
physical conditioning. It increases aerobic capacity (which is
the ability to turn oxygen into energy) and uses many muscle
systems in the body. It is especially good for strengthening the
legs. Running can be done almost anywhere and in almost all
weather conditions. Therefore, when people travel for vacation
or business, running is easy to continue. The only special
equipment required is a good pair of running shoes to support
the arches of the feet. The main disadvantage of running is that
it is somewhat taxing on the joints of the ankles, knees and hips.
Another disadvantage is that running decreases flexibility.

Swimming is considered the best overall body conditioner. It
increases aerobic capacity and exercises almost all of the major
muscle systems in the body. It is especially good for strengthening
the upper body and for increasing flexibility. Swimming can be
done indoors in a pool or outside in a pool or lake. Many people
swim year round, even when the water is cold. Swimming
requires a comfortable swim suit and a pair of water-tight
goggles. The disadvantages of swimming are that one must have
access to a pool or lake, and many people feel that it does not
control weight as well as other forms of exercise.

Conditions

Equipment

As with the previously marked passage on college choices, we had to invent repeatable category names. In this case, we used *conditions* and *equipment* as names for repeatable categories in paragraph two. These names were consistent with those supplied in paragraph one. Again, we used letters to designate the multiple details that pertained to a topic's repeatable category. For instance, the four benefits of swimming were marked a, b, c, and d. The representation corresponding to this marked passage is shown in Figure 7-19. Consistent with the representational principles introduced in Chapters 5 and 6, the topics appear along the top row, repeatable categories are listed down the left margin, and details are furnished in the cells intersecting the matrix's topics and repeatable categories.

Figure 7–19. *Running and Swimming Representation Constructed from Marked Text*

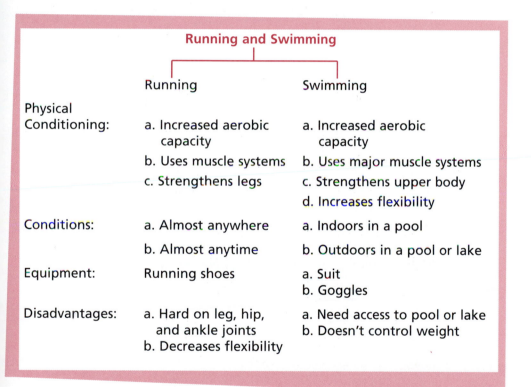

	Running and Swimming	
	Running	Swimming
Physical Conditioning:	a. Increased aerobic capacity	a. Increased aerobic capacity
	b. Uses muscle systems	b. Uses major muscle systems
	c. Strengthens legs	c. Strengthens upper body
		d. Increases flexibility
Conditions:	a. Almost anywhere	a. Indoors in a pool
	b. Almost anytime	b. Outdoors in a pool or lake
Equipment:	Running shoes	a. Suit
		b. Goggles
Disadvantages:	a. Hard on leg, hip, and ankle joints	a. Need access to pool or lake
	b. Decreases flexibility	b. Doesn't control weight

Passage 4

Experimental Procedure ★

Students first ^{1.} viewed the lecture either by taking notes in their
^{a.} conventional format, on the ^{b.} skeletal outline, or on the
^{c.} matrix framework. Following the lecture, students
^{2.} studied for 25 minutes either by ^{a.} reviewing their notes
or by ^{b.} writing an essay from their notes. Immediately
following, students were ^{3.} tested. First a ^{1.} synthesis test was
administered with a five-minute time limit. Next students had
ten minutes to complete an ^{2.} application test. Last, was a
^{3.} factual recognition test lasting five minutes. One week later, all
subjects returned to complete the ^{4.} delayed test. This was a
recall test and students had fifteen minutes to complete it.

This marked passage differs substantially from the previous marked
passages. First, because it has no repeatable categories, it has no circles.
Second, because there are several subtopics, it contains several boxes with
slash marks. For instance, students *studied* (the topic) by either *reviewing* or
writing an essay (the subtopics). Third, it contains numbers, because the four
topics are related sequentially and the three types of immediate tests (synthesis, application, and factual recognition) are also sequential.

Figure 7-20 shows the corresponding representation. Because there are
no matrix cells to present details, marked details appear in parentheses
along with the topics, subtopics, or sequence arrows.

Figure 7–20. *Experimental Procedure Representation Constructed from Marked Text*

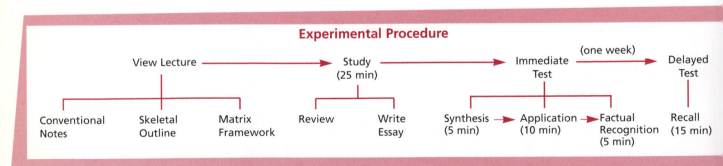

★

There are several different [types of test questions] that teachers can use to evaluate student learning. The two major types are short-answer and essay questions. Short-answer questions can be either select or supply type items. Select questions include true-false, multiple-choice, and matching items. In supply questions the answer is not provided and the student must recall the answer from memory. Essay questions involve the student recalling a great deal of knowledge rather than a specific bit of information.

This marked passage also has no repeatable categories and hence no circles. The information in this passage is hierarchically related. The topics were the two types of test questions, *short-answer* and *essay*. Subtopics pertaining to short-answer questions were *supply items* and *select items*. Subtopics pertaining to select items were *true-false, multiple choice,* and *matching*. In marking this passage, we took a few liberties that seemed within the guidelines of the marking system. First, we enclosed the title in brackets so that it was more apparent. Second, we used a box containing two slash marks to identify sub-subtopics (that is, the three types of select tests). Last, we drew an arrow between two details because one detail (*specific bit*) clarified what is *recalled*.

When you're marking text, you should add your own symbol markings and adapt some of ours to meet your needs. Just remember that a marked text should reveal the text's structure, players, and details, and be easily transformed into a representation. The representation for this passage appears in Figure 7-21.

Figure 7–21. *Types of Test Questions Representation Constructed from Marked Text*

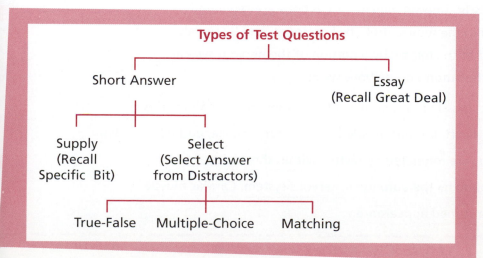

Exercise

Mark the biology passage below, which is about muscles. Construct a representation from your marked passage on a separate sheet of paper. We have marked the last paragraph for you.

Three Types of Muscle

The body contains three types of muscle—skeletal muscle, smooth muscle, and cardiac muscle. As the name implies, most skeletal muscle attaches to the bones of the skeleton. The contractions of skeletal muscle exert force on the bones and move them. Consequently, skeletal muscle is responsible for activities such as walking and manipulating objects in the external environment. Skeletal muscle is voluntary muscle—that is, its' contractions are normally controlled by the conscious desires of the individual. However, under many conditions, skeletal muscle contractions do not require conscious thought. For example, a person does not usually have to think about contracting the skeletal muscles involved in maintaining posture. Skeletal muscle contractions are regulated by signals transmitted to the muscle by a portion of the nervous system known as the somatic nervous system. When viewed microscopically, light and dark bands, which give the muscles a striped appearance, are visible.

Smooth muscle is so named because its cells lack the stripes found in skeletal muscle cells. Smooth muscle is involuntary muscle—that is, its contractions are not normally controlled by the conscious desires of the individual. However, under appropriate circumstances, a person can gain some voluntary control over smooth muscle. Smooth muscle contractions are regulated by factors within the muscle itself, by hormones, and by signals transmitted to the muscle by a portion of the nervous system known as the autonomic nervous system.

Cardiac muscle is a specialized type of muscle that forms the wall of the heart. Cardiac muscle is involuntary muscle, and its contractions are regulated by factors within the muscle, by hormones, and by the autonomic nervous system. Cardiac muscle cells have a striped appearance.

location   *type*   a.   b.   c.

Deploy Comprehension Strategies

Effective readers are strategic. They don't merely read. They engage in activities that ensure comprehension.

Effective readers are active readers who interact with the text. As they read, they raise questions, make predictions, organize ideas, generate elaborations, create summaries, and continually monitor understanding and strategy use. Although these comprehension strategies can be carried out inside your head, it is nevertheless better to convert them into physical actions, such as writing summaries and questions, either in the text's margins, or in notebooks, because text marking and notes are crucial to later review.

We discuss each comprehension strategy in turn. Later, we give you an example that shows how the strategies are applied collectively.

Raise Questions

Have you ever spoken with a three-year-old? If you have, you know that they are chock full of questions. Consider this exchange between child and adult:

Child: Why is a flower colored?
Adult: To attract bees.
Child: Why does the flower want to attract bees?
Adult: The flower needs to have its pollen brought to other flowers to make new flowers.
Child: What's pollen?
Adult: It's sort of like the flower's seeds.
Child: Do bees bring the pollen to other flowers?
Adult: Yes.
Child: Why do bees do that?
Adult: Bees do it by accident as they go from flower to flower sipping nectar.
Child: What's nectar?
Adult: It's a sweet juice that the flower makes and bees enjoy.
Child: Can we have nectar to drink with lunch?

Effective readers carry on an almost childlike inquisition with their texts. They are forever asking *who, what, where, when, why,* and *how* questions. Below is a short passage from a biology text about the nose's role in respiration. The portions in parentheses are the questions we raised.

Air enters through two nostrils (Why are there two?) and passes into the nasal passages (What happens in these passages? To

Effective readers are forever asking who, what, where, when, why, and how questions.

what do they connect?). Mucous membranes (What do they do?) containing many cilia (What do these look like and what do they do?) line the nasal passages. Bacteria and dust contained in the inhaled air is trapped and filtered by the cilia and the mucous secreted by the membranes (Is this why mucus blown from the nose is sometimes discolored?). Air is also warmed and moistened as it passes through the nasal passage. (What happens when someone has a cold and can't breathe through their nose? Are these advantages lost or does the mouth somehow serve the same functions? Are the nose strips that some football players wear effective?)

You'll note that many of our questions are basic *who*, *what*, *when* questions regarding function (for example, "What do mucous membranes and cilia do?") and structure (for example, "What do cilia look like? Where does respiration occur after the nasal passage?"). Some of our questions are *elaborative*, because they have personal relevance and extend beyond what the text is likely to report. Elaborative questions help you build external connections (as explained in Chapter 4) because they connect newly presented information with your prior knowledge. In this example, questions about dirty mucus, blocked nasal passages, and nose strips are elaborative questions. Elaborative questions and basic questions are effective because they both increase your attention while you're reading and aid your understanding as your questions are answered.

As you read, search for answers to your questions. In this case, questions raised about the functions of mucous membranes and cilia were later answered in the text. Don't discard your unanswered questions, such as "Why are there two nostrils?" Later, to increase your understanding, ask your classmates or the instructor.

Make Predictions

Predictions go hand-in-hand with questions.

The work of a meteorologist is one of prediction. Based on existing evidence (plummeting temperatures, a falling barometer, and northeast winds), past experiences, and a dash of intuition, meteorologists predict tomorrow's weather.

As an effective reader, you make even more frequent forecasts than do meteorologists. As you read, you predict a story's future events, the function of an elephant's floppy ears, and the structure of alveoli in the lungs.

Your predictions guide your reading because they encourage you to think ahead and later confirm or refute your predictions as you read. In short, predictions increase and focus your attention. Don't worry if your predictions turn out to be wrong. Leave the worrying to meteorologists who fail to predict rain and are likely to receive hate mail from picnickers caught in a sudden and unexpected downpour!

Predictions go hand-in-hand with questions. Predictions easily follow questions. Returning to the passage about the nose, we gaze into our crystal ball and make several predictions from the following questions:

Question	Prediction
Why are there two nostrils?	To determine an odor's direction.
What happens in the nasal passage?	Air is filtered.
To what are nasal passages connected?	A tube to the lungs.
What do cilia look like?	Tiny hairs or nets.
What if someone has a cold?	The mouth or air tube might do some filtering and warming.
Are nose strips effective?	They might open clogged nasal passages somewhat.

As with questions, seek to confirm or disconfirm predictions that aren't addressed in the text by discussing them later with fellow students and instructors. Although it's okay to live with unanswered questions and unconfirmed predictions for a while, don't live with them too long. Readers often hold tight to inaccurate conceptions or predictions (such as the one about air and food traveling along a single tube in the throat). To ensure greater comprehension, continue to seek knowledge by going beyond the text to ensure greater comprehension.

Exercise

Generate questions and predictions for the history passage below.

Raphael produced many paintings in his brief and brilliant career, nearly all of them models of the intellectual and technical achievements of the Renaissance. Raphael possessed an unerring sense of design and balance, and the capacity to reuse what others had devised. He never ceased to learn, but he never plagiarized. His many Madonnas are perfect jewels, but his masterpiece is the *School of Athens*. This is the ultimate statement of Renaissance classicism and the finest group painting of the age.[2]

---

[2]Adapted from A *History of a Western World*, 2nd ed., by C. Schuler, J. H. Claster, K. T. Beck, and W. E. Wright. Published by D.C. Heath and Company, A Division of Raytheon Education Company, Lexington, MA, 1969.

Organize Ideas

Throughout this book, you've seen that well-organized information bolsters comprehension and reveals the relations and patterns that are usually hidden in unorganized or linearly organized text. Remember that you learn more from looking at a completed puzzle than by studying its pieces. Effective readers build internal connections as they read; they assemble the puzzle. This section briefly describes how three now familiar strategies (questioning, predicting, and representing) help you organize text and build internal connections.

You can develop questions and predictions that pertain directly to the organization of ideas. For instance, when the text discusses short-term memory, question and predict the presence of a long-term memory. When a text that has described the function and structure of red blood cells introduces white blood cells, predict that the same repeatable categories (structure and function) are described for the new topic (white blood cells). When the text describes the first two stages in the respiration process, predict coverage of remaining stages. Don't wait for the text's organization to unfold. Aggressively seek and anticipate that organization through questions and predictions aimed at revealing it.

While you're reading, you can also determine the text's organization by marking it and constructing representations. When you're reading about the structure, secretions, and effects of duct and ductless glands, for example, represent this material as you see it done in Figure 7-22. Don't worry if your initial representation is incomplete. Try to at least develop the representation framework (topics and repeatable categories), such as the one in Figure 7-23, for comparing the nervous and endocrine systems. Complete the representation framework while you're either reading further or following reading.

Diagrams and graphs are also useful ways to organize text ideas. When reading about glands, for example, you might want to construct a simple diagram indicating the glands' locations.

Sketching a simple graph is also helpful. Suppose a psychology text on anxiety and performance states that performance is poor at low or high

Figure 7–22. *Representation Constructed While Reading Text*

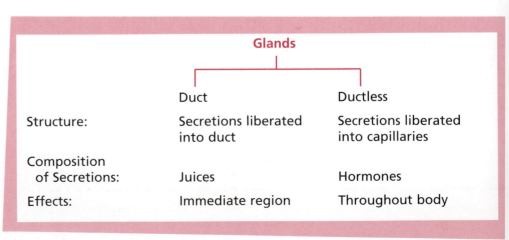

Figure 7–23. *Preliminary Representation Constructed While Reading Text*

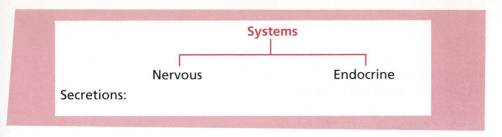

Figure 7–24. *Graph Constructed While Reading*

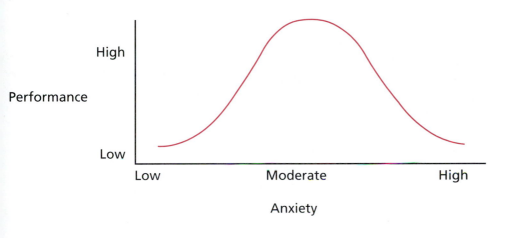

anxiety levels, but optimal at moderate anxiety levels. A graph like that shown in Figure 7-24 is useful in understanding the relationship between anxiety and performance.

As you read, sketch representations, graphs, and other displays (such as maps or pictures) that can capture the text's organization better than words alone.

Generate Elaborations

Elaborations are statements that extend beyond the information presented. They comprise *examples, comparisons* with previous knowledge, and *evaluations*. Constructing elaborations helps you build external connections or anchor new text information with previous knowledge and understand the new ideas better.

Salespeople are notorious elaborators. Consider the highlighted elaborations embedded in this sales pitch from a string salesperson:

Ordinary string *is the most important thing to have around the house* (evaluation). You'll need some from time to time *to tie up a box of pastries, pull a loose tooth, clean between more permanent teeth, or remember something important* (examples). *Staples or glue could never do that work, especially the tooth pulling* (comparison). String is, inch for inch, less expensive than tape

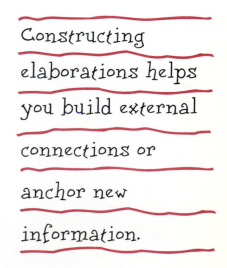

Constructing elaborations helps you build external connections or anchor new information.

Exercise

Construct a representation to organize the ideas presented in the following passage about the outcomes of young marriages.

The marriages with the poorest track records for success are those where each partner is below the age of eighteen. Also, when both partners are school dropouts, there is little chance for success. When the woman is pregnant prior to marriage, the prognosis for the marriage is also grim.

Marriages with an intermediate chance for success are characterized by females being age seventeen or older and males being age twenty or older. The female has dropped out of high school while the male has graduated from high school. The couple does not begin marriage with a pregnancy, but conceives a child immediately after the marriage.

Marriages with the best chance for success are those in which the partners are high school graduates. Pregnancy does not occur until at least one year after the marriage. The partners are older. The female is at least eighteen and the male is at least twenty.

---

and it's reusable (comparison). Why, I remember one time *dismantling my son's homemade walkie-talkies and using the string to stake tomatoes* (example). *Tape doesn't give you this kind of flexibility* (comparison). And, remember the best thing about string, *you just pull a few and you can get pretty much what you want* (evaluation).

Generate Examples   When reading text, you should not only note the author's examples, you should also develop your own. In a psychology class, you might learn that positive reinforcement is defined as the presentation of a stimulus following a behavior that increases that behavior. Along with that definition, the author is likely to present an example, such as Johnny raking his grandmother's leaves (the behavior), his grandmother

Figure 7–25. *Representation for the Concept Positive Reinforcement, Including Self-Generated Examples*

Positive Reinforcement

Definition: Behavior ⟶ Present Stimulus ➔ Behavior Increases
Example: Rake leaves ⟶ Receive $5.00 ➔ Rake more leaves
Own Example: Read book ⟶ Gain knowledge ➔ Read more books
Own Example: Compliment ⟶ People smile ⟶ Compliment more
    people   often

paying Johnny five dollars (the presentation of a stimulus), and Johnny returning soon thereafter to rake more leaves (an increase in behavior). The definition and example can be represented as shown in the top two rows of Figure 7-25.

To elaborate on this information, add your own examples to the representation. The examples should be ones that match the definition but involve situations that are different from those provided in the author's example(s). In Figure 7-25, the new situations involve reading and complimenting. If you create new examples involving new situations, it helps you to understand the concept, and later to recognize new examples on a test.

Make Comparisons   When you're learning new information, it is helpful to compare that information to familiar things. Comparisons help anchor the new information to existing knowledge and can actually prevent confusion. When you're learning about the operant concept of extinction, for example, it's helpful to compare it to the already acquired concepts of positive and negative punishment, which are similar to extinction. Figure 7-26 shows how the new information about extinction is added to an existing representation for punishment, thus aiding comparison.

From the representation, it is evident that all techniques decrease behavior. That is how they are similar. They are different in how the stimulus is manipulated. In punishment techniques, the stimulus is presented or removed. In extinction, the stimulus is withheld. Recognizing similarities and differences between the new concept (extinction) and the related concepts (positive and negative punishment) helps you understand the new concept and prevents you from confusing it with related concepts.

Figure 7–26. *Learning the New Concept Extinction Is Facilitated by Comparing It to Previously Acquired Punishment Concepts*

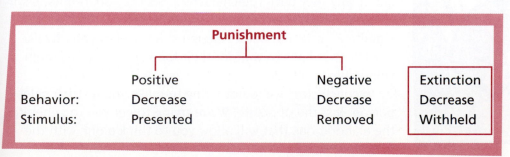

	Punishment		
	Positive	Negative	Extinction
Behavior:	Decrease	Decrease	Decrease
Stimulus:	Presented	Removed	Withheld

As another example: Suppose you were reading about spiders. A helpful elaboration involves comparing new information about spiders to already familiar, previous knowledge about insects. Many people confuse the two, believing that spiders are a type of insect. As you learn about the spider's characteristics, you can compare them to those of insects as shown in Figure 7-27.

Figure 7–27. *Representation Showing Comparison Between New Information About Spiders and Previous Knowledge About Insects*

	Insects	Spiders
Legs:	6	8
Body Parts:	3	2
Wings:	2	0
Eyes:	2	8

Evaluate Ideas Continually evaluate the merits of presented ideas. Do they make sense, are they logically derived, are they substantiated by evidence, are they important, and are they useful? In short, you should be a critical reader (and thinker) who challenges and evaluates ideas rather than swallows them hook, line, and sinker. For instance, when reading a psychology text, you might jot down evaluative comments like the following:

- "There is no evidence here to support this."
- "This finding occurred in a laboratory. I doubt it would hold up in a classroom setting."
- "This finding has implications for child-rearing."
- "I can use this technique to stick to an exercise program."
  - "This experiment would've been more convincing if the experimenters had included a group that hadn't recorded any notes."

When studying operant techniques like punishment and extinction, evaluate the techniques in terms of potential dangers ("Presenting a punisher might make the punished person respond aggressively"), or in terms of preference ("I would try extinction first, because it seems like the least offensive approach").

In evaluating information about spiders and insects, think about why they have the characteristics they do. "Perhaps spiders have eight eyes so they can see in several directions simultaneously and detect enemies. Since they can't fly like insects, they have to wait for their food, which makes them vulnerable to attack."

In conclusion, we're not trying to make you a string salesperson. Just the opposite. We're trying to get you to generate the elaborations that will allow you to think along with the

Exercise

Generate elaborations to help you understand and remember the passage below.

A recent experiment shows that memory is reconstructive, that we can remember things differently from how they occurred or in some cases even create "new" memories. The experimenter showed students a video of an automobile accident. A week later, the experimenter asked half of the students, "How fast were the cars going when they *bumped* into one another?" The other students were asked, "How fast were the cars going when they *smashed* into one another?" Although all students observed the same accident, on average, students given the leading question containing the verb *smashed* estimated higher speeds than the other students.

salesperson. Consider examples of how you might use the string. Compare its usefulness relative to other products. Evaluate both the string's worth and the salesperson's pitch. Learning to do all this makes you a better consumer—and, more to the point, a more aggressive, thoughtful, critical reader.

Create Summaries

How often do you read a page of text and then turn that page without having the foggiest idea what you just read? Perhaps too often. Many students fall into the trap of setting *time*, rather than *comprehension*, goals for reading. Your goal should never be, *read for two hours*. Your goal should be to *comprehend what's read*. Writing summaries is an excellent way to bolster and monitor your comprehension. Before you turn a page, summarize that page. Before you read a new chapter section, summarize the previous section. Before you close the book, summarize the completed chapter.

Write summaries, rather than saying or thinking them. One reason for doing this is that written page and section summaries help you to produce a final chapter summary. Another reason is that written summaries are permanent records. You can go back and read them weeks or months later when you're studying for a test or writing a paper. A third reason is that with a written summary, it's easier to detect gaps in your knowledge. As you write or review a written summary, what you don't know becomes obvious. A fourth reason is that you can exchange written summaries with study group members. A last reason is that writing summaries prepares you to answer essay questions. Many essay questions require a summary of text ideas.

The formula for writing effective summaries is as simple as 1-2-3: 1) report the main ideas, 2) combine ideas, and 3) leave out most of the details. This formula is applied below to generate a summary for the familiar story, "The Three Little Pigs."

> A hungry wolf went to the homes of three pig brothers in search of food. At each home he threatened to blow the house down and eat the pig. He succeeded at the first two homes, because the lazy pigs had built homes made of straw and sticks, respectively. He failed at the home of the third pig, which was built from sturdy bricks. In frustration, he came down the third pig's chimney, but ran off after landing in a kettle of boiling water prepared by the pig. The story's moral was to work hard.

Only the main ideas are reported, including ideas pertaining to the wolf's encounters with the pigs. Most details are left out. For instance, the pigs' farewell to their mother, which comes at the story's beginning, is omitted. Details of how the pigs happened upon the building supplies used to construct their homes are left out. Even the wolf's familiar threat, "Open the door and let me in!" was omitted.

Several ideas were combined: The first sentence reports that the wolf went to three pig homes. This information actually appeared in three different places in the story. The second sentence describes the wolf's intention at each home. Again, this information appeared in three separate parts of the story. The third sentence combines several ideas about the pigs' laziness, their poorly built homes, and the consequences of being lazy: being eaten by the wolf.

Notice also how relevant details are intertwined in the summary. The summary's first sentence, in addition to reporting that the wolf visited three pigs' homes, reveals the wolf's motivation (he was hungry) and the fact that the pigs were brothers.

How might you summarize the passage on lepidoptera, presented earlier on page 219? Below, we present a summary with our explanations in parentheses.

> Moths and butterflies are types of lepidoptera that share similarities and maintain differences (main idea). Both have two sets of

wings and progress through four stages of development (combine similar ideas and omit details). Differences lie in how they rest, when they fly, and their appearance (combine ideas about their differences; specifically combine the categories *color* and *antennae* into the new category *appearance*). Overall, a butterfly's characteristics are more pronounced than the moth's (main idea and omit details of differences).

When you're summarizing, your goal is to report the point of the story. You do this by capturing its main ideas, combining ideas, and omitting less-important details. Don't worry about leaving details out of your summaries. They are marked in your textbook and included in your representations for future reference.

Monitor Your Comprehension and Strategy Deployment

Think about all the rules that guide conversations: You must not speak too loudly or too softly, or while someone else is speaking. When others speak, you should look at them and appear interested by raising your eyebrows, nodding, or smiling. When you speak, you must watch the listener to see if your message is understood and accepted. You must ask questions when seeking clarification, and paraphrase the speaker's ideas when you're clarifying what's being said. These are just a few of the many rules.

Exercise

Write a summary summarizing this section about creating summaries.

As if it weren't difficult enough to apply all these rules when you're talking with somebody, you must also monitor your use of these rules. Silently and continuously you check your voice volume, turn-taking, non-verbal signals, and so on.

The same holds true when you're applying the comprehension strategies we've just described. You must monitor to ensure that you're using the questioning, predicting, organizing, elaborating, and summarizing strategies—and using them effectively.

Monitoring means having an ongoing dialogue with yourself about your use of comprehension strategies. For instance, you ask yourself "Am I looking for how these ideas are organized?" And you answer your question, "Yes, I am locating alert words." You comment on what you are doing ("I'm generating new examples for this term.") and how well you're doing it ("This is an excellent example. It matches the definition and applies the term in a new context."). Below is a list of some of the monitoring questions you might generate and answer while you're reading and deploying the various comprehension strategies described in this section.

Raise Questions
- Am I raising questions?
- Am I raising basic questions about the information's structure and function?
- Am I raising elaborative questions?
- Am I raising questions about the information's organization?
- Am I seeking answers to my questions?
- Is this answer accurate and complete?
- Where can I look for answers outside the text?

Make Predictions
- Am I making predictions?
- Am I transforming questions into predictions?
- Am I predicting future events?
- Am I predicting information about structure and function?
- Am I predicting the information's organization?
- Am I seeking to confirm my prediction?
- Was my prediction confirmed?
- Where will I seek information about my predictions outside the text?

Organize Ideas
- Am I marking the text?
- Am I determining the text's structures (hierarchy, sequence, and matrix)?
- Am I determining the text's "players" (topics, subtopics, and repeatable categories)?

- Am I determining the text's details?
- Am I generating representations, graphs, and other visual displays?

Generate Elaborations
- Am I generating elaborations?
- Am I generating examples?
- Am I generating comparisons?
- Am I evaluating text?
- Am I including elaborations in representations?

Create Summaries
- Am I summarizing at the end of pages, sections, and chapters?
- Am I reporting main ideas?
- Am I combining ideas?
- Am I omitting most details?

Monitor Strategy Use
- Am I monitoring strategy use?
- Am I comprehending?

How to Mark and Comprehend a Sample Passage

What follows is a short passage about rhinoceroses.[3] We have marked the passage and recorded a set of notes in the right margin to demonstrate how text-marking and comprehension strategies are applied collectively. Numbers in the passage refer to the notes and strategies shown in the right margin.

[3] Adapted from *Endangered Animals*, by Megan Stine. Published by The Trumpet Club, Inc., a subsidiary of Bantam Doubleday Dell Publishing Group, New York, NY, 1994.

★

Rhinoceroses come in different sizes and colors.[1] They also have either square lips or hooked lips,[2] and one horn or two.[3] It all depends on their species. There are five species in all.[4]

(Color) (Location) First, consider the black rhino of southern Africa.[5] Weighing between 2,000 and 4,000 pounds,[6] it is medium-sized for a rhino. It has two horns. The longer horn is in front and can measure up to 52 inches. The shorter horn is right behind it.[7]

(Social) (Habitat) Black rhinos are solitary. They like to stay in the jungle, rather than out in the open African plains.[8] It's probably just as well that black rhinos are loners, because they are known for having bad tempers. They charge more often than any other rhino species.[9]

(Temperament)

So how do you keep a black rhino happy? Leave it alone with plenty to eat. Its favorite foods are juicy twigs from trees and fresh young shoots from bushes. Black rhinos are picky eaters, which is why their hooked lips come in handy. They use their hooked top lip to feel around for food and grab it.[10] Then they chomp down with their teeth.[11]

(Color) (Temperament) White rhinos,[12] on the other hand, are more easygoing than black rhinos. And it's a good thing, too, since white rhinos are almost twice as big.[13] They weigh between 5,000 and 8,000 pounds. These truck-sized animals are friendly with each other. They live in small family groups of three, four, or five. The bulls will charge one another to defend their

(Size) (Social)

1. (Org.) Size and color are repeatable categories.
2. (Ques.) Why square or hooked lips? (Elab.) Cows have square lips for grazing. (Pred.) Lip structure based upon eating habits. (Org.) Lips and horns are repeatable categories.
3. (Ques.) Why one or two horns? (Pred.) Deals with fighting or mating.
4. (Org.) Initial framework

Rhino Species

1 2 3 4 5

Size:
Color:
Lips:
Horns:

5. (Elab.) Many jungles in southern Africa.
6. (Elab.) Weighs as much as large car.
7. (Ques.) Why does it have two horns? Why the difference in size?
8. (Elab.) Probably easier to be solitary in jungle.
9. (Ques.) Is there a relationship between being solitary and ill-tempered? (Pred.) Solitary nature means it does not tolerate "intruders."

10. (Ques. Ans. + Org.) They do use hooked lips for eating twigs and shoots.
11. (Summary) Black rhinos live alone in jungles where they use hooked lips to eat twigs. They are medium sized but the fiercest of rhinos. Perhaps their two horns are used for charging.
12. (Pred. + Org.) Same repeatable categories for this topic.
13. (Org. + Pred.) Maybe size and temperament are inversely related. Bigger rhinos need not be aggressive. while smaller rhinos must.

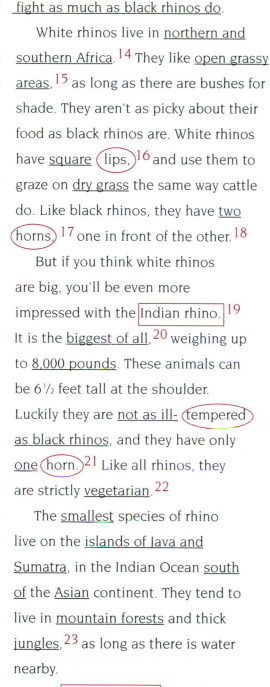

home-range territory, but they <u>don't</u> <u>fight as much as black rhinos do.</u>

(Temperament)

White rhinos live in <u>northern and</u> <u>southern Africa.</u>[14] They like <u>open grassy</u> <u>areas,</u>[15] as long as there are bushes for shade. They aren't as picky about their food as black rhinos are. White rhinos have <u>square</u> (lips,)[16] and use them to graze on <u>dry grass</u> the same way cattle do. Like black rhinos, they have <u>two</u> (horns,)[17] one in front of the other.[18]

(Location)
(Habitat)
(Food)

But if you think white rhinos are big, you'll be even more impressed with the Indian rhino.[19] It is the <u>biggest of all,</u>[20] weighing up to <u>8,000 pounds</u>. These animals can be 6½ feet tall at the shoulder. Luckily they are <u>not as ill-</u> (tempered) <u>as black rhinos</u>, and they have only <u>one</u> (horn.)[21] Like all rhinos, they are strictly <u>vegetarian</u>.[22]

(Size)
(Food)

The <u>smallest</u> species of rhino live on the <u>islands of Java and</u> <u>Sumatra,</u> in the Indian Ocean <u>south</u> <u>of</u> the <u>Asian</u> continent. They tend to live in <u>mountain forests</u> and thick <u>jungles,</u>[23] as long as there is water nearby.

(Size)
(Location)
(Habitat)

The Sumatra rhino is small, weighing an <u>average of 1,500 pounds,</u> and both males and females have <u>two</u> (horns.) The Java rhino weighs as much as <u>one ton</u>. The <u>males have one</u> (horn,) but <u>some females have no horn</u> at all.[24]

(Size)
(Size)

14. (Ques.) What is it about northern Africa that is inviting to white but not black rhinos?
(Pred.) Fewer jungles in the north.
15. (Pred.) They have square lips.

16. (Pred.) Prediction confirmed.

17. (Ques.) Why two horns?
(Ques. Ans.) Does not seem to deal with aggressiveness.
18. (Org.)   Rhinos

	Black	White
Color:	Black	White
Size:	2,000–4,000	5,000–8,000
Lips:	Hooked	Square
Horns:	Two	Two
Location:	S. Africa	N. & S. Africa
Social:	Solitary	Small Groups
Habitat:	Jungle	Grasslands
Temperament:	Mean	Easygoing
Food:	Twigs	Grass

(Summary) Compared to black rhinos, white rhinos are bigger, more social, and less aggressive. They have square lips useful for grazing in both N. and S. Africa. Both have two horns.
19. (Pred.) From India.
20. (Elab.) This is opposite for elephants. African elephant is bigger than those from Asia.
21. (Ques.) Why only one horn?
22. (Org.) Lots of missing information.
(Elab.) Author not even true to initial framework about lips and color.
(Summary) Indian rhino is largest and unlike others has only one horn.

23. (Pred.) Eats twigs and shoots with hooked lips like black rhino because they live in jungle.

24. (Elab.) If some females are without horns, then function of horns might be in part ornamental like the bright colors of male birds.
(Summary) The island rhinos are smaller than others, live in jungles and have two, one, or no horns.

Exercise

Use your text-marking and comprehension strategies on the following excerpt from a psychology text.

Shaping and Chaining

Shaping is a process by which students' approximations of a behavior are reinforced, in an effort to gradually lead the student toward mastery of that behavior. Rather than expecting perfect performance immediately, shaping stresses gradual but steady improvement. To implement shaping in the classroom, a desired level of competence for a particular skill must first be determined. Next, students are assessed to determine their initial competence level. The teacher then sets goals for the students that are just beyond—but within reach of—students' current performance. Students are reinforced each time their performance matches the current standard set by the teacher. When a student regularly meets or exceeds a given standard, the teacher raises the student's goal, and the cycle begins again. The cycles of setting standards for student performance, and then raising the standards once they have been met, gradually moves students from the initial competence level to the desired competence level.

For example, Mrs. Petrie, a second-grade teacher, wants her students to be able to compose stories that are creative, grammatically correct, and neatly written. She wants them to be able to do this by the time the school year has ended. She starts at the beginning of the year by encouraging her students to write down their stories freely, without regard for grammar or handwriting. She reinforces students when they generate stories that are original, elaborate, or unique. As the year progresses and the students become proficient at producing what Mrs. Petrie views as creative stories, she begins to work with them on their handwriting. She gives them explicit instruction in letter formation and has them rewrite their stories to improve their penmanship. Finally, as good handwriting and creativity become more and more common in students' compositions, Mrs. Petrie begins to use their stories as an opportunity to demonstrate the rules of good grammar. She helps students reword or restructure the sentences to conform to grammatical rules. By the end of second grade, guided by the process of shaping, most of Mrs. Petrie's students are capable of composing stories that achieve her goals.

Chaining is the technique by which the simple components of a behavior are built up into an integrated performance of the original, complex behavior. The components are linked together by starting with a single unit and then adding one new component at a time until the entire sequence, or chain, is complete.

In "forward chaining," the teacher begins by reinforcing correct performance of the first behavior in the sequence, and continues to reinforce that behavior until it is well established. When the step is mastered, the teacher introduces the second step, and the student learns to use both steps together. For instance, a teacher sets the goal of having Bill write his name. If the teacher were going to do forward chaining with this particular task, he or she would reinforce the student's correct formation of the tall, straight line in the letter "B." Once that step was mastered, the half circles would be added and reinforced, and so on with each letter until Bill could successfully write his entire name.

We can link the steps of a task together either by moving from first to last, as we just did, or from last to first. This latter process is called "backward chaining." If a kindergarten teacher wanted his students to put their heads down on their desks and be quiet before lining up for recess, it would make sense to teach them how to line up first. Appropriate lining-up behavior would be reinforced by dismissing the students to recess. Once they had learned to line up properly, they could be taught to quietly rest their heads prior to lining up. Recess would once again reinforce the appropriate behavior—in this case, a simple two-link chain.

What to Do After You Read

After surveying and marking the text and recording text notes, your job as reader is almost complete. There are three tasks remaining: After you've finished reading, generate representations that highlight and organize the important text ideas, generate a final summary, and compile a list of unanswered questions that you might be able to answer through additional reading or conversations with students or the instructor.

Generate Representations

Generate completed representations following reading. We recommend that you at least construct representation frameworks while you're reading, perhaps showing the topics and repeatable categories, and then generate complete and improved representations following reading.

Let's return to the passage about rhinoceroses. Here, we generated an initial framework after reading the introductory paragraph and a preliminary representation comparing black and white rhinos. Now we revisit the marked passage and our preliminary representation and construct the "complete" and improved representation that you see in Figure 7-28.

The representation in Figure 7-28 is as complete as possible from reading the text—but the text obviously left out a great deal of information. Those omissions make it difficult to identify relations and patterns among the five species of rhinos. Later, we'll ask questions about those missing details and look for answers either through additional readings or in consultations with students and faculty.

The representation is improved, because it's better organized than either the text or the preliminary representation generated after first reading about the black and white rhinos. One improvement is that topics are now grouped by location (Africa and Asia). You'll notice, though, that a question mark follows the location "India" for the Indian rhino. This is because the author never stated that the Indian rhino lives in India. This is our assumption, based upon its name. The question mark is a signal indicating that this information is not confirmed and should be verified. The representation might also be improved by rearranging the topics (the five rhinos) by their increasing size. It is difficult to know at this point what topical organization is best, given the many missing details.

Another improvement is the reordering of repeatable categories. We grouped related repeatable categories, such as location and habitat; habitat and food; food and lips; and social group, temperament, and size.

The reading process does not end when the last word is read

Figure 7–28. *Representation of Rhinoceros Passage Constructed from Text Markings and Preliminary Representation in Notes*

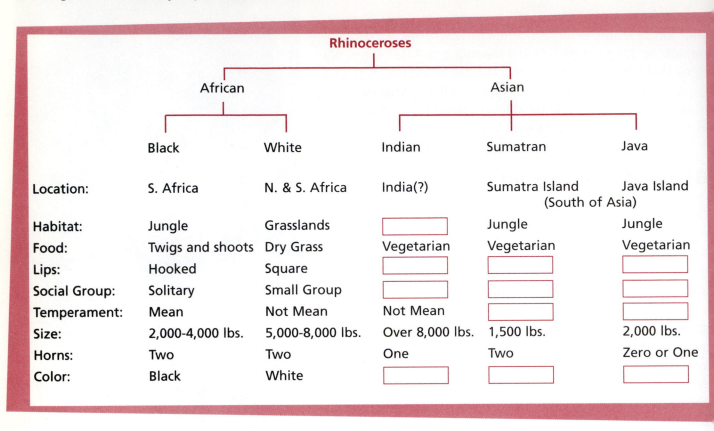

	African		Asian		
	Black	**White**	**Indian**	**Sumatran**	**Java**
Location:	S. Africa	N. & S. Africa	India(?)	Sumatra Island (South of Asia)	Java Island
Habitat:	Jungle	Grasslands	☐	Jungle	Jungle
Food:	Twigs and shoots	Dry Grass	Vegetarian	Vegetarian	Vegetarian
Lips:	Hooked	Square	☐	☐	☐
Social Group:	Solitary	Small Group	☐	☐	☐
Temperament:	Mean	Not Mean	Not Mean	☐	☐
Size:	2,000-4,000 lbs.	5,000-8,000 lbs.	Over 8,000 lbs.	1,500 lbs.	2,000 lbs.
Horns:	Two	Two	One	Two	Zero or One
Color:	Black	White	☐	☐	☐

Diagrams are another helpful representation for learning this information about rhinoceroses. You can sketch a diagram showing a single rhino or comparing two or more rhinos. A diagram for the black rhino might highlight its black color, two horns, and hooked lips. More abstract characteristics, such as location, can be illustrated by positioning the rhino in the southern portion of an outline drawing of Africa, as in Figure 7-29. A comparative diagram might show the larger white colored rhinos in small groups grazing upon grass with square lips while the smaller black colored rhino stands alone, munching twigs with hooked lips.

You might also construct a representation that combines information from various text sections. Suppose the passage about rhinoceroses was only one section of a chapter about wild animals. In this case, a representation comparing the different types of wild animals is also appropriate. The more general representation might have a framework like the one you see in Figure 7-30.

Generate a Final Summary

It is important to generate a final chapter summary drawn from the chapter representations and preliminary page and section summaries you've made

Figure 7–29. *Diagram Showing the Black Rhino's Location*

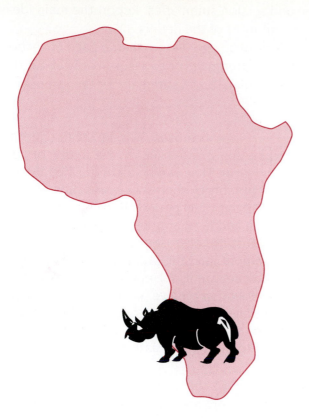

Figure 7–30. *Overarching Representation for a Chapter on Wild Animals*

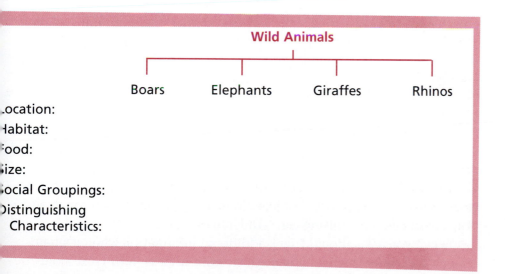

Wild Animals

Boars   Elephants   Giraffes   Rhinos

Location:
Habitat:
Food:
Size:
Social Groupings:
Distinguishing
   Characteristics:

while reading. This final summary is useful to have while you're studying, but it is also useful to create because creating a summary forces you to identify the chapter's most important ideas and discern the relations among them. For this reason, you should generate your own summary rather than rely on one produced by the author. In addition, given the reading strategies and activities you now have at your disposal, you might produce a better summary than the author.

Follow the same formula for generating a chapter summary as you do for generating page and section summaries. Report the main ideas, combine ideas, and leave out most of the details.

A chapter summary is, of course, longer than a page or section summary. In most cases, a handwritten page or two is probably about the right length for most chapter summaries. A summary for the rhinoceroses passage appears below:

> There are five species of rhinoceroses. Two are located in Africa (black rhino and white rhino) and three in Asia (India) or nearby islands (Sumatra and Java). They can be distinguished by several characteristics, most notably by their size, horns, lips, food and habitat. Rhinos range from 1,500 pounds to 8,000 pounds. The island rhinos (Sumatra and Java) are the smallest and the white rhino is the largest. Most rhinoceroses have two horns, except for the Indian rhino (one horn) and the Java rhino (zero or one horn). Rhinos have hooked or square lips. Hook-lipped rhinos like the black rhino eat twigs found in jungles, while the square-lipped rhinos like the white rhino graze on grasses found in the plains. It should be mentioned that the black rhino is the fiercest rhino. This might be related to his solitary nature.

The final summary above follows the formula for summary generation. It reports the main idea—that there are five species of rhinoceroses that are distinguished by size, horns, lips, food, and habitat. It combines ideas, for example, by specifying that two rhinos are from Africa and three are from Asia, or by mentioning that both island rhinos are relatively small. Most importantly, the summary combines ideas that convey important relationships, such as that among food, lips, and habitat. The summary, however, omits most details. It includes only an important few, which clarify important ideas such as the size range among rhinos.

Compile Questions

Based on questions you generated during your reading that were not answered in the text, and based on gaps you find in the representations you construct, compile a list of questions. Find the answers through additional readings or by talking with students or instructors.

"Why," you ask, "should I seek additional information when it's hard enough and time-consuming enough to learn what is in the text alone?" Good question, but now you probably know the answers.

One reason is that if your questions go unanswered, you have an unfinished puzzle. And try as you might, you cannot complete that puzzle if pieces are missing. You certainly can guess or assume what those missing pieces look like, but you should confirm those hunches. Just as a physician wouldn't make a diagnosis with incomplete data, a reader shouldn't reach unconfirmed conclusions.

Exercise

Before you read the summary at the end of this chapter, try generating your own. Use the three summary writing rules. Compare your summary to the one we provide.

Said another way, the "additional information" you seek is not "additional" at all. It's vital to understanding what is there. Do you remember the example in Chapter 4 about northwest coast Indians living in homes with slant roofs made from wood planks? Missing information about the environmental conditions along the northwest coast made it difficult to understand why houses were built as they were. Additional information about the northwest coast's high rainfall average and timber availability makes the existing information (homes with slant roofs made from wood planks) more understandable. Additional information about the lips, foods, and habitat of the Asian rhinos would confirm whether there were indeed a relationship among lips, food, and habitat, as appears to be the case based on what is known about African rhinos. That is, African rhinos living in jungles eat twigs with hooked lips, whereas African rhinos living in grasslands eat grass with square lips. If this relationship is confirmed for all five rhinos, then it is possible to learn and remember fifteen facts that pertain to the habitat, food, and lips for the five rhino species by simply remembering the relationship and where each rhino lives (five facts).

A last reason you should seek additional information is because your purpose for learning should extend beyond answering test questions to mastering a field of study. Should you ever require heart surgery, would you prefer a surgeon who merely passed medical exams, or one who initiated and answered important surgical questions beyond the scope of a unit test? And what about the significant contributions of Galileo, Mozart, and Madame Curie? Were they made while these people prepared for exams? No, their contributions were the pinnacles of understanding built on questions that they raised and sought to answer.

Returning to the material on rhinoceroses, you can generate questions that correspond to the matrix's empty cells (see Figure 7-28) and from those unanswered questions that you generated during your reading. Below is a compilation of questions that you can research, discuss with classmates, or ask of instructors.

- What is the location and habitat of the Indian rhino?
- What type of lips do Indian, Sumatra, and Java rhinos have?
- What is the social group for Indian, Sumatra, and Java rhinos?
- What is the color of those rhinos?
- What is the temperament of Sumatra and Java rhinos?
- Why do rhinos have horns?
- Why are there different numbers and sizes of horns?
- Why is the black rhino ill tempered and solitary? Is there a relationship between these characteristics?
- Why do black rhinos live only in southern Africa?

Exercise

Make a list of unanswered questions from this chapter. Consult with fellow students and your instructor if necessary, to answer these questions and gain fuller understanding.

Summary

Students often use weak, passive reading strategies, such as rereading and highlighting. They read a textbook as if they were reading a newspaper. Effective readers read aggressively.

To become an effective reader, set the mood for reading by planning to read the text actively and comprehend it fully. Next, survey the chapter. Using text aids such as overviews, headings, and summaries, establish the text's structure and anchors (or familiar ideas) for better comprehension.

While reading the text, mark the text's organization. Use a simple marking system that highlights titles, topics, subtopics, repeatable categories, and details.

While you're reading, also use a powerful arsenal of comprehension strategies, such as questioning, predicting, organizing, elaborating, summarizing, and self-monitoring. These help you focus on key ideas, build internal and external connections, and monitor comprehension and strategy deployment.

After reading, transform the marked text into representations that reveal relationships. Also, generate a final summary and compile a list of unanswered questions. Consult books, other students, and your instructors to find answers to your questions.

Answers to focus questions

1. Low-achieving students used passive reading strategies, such as highlighting and rereading. They focused on one idea at a time. In contrast, high-achieving students were active readers who organized ideas and related them to past knowledge.

2. The benefit of text aids are as follows:

    Highlighting—Highlighting draws attention to important ideas.

    Overviews and Summaries—When examined prior to reading, they draw attention to important ideas. They also show how ideas are organized.

    Headings—Headings guide attention and show the text's organization.

    Objectives and Questions—Objectives and questions guide attention and help students monitor comprehension.

    Representations—Representations organize information.

    Examples—Examples help in making external connections between the new ideas and past knowledge.

3. When surveying a chapter's structure, you should learn how the chapter is organized and identify the topics, subtopics, and repeatable categories that make up the structure.

4. You should survey the chapter to establish its structure, focus attention, budget your reading time and effort, and establish anchors (external connections) for learning the text information.

5. A marked text reveals the text's structure (hierarchy, sequence, or matrix), the players (topics, subtopics, and repeatable categories), and important details.

6. Text marking symbols:

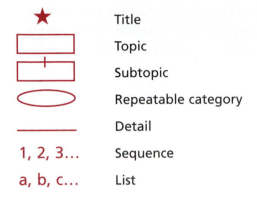

★	Title
☐	Topic
☐	Subtopic
⬭	Repeatable category
——	Detail
1, 2, 3...	Sequence
a, b, c...	List

7. Repeatable category labels.

   A. Medication

   B. Year

   C. Vegetation

   D. Transportation

8. Comparative Psychologists versus Ethologists

Comparative Psychologists versus Ethologists ★

Comparative psychologists can be compared with ethologists along several dimensions. Comparative psychologists study animal behavior in laboratory settings. They conduct diligent experiments on a few animal species trying to uncover general learning principles common to all animals. The American psychologists believe that behavior is learned. *(Methods, Purpose, Animals Studied, Origin)*

Ethologists, on the other hand, study animal behavior in the animal's natural surroundings. Their methods are less rigorous. They usually observe animals. The ethologists study many animals to learn how each behaves. These European psychologists believe that behavior is innate. *(Setting, Purpose, Animals Studied, Origin)*

9. Comparative Psychologists versus Ethologists

Comparative Psychologists versus Ethologists

	Comparative Psychologists	Ethologists
Study:	———— Animal Behavior ————	
Setting:	Laboratory	Natural surroundings
Methods:	Experimental	Observation
Animals Studied:	Few	Many
Purpose:	Determine general laws	Learn how each animal behaves
Behavior:	Learned	Innate
Origin:	America	Europe

10. Answers to Matching Item.

1. c, 2. d, 3. a, 4. b, 5. f, 6. e

11. Questions generated while reading are easily followed with a prediction about the question's solution.

12. Show the organization of text ideas by marking the text and by generating representations.

13. Elaborations are easily noted in text margins as you generate examples, evaluate ideas, or argue with the author. Elaborations can also be added to representations.

14. The formula for writing effective summaries includes: reporting main ideas, combining ideas, and omitting most details.

15. Readers should monitor both their comprehension and their use of comprehension strategies, such as questioning, predicting, organizing, elaborating, summarizing, and self-monitoring.

16. Following reading: generate representations, create a final summary of the reading material, and compile a list of unanswered questions to be researched.

chapter 8
Learning from Lectures

OVERVIEW

Focus Questions

Introduction

What to Do Before the Lecture
    How to Prepare Emotionally
    How to Prepare Physically
        Attend Class
        Be on Time
        Sit Up Front
        Sit on the Edge of Your Seat
        Have Materials Ready
    How to Prepare Mentally

What to Do During the Lecture
    How to Record Complete Notes
        Record Main Ideas, Details, and Examples
        Record Abbreviations and Notations
        Influence the Lecturer
        Follow Importance Cues
        Self-Monitor
        Repeat the Lecture
    How to Record Organized Notes
    How to Record Elaborate Notes

What to Do After the Lecture
    Make Your Notes More Complete
    Make Your Notes More Organized
    Make Your Notes More Elaborate
        Add Elaborative Comments
        Write a Summary
        Generate Questions

Summary

Answers to Focus Questions

focus questions

1. Where is the best place to sit during a lecture, and why?
2. What tools should you have available for lecture note-taking?
3. How can you prepare mentally for a lecture?
4. What are the two functions of note-taking?
5. Are students generally good note-takers?
6. How important is complete note-taking?
7. What constitutes complete notes?
8. Can you supply note-taking abbreviations or symbols for the following terms or phrases?
   A. minute
   B. pound
   C. and so forth
   D. and others
   E. for example
   F. without
   G. therefore
9. What should you do if the instructor displays a slide and talks about the slide at the same time?
10. How can you take more complete notes?
11. How would you generate the representation framework you would construct in notes if your lecturer said the following?
    A. "Today, we're going to discuss five famous creators. We'll examine their products and the processes they used to create them."
    B. "Today, we'll cover three chess tactics: the pin, fork, and skewer. I'll define each and show you several examples and non-examples of each."
    C. "Let's start with the blue whale. It is the largest mammal."
    D. "Asperger's Syndrome differs from autism along several dimensions."
12. How can you determine the lecture's organization?
13. While recording lecture notes, should you record ideas not presented by the lecturer, or record only the things said?
14. What should you do with your notes following the lecture?

Lanny glances nervously at his watch as he approaches the double doors of Lecture Hall 338. "Seven minutes past nine. I'm late for history class!" Still puffing from dashing across campus and running up three flights of stairs, Lanny fills his lungs with oxygen and his heart with courage, and then slowly pulls open a door.

The door creaks and groans like a wood floor protesting under steps in the night. Instantly, two hundred sets of eyes turn and flash at him, paralyzing him like a frightened deer frozen in a car's headlights. Another deep breath. Lanny shuffles down the aisle and across a crowded row toward a vacant seat. He utters a litany of "Excuse me" and "I'm sorry" as he jostles three desks and stamps the feet of would-be note-takers.

Lanny sifts through his bulging backpack, looking for his history notebook. "Chemistry . . . literature . . . algebra . . . why do they all look alike? . . . Ah! history!" Lanny flips to a page free from half-written letters and phone numbers. He rustles through his backpack once more, searching for a pen. A well-chewed ballpoint surfaces—but it has no ink in it. More rummaging. Finally, a pencil stub emerges. Predictably, it has a rounded point and no eraser.

At last, Lanny tunes in the instructor, who is droning on about Constantine the Great. "I've never heard this name before. How great could he be?" Lanny wonders. "Maybe the instructor introduced this character during the last lecture when I overslept and missed class altogether . . ." Lanny muses.

The next several minutes are abuzz with names, dates, and places . . . Diocletian, Byzantium, Julian the Apostate, Armenia, Persians in 364, Theodosius I in 395, Constantinople and Honorius, the Visigoths, and Alaric's brother, Ataulf. Lanny hasn't been this confused since he attended the wedding of his third cousin, Leopold Appolinaris, who married Sasha Vivenski.

The instructor now flips on the overhead projector, showing a time line. Lanny strains to make out the distorted image, which seems light years from where he's sitting at the rear of the lecture hall. He tilts his glasses nearer his eyes, hoping he can focus the image. He begins to copy what little he can see. Meanwhile, the instructor jabbers on about the significance of these events. Lanny copies, listens, copies, listens. Having only one brain, he does neither very well. Then, before he can fully observe it, the time line slide flickers and goes black, like a falling star in the night sky.

On and on the lecturer drones about the House of Theodosius, Sister Pulcheria, and husband Marcian. Lanny's attention shifts about the room to swinging legs, tapping pens, chesty coughs reminiscent of his bout with bronchitis, and the rustle of newspapers. "At least I'm trying," Lanny mutters dejectedly.

Lanny's anguish and frustration though is quickly buoyed by the sound of the closing bell. He inspects his notebook page, which contains about a half-page of notes—mostly names he cannot pronounce, spell, or explain—and proudly closes his notebook. "Literature begins in ten minutes," he thinks. "That gives me enough time to cash a check and run to the snack bar for a soda and bagel. Lectures sure are draining!"

> *Students who record complete, organized, elaborate notes perform better on tests.*

anny's fictional nightmare is, unfortunately, a reality for many college students who fail to learn from lectures because they make poor choices (such as coming late to class and sitting in the rear of the room) and use ineffective strategies (such as recording incomplete notes).

Unlike a textbook, in which the study content stays put, a lecture is fleeting. You must do everything possible to record effective notes during the lecture. Students who record complete, organized, elaborate notes perform better on tests than students who record incomplete, disorganized, and unelaborated notes. If you're absent or late to class, that diminishes your note-taking. So too do inadequate background knowledge, a negative mood, a lousy seat, weak strategies, and a host of other factors.

This chapter explains and demonstrates how to improve note-taking and lecture learning. This chapter's organization is similar to that of the previous chapter on text learning: You are instructed in what to do before, during, and after the lecture. This chapter's main message is also similar to that of the previous chapter: Engage in active, even aggressive, strategies to maximize lecture learning.

What to Do Before the Lecture

Come to a lecture prepared to learn. Lanny, the student portrayed at the beginning of the chapter, was pitifully unprepared. Proper preparation takes three forms: emotional, physical, and mental. Emotional preparation means you are excited and motivated to learn. Your mood is positive. Physical preparation means that you have prepared your body and its physical surroundings. Like the well-conditioned third baseman pounding his fist in his faithful glove and creeping in for an anticipated bunt, you've got to be positioned for success. Mental preparation means you have filled your mind with the knowledge necessary to support new learning. You've developed a framework for organizing information and an anchor for supporting lecture ideas.

How to Prepare Emotionally

Some students sabotage their academic success by dampening their mood and motivation for lecture learning. Their DIFS (desire, intention, focus, and sustain) are all wet. In terms of **desire**, their goal is simply to show up for lectures in hopes that instructors fill their minds with knowledge the way bakers fill a cake mold. Their **intention** or plan is poorly developed. They think, "I'll try to attend most lectures and jot down some terms I don't know." Their **focus** is poor. They miss lectures, daydream when they are present, and only occasionally tune in—as if they were watching an old movie. Their half-page of unfamiliar terms provides them with a minimal resource for test preparation. Poor comprehension and low test scores **sustain** or reduce the student's already suffering motivation. The unsuccessful student continues to record incomplete notes, or perhaps abandons lectures and note-taking altogether. In short, the student sustains a defeatist attitude.

If you're going to be successful at lecture learning, a positive mood is essential. Consider Nancy, a former student of ours, whose desire, intention, focus, and sustainment fanned her lecture activities and ignited her academic success. Nancy got "pumped up" for a lecture. Her desire was to record the best set of notes possible. She envisioned herself recording many complete, well-organized, elaborate notes. Her intentions were clear. Before a lecture, she would read and review course material, which enabled her to record effective notes. She planned to arrive early for class, secure a front row seat, and use an arsenal of strategies geared to maximizing note-taking and facilitating comprehension. Nancy's focus was unwavering. Her attention was riveted on the lecture and on her note-taking strategies. There was no opportunity for Nancy to daydream or become bored, because her focus was entirely on recording excellent notes. Nancy sustained these activities and her high-flying motivation throughout her college career. She was rewarded with high grades and a level of understanding reserved for those who combine effective strategies and hard work.

GET "PUMPED UP" FOR LECTURES

Approximately half of the course material you must learn stems from lectures. This information disappears fast, therefore it must be recorded immediately. So get ready. A lecture is like a burning building: You can stand back and watch it burn, or you can hoist a ladder, wield an ax, or carry a hose to douse the flames. Of course, firefighting is best done by trained personnel. You'll need more than emotional preparation. You must also be prepared physically and mentally.

How to Prepare Physically

How often have you witnessed a college football team before the big game as it explodes from the tunnel, thunders down the field, leaps into a circle of adjoining arms, bangs helmets, joins in a chorus of grunts and snorts, and then promptly gets blown out, 52–7? Clearly, the emotion was there. Allowing eleven quarterback sacks, giving up 500 rushing yards—275 in the last quarter—and having a parade of players limp from the field with leg cramps, are clues that their physical preparation was inadequate. Physical preparation is crucial for winning in football—and just as crucial for winning in the classroom. You must be prepared physically to record notes and learn from lectures. Following are a few tips for physical preparation.

Attend Class

You must physically be there in class to learn from lectures. Course handouts, the textbook, and even fellow students' notes cannot completely recapture missed lecture information. Furthermore, your absence means you forfeit your opportunity to ask questions and contribute to class discussions. Classes should be experienced, not just attended. Are you as satisfied having a friend tell you about a play that you missed as you would be if you experienced it yourself?

Sure, students have reasons for missing class, such as a dead car battery, a scheduled job interview, and illness. But are these reasons—or excuses? If you discover that your car's battery is dead, run or ride a bike to class, or call for a cab. Who scheduled the interview . . . the Governor? No matter how important they are or seem to be, schedule other commitments outside class hours. If you're really sick, then stay home and do all that you can to recover quickly. Arrange for a classmate to tape-record or videotape the lecture, and for several students to share their notes with you. But—if your illness is not contagious and you can sit up in bed, then you probably can sit up in class and should be there.

Be on Time

If your class begins at 9:00 A.M., then be there at 8:50. Being "on time" for class means being there at least ten minutes before the lecture whenever possible. Spend this time preparing your note-taking materials and reviewing previous notes. Furthermore, slipping in to class late is inconsiderate to fellow students and the instructor, all of whom are hard at work.

As is true with absences, if you're late, then you cannot physically be in your seat and recording notes. Thus, you cannot learn. Just as absences and lateness can doom you in the workplace, they can doom you in the classroom as well.

Sit Up Front

If you were going to camp out for two days and nights so you could be among the first to purchase concert tickets to your favorite music group, when you got to the ticket window, which seats would you choose? Probably front row, center. There you could study how the musicians' fingers strum difficult licks and watch the perspiration run down their foreheads. As for sound, you wouldn't miss a note. And yet where do students arriving early to a class choose to sit? They grab the seats in the rear of the classroom or along the sides—places with lots of distractions. Places where they can't see or hear well.

Sit toward the front of the classroom where it's easier to focus attention. If you sit toward the back, there are more potential distractions between you and the instructor. As students in front of you rock in their seats, tap their pens, or swing their legs, your attention is drawn to their movement.

If you're sitting in the rear of the room, it's also harder for you to hear the instructor. You can also be more easily distracted by the occasional whispered comments or conversations of other students in the classroom—particularly in the back.

When you sit toward the front, you get the feeling that the instructor is actually talking to you. Your attention is focused on what the instructor is saying. You're more likely to take complete notes. Serious students and concert goers know the best place to sit: front and center.

Sit on the Edge of Your Seat

It does no good to go to class, get there early, grab a front row seat—and then sit passively throughout the lecture as if you were a zombie. Instead, you should be right on the edge of the seat, as if you were watching the final, heart-wrenching scene in *Romeo and Juliet*. Lean into the lecture as if you were trying to hear Romeo's dying words. Listen to and watch the instructor as intently as if he were Friar Laurence eulogizing the dead lovers, and pause only to record lecture notes.

It's important to maintain concentration throughout the lecture. It's common for students to take fewer notes in the second half of lectures because they tire, lean back in their seats, and begin to listen for the final bell. Stave off fatigue by being in top condition to attend lectures. Get plenty of sleep, exercise regularly, and go to class neither too hungry nor too full to concentrate.

Have Materials Ready

A fighter once came out of his corner having left his mouthpiece behind. He promptly took a hard right to the jaw. Amidst blood and spewed teeth, the fight was immediately halted. Fighters must be prepared with the right materials, and like boxers, students must also come out of their corners with the right materials, ready for lecture learning.

Use a separate notebook for each subject. A three-ring binder is probably the best, because you can easily add and remove pages. Handouts tucked inside a spiral notebook usually fall out and are either misplaced or lost.

Clearly mark each notebook's subject on the cover so that you don't carry the wrong notebook to class. Notebooks should also include your name, address, and telephone number on the inside cover in the event they are left behind, temporarily appropriated by a foreign agent, or abducted and held for ransom.

Come to your lectures equipped with an arsenal of working pens and pencils. Don't be like Lanny at the beginning of the chapter, whose only pen was dry and whose only pencil was worn to an eraserless nub. Also remember that you need both blue and red pens, because lecture notes should be recorded in two colors, as we explain below.

Have the class textbook and handouts available at lectures, too. Occasionally, instructors refer to diagrams, graphs, or assignments found in the text, or follow course outlines or objectives they provided earlier.

Finally, have available any special tools or materials appropriate to the class. Your math instructor, for example,

may suggest that you bring a calculator to class. In your design class, special drawing instruments and sketch pads might be necessary.

Have your notebook and other materials on your desk and ready to go before the lecture. When the bell rings to begin the round, you'll be ready to come out swinging.

How to Prepare Mentally

Let's face it. Lecture learning is a brain drain because lectures are usually delivered at top speed, lack organization, and contain many unfamiliar terms. Prepare your brain for lectures by reviewing previous notes and reading related text chapters ahead of time. These activities can be carried out at your own pace, and they can provide you with a framework for selecting, organizing, and applying important lecture ideas.

Suppose today's lecture topic in psychology is about long-term memory. Reading the chapter on long-term memory in advance of the lecture helps you establish a framework. The text's organizing structure—examining the encoding, storage, and forgetting aspects of long-term memory—is useful in helping you select and organize lecture ideas. The text's descriptions of memory failure among head trauma patients and those with Alzheimer's disease also give you contexts for anchoring future lecture ideas. If you review your previous lecture notes about short-term memory prior to the new lecture, that too prepares you to compare short- and long-term memory as the new lecture is presented.

For example, if you're preparing for a biology lecture on sexual reproduction in plants, review your recent notes about parts of the plant and their functions. Also review your not-so-recent notes on animal reproduction to reactivate your general knowledge about reproduction, and as a means for comparing animal and plant reproduction. Read the chapter on plant reproduction before the lecture. For example, if you familiarize yourself with important terms, the plant's reproductive sequence, and interesting accounts about seed dispersal, it can be very helpful to you in selecting, organizing, and applying lecture ideas.

Don't go into a lecture mentally unprepared. The lecturer is going to strap on the crash helmet and put the pedal to the metal. The degree to which you are able to follow along depends entirely on your level of understanding going in. If the gap between your knowledge and the lecturer's starting point is too great, you'll be left behind in a puff of smoke. Read, review, and be ready to roll.

Prepare for lectures by reviewing previous notes and reading related text chapters ahead of time.

Exercise

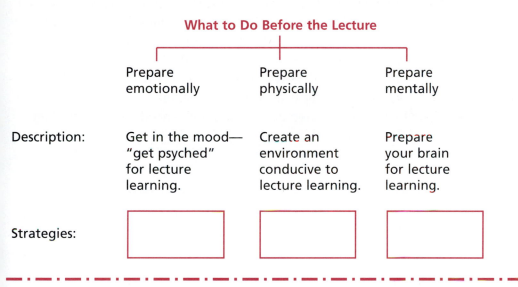

Below is a matrix framework to use as a way to summarize this section. Include the strategies we've mentioned, and add others you might have or think of for increasing your emotional, physical, and mental preparation for a lecture.

What to Do Before the Lecture

	Prepare emotionally	Prepare physically	Prepare mentally
Description:	Get in the mood—"get psyched" for lecture learning.	Create an environment conducive to lecture learning.	Prepare your brain for lecture learning.
Strategies:			

What to Do During the Lecture

Your primary objective during the lecture is to record an effective set of notes. This means notes that are complete, organized, and elaborate. Effective note-taking has two advantages: better understanding during the lecture, and a set of notes useful later for review.

Lecture note-taking is important for two reasons. First, because recording notes increases your attention and aids your memory. When you record copious notes, you cannot be bored and you cannot daydream. You're focused on the lecture. Recording notes also helps store information in your memory. Students who record notes (but then don't review them) remember more lecture ideas than students who listen to the lecture but don't record notes.

The second and primary benefit of notes is reviewing them. Students who review notes invariably outperform students who don't review notes. Review helps you store information permanently in your memory. The more complete, organized, and elaborate the notes you record, the better your learning during the lecture *and* during your review.

Following are strategies for recording complete, organized, and elaborate notes.

How to Record Complete Notes

Most students record too few notes. Many students record only 30 to 50 percent of lecture points. Some first year students record only 10 percent of lecture points. This level of note-taking is far too low. Lecture information that is not recorded in notes stands only a 5 percent chance of being recalled later on a test. Information contained in notes is about ten times more likely to be recalled.

Because a lecture is as fleeting as a parking space on your college campus, you must record adequate notes during the lecture. To imagine you'll recall lecture points later without noting them is wishful thinking. Even the most unforgettable information requires a note for remembering. Was it perhaps the king in one of Lewis Carroll's *Alice* stories who remarked, "The horror of the moment I shall never forget!" and the queen responded something along the lines of, "But you will unless you make a memorandum of it." We forget what isn't written down—as is evidenced by the partial recall of the quotation and its source.

Here are strategies for increasing the number of lecture points in notes.

Record Main Ideas, Details, and Examples

Many students record only the information they do not understand. When they later review, all they have to study is a bunch of information they still don't understand. Others jot down just the main ideas. They leave out all the details, hoping that the main ideas will help them recall the details. But unless the details are recorded, they won't be recalled. Still other students record main ideas and details—but then they leave out examples. As soon as the lecturer begins a "story" or example, many students drop their pens, lean back in their seats, and enjoy the stories and examples, which they believe are just incidental to the lecture. In fact, examples are crucial for full understanding of new concepts and good performance on some types of tests.

To illustrate the interplay and importance of main ideas, details, and examples, suppose that your psychology instructor reported that short-term memory has a limited capacity. You should note this main idea. The instructor then mentions that short-term memory has a capacity of approximately seven bits of information. You should note this detail. The lecturer then remarks that telephone numbers and zip codes were developed not to exceed the capacity of short-term memory. You should note these examples. The resulting notes might look like this:

Short-term memory (STM) = limited capacity

- 7 bits
- Ex. Telephone #s   {within STM limits}
     Zip codes

The purpose of note-taking is to record a complete account of the lecture. From your notes, you should be able to recreate the lecture months later. This is not to suggest that you should record the lecturer's every word; instead, you should record all the main ideas, details, and examples presented. Although these don't need to be recorded in sentence form, they should be recorded completely enough so that you can understand them later, as we showed you in the sample notes for short-term memory. Notice that phrases, symbols, and abbreviations are used, rather than complete sentences.

What follows is a portion of a lecture on creativity. Try recording a complete set of notes that contains main ideas, details, and examples. Then examine the notes we prepared.

> Expressive creativity is defined as the ability to make a quick, or a series of very quick, responses in a situation. The time necessary to produce the creative response is only a few seconds. Examples include a boxer adjusting his techniques to beat his opponent, an actor improvising in the theater, or a comedian reacting to an audience. In each case, the person makes a series of responses that appear spontaneous or unrehearsed. In actuality, the expressively creative person has made a very similar response in very similar situations before. Thus, an important characteristic is the ability to see very rapidly how a new situation is similar to an old situation. Returning to the example of the comedian, a heckler in the audience might "put down" the comedian. The comedian, however, seeing the relationship between what this heckler has said and previous situations involving hecklers, is able to "put down" or respond to the heckler quickly. The time necessary to develop this sort of creativity is usually eight to twelve years. Another characteristic associated with expressive creativity is timing. The person has to learn when to make the responses.

Our notes on this lecture look like this:

CREATIVITY

Expressive

    Def—making very quick response(s)
    Time to respond—few s.
    Ex—boxer adjusting technique
        actor improvising
        comedian reacting
    Responses—appear spontaneous, unrehearsed, actually similar
          response to similar situation
    Characteristic—see rapidly how two situations are alike
    Ex—comedian's response to heckler seems spontaneous but is
        similar to other responses to other hecklers
    Time to develop—8–12 yrs.
    Characteristic—timing, when to make response

These notes contain the main idea (the definition), details (such as time to respond, responses, characteristics, and time to develop) and examples that are paraphrased, rather than word for word. The notes are brief, but complete enough to reconstruct the lecture. The notes also contain abbreviations and notations, which are both helpful and efficient for recording a complete set of notes.

Exercise

Below is another portion of a lecture. Construct a set of lecture notes. Indicate whether each note is a main idea, detail, or example.

To the human eye, stars seem to be about the same size. In truth, many stars are larger than our sun. They appear small because of their great distance.

Stars seem to vary in brightness. This is due to their distance, size, or temperature. A very large star such as Sirius, the Dog Star, appears bright because it is close and very hot. The star Vega, in the Harp constellation, is three times farther away than Sirius, but appears just as bright because of its extreme heat. Rigel, in the constellation Orion, is 540 light-years from earth, but because it is very large and very hot, it appears as one of the brightest stars. In the same constellation, the star Betelgeuse is only 270 light-years away, and while not as hot as Rigel, it appears nearly as bright. This is because of its immense size.

Record Abbreviations and Notations

To help compensate for rapid lecture rates, use abbreviations and notations while recording lecture notes. Some common abbreviations and their translations are listed in Figure 8-1

Probably the most useful abbreviations are those you construct within a unit of instruction. For example, in a unit on behavioral psychology, you might use the abbreviations in Figure 8-2. Be certain to write the term in full along with its abbreviation [for example, positive reinforcement (PR)] the first time through so that you can remember what the abbreviation means when you're studying your notes later.

Certain notations or symbols are useful, too. Some common ones are shown in Figure 8-3.

Figure 8–1. *Some Common Abbreviations*

Abbreviations	Translations
cf.	compare
e.g.	for example
ex.	for example
etc.	and so forth
i.e.	that is
vs	versus
et al.	and others
w/out	without
cm	centimeter
s	second
min	minute
lb	pound
ft	foot
Mon	Monday
'98	1998

Figure 8–2. *Abbreviations Developed for a Unit on Behavioral Psychology*

BP	Behavioral Psychology
PR	Positive Reinforcement
NR	Negative Reinforcement
PP	Positive Punishment
NP	Negative Punishment
EX	Extinction
S	Stimulus
R	Response

Figure 8–3. *Some Common Notations for Note-Taking*

Notations	Translation
Ψ	Psychology
=	Equal to
≈	Approximately
∴	Therefore
↑	Increase
→	Leads to
#	Number

Exercise

Make a list of other common or special abbreviations and notations you might use when recording lecture notes for the courses you're taking.

Influence the Lecturer

Suppose you were at a raffle and the prize was a $1,000 mountain bike. The raffler draws a slip of paper from a large barrel and reads the eight-digit number of the winner over the public address system. The quality of the system is terrible, due to low volume and a crackling noise, so the numbers are barely audible. You decipher a few numbers that match those on your ticket. But when the raffler has read the number, no one steps forward to claim the prize. What do you do?

The solution is obvious. You ask the raffler to repeat the numbers. The possible consequence of mishearing the numbers is too severe to take the chance of not hearing them again.

But students attending lectures rarely ask instructors to repeat information they do not hear clearly—information that is critically important to understanding the lecture.

Assert yourself in lecture settings. Be polite, but forceful. If the instructor speaks too rapidly or too quietly, for example, ask the instructor to repeat the information. If there's information you don't understand, you can ask the instructor to clarify it by rephrasing or explaining it. Better yet, ask the instructor a question about the information. For example, "You mentioned that this related to reinforcement theory. Could you explain how?"

What do you do when the instructor is displaying a detailed slide or overhead on a screen and continues to lecture? Do you record the lecturer's words or pay attention to the visual display? You can influence the lecturer by asking for a quiet moment to record notes on the visual display. If the instructor refuses to stop lecturing, then record the spoken lecture in notes and influence the lecturer after class by asking to see the display and taking notes on it then.

Remember that successful lecture learning depends on recording complete notes. Treat all lecture information as if it could be your winning number in a lottery. If you don't exercise some responsibility in how the lecture is delivered, you are going to pay the consequences of missing valuable information.

INFLUENCE THE LECTURER

Follow Importance Cues

Lecturers use many cues to signal important ideas. It is crucial that you record these highlighted ideas in notes, and mark them with an asterisk or some other symbol that signals their importance. Cues can be nonverbal, spoken, or written.

One college instructor we know emphasizes important points by resting his chin in his hand, jutting out his bottom lip, arching his eyebrows, and nodding his head vehemently. His students are alert for this cue and write feverishly when they see it. Other nonverbal cues might include pointing, clapping, finger-snapping, hand-waving, a piercing glance, an extended pause, or variations in voice pitch, volume, cadence, or speed.

Spoken cues can signal importance, such as when an instructor says that a point is "noteworthy," "critical," "important," or "imperative." The not-too-subtle phrase "This will be on your test," of course, should not be overlooked.

When an instructor repeats a term or phrase this also signals importance. Be sure to note this important information along with an asterisk or other symbol to indicate its importance.

Written cues are those that appear on the chalkboard, an overhead, or a handout. Take special note of these. If instructors bothered to write this information, you can believe it really is important.

Most students are well aware of the importance of chalkboard information. We have observed many students recording the scribbles left behind from the previous lecturer, who forgot to erase the board.

When instructors prepare written outlines, questions, or objectives, read them in advance of the lecture and make detailed notes related to these lecture aids. These aids are provided to signal important ideas and guide note-taking.

Self-Monitor

Heavyweight boxing champion Michael Moorer was convincingly beating 45-year-old George Foreman, who had been champion twenty years before. For nearly ten rounds, Foreman looked like an overweight, undertrained shadow of his former self. Moorer was giving the former champion, who most thought should be home playing with his grandchildren, a real licking. But before the tenth round ended, Foreman's unexpected right hook sent Moorer crashing. Amazingly, Foreman had regained the title. The lesson here is that the fight doesn't end until the final bell sounds. Perhaps Yogi Berra said it best, "It ain't over 'til it's over."

In classrooms, students often begin to pack up in anticipation of the final bell, although the instructor is still lecturing. It is no wonder that students take fewer notes during the second half of lectures relative to the first half.

This note-taking decrease is only partly due to notebooks closing prematurely. Many students allow their minds to wander. Or they become bored or restless as the lecture stretches on. Remember, though, that letting yourself become inattentive, bored, or restless are choices *you* make. You can just as easily choose to record a set of quality notes—a practice incompatible with inattentiveness, boredom, or restlessness.

How can you be certain to continue a high level of note-taking throughout the lecture? The solution is to self-monitor. While you're recording lecture notes, monitor your note-taking process. Ask yourself questions like these:

1. Am I recording complete notes?
2. Are my notes detailed?
3. Do they contain all the provided examples?
4. Am I influencing the lecturer?
5. Am I searching for cues?
6. Am I emphasizing the important points?

Self-monitoring is important throughout the lecture, but particularly during the latter stages when it's normal for you to feel a little tired. Monitor your note-taking throughout the lecture and monitor your monitoring. That is, be sure that you are evaluating your note-taking. Don't be caught with your guard down before that final bell sounds.

Repeat the Lecture

If at first you don't succeed—repeat the lecture.

Perhaps you've followed the tips for complete note-taking described here and still record notes that are relatively incomplete. Incomplete note-taking might result from the lecture being presented rapidly, or containing too many noteworthy details, or being poorly organized. In any event, there is something else that you can do during the lecture to ensure that you have complete notes later.

When it is difficult to record complete notes, tape record (or videotape) the lecture and play it back one or more times following the lecture. As you replay the lecture, add to your existing set of notes. Doing so helps you record more notes—particularly details—and recall more lecture points than if you hear a lecture only once and record only a single set of notes. The first time you hear a lecture, you are likely to note the lecturer's main points but miss many important details and examples. These are easily added to your notes when you hear or review the lecture again.

Listening to a lecture more than once helps you record more complete notes, and recall more lecture points when tested

How to Record Organized Notes

It is important that notes are complete. But it's just as important that they be well organized; they should help you build internal connections among lecture ideas. Well-organized information is simpler to learn, understand, and remember. You can ensure the organization of your notes through activities carried out during the lecture.

Try to determine the lecture's organization at the start. Sometimes instructors convey the organization directly by using a lecture organizer that is written on the board or distributed to students. The organizer we've provided in Figure 8-4 shows marketing students the details they must record and their organization.

Some instructors provide verbal cues early in the lecture that give you the lecture's overriding organization. The instructor, for example, says, "We will cover Piaget's four stages of development," or "We will discuss two types of peptic ulcers." Given these cues, you're aware that the overriding organization of the Piagetian lecture is sequential (given the alert word *stages*), and the overriding organization of the lecture on ulcers is hierarchical (given the alert word *types*). (See Chapters 5–6 for reminders about alert words and representations.) Also pay attention to early verbal cues that establish the lecture's repeatable categories. For example, the instructor who is discussing Piaget might say, "Piaget's stages are described with respect to age of onset, length of stage, characteristics, examples, and limitations." The instructor discussing peptic ulcers might comment that "throughout the lecture the location, rate of occurrence, cause, and treatment of ulcers are described."

Hopefully, you can construct organizational frameworks similar to those shown in Figure 8-5 and Figure 8-6 at the start of lectures and add to and complete them during the lectures.

Figure 8–4. *Lecture Organizer for Types of Market Structures*

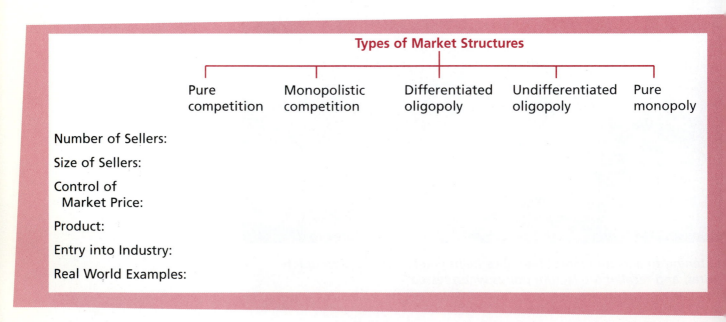

Types of Market Structures

	Pure competition	Monopolistic competition	Differentiated oligopoly	Undifferentiated oligopoly	Pure monopoly
Number of Sellers:					
Size of Sellers:					
Control of Market Price:					
Product:					
Entry into Industry:					
Real World Examples:					

Figure 8–5. *Note-Taking Framework Based on Lecturer's Cues*

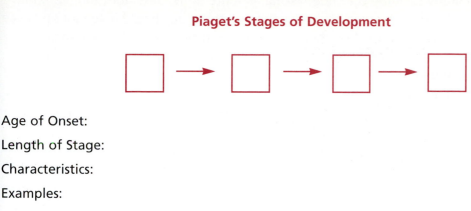

Piaget's Stages of Development

Age of Onset:

Length of Stage:

Characteristics:

Examples:

Limitations:

Figure 8–6. *Note-Taking Framework Based on Lecturer's Cues*

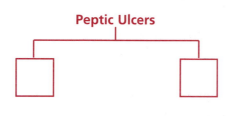

Peptic Ulcers

Location:

Rate of Occurrence:

Cause:

Treatment:

In cases where instructors provide no written or verbal organizer at the start of the lecture, try anticipating the lecture's structure. You can do this by recalling previous lectures and readings, and by considering the overriding structure of the field of study.

In a psychology course, for example, the previous lecture might have been on behavioral theory. In that lecture, the following information was discussed: the theory's founder, the year it was founded, the central idea, major principles, research evidence, and implications for learning. If today's lecture pertains to cognitive theory, then you can anticipate that the same dimensions (or repeatable categories) will probably be used to describe cognitive theory as for behavioral theory.

In an exercise physiology class, you read the chapter about vitamin supplements prior to a lecture on that topic. The text described how various vitamins affect aerobic capacity, anaerobic performance, muscle development, and general health. You can anticipate that the lecture will follow more or less the same organization.

In other cases, you might rely on your general knowledge about a field of study to guide your note-taking. In a literature class, for example, while you're taking in a lecture about a short story, you should listen for and note ideas about *plot*, *setting*, *characters*, *conflict*, and *resolution*. All short stories share these dimensions. In a history class, while the lecturer is discussing a previously unknown event, you should listen for and note information about *where* the event took place, *who* was involved, *when* and *why* it occurred, *how* it happened, and *what* actually occurred. These dimensions cut across or describe all historical events.

While the lecture is proceeding, the best clue for organizing lecture ideas comes from the notes you've already recorded. For example, return to the notes you've taken about expressive creativity, and see if you can anticipate the repeatable categories the lecturer might use to describe the next type of creativity. You should anticipate noting the *definition*, *examples*, *time to respond*, *time to develop the response*, and *characteristics*.

Below is a continuation of the creativity lecture. This section is about innovative creativity. Does the lecturer address the repeatable categories you anticipated?

Innovative Creativity

Innovative creativity is the ability to significantly change ideas, beliefs, or products. Examples of innovative creativity include inventors who improve products, writers who alter styles, and scientists who discover cures for illnesses. Innovative creativity is only possible among those who have a great deal of knowledge in a domain, and who find fault with existing ideas or products in that domain. Innovative creativity is a lifetime endeavor. Most significant products or ideas are produced by those who commit their lives to their creations.

The lecturer did address the identical repeatable categories except for *time to develop*. If other types of creativity are presented, anticipate that the lecturer will discuss the same dimensions or repeatable categories.

Your ability to recognize the lecture's organization prior to or during the lecture leads to an important question: Should you generate representations while you record notes? Our answer is "Yes, if you can." Students in our classes who have practiced constructing representations often generate representations while recording lecture notes.

Usually, however, a lecture is presented rapidly, without advance warning about its organization. In such cases, record the important lecture ideas in a linear form, sketch an occasional representation framework when you can, and construct complete representations following the lecture.

To show you that it is possible to construct representations during the lecture, on pages 273–274, a sample lecture on brakes appears in the left column, while our corresponding lecture notes appear alongside in the right column.[1]

Notice that our lecture notes include hierarchies, sequences, and matrices. All of the lecture information can be easily represented using these three patterns. Following the lecture, we'll organize our notes even better, and we'll add diagrams to further organize lecture points.

[1] Adapted from *World Book Encyclopedia* (1989). Scott Fetzer Co., New York, NY. Volume 2, pp. 570–572.

Lecture

A brake is a device that slows or stops the movement of a wheel or engine of an entire vehicle.

Most brakes have a fixed part called a brake shoe or block that presses against a turning wheel to create friction.

This friction causes the wheel to stop or slow down.

There are three major kinds of brakes: mechanical, hydraulic and air. Other common types include power brakes and electric brakes.

Mechanical brakes have cables that push the brake shoes close to the wheel.

Most lightweight bicycles use a mechanical brake called a caliper brake.

It consists of two rubber brake shoes, one on each side of the wheel rim.

Cables connect the shoes to the brake levers located on the handle bars.

When the rider squeezes its levers, the cables force the shoes to press against the wheel rim. This action slows or stops the bicycle.

Notes

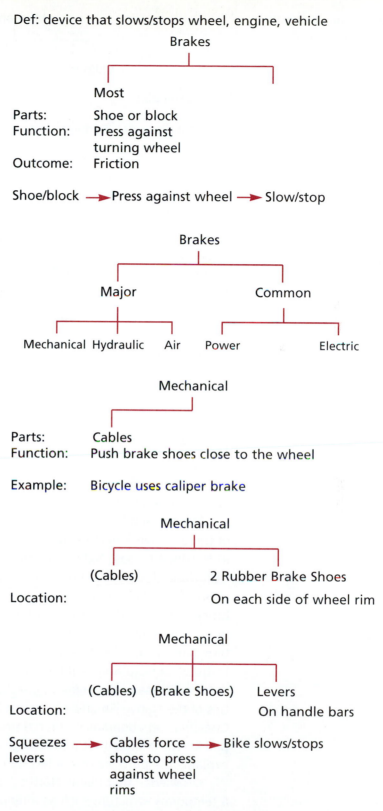

Def: device that slows/stops wheel, engine, vehicle

Brakes
— Most

Parts: Shoe or block
Function: Press against
            turning wheel
Outcome: Friction

Shoe/block ⟶ Press against wheel ⟶ Slow/stop

Brakes
— Major — Common

Mechanical Hydraulic   Air   Power   Electric

Mechanical

Parts: Cables
Function: Push brake shoes close to the wheel

Example: Bicycle uses caliper brake

Mechanical

(Cables)   2 Rubber Brake Shoes
Location: On each side of wheel rim

Mechanical

(Cables)   (Brake Shoes)   Levers
Location: On handle bars

Squeezes ⟶ Cables force ⟶ Bike slows/stops
levers   shoes to press
           against wheel
           rims

Lecture

Automobiles are equipped with another kind of mechanical brake, which is called an emergency brake.

This brake is also known as a parking brake, because it helps prevent a parked car from rolling away.

When the driver applies the emergency brake, a system of levers, rods, and cables exert pressure on the brake shoes of the rear wheels.

Notes

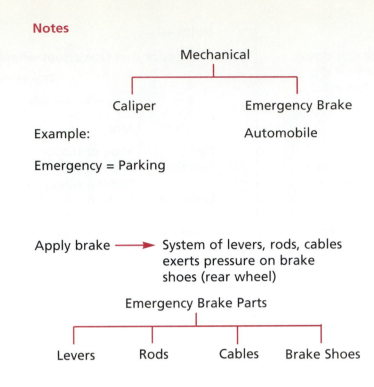

How to Record Elaborate Notes

There is a widely held belief among educators and students that *less* is easier to learn than *more*. That makes sense. However, in cases where additional information elaborates on or meaningfully extends the to-be-learned information, learning *more* is easier than learning *less*.

As an example, suppose that you were asked to learn about the homes of three Native American groups. You are told by the lecturer that a) Northwest Coast Native Americans lived in homes made of wood planks with slanted roofs, b) Plains Native Americans lived in teepees, and c) Southern California Native Americans lived in houses made of dirt and brush. Although this information is memorizable, it has no apparent rhyme or reason. Why did the different groups live in such homes? That information is not provided. It would be easier to learn the information about Native American homes if the lecturer gave you more information about the conditions in the areas where the homes were built, or the characteristics of the Native Americans themselves. Learning that the Northwest Coast has an abundance of large trees provides a rationale for using wood planks. Knowledge that it rains a great deal along the Northwest Coast explains the purpose of slanted roofs.

Knowledge that Plains Native Americans were mobile makes the use of a temporary structure such as a teepee more understandable. Furthermore, it makes sense for them to use teepees, since there is a shortage of trees and an abundance of buffalo and deer (skins). Dry conditions and few trees in Southern California help explain why Native Americans there used dirt and brush for home building.

Exercise

Record a set of lecture notes for the portion of the lecture below. Construct representations whenever possible.

Large storms that cross the United States are termed "cyclones." Don't confuse cyclones with tornados. Tornados are small, violent winds that form a funnel-shaped cloud. Tornados are the most destructive winds on earth. The wind in a tornado's funnel moves at a rate of four or five hundred miles per hour. The air blows with a twisting motion and whirls upward. It has tremendous force, and can wreck homes and trees and carry them off like matchsticks. A tornado's funnel is usually not more than a hundred feet wide, and a tornado rarely remains in contact with the ground for more than a mile. A cyclone, in contrast, can cover an area of five hundred to a thousand miles, and cross the United States in four to eight days.

Hurricanes are similar to cyclones, except they are smaller and move at higher speeds. Hurricanes can move at speeds of a hundred miles per hour. In the center of the hurricane, there is an "eye," a calm area caused by rising air. Hurricanes are common along Atlantic shores, whereas tornados usually appear inland and are most common in the midwest. Hurricanes are destructive because of their high winds and flooding due to heavy rains and rising tides.

Another example in which more is better than less comes from the use of examples for learning concepts, which you read about in Chapter 7. Suppose that you had to learn several of Freud's defense mechanisms such as:

Repression—Memories associated with a traumatic event are repressed or covered up, and are not readily retrievable.

Sublimation—The channeling of sexual energies into socially acceptable activities.

Definitions of concepts such as these are much easier to learn if you can learn examples along with the definitions. The examples help you understand and remember the definitions. An example for each defense mechanism follows:

Repression—John rarely thinks about his old girlfriend Samantha, who broke up with him just prior to their senior prom. He cannot recall the situation that caused their break-up.

Sublimation—Marcy reads incessantly while her boyfriend studies overseas for one year.

Sometimes you can take elaborate notes when the lecturer anchors the teaching or learning of an entire lesson to some previously learned material. For example, many psychologists have found it effective to teach about the structures and processes of memory by using the structures and processes of a computer as a model or anchor. Both computers and human memory have limited working memories in the areas where computations occur, and large long-term memories for information storage. Both encode information and retrieve it from memory. Elaborating upon the new information about memory by connecting it to familiar information about computers facilitates the new learning.

What all of this means is that lecture notes are best when they include elaborations. You should, when possible, record related ideas and examples you develop yourself. When you jot down elaborations, you are building external connections by relating lecture ideas to familiar knowledge. This bolsters your comprehension and improves your retention. As you listen to a lecture, elaborate on the lecture points by jotting personal comments, questions, examples, and evaluations of lecture ideas.

As graduate students, this book's authors both took notes with two colored pens. A blue pen recorded the lecturer's points. A red pen recorded thoughts about the lecture points. Our red "thinking" pens wrote down questions about the lecture material (for example, "How long do brake shoes last? Do foot brakes on a bicycle operate the same as hand brakes?"); related lecture information to background knowledge (for instance, friction is responsible for making everything stop—all braking systems must create friction); generated novel examples (for instance, a motorcycle and baby carriage both have mechanical brakes); made inferences (for instance, mechanical brakes can probably snap and therefore

After the lecture, meet with other students to improve your lecture notes

work best on lighter objects); and evaluated ideas (I disagree that electric brakes are common).

Of course, you can elaborate on the ideas you've noted after the lecture, when you have more time. Nevertheless, it is important to record brief elaborations during the lecture while the thoughts are there; otherwise you may forget them.

What to Do After the Lecture

Your goals after the lecture are to produce a set of complete, organized, and elaborate notes that will be useful for review. After the lecture, take additional steps to ensure that notes are complete, organized, and elaborate. Fortunately, this is now accomplished without the time pressures and frenzy associated with note-taking during the lecture.

Make Your Notes More Complete

Remember that most students are notoriously incomplete note-takers recording, on average, about 30 percent of lecture ideas. Although the strategies presented for complete note-taking during the lecture should significantly bolster your note-taking abilities, it is still likely that you left out some critical ideas from your notes.

After the lecture, make sure notes are complete, organized, and elaborate.

To make your notes as complete as possible, meet sometime during the next few days after the lecture with a few students from the class. You and your fellow students should take turns reading portions of your notes aloud. Group members should add missing points to their notes and offer noted points to help others complete their notes. If your group is still missing lecture information after you meet, then ask your instructor to help you fill in the gaps.

During group sessions, you can also correct your notes. For instance, you might occasionally record misinformation during the lecture in your haste to record complete notes. You might, for example, note during a psychology lecture that proactive interference is interference occurring *after* other material is learned. Actually, proactive interference is interference occurring *before* other material is learned. It's an easy mistake to make, and the group session is the perfect place to make the correction.

Make Your Notes More Organized

After a lecture, construct representations or other visual aids, such as graphs, pictures, or maps that capture the organization among lecture ideas. The methods for constructing representations were introduced in Chapter 5 and demonstrated further in Chapter 6. Completed representations for the lecture material on creativity is shown in Figure 8-7. Representations for the material on brakes is shown in Figures 8-8, 8-9, and 8-10.

Figure 8–7. *Organized Lecture Notes on Creativity*

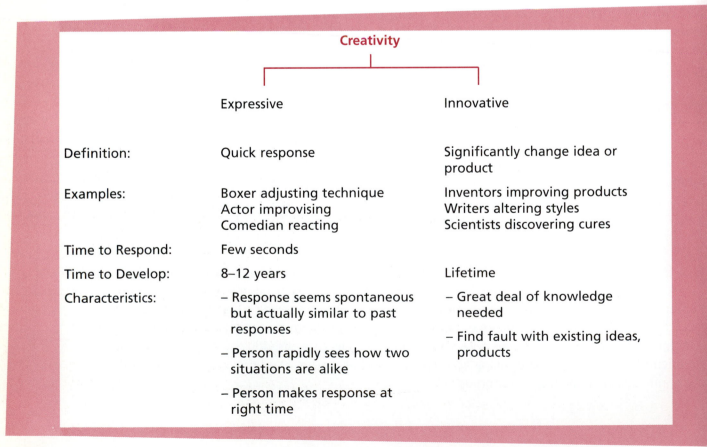

	Expressive	Innovative
Definition:	Quick response	Significantly change idea or product
Examples:	Boxer adjusting technique Actor improvising Comedian reacting	Inventors improving products Writers altering styles Scientists discovering cures
Time to Respond:	Few seconds	
Time to Develop:	8–12 years	Lifetime
Characteristics:	– Response seems spontaneous but actually similar to past responses – Person rapidly sees how two situations are alike – Person makes response at right time	– Great deal of knowledge needed – Find fault with existing ideas, products

Figure 8–8. *Organized Lecture Notes on Brake Types*

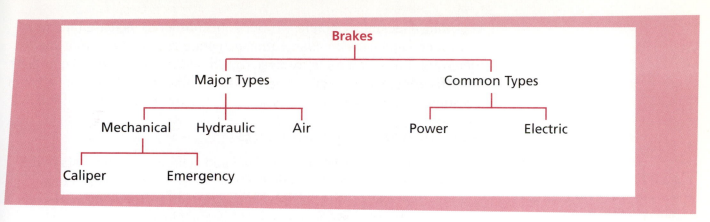

Figure 8–9. *Organized Lecture Notes on Mechanical Brakes*

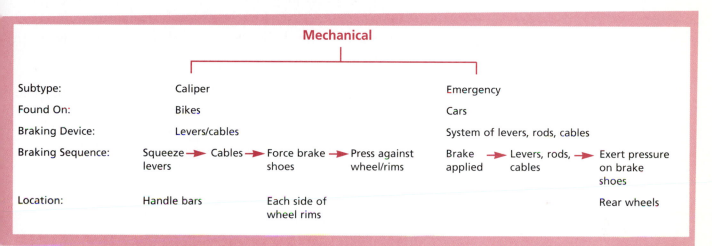

Figure 8–10. *Diagram of Mechanical Brakes*

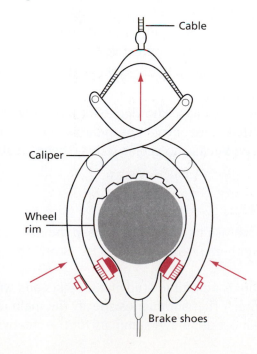

When the rider squeezes the levers, The cable forces the shoes to press against the wheel rim. This action slows or stops the bicycle.

Make Your Notes More Elaborate

Following a lecture, elaborate on your notes further to increase (and monitor) your comprehension. Elaboration activities following a lecture are identical to those following reading. You should add elaborative comments (such as examples and evaluations), write a summary, and generate a list of questions.

Add Elaborative Comments

Read your notes following a lecture and add elaborative comments in red pen. Remember, the red pen signifies that these are your ideas or comments rather than the lecturer's. Adding elaborative comments makes lecture information more meaningful and memorable to you.

Think of elaborating as having a conversation with your notes. Argue with your notes. Evaluate an idea's merits. Relate the information to past knowledge. Sprinkle in a few examples, and raise some questions.

Returning to the creativity material, you might add elaborations like the following:

> *Think of elaborating as having a conversation with your notes.*

- David Letterman displays expressive creativity when he reacts spontaneously to someone in the audience.
- Expressive creativity requires quick responses. Police officers must make split-second decisions whether to fire a weapon.
- Seems like the key to expressive creativity is quickly recognizing the pattern that exists.
- Seems like most people become expressively creative in an area they know a lot about.
- Robin Williams seems like an especially expressively creative person.
- What is meant by a significant change for innovative creativity? Significant by whose standards?
- Are the people who "discover" all these odd devices, like a clamp to open soda bottles, innovatively creative?
- Freud, who developed the field of psychoanalysis, was innovatively creative.
- If it takes a lifetime to amass knowledge for innovative creativity, does that mean that someone can be creative in only one area? What about Leonardo da Vinci, who seems to have been creative in several areas?

Write a Summary

Writing a summary forces you to identify and grasp the most important lecture ideas as you weave them into a clear, concise "story" that you can easily tell to a friend.

The written summary is helpful in studying for tests and writing papers. You'll recall from Chapter 7 that summaries specify the main ideas, combine ideas, and delete most details. A summary for the creativity material appears below.

There are two types of creativity: expressive and innovative. Both take many years to develop as the creative person acquires the knowledge and skill necessary. Expressive creativity involves a rapid response in what seems like a new situation. Actually, the "new" situation is similar to previous situations. The person draws upon the knowledge of past experiences to act creatively now. An example is a seasoned comedian who reacts to a heckler based on past experiences.

Innovative creativity involves making a significant change in an idea or product. Discovering a cure for a disease is an example.

Generate Questions

Although lectures should answer many of the questions you might have about a topic, they should prompt you to raise many more. As questions pop into your mind during the lecture, you should ask them of the lecturer. A lecture is an interactive process, and most instructors enjoy and invite questions.

If, for some reason, questioning is inappropriate during the lecture, then write your question in your notes (in red pen). Following the lecture, review your notes and record additional questions you might have. Ask these questions of classmates during study sessions, or seek answers from your text, additional readings, or the instructor.

Don't be bound by the information provided. Ask questions and seek fuller and greater understanding. Questioning and searching for understanding are characteristics common among knowledgeable, creative people.

A list of questions stemming from the creativity material follows:

1. If a comedian uses the same put-down repeatedly to rebuff a heckler, is that response creative?
2. Must the comedian invent the response to the heckler, or can he or she copy one used by another comedian?
3. Does the response seem spontaneous to those who follow the comedian faithfully? Do they recognize the response as similar to another comedian's?
4. What constitutes a significant change?
5. Are the discoveries of "odd devices" creative?
6. Must innovative creativity stem from dissatisfaction?
7. Does innovative creativity extend beyond one area for a person? Wasn't da Vinci creative in several areas?
8. Isn't there a difference between someone building a better mousetrap and someone inventing a new style of music or painting? Is there another, more sophisticated, form of creativity beyond innovative creativity?

Exercise

1. Return to the notes you made earlier about stars and about storms. Make those notes more organized and more elaborate.

2. Try recording complete, organized, and elaborate lecture notes in class. Compare these new notes to those you recorded previously. Do the new notes contain more main ideas, details, and examples? Are they more organized and more elaborate? Are they more useful for review?

3. To help you integrate and apply the ideas presented in this chapter, complete the following matrix framework.

Strategies for Better Note-taking

	Complete Notes	Organized Notes	Elaborate Notes
Strategies used before lecture:			
Strategies used during lecture:			
Strategies used after lecture:			

Summary

Students are notoriously poor note-takers. They record only about 30 percent of the points covered in a lecture even though they stand only a 5 percent chance of later recalling a non-noted idea. Students' brief notes are usually linearly organized and aren't elaborated. Students should strive to record complete, organized, and elaborate lecture notes.

You can do several things to make notes more complete. Before a lecture, prepare emotionally by "psyching yourself up" for complete note-taking. Prepare physically by attending class on time, sitting in the front row, and having note-taking materials ready to go. Prepare mentally by reading assignments and reviewing previous lecture notes before the lecture.

During a lecture, record complete notes by noting main ideas, details, and examples. Follow the lecturer's cues for noting these important ideas. When lectures are too rapid, use abbreviations and notations to speed note-taking and slow down a fast-talking lecturer with comments, questions, and requests. Also, try tape-recording lectures and replaying them after the lecture. You can also bolster note-taking after the lecture by examining the notes of fellow students.

Capture the lecture's organization by generating representations during and after the lecture. Instructors often provide spoken or written cues that signal a lecture's organization. Otherwise, anticipate the lecture's organization by reading the text and reviewing previous lecture notes before the lecture.

Elaborate on notes during and after the lecture. Elaborations are ideas that extend beyond the lecturer's ideas. Elaborations include examples, related ideas, comments, questions, summaries, and evaluations of what's said. Use blue or black pen for noting the lecturer's ideas and a red "thinking" pen for noting elaborations.

Finally, remember that note-taking improves your achievement in two ways. The process of recording notes improves your attention and aids your memory. Having notes to review later helps you store information more permanently in memory. How to review notes is the topic of Chapter 9.

Answers to focus *questions*

1. The best place to sit during a lecture is in the middle of the front row. Sitting farther back, there are more distractions between you and the instructor. Toward the back, your attention is easily drawn to movements and sounds around you. The instructor is also more difficult to see and hear. When you sit in the front row, you feel as though the instructor is talking to you. You listen better and take more complete notes.

2. Come to lectures prepared to learn and record notes. Have your loose-leaf binder for that class, several sharpened pencils, and smooth writing pens—blue and red. Also carry the text, course handouts, and special tools, such as calculators, to class. Have your materials out and ready to go.

3. Mental preparation involves "getting up to speed" for the lecture. Do this by reviewing previously recorded lecture notes and reading related chapters prior to the lecture. Doing so helps you better understand the lecture.

4. Note-taking serves two functions. First, the process of recording notes focuses your attention during the lecture and helps you store lecture ideas in your memory. Second, the recorded notes are available for your later review. Without notes for review, you'll forget many of the lecture ideas.

5. Students are generally poor note-takers. Most students record only 30 to 50 percent of lecture points. Some first year students record only about 10 percent of lecture points.

6. Complete note-taking is crucial. You are apt to recall only about 5 percent of lecture information that you didn't write down.

7. Complete notes include main ideas, details, and examples.

8. Note-taking abbreviations or symbols:

   A. minute   min.
   B. pound   lb.
   C. and so forth   etc.
   D. and others   et al.
   E. for example   e.g.
   F. without   w/out
   G. therefore   ∴

9. When instructors present visual and oral messages simultaneously, recording notes about both is impossible. Politely ask the instructor for time to record the visual message before it is discussed. If the instructor won't allow that, then record the instructor's verbal message as it is presented and ask to record the visual message after class or during office hours.

10. Take more complete notes by using abbreviations and notations, influencing the lecturer (for example, asking her to slow down), following note-taking cues (for instance, spoken cues such as the instructor repeating a phrase), self-monitoring your note-taking, and tape-recording the lecture so you can add to your existing lecture notes when hearing the lecture a second (or third) time.

11. Lecture Frameworks

    A.
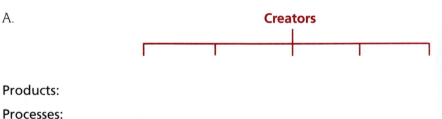

    Products:

    Processes:

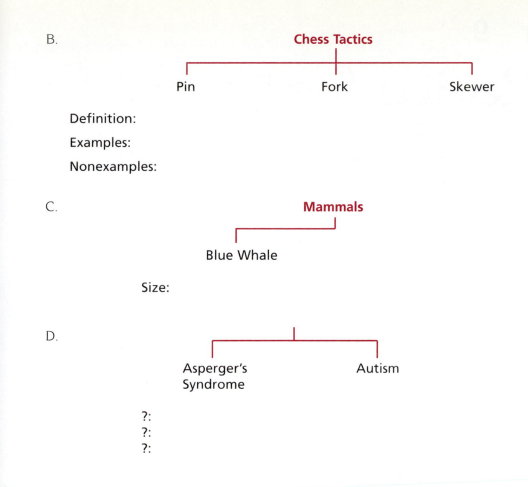

B.

Chess Tactics

Pin   Fork   Skewer

Definition:

Examples:

Nonexamples:

C.

Mammals

Blue Whale

Size:

D.

Asperger's   Autism
Syndrome

?:

?:

?:

12. You can determine the lecture's organization by listening or looking for organizational cues at the start of the lecture. Instructors often provide the lecture's organization orally (for example, "Today we'll cover three chess tactics . . ."), or by writing it on the board, or by including it in lecture handouts. Previous lectures and assigned readings also provide clues about the lecture's organization.

13. While recording lecture notes, you should elaborate on the presented ideas. We recommend using a red "thinking" pen for this. Use the red pen to record occasional questions, related ideas, examples, inferences, and evaluations that you think of. Elaborations help you follow and understand the lecture better.

14. Following the lecture, make sure your notes are complete and correct by reviewing them with study group members. To make your note organization better, generate representations and other visual displays. Last, elaborate further on notes by adding more elaborative comments, writing a lecture summary, and generating a list of questions. You can answer your questions by consulting a textbook, fellow students, or the instructor.

chapter 9
How to Review for Exams

OVERVIEW

Focus Questions

Introduction

Why You Should Review

Where You Should Review

When You Should Review

With Whom You Should Review

What You Should Review

How You Should Review
  Prepare the Content
  Build Internal Connections
  Build External Connections
  Conduct Test-Appropriate Practice
    Practice for Fact Items
    Practice for Concept Items
    Practice for Skill Items

Summary

Answers to Focus Questions

focus questions

1. Why should you review regularly, not just for exams?
2. Who are the "Lounge Scroungers" and what do they do?
3. When should you review for exams?
4. How should study groups operate?
5. What should you review for exams?
6. Can you identify the following test items as assessing skill, concept, or fact?

   A. $847 \div 9 = ?$
   B. Who was the sixteenth president?
   C. Look at this chess diagram and circle the piece being pinned.
   D. Write the steps for solving quadratic equations.
   E. Read the examples below and underline the one that shows a monopoly.
   F. Generate a representation for the passage below.

7. What are the four steps followed in reviewing for tests?
8. What special things should you do when you're studying facts?
9. What special things should you do when you're studying concepts?
10. What special things should you do when you're studying skills?

The coffee pot is working overtime. As Roger sips the night's fifth cup, the digital clock blinks 3:22 A.M. Later this morning, at 10:00, Roger will take his second biology exam. Roger began studying at 7:30 P.M.—nearly a full eight hours ago—in hopes of posting a good grade. He needs one. Roger notched only a 62% on the first exam. But last time, Roger only studied until three in the morning. This time he's pulling an all-nighter.

Roger began this night's study by reading Chapters 4 through 8 in the residence hall study lounge. He prefers to save reading assignments till the night before, so that the material is fresh in his mind. Roger was distracted a few times, though, by friends who just wanted to talk, and by folks circulating through the lounge checking to see who was there.

Later, Roger met with six classmates to study. But by the time they'd finished griping about the instructor's boring lectures and lousy tests, the group members scarcely had time to exchange and copy each other's notes for missed lectures. Roger copied notes for three missed lectures. One classmate needed notes for fourteen lectures. She carted notebooks to a copy machine and dropped in about $20 in change to make copies. The group thought this was a hoot.

Now Roger is in his room, lying on the bed, rereading lecture notes and highlighted portions of the text for about the sixth time. He recites the definitions of new terms like *mitosis*, *meiosis*, *genotype*, and *phenotype*. Roger dozes until the last drops of coffee sizzle in the pot, waking him from a DNA nightmare. The sun now lights the clock, which reads 9:25 A.M. Roger wipes the sleep from his eyes and concludes he's not cut out for all-nighters. He takes a quick shower, grabs a doughnut and cup of coffee, and heads to the exam.

Again, the exam is not what Roger expected. He doesn't have to define terms like *mitosis* and *meiosis*, but he does have to identify new examples from illustrations. He doesn't have to define *genotype* or *phenotype*, but he does need to use these ideas to predict an offspring's characteristics. "Where does the instructor come up with these questions?" Roger wonders. Midway through the exam, Roger realizes he's toast and that even a C on this exam is a long shot. Roger yawns, pencils in another guess, and hopes he can hang on to his D average.

This chapter is about review. It covers *why* to review, *where* to review, *when* to review, *with whom* to review, *what* to review, and most importantly, *how* to review.

Too often, college students make the same poor review choices as Roger did. They review the night before the test (when) in crowded lounges (where) with other underprepared students (who) solely to pass a course exam (why). They review lecture notes and the text (what) by rereading and reciting definitions (how). In this chapter, you'll learn why these are poor review choices.

Some of the strategies for the *why*, *where*, *when*, *with whom*, *what*, and *how* of reviewing are already familiar, because you've read about them in earlier chapters. But the last section, which tells you how to review for various exams, will probably be new to you. You probably haven't been taught how to study differently for different types of exams. In fact, most students, like Roger, aren't even aware that there *are* different types of exams. An exam could require the recall of facts, recognition of concepts, or application of skills. Some may even require all three.

Before we talk about how to review for different types of exams, we'll look at the more general issues of why, where, when, with whom, and what to review.

Why You Should Review

Reviewing is something you should do throughout the semester on a daily basis, because it keeps you current.

Certainly you should review to pass or "ace" course exams. Exams are the yardstick of learning—but are they the only yardstick? As the Gershwin song says, "It ain't necessarily so."

We know a former graduate student who received a perfect score on a six-hour statistics exam that covered regression analyses. His perfect score was the first ever in this course at his university. The student, though, when later confronted with authentic statistical problems as a researcher, admitted that he had little idea when to apply regression techniques or how to use them. Outstanding preparation for the test somehow resulted in restricted knowledge for real-world problems.

Suppose that your physician, your next airline pilot, or your child's first-grade teacher had passed the necessary qualifying exams, but was unable to apply the learned information meaningfully. Those are frightening thoughts!

Although it's important to prove your mettle by zapping exams, your eyes should be set on wider horizons. You should want to master a course, and you should also want to ensure that you can use its ideas and skills in the future. College courses are the foundation for your later success as a researcher, teacher, pilot, physician, or whatever work you choose. As you learn and review, do so with one eye on the impending test and the other eye on real-world considerations. When you strive to really understand and apply information, you'll find that passing tests is a minor hurdle on your way toward achieving expertise in your field.

Exercise

Generate a list of reasons why you want to perform well in your courses, other than to receive high grades. Having alternative reasons to learn should improve your desire to review effectively.

Where You Should Review

BEWARE THE LOUNGE SCROUNGERS!

Prepare a special place for studying. Perhaps you're fortunate enough to have a quiet haven in your residence hall, apartment, or house that will serve this purpose. Your special study sanctuary should include a large desk or table with nearby storage for books, materials, and supplies. Keep your work surface uncluttered. Remove books and materials that don't have anything to do with your immediate work. Banish unpaid bills and unfolded laundry to a dark corner elsewhere. Have support materials, such as paper, pens, and reference books, close at hand on shelves, or in nearby drawers or cabinets. Make sure you've got plenty of good light. Create a comfortable study environment, since you'll be spending a lot of your time there.

Why is a quiet place so important? Think of it this way: Oxymorons are figures of speech in which incongruous or contradictory terms are combined, such as "deafening silence" or "jumbo shrimp." An oxymoron prevalent on college campuses is the "study lounge." Who came up with this architectural blunder . . . Frank Lloyd Wrong? It's crazy to expect students to study in a large open room stocked with soft couches and easy chairs, and brimming with distractions.

Study lounges are about 10 percent study and 90 percent lounge. Lounges are full of chatting, coughing, sniffing, and snoring sounds, and with "Lounge Scroungers," students who pop in just looking to gab or to lure a would-be studier downtown for frozen yogurt. Avoid study lounges as scrupulously as you would the dining hall's meat pie medley.

Also avoid your bed when you're studying. There exists a high correlation between lying in bed and sleeping—except for two-year-olds. Study in an upright position at a desk or table, away from annoyances. This might be in your room while your roommate is in the kitchen inhaling pizza or at a quiet study carrel in the library. Or maybe you can study in more offbeat locations, such as vacant classrooms, in your garage, or at a picnic table in a quiet park. One student studied routinely in a vacant section of the college library that was undergoing renovation, and on the soccer bleachers on warm autumn afternoons. When distractions are difficult to escape (such as the audible snarfing of a pepperoni pizza), try to get rid of them with the hum of an electric fan or with soothing instrumental music.

Prepare a quiet and uncluttered study space

Exercise

Check to see if you have these materials and supplies available in your study area.

- [ ] paper
- [ ] pens
- [ ] pencils
- [ ] pencil sharpener
- [ ] stapler
- [ ] paper clips
- [ ] tape
- [ ] scissors
- [ ] markers
- [ ] calculator
- [ ] ruler

- [ ] dictionary
- [ ] thesaurus
- [ ] grammar book
- [ ] computer program guides
- [ ] bookshelves
- [ ] desk organizers
- [ ] file folders
- [ ] file labels
- [ ] file drawers
- [ ] adequate lighting

When You Should Review

Be completely prepared for the exam at least three days in advance.

First, let's discuss when *not* to review. You should study very little in the three days just before an exam. No, this is not a misprint. Be completely prepared for the exam at least three days in advance. If you are, you'll be less anxious. In the days immediately preceding the exam you're more anxious and distractible. It's hard to concentrate on studying when the test is just around the corner. Trying to study the night before a test is like trying to sleep the night before Christmas.

If you're prepared at least three days in advance, you're also less at the mercy of unexpected events. All too often, students get sick, have accidents, or get troubling news from home just before exams, and so they're unable to study as planned. Instructors are usually not sympathetic. They've heard all the variations of the "sick grandmother" story that have ever been invented, and they know that students actually had weeks to prepare.

Studying should be done throughout the semester on a daily basis. (Remember to *invest daily* and *invest early*.) Don't try to cram it all into a few hours or days before the test. The same way that daily running workouts strengthen your body for longer and faster runs, regular studying strengthens the knowledge and skills that support your additional learning. If you don't exercise regularly, you're not prepared for more demanding workouts later. Similarly, when you fail to study regularly and stay current with your lecture content, you're unable to grasp new information. The instructor has zoomed ahead and you're left in a cloud of dust, gasping for breath, unable to catch up.

The chief reason for studying throughout the semester is that you can't apply the learning strategies described in this book in just a few days' time. Just as Rome wasn't built in a day, representations and summaries are not generated and reviewed overnight.

For example, let's go back to the puzzle analogy presented in Chapter 5. A puzzler working for a short time might only examine the puzzle pieces as each one is turned up, and then assemble a corner or two. But the puzzle's theme and patterns aren't immediately observable. They only emerge after considerable time and work. But once the puzzler can see them, the themes and patterns are meaningful and memorable. Good review strategies also require time and effort to produce meaningful and memorable knowledge.

Another guideline involves developing substantial time blocks for studying. As much as possible, arrange to set aside one- to four-hour time blocks for studying. With longer time blocks, there are fewer start-up periods—which include packing books, walking to the library, assembling materials, and planning review activities—and a greater likelihood of relating information. For instance, if you're studying about black and white rhinos during the same session, you are much more likely to note their similarities and differences than if you studied them in separate study sessions three days apart.

You can also see advantages of extended study sessions if you think about them relative to automobile maintenance. It takes less time for a mechanic to change the oil, lube the chassis, rotate the tires, and check the brakes during a single service visit than if she were doing the work over several visits. The mechanic only needs to jack up the car once. She can lube the chassis while the oil drains, and remove the tires only once for both rotation and brake inspections. In fact, if she's working on brakes and tires during the same visit, the mechanic is more likely to notice the relationship between the brake's damaged rotor and the tires' uneven wear pattern.

This is not to say that you should only use big blocks of time for studying. Not so! Use your spare moments, too—the ones you spend waiting for rides, appointments, or slow cashiers. (Remember to *invest wisely*.) These portholes of opportunity are ideal for reviewing definitions or answering study questions listed on cards. Together with longer study sessions, brief study periods keep you thinking and involved in learning.

A last guideline concerns arranging an optimal time to study. Arrange study slots outside your class schedule and life commitments (like work and band practice), as specified in Chapter 3. To the extent possible, arrange substantial study time in the morning. People are generally fresher and more alert in the morning, following a restful night's sleep, and mornings are usually quieter and have fewer distractions than other times. The sound of morning showers, for example, is music when you compare it to the blare of nighttime stereos or the bedtime arguments of children or the uneven snoring of a spouse.

If you must study at night, be sure to wind down before turning in. When you study right up until bedtime, you might have trouble relaxing and falling asleep. Right before bed, some light reading or mindless television viewing (choose any channel) can relax you and pave the way for sleep.

STUDYING IS MORE EFFECTIVE IN PLACES AND AT TIMES WHEN FEW DISTRACTIONS ARE LIKELY.

With Whom You Should Review

For the most part, studying is a solitary act. Conjure up an image of studying and you visualize a solitary figure seated at a desk, poring over stacks of books and papers. The only light comes from a small desk lamp in an otherwise darkened room.

Top students do spend the bulk of their study time working alone. But they also spend substantial time working in study groups where they share materials, clarify ideas, and test one another on a regular basis. Group study—when done appropriately—is highly effective. In this section, we offer eight guidelines for developing and conducting study groups.

A well-functioning study group is a key to college success

Exercise

If you haven't yet completed the time-management block schedule suggested in Chapter 3, then do so now to ensure that you plan sufficient time for studying. Below is a blank block schedule. Review the guidelines in Chapter 3 and complete the block schedule by including classes and commitments, chores, study periods, and leisure activities.

BLOCK SCHEDULE

	Sunday	Monday	Tuesday	Wednesday	Thursday	Friday	Saturday
6:00–7:30							
7:30–8:30							
8:30–9:30							
9:30–10:30							
10:30–11:30							
11:30–12:30							
12:30–1:30							
1:30–2:30							
2:30–3:30							
3:30–4:30							
4:30–5:30							
5:30–6:30							
6:30–7:30							
7:30–8:30							
8:30–9:30							
9:30–10:30							
10:30–11:30							

Form a study group for each class If you are taking math, English, science, and history courses, then form a separate study group for each class that includes members from that class.

Include three to five serious members Your study group shouldn't be either too big or too small. Too big, and responsibility gets sidetracked because members think that someone else will do the work. Too small a group, and the benefits of sharing work and ideas are lost. A study group including between three to five members seems ideal—neither too big nor too small.

Include only serious members who pledge to attend all sessions, complete all assignments, and work toward mastering the course. Anyone who cannot make this pledge is more of a hindrance than a help.

Schedule weekly meetings Begin meeting the first week of the semester (remember to *invest early*) and meet regularly (remember to *invest daily*) throughout the semester. We recommend once-a-week meetings that last about one to two hours. Don't skip sessions because the next test is weeks away. Cramming is as ineffective for your group as it is for you alone. Your group benefits by completing and sharing work throughout the semester.

Make written assignments At the conclusion of each session, each group member should be asked to complete a written assignment. Assignments might involve marking text, constructing representations, formulating practice tests, and generating summaries. Completed assignments are photocopied and shared among your group at subsequent sessions.

Be prepared for study sessions Study sessions should be a sharing of knowledge rather than a sharing of ignorance. Your group must be as prepared for study sessions as ski bums for snow. Complete all readings, attend all lectures, and finish all written assignments (such as summaries, test questions, and representations) prior to group meetings. Members should make legible copies of assigned work and distribute them to the others in the group.

Stay on task Your job is to study, not to socialize or gripe about the class. Don't tolerate chatterboxes and complainers. Remember, this is a study group, not a support group.

Be cooperative, not competitive When a basketball player makes a basket, it's usually because her teammates made a good pass, set a pick, or cleared a zone. Teamwork is as essential to winning study groups as it is to winning basketball. Work cooperatively in groups by openly sharing materials and ideas.

It is vital that your group cooperate, rather than compete. Competition divides and destroys groups. Members should do their best and help others to do *their* best. Try something that has been a hallmark of the University of North Carolina's basketball team: When a player makes an unselfish pass leading to a basket, the scorer points to that player to acknowledge the pass. During study sessions, point to the person who passes you helpful information.

While it is important to act cooperatively and supportively, your group must also be honest and up-front with one another. When a member's representation is incomplete and disorganized, or his summary is incomprehensible and overstuffed with details, you should tell him why his work is inadequate. In fact, accepting substandard work not only hurts the person who produced the work, it hurts all the group members. The other person has no idea that his work needs correction. He only finds that out when it's tested in an exam—and by then, it's too late. Further, if group members keep silent because they don't want to hurt someone's feelings, then the group is undoubtedly going to receive substandard work thereafter. Constructive criticism is necessary to improve both individual and group performance.

On the other side of the coin, if you're the person receiving criticism, then recognize its value. Without constructive criticism, your errors go undetected and uncorrected. Your group's members should not merely tolerate criticism, but invite it. Like most medicines, it might not taste good, but it's good for you.

Dismiss noncontributors Fellow members who don't hold to the study group guidelines—by skipping meetings, not completing assignments, or behaving uncooperatively—should be asked to leave the group. The group is optional and should only be for those who are seriously committed to it. Agree at the beginning to provide only one warning. If there's a second offense, then drop the person who does not comply. Otherwise, the person will grind your whole group to a halt.

> Constructive criticism is necessary to improve both individual and group performance.

Exercise

Based on the study group guidelines, write an informal "contract" that might be signed by all study group members. The "contract" should specify all the expectations of belonging to and participating in the group.

What You Should Review

Now that you've developed representations, summaries, and questions from lectures (as shown in Chapter 8) and texts (as shown in Chapter 7), these, along with additional study notes you'll construct, become the primary materials for review.

Most students don't know this. To prove the point, amble into any study lounge on any campus and locate a studier (not a lounger). Observe what the studier is studying to prepare for a test. We'll bet dollars to doughnuts (actually, a fairly even bet these days!) the studier is poring over textbooks and lecture notes. We hope you won't have to do the same.

Would you rather eat flour, water, yeast, and salt . . . or bread? Would you rather look at negatives or colored photographs? Why read the rough draft if you can read the polished work? And why study lecture notes and texts after you've transformed them into representations and summaries that are ideal for review. Certainly, you need to refer occasionally to lecture notes and texts for clarification and detail, but for the most part, these original sources are obsolete because you've got your newly prepared representations, summaries, and other study aids.

How You Should Review

Many students review by rereading, recopying, reciting, and regurgitating—which is *re-diculous*. As you know now, repetition strategies don't support understanding or promote long-term retention, and they're especially worthless if you're preparing for tests that require recognizing new examples or the application of ideas. Recall from the beginning of the chapter that Roger's repetition strategies (rereading and reciting) were useless for identifying examples of mitosis and meiosis, or for predicting an offspring's characteristics from genotypes and phenotypes.

Remember, too, that Roger was surprised by these questions. He expected to define terms, not identify them among novel examples or use them to solve a problem. Like Roger, many students are not aware of the various types of test questions and the review methods that are appropriate for each.

We provide a four-step review model that prepares you for all test types. The model, shown in Figure 9-1, is called the **PIE TAP** review model. (Yes, you guessed it: This is an acronym that's also a mnemonic.) The first three steps are always the same, regardless of the test type you expect. You must prepare (**P**) the content, build internal (**I**) connections, and build external (**E**) connections. If you followed instructions for how to record text notes (Chapter 7) and lecture notes (Chapter 8), you have already completed these three steps. Thus, the first three steps are as easy as PIE!

The last review step is test-appropriate practice (TAP). Tests often TAP your knowledge of facts, concepts, or skills. Each test requires somewhat different practice methods. You must practice for these different test items appropriately otherwise the band will blow TAPs at your graduation. Each review phase is now described in turn.

Figure 9–1.

Figure 9–1. *The PIE TAP Review Model*

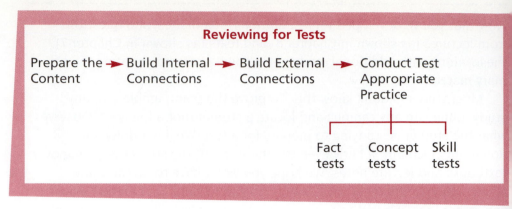

Prepare the Content

> *The first step in review is to prepare a complete, well-organized set of notes to study.*

The first step in review is to prepare a complete, well-organized set of notes to study. *Complete* means that notes contain all important information. Notes should include key terms, definitions, examples, and details. *Organized* means that notes appear in a spatial form whenever possible. By "spatial" we mean using a hierarchy, sequence, matrix, graph, or diagram so that you can easily draw relations among ideas. If you followed our instructions for recording text and lecture notes in Chapters 7 and 8, then you already have a complete and organized set of notes available for further review.

Suppose that you've recorded a set of lecture notes, but it's incomplete and not well organized, like the notes on operant conditioning below. How would you prepare these notes for review?

Operant Conditioning (OC)

OC—a process that increases or decreases behavior by presenting or removing a stimulus following the behavior

Two types—

Reinforcement—inc. in beh.

Punishment—dec. in beh.

Reinforcement—Pos. (PR) + Neg. (NR)

PR— inc. in beh. due to pres. of stimulus following beh.

Ex. Worker works late, boss praises worker, worker works late more often

rat presses lever—?—

Possible side effect is satiation if too much of reinforcer is given.

NR— inc. in beh. due to removal of stimulus following beh.

Side effect is that NR can cause escape beh. or aggression

        Ex. (Worker is under threat of dismissal) worker works late,
            boss removes threat, worker works late more often
        (rat is being shocked) rat presses lever, shock is elimi-
            nated, rat presses lever more often
    Punishment—Pos (PP) + Neg (NP)
        PP— dec. in beh.—?—
            Ex. Worker goofs off, is reprimanded, stops goofing off
            rat presses lever, is shocked, stops pressing lever
            Can cause aggression and modeling of punisher
            Ex. spanked child may hit dog or baby sitter
        NP— dec. in beh. due to removal of stimulus following beh.
            Ex. Worker goofs off, money is deducted, worker stops
                goofing off
            rat presses lever, water is removed, rat stops pressing lever
            Also produces—?—

First, make sure your notes are complete. Meet with your study group
(or a small group of students from the class) within a day or two of the lecture, while your recollection of the lecture is still fresh. Read the lecture
notes aloud and fill in gaps in your notes. Be sure you've recorded the
names of presented terms (such as *positive reinforcement*), their definitions
(*increase in behavior due to presentation of stimulus following behavior*) examples
(such as those about the worker and the rat) and related details (*positive
reinforcement can cause satiation*).

Notice that this student's notes contained question marks to designate
where lecture information was knowingly missed, perhaps because the student couldn't hear the lecturer, or record notes fast enough, or maybe he
broke a pencil point. Ask your group or instructor about missed information designated in your notes, and add it to your notes.

Second, strive to organize lecture ideas using spatial patterns, such as
hierarchies, sequences, matrices, and diagrams. You'll find organized representations for the lecture notes above in Figures 9-2 and 9-3.

Figure 9-2 shows the important terms (such as positive and negative
reinforcement), their definitions, and related details about side effects. The
examples could easily have been included in this representation, but a second representation, Figure 9-3, better emphasizes the sequence of events
inherent in the definitions and their corresponding examples.

Build Internal Connections

Now that notes are complete and well organized, you might believe that
the relations and patterns inherent in the notes will scream out at you.
Wrong. The student studying the operant conditioning representations in
Figures 9-2 and 9-3, for example, will not recognize the similarities and dif-

Figure 9–2. *Organized Notes Prepared from Lecture Notes*

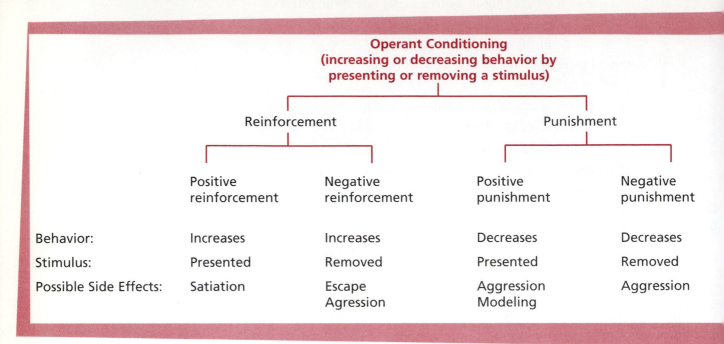

Figure 9–3. *Organized Notes Prepared from Lecture Notes*

Positive Reinforcement

Definition:	Behavior	→ Presented stimulus	→ Increased behavior
Example 1:	Work late	→ Praise	→ Work late more often
Example 2:	Rat presses lever	→ Receives food	→ Keeps pressing lever

Negative Reinforcement

Definition:	Behavior	→ Removed stimulus	→ Increased behavior
Example 1:	Work late	→ Threat of dismissal removed	→ Work late more often
Example 2:	Rat presses lever	→ Shock removed	→ Keeps pressing lever

Positive Punishment

Definition:	Behavior	→ Presented stimulus	→ Decreased behavior
Example 1:	Worker goofs off	→ Reprimanded	→ Stops goofing off
Example 2:	Rat presses lever	→ Shocked	→ Stops pressing lever

Negative Punishment

Definition:	Behavior	→ Removed stimulus	→ Decreased behavior
Example 1:	Worker goofs off	→ Money deducted	→ Stops goofing off
Example 2:	Rat presses lever	→ Water removed	→ Stops pressing lever

Exercise

Below is a set of notes. Prepare this content for review by organizing it.

Prejudice and Discrimination

Discrimination—an action, unfair treatment toward someone
Prejudice—an attitude, a prejudging
    Positive prejudice—exaggerates the virtues of a group
    Negative prejudice—prejudgment that groups are inferior
Discrimination usually the result of prejudice
Sometimes prejudice and discrimination match or don't match

1. All-weather bigot—prejudiced and discriminates. Person might say "Of course I discriminate—they deserve it."

2. Fair-weather bigot—prejudiced but does not discriminate. "I don't like them, but I can't turn them away."

3. Fair-weather liberal—not prejudiced but does discriminate—A server at a restaurant may be told to provide slower service to a group. Doing so, the server might remark "What can I do? I don't want to get fired."

4. All-weather liberal—not prejudiced and does not discriminate. "Everyone should be treated equally. Anything less is un-American and immoral. I would never be part of it."

---

ferences between the operant terms if she looks at each one separately. Remember that examining individual puzzle pieces never reveals the puzzle's theme. The pieces must be assembled to recognize the big picture.

Building internal connections is the single most important aspect of review. Building connections is crucial because it is far easier to learn a few meaningful chunks of information than many isolated facts. Recall from Chapter 4 that recognizing that butterflies have more pronounced characteristics than moths made it easy to remember the simple facts that butterflies are more colorful, fly by day instead of night, have long antennae with knobs versus feathery antennae, and outstretched wings rather than wings drawn in.

Search for relations and patterns in information—because they are always there. The world and its information are systematic, not random. If there is a rhyme, there is a reason. A certain fish has a black top because it is a bottom dweller. Its black top camouflages it from its prey above. Frogs have long sticky tongues because this is the only way they can catch flying insects. When there is an event, there is always a preceding event and a consequence to that event. Food, for example, is digested in your stomach only after it is chewed and swallowed, and before it proceeds to the intestines.

There are also varying types of things. If there are mammals, there are nonmammals and there are various types of mammals. If there are snakes, there are various types of snakes. If there are rattlesnakes, there are snakes without rattles. The world and its information are inherently organized. As a learner, you must seek information's organization and relations.

If you look carefully at Figure 9-2, several internal connections become apparent. First, note that there are two types of operant conditioning (*reinforcement* and *punishment*) and that each type has positive and negative subtypes. These hierarchical relations appear in the top portion of Figure 9-2.

Next, note the coordinate relations in the row labeled "behavior." Reinforcement results in an *increase* in behavior. Punishment results in a *decrease* in behavior.

Next, note the coordinate relations in the row marked "stimulus." Positive techniques involve a *presented* stimulus. Negative techniques involve a *removed* stimulus.

Putting these two ideas together, it is easy to define the four terms. Negative reinforcement, for example, must involve an *increase* in behavior because it is a form of reinforcement and the *removal* of a stimulus because it is a negative technique.

Last, note the coordinate relations in the row labeled "side effects." Negative reinforcement and both forms of punishment may result in aggression. The side effects for all four techniques are negative.

Now examine Figure 9-3 and note the internal connections you find there. First, note that the definitions for all four terms are sequential. All definitions involve three factors: a behavior, a presented or removed stimulus, and an increase or decrease in behavior. Figure 9-3 also reveals, as did Figure 9-2, that reinforcement techniques involve an *increase* in behavior, whereas punishment techniques involve a *decrease* in behavior, and that positive techniques involve the *presentation* of a stimulus, but negative techniques involve the *removal* of a stimulus.

Next, note the relations between example and definition parts for each term. Examining positive reinforcement, for instance, you see that working late is a behavior, praise is a presented stimulus, and working late more often is an increased behavior. When you can see how the examples match the definitions, it helps you recognize new examples on a concept test, as you'll soon see.

> The world and its information are inherently organized.

Exercise

Return to the organized content on prejudice and discrimination that you prepared previously. Now, build internal connections.

Build External Connections

Build external connections by relating presented material to previously acquired background knowledge. When you connect new information to your background knowledge, you understand the new information better and remember it more easily.

Form external connections by generating personal examples that apply presented ideas in new settings, and by evaluating the merits of the presented ideas.

Figure 9-4 shows how personal examples are easily added to study materials. It shows a portion of Figure 9-3 along with personal examples of positive reinforcement in varying settings.

Figure 9–4. *Study Notes Containing External Connections*

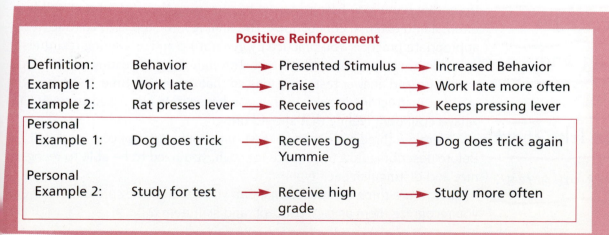

Exercise

Return to your organized notes on prejudice and discrimination. Add a boxed section, as we did in Figure 9–4, that includes external connections.

While studying the operant conditioning material, you could also build external connections by evaluating the merits of each technique. For instance, you might prefer using positive reinforcement over negative reinforcement when you want to increase behavior, because the side effects of positive reinforcement are less damaging. When you want to decrease behavior, you might prefer using negative punishment over positive punishment, because you favor removing a favorable stimulus like water over presenting an aversive one like shock. You can easily add these evaluations to Figure 9-2 by including a new repeatable category called "Preference."

Conduct Test-Appropriate Practice

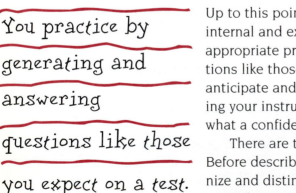

Up to this point, you have reviewed by preparing the content and building internal and external connections. The final review step is to conduct test-appropriate practice. You practice by generating and answering test questions like those you expect on a test. Through this self-testing process, you anticipate and answer test questions so that come test-time, there is nothing your instructor can ask you that you haven't already asked yourself. Oh, what a confident feeling that should bring!

There are three main types of test questions: fact, concept, and skill. Before describing how to practice for each, you need to be able to recognize and distinguish each type.

Below are three test questions. Can you tell how they are different? Can you recognize them as fact, concept, and skill items?

1. Define the mean.
2. To find out how students, in general, did on the test, Mr. Marsh added all the scores and divided by the total number of scores. What did Mr. Marsh find?
3. Calculate the mean for the following scores: 7, 9, 3, 6, 5.

The first item is a *fact item*. Fact items require you to provide information previously presented. In this case, you must provide the definition for the term *mean*.

The next item is a *concept item*. Concept items require you to classify a new, previously unencountered example into a category. In this case, you must classify the new example into the category mean.

The last item is a *skill item*. Skill items require you to apply a rule or procedure to solve some problem. In this case, you must apply the procedure for calculating the mean. You must add the scores and divide the sum by the number of scores.

At first glance, all three items look very much the same. After all, they all pertain to the mean. But if you look more carefully, you'll notice that the items increase in complexity. The fact item is the simplest. It requires you to give a memorized, previously presented definition. A parrot or a two-year-old could state the definition. However, neither could recognize the previously unencountered example of the mean (concept item) or calculate it (skill item) from a sample set of scores. Even the seemingly simple skill of calculating the mean involves applying several operations, such as adding, carrying, dividing, and rounding. This means that being able to define a concept is no guarantee for recognizing it or applying it to solve a problem.

Consider the three types of test items relative to geometry.

1. What is the formula for calculating perimeter?
2. Trace the perimeter with your pencil in the figure below.
3. Calculate the perimeter in the figure below.

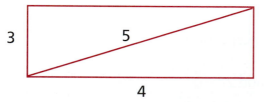

The first item is a fact item. You must recall a previously presented formula. Notice that you simply recall the formula, you don't apply it.

The second item is a concept item. You must examine this new figure and, based on the definition of perimeter, identify its perimeter (as opposed to its length, width, diagonal, or area, for example).

The last item is a skill item. Solving this item requires a procedure involving several steps, including those associated with Questions 1 and 2. First, you identify the perimeter (as in Question 2). Next, you recall the formula for calculating it (as in Question 1). Next, you determine the lengths for the unknown sides by recognizing that the figure is a rectangle and by applying the rule that rectangles have opposite sides of equal length. Last, you sum the length of each side to calculate the perimeter.

Practice for Fact Items

Most test items are fact items that test your memory for previously presented information. Fact items are likely to turn up in all courses, from art history to zoology. They are most prevalent in information courses like history, psychology, sociology, and philosophy. They are least prevalent in skill courses, like math or chemistry.

Practicing for fact items involves generating and answering test questions and using mnemonics, if necessary. There are three different types of fact items that might appear on your test: single-fact, within-topic, and across-topic. Create and answer all three types.

Single-fact items require you to recall a single fact. Generate single-fact items by asking for details associated with a topic and repeatable category. Returning to Figure 9-2 about operant conditioning, you can see that several single-fact questions are generated, such as the following:

1. What happens to the behavior (repeatable category) when negative reinforcement (topic) is applied?
2. What is the side effect (repeatable category) of negative punishment (topic)?
3. Positive punishment (topic) is characterized by a _____ in behavior (repeatable category).
4. In positive reinforcement (topic), the stimulus (repeatable category) is _____.

Exercise

Identify the following test items as being fact, concept, or skill items.

Insert quotation marks if appropriate in Items 1 and 2.

1. Making fun of Cooper, Mark Twain said, He saw nearly all things as through a glass eye, darkly.
2. Mark Twain said that Cooper saw nearly everything darkly, as if he were looking through a glass eye.
3. Name the three instances when quotation marks are necessary.
4. When are double quotation marks used?
5. Should the following sentence contain quotation marks?
   The poem Twas the Night Before Christmas is a holiday favorite.

Notice that each of these questions required a single fact related to a given topic and a repeatable category.

Within-topic items require that you recall two or more facts within a certain topic, such as negative reinforcement. Examples of within-topic items that you could generate from Figure 9-2 include:

1. What are the characteristics of negative reinforcement?
2. In negative punishment, behavior _____ as the result of a _____ stimulus.
3. Although behavior _____ when positive punishment is applied, the side effect of _____ is possible.
4. What are the defining characteristics of positive reinforcement?

Across-topic items require you to compare across two or more topics (for example, positive reinforcement and positive punishment), along one characteristic (such as *stimulus*), or multiple characteristics (such as *stimulus* and *behavior*). The across-topic items below were constructed from Figure 9-2.

1. How are positive reinforcement and positive punishment alike?
2. Which operant techniques involve an increase in behavior?
3. Which operant techniques involve aggression as a side effect?
4. Explain how negative reinforcement and negative punishment are similar and different.

If, after all these review activities, there are still some facts that you haven't learned well, then it's time to go to your bullpen and bring on your ace relief pitcher—mnemonics. Remember from Chapter 4 that mnemonics are memory tricks or devices for remembering stubborn bits of information that you can't easily connect with other ideas or that aren't inherently meaningful.

However, mnemonics are not so much a last resort as they are the icing on the cake. Mnemonics can help ensure memorability. But note their place in the pecking order of learning and review strategies . . . last. Unlike other study-skills texts that teach mnemonics as the best or single strategy, we contend that other strategies, such as building connections and generating test items, are far more meaningful and helpful than mnemonics.

How can mnemonics help you remember facts? To remember that positive techniques involve the presentation of a stimulus, you could perhaps draw and later imagine a picture of a gift, a present (for presentation) with crossing ribbons that form the symbol for positive (+), such as the diagram in Figure 9-5.

To remember that reinforcement techniques involve an increase in behavior, you could think about the word *reinforcement* relative to a construction project. If you reinforce a wall or fence, you increase its strength.

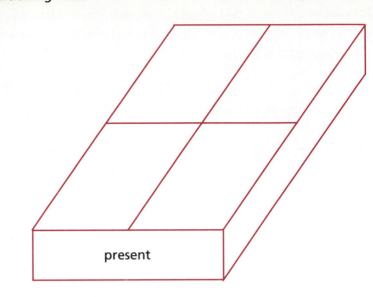

present

You can also construct sentences (sometimes, the sillier they are, the easier they are to remember) from the first-letters associated with the operant terms and their characteristics to help recall facts. For example, you could use the sentence "Peter (P) Piper (P) does (D) peppers (P)" to remember that positive punishment (PP) decreases (D) behavior due to a presented (P) stimulus. Similarly, the sentence "Put (P) robbers (R) in (I) prison (P)" can be used to recall that positive reinforcement (PR) increases (I) behavior due to a presented (P) stimulus.

Exercise

Return to your notes on prejudice and discrimination. Prepare fact test items to aid your review. Also use mnemonics to associate each of the four names (for example, "Fair-weather bigot") with its definition (that is, *prejudiced, but does not discriminate*).

Practice for Concept Items

Look at the four pictures below. Pick out the one that is a chair.

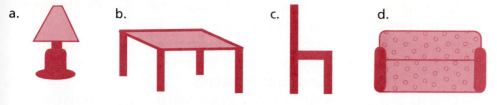

a. b. c. d.

Did you pick letter *c*? If you did, it was because you've acquired the concept of *chair*. You are able to identify new (previously unencountered) examples of *chair*. You probably identified the other concepts as well: *lamp, table,* and *couch*; letters a, b, and d, respectively.

You began learning concepts as an infant. Before you could even talk, you knew concepts like *blankie* and *bottle*. Asked to touch the *blankie* you touched the blanket, rather than another object. Some other concepts you learned early included *doggy* and *kitty* and *cup* and *shoe*. You even learned more subtle concepts, like *touch* and *pat* and *big* and *small*.

By now, you've learned to recognize thousands of concepts. Walking across campus, you note *high-top sneakers, parkas, mountain bikes,* and *white pines.* You point out *backpacks, textbooks, trash cans,* and *vines.* Speaking to friends, you identify *traces of anguish, remorse, lethargy,* and *despair.* Fortunately, you acknowledge their *joy, conviction, buoyancy,* and *flair.* Driving home, you see *Broncos, Mustangs, Cavaliers,* and *Fords,* as well as *Jettas, Tercels, Fiats,* and *Accords.* At home, you reluctantly recognize *dirty dishes, junk mail,* and *milk that's gone sour,* but gleefully acknowledge *frozen dinners, grape juice,* and one *very hot shower.*

Many college courses are replete with concepts. A study skills course based on this book might require students to identify *representations (hierarchy, sequence, matrix,* and *diagram), alert words, internal and external connections, faulty repetition strategies, topics, subtopics, repeatable categories,* and *details, block schedules, daily schedules, early and wise time investments, excuses, focus,* and *intention,* and *fact, concept* and *skill* test items.

Biology is a course involving considerable concept learning. Biology students might identify novel examples of *absorption, alveoli,* a *biotic community, bronchial tubes, chilopoda, commensalism, cytoplasm, duct glands, Dutch elm disease,* and the *dominant species,* just to name a few.

Psychology is another course laden with concepts, such as *reinforcement, punishment, proactive and retroactive interference, primary and recency, independent,* and *dependent variables.*

In architecture classes, students must identify various architectural structures, such as *Gothic, Colonial,* and *Tudor.* In music classes, students classify musical compositions by period (such as *classical* and *Romantic*) and by composer (for example, *Bach, Haydn,* and *Stravinsky*). In art classes, artistic styles are identified (such as *cubism* and *impressionism*) as are obscure works of artists such as *Van Gogh* and *Rembrandt.* In literature, a student might have to classify the form of poetry (*narrative, dramatic,* or *lyric*) or recognize the style of *Emily Dickinson* or *Walt Whitman.* Mathematics, too, is rich with concepts. Geometric shapes such as *circle, square, ellipse,* and *parallelogram* are identified.

Students must recognize problem types so they know what method or formula to apply. In the problem, "John had fourteen marbles and gave seven to Bill. How many marbles did John have left?" the student must recognize this as a subtraction problem. If the student misclassified the problem as an addition problem, he will get the wrong answer even though he knows how to subtract. Oftentimes students who know how to carry out math computations get the wrong answer because they misclassify the problem. They fail to recognize math concepts.

Concept test items require you to identify and perhaps also classify a new, previously unencountered example. Most concept items appear as multiple-choice questions. The multiple-choice format allows the test constructor to assess how well you distinguish one particular concept from similar concepts. For instance, earlier you identified the concept of *chair* among similar concepts (*lamp*, *table*, and *couch*).

A multiple-choice item can present the novel example in the question's stem and require you to choose the corresponding concept name, as in Item 1 below, or can present the concept name in the stem and require you to choose the corresponding example among several distractors, as in Item 2 below.

1. "Alan ate eighty ants" is an example of which literary style?
   a) hyperbole
   *b) alliteration
   c) oxymoron
   d) simile
2. Which of the following is an example of alliteration?
   a) The rain came down in buckets.
   *b) Sally sang silly songs.
   c) There was a deafening silence.
   d) His demeanor was like that of a dog caught napping on the couch.

A concept item's form is irrelevant. The bottom line is that all concept items require recognizing new types of examples—examples that you've never seen before. That's why concept items are difficult for students who memorize a concept's definition, but ignore provided examples and nonexamples. The definition alone just is not sufficient for identifying new examples.

Even the simple concept of square is not easily learned with the definition alone: "A closed, four-sided figure, with all sides of equal length and four right angles." The learner might be unable to recognize a closed figure, right angles, or equal sides, and mistakenly identify the three figures below as squares.

A.   B.   C.

Although the concept definition helps in learning concepts, it is not enough. Often, learners can state the definition but they can't recognize new examples. Consider the biological definitions below. Based solely on the definition, can you identify new examples of these in illustrations or among live plants?

Stamens	Located inside the corolla in a ring formation, stamens are the flower's male organ.
Anther	A knob-like sac at the top of the stamen. The anther produces pollen.
Stigma	Extended from the pistil, it has a sticky top to receive pollen.
Style	Connects the stigma to the ovary.
Ovary	The enlarged base of the pistil.

Concept learning depends largely on your experience with a wide range of examples. This is logical, since you must ultimately identify new examples.

Return to the concept of *chair*. If, when you learned this concept, you were shown a single example of chair (perhaps one of medium size, made from wood), you might believe that all chairs look that way. You might not recognize a tiny chair from a dollhouse or a huge stuffed armchair from a furniture store. You might not recognize one made from plastic, or one with a cloth covering. Your chair concept would be very restricted.

Children often have restricted concepts. Suppose a child learns the concept *car* through experience with just the family car (perhaps a tan, two-door Ford). Not having been exposed to a variety of cars, the child might believe that all cars are like hers. She would not identify a red, four-door Chevy, for example. It is important that she experience a wide range of examples—cars of varying color, size, and styles—so she can recognize the critical attributes that all cars have (four wheels, motor, carries two to six passengers) and dismiss irrelevant attributes, such as size, style, and color.

A physician friend of ours had a restricted concept and it cost him a fair amount of money and pride. Two years out of medical school, Tom was a 35-year-old physician working at a medical clinic when he developed a rash on his chest. He was unable to diagnose the rash. He asked two colleagues with whom he worked to examine the rash. They, too, were unable to make a diagnosis. Tom then made an appointment with a specialist in dermatology. The specialist, in an eye blink, diagnosed the rash as shingles. The diagnosis cost Tom $100 and the embarrassment of not diagnosing an ailment he had seen among patients several times.

WEATHER FORECASTING
– AND ALL OTHER ENDEAVORS –
DEPENDS ON CLASSIFYING CONCEPTS

Why was Tom unable to make a diagnosis? The reason is that he'd only seen elderly patients with the disease in its advanced stages. Tom had never before seen the disease in its early stages, or among young patients. Had Tom experienced a range of examples in medical school (the disease at varying stages and afflicting various-age patients), he would have learned the concept and been able to make the diagnosis.

Along with examples, it's helpful to note and recognize nonexamples. One reason is that nonexamples help learners to discriminate the concept from similar concepts. A child who's acquiring the concept *car* might easily mistake a bus, motorcycle, or van for a car. Similarly, a lamp, couch, or table might be mistaken for a chair. A range of examples helps set a concept's boundaries, whereas nonexamples specify the concept's limits. Nonexamples show where one concept ends and another begins.

A second reason why nonexamples are important is because concept identification on tests and in the real world occurs against a background of related concepts. When you're identifying cars, for example, you know that the natural context for cars is a roadway containing trucks, vans, motorcycles, and buses. In the real world, you need to distinguish cars from these nonexamples of cars. Dermatologists who diagnose shingles must do so relative to similar rashes and skin disorders, such as eczema, hives, and impetigo. In school settings, your concept of capitalism is generally going to be tested relative to the similar concepts of communism and socialism.

Because concept learning depends on recognizing new examples from nonexamples, you can benefit by generating and answering your own test questions. But, because your own items cannot truly contain novel examples and nonexamples (after all, you developed them!), you should share practice items with study group members. That way, all study-group members get practice generating and answering a wide range of concept items.

When you're generating concept questions, remember a few simple guidelines: First, be sure the item is a *concept* item and not a *fact* item. Concept items require the identification of novel examples rather than the recall of facts. To emphasize the difference, consider Item 1, below.

1. When Billy did good things, the teacher presented a stimulus to increase those behaviors. This is an example of
   a) positive reinforcement
   b) negative reinforcement
   c) positive punishment
   d) negative punishment

Item 1 is not a concept item because there really is no example. The question states the concept characteristics (*present stimulus* and *increase behavior*) rather than exemplifying them. A true concept item presents the concept characteristics in disguise. It doesn't state them explicitly. A true concept item that uses the concept of positive reinforcement appears in Item 2, below.

Nonexamples specify the concept's limits, and show where one concept ends, and another begins.

2. Billy read three pages of his new book on Tuesday. The teacher praised Billy for reading. On Wednesday, Billy read sixteen pages. This is an example of
    a) positive reinforcement
    b) negative reinforcement
    c) positive punishment
    d) negative punishment

Second, be certain your item requires that a novel example be identified. Item 3, below, is not truly a concept item because it incorporates an example presented during instruction.

3. A rat presses a lever and receives food. Subsequently, the rat presses the lever more often. This is an example of
    a) positive reinforcement
    b) negative reinforcement
    c) positive punishment
    d) negative punishment

Remember that "cosmetic" changes to previously encountered examples are not really novel either. By a cosmetic change, we mean doing something like changing the rat to a mouse, which doesn't really result in a novel example. Strive to create items that vary widely from provided examples.

Item 4 is a concept item that varies widely from provided examples of positive reinforcement because it involves a behavior (hitting) and a stimulus (yelling) considered aversive. Still the item is an example of positive reinforcement because it meets the definition: A behavior occurs, a stimulus is presented, and the behavior increases.

4. Tommy hits his sister Ericka. Mother yells at Tommy for hitting. Tommy, then hits Ericka again. This is an example of
    a) positive reinforcement
    b) negative reinforcement
    c) positive punishment
    d) negative punishment

When creating a practice concept test, remember to mix your items on the test so that their placement does not cue the answer. For instance, don't provide your study partners with a concept test in which the first six items pertain to positive reinforcement and the next six items pertain to negative reinforcement.

When you're answering concept questions that you or your group has generated, flag those items that do not adequately test the concept, such as Items 1 and 3 above. Notice that Item 5 is also a poor item. The example does not fit with any of the operant concepts because it is not clear whether the behavior is increased or decreased. The student who wrote practice Item 5 must not have a clear understanding for operant concepts. Help students who generate faulty practice items by pointing out mistakes.

5. Sally gets all items correct on her spelling test and her teacher gives her M&Ms. This is an example of
   a) positive reinforcement
   b) negative reinforcement
   c) positive punishment
   d) negative punishment

Exercise

Return to your study notes on prejudice and discrimination, and develop concept test items for review.

Practice for Skill Items

What is the solution to this problem: $5 + (8 \times 7) = \square$? Is it 91 or 61? The answer is 61. The correct solution involves multiplying 8 and 7 and adding the product to 5. But how do you know that you should multiply 8 and 7 first, rather than add 5 and 8 first? You know because you learned a **rule** that governs solving all math operations that use parentheses: "Do what is in the parentheses first." Rules are one form of skill knowledge. The application of rules is one type of skill item.

What is the solution to this problem: $2 \frac{2}{3} + 2 \frac{1}{4} = \square$? The solution is $4 \frac{11}{12}$. The correct solution involves applying a **procedure**. The procedure for adding mixed fractions is illustrated in the series of steps shown in Figure 9-6. These same steps are used for adding all mixed fractions.

Procedures, then, are a second form of skill knowledge and the application of procedures is a second type of skill item. The common element in rules and procedures is that they are applicable in a wide range of new situations.

Let's look at some common rules that govern behavior across settings. In conversation do you ask, "John went to the store for who?" or "John went to the store for whom?" Whom is correct according to the rule, "whom should be used in the objective case." The objective case applies when a word is an object of a preposition such as with, for, to, and between. Should you say, "To who will you send it?" or "To whom will you send it?" The same rule governs your behavior: Use whom because it is the object of the preposition to. If you can apply this rule correctly, you should never make a faux pas regardless whom you speak to.

Figure 9–6. *Procedure for Adding Mixed Fractions*

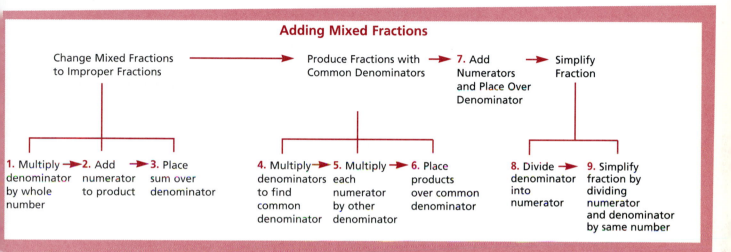

How do you solve this math problem: $7 - {}^-10 = \Box$? The solution is 17. This problem, and others involving the subtraction of a negative number, is easy to solve if you apply the rule "If you are subtracting a negative number, then switch the negatives to positives so you are adding a positive number." If you've acquired this rule you should easily solve this problem as well: ${}^-13 - {}^-13 = \Box$.

Another common rule is the spelling rule "i before e except after c." By applying this rule, you know how to spell tricky words like *receipt* and *receive*.

Rules also help in pronunciation. The "o" in bone is long, because the word ends in "e." The "i" in line is long for the same reason. The rule is that one-syllable words following the form "consonant, vowel, consonant, e," have long vowel sounds and a silent ending "e."

Rules govern all aspects of our lives. The Ten Commandments are a good example of rules.

Several rules should also govern your learning. A few we suggest are listed below.

- If the material is comparative, then generate a matrix.
- If the lecturer speaks too fast, then ask the lecturer to slow down.

- If you are studying for a concept test, then practice identifying novel examples of concepts.
- If you know you're going to have a test months later, then invest early and invest daily.
- If you must remember arbitrary facts, then use mnemonics.
- If you locate topics while reading, then place a box around them.
- If you locate repeatable categories while reading, then circle them.

Notice that all the rules above follow the same form. All are if/then statements. If a certain condition exists (for example, repeatable categories), then you should take a certain course of action (for example, circling repeatable categories).

Identifying the *if* portion of the rule (for example, the rapid lecturer) is recognizing a concept. Thus, you can see that concept identification is an important part of using rules.

Skill knowledge is often more complex than applying single rules. Skill knowledge also requires you to apply a procedure composed of several rules and concepts. The procedure for adding mixed fractions presented in Figure 9-6 involved several rules and concepts. In terms of concepts, the solver must identify whole numbers, numerators, denominators, common denominators, products, and sums. In terms of rules, the solver must apply rules of multiplication, addition, division, finding common denominators, and simplifying. All of these concepts and rules were applied following a strict sequence or procedure.

Consider another mathematical problem: Finding the hypotenuse of a right triangle as in the problem below.

Find the length of the missing side.

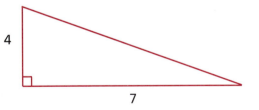

The procedure used to solve this problem involves the following steps comprised of concepts and rules:

1. Identify the figure as a right triangle (concept).
2. Identify the hypotenuse (concept).
3. Identify the length of the given sides (4, 7) (concept).
4. Square the given sides ($4^2=16$, $7^2=49$) (rule).
5. Sum the squares ($16+49=65$) (rule).
6. Find the square root of the summed squares by division ($\sqrt{65} = 8.06$) (rule).

Again, this procedure, known as the Pythagorean Theorem, is applicable for any problem aimed at determining the length of a right triangle's unknown side.

Procedures are most common in math, science, and English courses. In math, a student must apply procedures to solve quadratic equations, determine ratios, compute the area of a triangle, do long division, and calculate percentiles. All of these require procedures. In science, a student must employ experimental methods (for example, state the problem, plan a solution, predict outcomes), balance chemical equations, dissect frogs, compute genetic makeup, and calculate force. All of these require procedures. In English, a student must demonstrate rules for pronunciation, spelling, punctuation, forming plurals, and using the possessive case.

Procedures are very common in math, science, and English courses. But you also need to acquire several procedures for study skills. You must, for example, learn to mark a text, construct a representation, prepare a block schedule, and study for a fact test.

Notice that skill tasks do not involve *knowing* something. They involve *doing* something. In study skills, the student does not state rules for generating representations; the student, given new material, constructs representations.

Often, rules and procedures are not learned in isolation but in families, as was true with facts and concepts. Learning several rules and procedures together is simpler than learning them separately. When they're learned collectively, it is easy to construct internal connections by noting similarities and differences among them. Learning rules and concepts collectively also reduces confusion.

Consider the rule for using commas: "If there is a coordinating conjunction joining main clauses, then use a comma." If you're like most people, you could state this rule (fact knowledge) but not demonstrate it (skill knowledge). You probably couldn't identify a main clause or a coordinating conjunction (concept knowledge). Look what happens, though, when this rule is shown along with the rule for using semicolons, and when both rules are illustrated, as in Figure 9-7.

Although the rule for comma usage is confusing, some confusion is reduced by comparing it to the rule for semicolon use, which appears on the right side of Figure 9-7. The two rules are similar, because both involve two main clauses. The rules are different, because commas are used with coordinating conjunctions and semicolons are used without coordinating conjunctions.

The two rules come into sharper focus when each example is considered relative to its rule (within-topic connections) and relative to each other (across-topic connection). From the examples it is evident that main clauses are sentences in themselves, such as "Paradise was an exclusive country club" and "The gates of hell were open." Coordinating conjunctions are connecting words such as *but* and *while*. Collectively, the rules are easily understood. When two main clauses are joined by a coordinating conjunction, a comma is appropriate. When main clauses are not joined by a coordinating conjunction, then a semicolon is appropriate.

The problem is that rules such as these are usually taught separately, in isolation. We inspected several grammar texts and found that the rules for

Figure 9–7. *Matrix Representation Helpful in Learning a Family of Rules*

	Comma	**Semicolon**
Rule:	If there is a coordinating conjunction joining two main clauses, then use a comma.	If there is not a coordinating conjunction joining two main clauses, then use a semicolon.
Example:	Paradise was an exclusive country club, but the gates of hell were open.	Paradise was an exclusive country club; the gates of hell were open.

internal punctuation, such as commas, semicolons, colons, and dashes were taught over several chapters, rather than collectively. We hope you now recognize the importance of learning facts, concepts, rules, and procedures in families, rather than separately.

The three keys to acquiring skills are practice, practice, and practice. Skills become more accurate, faster, and increasingly automatic the more they are practiced. Chess champions, for example, make fewer errors, play more rapidly, and can play against a dozen or more players simultaneously, because they have internalized chess rules and procedures through years of practice.

The adage that practice makes perfect is almost correct. Perfect practice makes perfect results. Playing chess or playing golf incorrectly results in minimal improvement. Correct practice in chess or golf depends on feedback from an expert chess player or golf pro. Although he hates to admit it, one of this book's authors played golf for sixteen years without instruction.

Practice makes chess skills—and all skills—automatic

His scores hovered around 160 for eighteen holes. Only after a golf pro tinkered with his game—having him grip the club at the proper end, remove head covers before striking the ball, and aim toward the hole rather than playing partners—did his scores fall below 140, thanks to these subtle adjustments.

Learning academic skills also depends on practice and feedback. Therefore you should practice using skills and ask for feedback about your performance. Do so by generating practice problems, sharing problems with study group members, answering the problems, and asking for feedback on the correctness of solutions.

Returning to the material on operant conditioning, procedural items are developed and addressed such as those below.

1. You are a parent concerned that your children are watching too much television. Explain how you might decrease television viewing and increase time spent on homework through the use of operant techniques.
2. As a classroom teacher you notice that many students are handing homework in late and in messy condition. Explain how you might turn this situation around using operant techniques.
3. Using operant conditioning techniques train a dog to offer its paw on command.

By exchanging items with study partners, you're given several opportunities to practice skills in various settings (such as parenting, teaching, and dog training).

Exercise

1. Develop several skill items for you and fellow students to practice on in preparation for a test on this chapter.

2. Suppose that Roger, who was introduced to you in the boxed section at the beginning of this chapter, is a friend of yours. Be a candid and helpful friend by telling Roger each thing he is doing wrong in reviewing for his biology exam. Provide specific alternatives to replace each of his ineffective study behaviors.

Summary

This chapter addresses several important questions about how you should review. It explains that you should review for exams, but also to learn and apply new ideas (why?). It points out that you should review in quiet, isolated areas (where?) during designated time blocks and when brief opportunities arise, such as while waiting for a bus (when?). And it explains that you should review study notes comprised of representations, summaries, and practice questions (what?) both alone and with study partners (with whom?).

The most important question addressed in this chapter is "How do you review?" You must recognize and anticipate three types of test items—fact, concept, and skill—and prepare accordingly for each. Fact items require recognizing or recalling presented facts. Concept items require identifying new examples. Skill items require applying rules or procedures.

Review involves four steps: preparing the content, building internal connections, building external connections (PIE), and conducting test-appropriate practice (TAP). Remember these four steps by remembering PIE TAP. The first three steps are used for any test type. Test-appropriate practice is aimed at preparing for fact, concept, or skill tests.

Prepare the content by developing complete and organized study notes—often by creating representations. Build internal connections by relating information within and across topics. Build external connections by relating information to background knowledge. Do so by generating personal examples and evaluating the merits of presented ideas. Last, conduct test-appropriate practice by generating and answering fact, concept, and skill items. Also use mnemonics—memory tricks—to remember facts.

Answers to focus *questions*

1. You should review for exams, of course, but you should also review to understand and apply worthwhile ideas.
2. The "Lounge Scroungers" hang out in study lounges and distract would-be studiers. Avoid them by studying in quiet out-of-the-way places.
3. You should review early and often in preparation for exams. Cramming is not where it's at. Be prepared for a test at least three days in advance. Studying should ideally be done in extended time blocks during the morning and daytime hours, and also in your spare moments.
4. You should form study groups for each class. They should include between three and five serious members who meet weekly to

exchange and discuss study materials they generate. The group should work cooperatively and dismiss any members who fail to contribute adequately.

5. You should convert lecture and text notes into study notes. Study notes include representations, summaries, and questions and answers. These study materials should be reviewed extensively. Make occasional references to the original lecture or text notes for clarification or additional details.

6. The type of test items are as follows:
   A) skill, B) fact, C) concept, D) fact, E) concept, and F) skill

7. The four review steps are prepare the content, build internal connections, build external connections, and conduct test-appropriate practice.

8. Special things to do when studying facts are to remember that facts are best learned when connected to other facts. To learn facts, generate representations and build internal and external connections. Internal connections are the within- and across-topic relationships found in the representations being reviewed. External connections are relationships made between the new material and past knowledge. In addition, practice for fact tests by generating and answering fact questions and using mnemonics.

9. Definitions and examples are the special keys to studying concepts. Prepare by recording a concept's definition and a wide range of examples and nonexamples. Do not learn a concept separately, however. Represent the definition, examples, and nonexamples for a family of related concepts. Examine the representation and build internal connections within and across concepts. It is especially important to note how concept examples correspond with concept definitions, and how concepts are similar and different. It is also helpful to build external connections—new examples and nonexamples of these concepts. You can easily add these to representations. Finally, practice for concept tests by generating concept items and answering the concept items generated by others.

10. One special key to preparing for a skill test is representing the procedure along with worked examples. Portions of the worked examples appear beneath the corresponding steps in the procedure. Initially practice new problems with the help of this representation, and practice later without assistance.

    It is also helpful to learn and represent skills as a "family." Doing so helps you compare and contrast the skills. Because skills are used under certain circumstances, it is important to employ concept learning strategies to recognize the conditions under which a skill is warranted. Also, practice by generating and answering skill items.

chapter 10
Taking Tests

OVERVIEW

Focus Questions

Introduction

How to Prepare for Tests
   How to Prepare Mentally
   How to Prepare Physically
   How to Prepare Emotionally
      What Is Test Anxiety?
      How Anxiety Can Help
      Causes of Test Anxiety
      How to Cope with Test Anxiety
      How to Defuse Anxiety

Use General Test Strategies

Use Specific Item Strategies
   Use Item-Type Strategies
      Strategies for Answering Fact Items
      Strategies for Answering Concept Items
      Strategies for Answering Skill Items
   Use Item-Form Strategies
      Strategies for Answering Multiple-Choice Items
      Strategies for Answering Matching Items
      Strategies for Answering True/False Items
      Strategies for Answering Short-Answer Items
      Strategies for Answering Essay Items

How to Analyze Test Errors (Error Analysis)

Summary

Answers to Focus Questions

focus questions

1. Generally speaking, where is the best place to sit during an exam?
2. Why are most students test-anxious?
3. Can test anxiety be good?
4. What causes test anxiety?
5. What are some simple ways to defuse test anxiety?
6. Can you list ten general strategies for test-taking?
7. What is meant by item form and item type?
8. Can you match the item types on the left with their examples on the right?

   1. Fact
   2. Concept
   3. Skill

   a) What is the relationship between interest rates and inflation?
   b) Determine the rate of interest if an investment of $1,000.00 grows to $1,200.00 in three months.
   c) The Taylor's house is worth $40,000 more today than five years ago despite making no improvements. This is an example of _____.

9. What are the recommended general strategies for answering fact, concept, and skill items?
10. How should you begin approaching or answering multiple-choice items?
11. What are some guidelines for eliminating alternatives in a multiple-choice item?
12. What are some important strategies for answering matching items?
13. What are some important strategies for answering true/false items?
14. What are some important strategies for answering short-answer items?
15. What five steps should you follow when writing an essay?
16. How important is it to write essay answers neatly?
17. What two things do you learn through error analysis?

Have you had one of those experiences where everything you do is wrong and everything goes wrong? It's like you're hit with Excedrin® headaches seven through twenty-three all at once. Donna had such an experience.

The whole horrible thing began when Donna fumbled with her alarm and dropped right back to sleep. She was nearly comatose from cramming through the night for her psychology test. When she finally woke up she threw on the official college test uniform—sweats and a ball cap—and dashed to the test. There was no time for breakfast.

Donna arrived about ten minutes early. Amid the buzz of independent variables and cognitive theories, she whipped out her notebook and began rereading her notes—a continuation of last night's activities, when she read them nearly thirty times. A panicked student on her left interrupted, inquiring about proactive and retroactive interference.

"What are those?" Donna asked, her voice rising and confidence shrinking.

"Types of forgetting . . . like decay and retrieval-cue failure," shot back a more confident voice from the right. "Decoy cues." The absurd image of a line of fake ducks floated through Donna's mind. "What are decoy cues?" she wailed. "I don't have that stuff in my notes!"

Before anyone could answer Donna, the instructor burst through the door and banged a huge pile of exams on the desk. "Fifty short answers and two essays" he announced in a frosty tone. "You've now got . . . forty-eight minutes."

The instructor's icy directives hit Donna like a slushball in the face. Her brain, having an apparent out-of-body experience, left the room, screaming. "I don't know this stuff . . . I'm going to do terribly . . . I got a C last time, I need an A this time . . . My sorority will place me on probation . . .

My parents will disown me . . ." Donna's body, trapped in its seat, showed signs of anxiety too. Her heart fluttered like a hummingbird's wings, and her throat felt drier than a rain gauge in Arizona.

The test fell to her desk like a hammerblow. The reverberation summoned her brain but accelerated her heart into warp drive and squeezed the last molecule of moisture from her throat. Her pencil bounced as she scribbled her name on the test. At this point she thought, all too prophetically, "It will all be over soon."

To regain some confidence, Donna shot past the directions for Part One and set to work on the first of several multiple-choice items. She read the first item and then read it again, and again, and then again. Donna was stumped. In desperation, Donna selected a term she did not recognize. "This must be right," she hoped. Item two was simpler. Immediately, she recognized that the answer was A. She circled it and read no further, ignoring the preferred answer below it. Donna struggled with items 3 through 5 the way a three-year-old struggles with buttons . . . spending about three minutes on each. As Donna plodded through the remaining multiple-choice items, she found herself guessing at several.

Her confidence almost sunk by the "tricky" multiple-choice items, Donna's spirits began to rise when she spotted the oasis of true/false items before her. Again, she bypassed the directions and dove headlong into the items. The true/false items were a snap, she thought. She sped through them at Warp 7, barely noticing that she marked eight of the ten items "false."

Poised to begin a string of matching items, Donna noticed a low rumbling sound building in the distance and moving closer. She glanced toward the window and blinked at the bright morning sun. "Strange," she thought. Nearby students turned a sharp glance toward Donna. Some covered their ears seeking solace. Donna, having now traced the disturbance to her own tummy, gently rubbed it and wished she had not skipped breakfast. Her mind turned to raisin-studded oatmeal.

Next, Donna skimmed the directions for the matching items. "These should be simple," she reasoned. "I just have to figure which answer goes where." Donna couldn't find a match for the first item. She made her best guess and then wound her way through the matching portion the way Godzilla winds his way through a Japanese city. Donna side-stepped a few tough ones and stumbled over most. In the end, however, she eliminated each answer, leaving no survivors.

Having completed the objective portion of the test, Donna decided not to recheck previous items. She remembered someone once telling her it's best to trust your first impression. Perhaps this advice came from someone selling white carpeting.

Now only twelve minutes remained. Donna reached the essay portion. She noted that each of the two essay items was worth twenty points. "That's almost half the points and you left yourself a lousy twelve minutes!" shouted an obscure portion of Donna's brain, unwilling to share responsibility for falling behind. "We can still do it," the rest of her brain argued weakly, like a dispirited coach whose team trails by forty points at the half.

The first essay question asked for a description of proactive interference and the research studies supporting it. She threw a quick glance to her right and saw the confident student over there writing feverishly. Donna wrote that proactive interference is a type of forgetting different from retroactive interference and decoy cues. A "fact" sure to amuse even her dour instructor. Knowing nothing more about proactive interference, Donna shifted gears and filled the page with personal accounts of forgetting in general. Her showcase example was the time she forgot

to put the lid on the blender while preparing a raspberry margarita.

Four minutes remained, and the room was already two-thirds empty. The last item asked how short- and long-term memory compare and contrast. Donna knew this stuff better than her roommate's sweaters. Quickly she scribbled a list of facts pertaining to short-term memory, then a second list of facts pertaining to long-term memory. "It's nice to end on a high note," Donna reasoned, just before the bell screamed shrilly.

The testing ordeal now finished, Donna left the room feeling pretty good about her performance.

During the next class period, the instructor went over the test, item by item. Donna was absent, preferring to study for her chemistry test later that day. Donna's absence meant that she could only get her grade. By her absence, Donna forfeited any opportunity to receive specific feedback about her performance. This is like experiencing labor and then only seeing the baby's picture. Had Donna attended, she would have learned more than her score, which was a D. For instance, Donna would know that her answer to Item 1 was wrong. The instructor admitted that he occasionally concocted fake terms to distract students. Donna would know that A was not the best answer for Item 2. B was. The instructor reminded students that the directions for multiple-choice items called for the best answer in those cases in which an item could have several correct answers.

Had Donna attended, she would have known that only a handful of students lost points on the true/false items for not correcting fake statements as instructed, and on the matching items for not paying attention to the instructions that an item might be used more than once, or maybe not at all. Donna would also know that the instructor graded essays very hard. Essays filled with personal accounts rather than research evidence received no credit. Even essays that listed facts, but didn't compare and contrast them as directed, were penalized harshly.

Last, Donna would know that the instructor allowed those who attended class that day to attempt a bonus essay worth twenty points.

onna messed up. She was not mentally, physically, or emotionally prepared for the test. Donna's mental preparation was poor. She didn't know the material because she used weak strategies like rereading notes. Physically, she was tired and hungry and thus in a weakened state. Emotionally, she was anxious. She couldn't control her irrational thoughts or her physical stress reactions. Donna also ignored several general test strategies. For instance, she didn't bother to read directions and she mismanaged the time allotted for the exam.

Donna also ignored several item-specific strategies—guidelines for answering different forms of questions (for example, multiple-choice and essay) or type (for example, fact and concept). Donna failed to consider all the possible options for multiple-choice items, or to reconstruct representations when she answered fact items.

And Donna failed to analyze her errors. She never learned what was wrong or where she went wrong. For instance, was her limited knowledge about forgetting a function of ineffective note-taking or poor review? Without error analysis, no student can recognize or correct mistakes.

You've come too far in acquiring sophisticated learning strategies to let your hard work be destroyed by poor test-taking strategies. Test-taking is just another academic area (like time management, note-taking, and review) that you can bring under your control. To help you do this, this chapter covers all aspects of test-taking: preparation, general test strategies, specific item strategies, and error analysis.

How to Prepare for Tests

Eavesdrop on any basketball coach readying her team and you'll hear her harp on three types of preparation. "A winning player," she'll say, "is mentally, physically, and emotionally prepared. Mentally, the winning player knows the plays, the opposition's plays, and what to do in any situation imaginable. Physically, the player has become strong and agile. She's rested and properly warmed up. Emotionally, she is fire under control. There's no stress, only nerve. There's no crack in her confidence."

Test preparation involves the same three components. The winning student is mentally, physically, and emotionally prepared for tests. The student knows her stuff, she's rested and alert, and she's confident she'll do well. She quickly dismisses any negative thoughts and tension if they intrude.

We discuss each type of preparation in turn.

How to Prepare Mentally

If you're mentally prepared, you should perform well on a test despite other factors, such as fatigue, anxiety, and poor test-taking strategies. It's not that test-taking strategies can't improve your test performance—they can—it's that proper test preparation is of uttermost importance. Sound mental preparation makes your tiredness irrelevant, turns your anxiety into energy, and gives you the knowledge that can guide you through any test item type or form.

Students often blame poor test performance on carelessness or anxiety. On closer examination, it's clear their problem stemmed from poor mental preparation. The students simply did not know the material well enough. But being more careful and less anxious aren't going to make much difference if the student's mental preparation is inadequate. In fact, test anxiety, as you'll soon learn, is often the result of inadequate mental preparation. Most students who are test-anxious should be. They are woefully underprepared.

The myriad strategies that result in good mental preparation fill this book's first nine chapters. Here in this chapter, we highlight a few key principles and strategies that prepare you mentally for tests.

1. Invest time, invest it early, and invest it daily. Spend a lot of time studying. Begin studying at the start of the semester and study regularly throughout. Cramming is forbidden. Be fully prepared at least three days before any test.

2. Record complete notes. During lectures and while reading texts, record complete notes that include topics, subtopics, repeatable categories, details, and examples. If it's not noted, you probably won't remember it. Your notebook is your memory's safe deposit box.

3. Organize notes spatially. Lists, outlines, and paragraphs obscure relations and represent information in a piecemeal fashion. Whenever possible, organize notes spatially. Use hierarchies, sequences, matrices, diagrams, maps, and graphs so that relations are apparent.

4. Build connections. Learning involves connecting new ideas to one another and to ideas you learned previously. Build connections by searching out representations for relations and patterns. Search for hierarchical and sequential relations. Determine how things are similar and how they are different.

5. Practice in a test-appropriate way. Prepare for fact items by building connections and using mnemonics to remember details. Prepare for concept items by studying a concept's definition, range of examples, and nonexamples. Prepare for skill items by practicing the procedural steps in worked problems. In all cases, learn facts, concepts, and skills in families. Generate and answer practice questions.

6. Study in a group. Share study materials and test items with other serious students. Doing so improves your test performance, makes studying more fun, and provides a reliable gauge for measuring test readiness. Group members test each other so thoroughly that there is nothing the instructor can ask them that they haven't already asked each other.

> Proper test preparation is of uttermost importance.

7.   Hurdle barriers. There are bound to be problems. Illness, early class-es, large classes, boring instructors, visiting relatives, missed rides, and lousy moods creep into every college student's life from time to time. Recognize that these barriers are surmountable. Rather than roll over and play dead, devise a solution to any problem that arises. When classes are too early, for example, go to bed earlier, exercise in the morning, or take afternoon naps. Whoever, whatever the enemy, defeat it.

How to Prepare Physically

You're not swimming the English Channel, running the Boston Marathon, or riding a bike in the Tour de France. You're only taking a test. Still, physi-cal preparation is important to success. Some suggestions are on the next page.

Exercise

Below is a checklist based on the PIE TAP model for review, which we presented in Chapter 9. Use this checklist as a gauge to deter-mine if you are prepared mentally for an upcoming test.

Prepare the Content
    Study notes contain important terms
    Study notes contain definitions
    Study notes contain examples
    Study notes contain details
    Study notes are well-organized, using representations
Build Internal Connections
    Build hierarchical relations
    Build sequential relations
    Build coordinate relations (compare and contrast topics)
Build External Connections
    Relate to past knowledge and experiences
    Develop new examples
    Evaluate ideas
Conduct Test-Appropriate Practice
    Develop and answer fact questions
    Develop and answer concept questions
    Develop and answer skill questions
    Develop mnemonics

1. **Get a good night's rest.** Tiredness diminishes the brain's performance. When you're tired, it is more difficult to concentrate, read with comprehension, perform mathematical calculations, or organize your thoughts. One author knows the relationship between fatigue and mental ability firsthand: In the early stages of a marathon, he can easily calculate his pace and projected times for any mile forthcoming. In the latter stages of a marathon, he can scarcely add whole minutes to his present time.

2. **Eat properly.** When your blood sugar level drops, so does your concentration. When your tummy is empty it writhes and groans, drawing your attention away from the test. Pacify your stomach before the test by eating a nourishing snack or a good meal about an hour beforehand. Avoid sweets like soda, candy, and cake, which provide a surge of energy and soon shortcircuit like a string of Christmas lights with a bad bulb. Choose grains, fruits, vegetables, and especially proteins (such as meats and cheeses), all of which have proven staying power.

3. **Exercise beforehand.** Light exercise relaxes you and relieves stress. It also wakes up your brain and readies it for the test. One author jogs before big presentations. While he runs, he mentally delivers his talk and envisions himself presenting it successfully. Several world chess champions, such as Bobby Fischer, rely on daily exercise to help play their best.

4. **Choose a good seat.** Part of physical preparation is sitting in a comfortable seat in a location that's relatively free from distractions. In a test environment, every sound is amplified, every movement exaggerated. A sniffle sounds like a shop vac, a blown nose like a tuba. Students packing up and leaving early take on the proportions of floats in the Macy's Thanksgiving Day Parade.

   Remember, the best seat for lectures is front and center. That's not a bad location for testing—but you can do better. We recommend a seat away from other students (whenever possible), along a side wall, and away from the door. In Figure 10-1, the optimal seats are designated with Xs. If possible, angle your seat toward the wall to further block distractions.

   Beware, however, of test circumstances that might dictate that you choose another seat. For example, if the proctor invites students to come forward, either with questions or to turn in exams, a seat near the proctor is one that will be chockful of distractions. Exam proctors should (although they don't always) arrange a test environment nearly distraction-free. If you are distracted by gum-chewers, questioners, test completers, or the proctor's conversations, then voice your concern to the proctor and request assistance.

CHOOSE A QUIET SEAT AWAY FROM DISTRACTIONS WHEN TAKING A TEST

Figure 10–1. *Typical Seating Plan. Seats Relatively Free from Distractions Are Marked with X.*

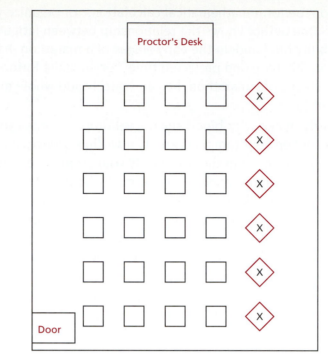

5. **Have necessary materials available.** Have plenty of pencils and pens with you. You need pencils for marking computer sheets or figuring math problems and pens for writing essay responses, and you definitely don't want to be slowed down by a broken pencil or a pen whose ink supply runs out in the middle of the test. Take along scrap paper, too.

   Know in advance what other supplies are required or recommended, such as "blue books" for essay responses, a calculator, ruler, compass, protractor, or dictionary. If the test is an open-book exam, then have all allowable reference materials available and clearly marked for easy access. Finally, wear a watch to monitor the time. Not all classrooms have clocks that work.

How to Prepare Emotionally

"We experience moments absolutely free from worry. These brief respites are called panic."

—Cullen Hightower

Do you shiver at the mention of a test and quake when you take one? When you're taking a test, do your hands tremble, teeth chatter, and head sweat as if you gulped a jalapeno pepper? Do you encounter mental blocks, surges of panic, or waves of self-doubt? If you experience any of these symptoms, you might have test anxiety.

Exercise

This exercise demonstrates the bad effects of being tired and the refreshing effects of exercise.

Below are two problems, each of which has three parts. Attempt one problem when you are mentally exhausted. For example, following a marathon study session, after completing your tax return, or after "reasoning" with your 2-year-old. After you complete the first problem, take a brisk walk outside or do some physical exercise for at least twenty minutes. Then try the second problem.

When you do the problems, do them in your head without writing down your answers. After you complete part one of each problem, cover that part so that you don't refer to it when you're trying the other parts. Time it to see how long it takes you to complete each problem successfully.

Our prediction is that mental fatigue will slow down your mental calculations, and moderate exercise will "clear" your brain while you carry out the calculations. The results should show you that a "clear" mind is important for classroom learning, studying, and test taking.

Problem 1

Joan runs the first five miles of a thirteen-mile race in 27:45. What is her pace per mile?

Joan maintains this pace for each of the next three miles. What is her time at the eight-mile mark?

Joan hopes to run a faster pace over the last five miles of the race. She hopes to run each of the last five miles four seconds faster than the mile before it. How fast will she run the last five miles?

Problem 2

Greta runs the first five miles of a thirteen-mile race in 26:05. What is her pace per mile?

Greta maintains this pace for each of the next three miles. What is her time at the eight-mile mark?

Greta hopes to run a faster pace over the last five miles of the race. She hopes to run each of the last five miles six seconds faster than the mile before it. How fast will she run the last five miles?

What Is Test Anxiety?

Test anxiety is a physiological reaction to test situations. The anxious reaction manifests itself in many ways, including: accelerated heart rate, heavy breathing, blinking, teeth grinding, sweating, fainting, confusion, mental blocks, panic, headaches, crying, and upset stomach. However, in our combined forty-plus years of college teaching, we've observed fewer than five classic cases of test anxiety. In classic cases, the anxiety stems from a gen-

IN THE GRIP OF TEST ANXIETY

uine fear of tests. Any test, *all* tests, produce anxiety, even for top students. Most students experience "restricted" test anxiety: Their anxiousness appears only when they are unprepared for a test.

The milder forms of anxiety that most students feel—the sweaty palms, butterflies, occasional goose bumps, and the like—are not all bad. It is natural to be nervous before important events—be they tests, a trumpet solo, or a marriage proposal. Some nervousness is your body's way of warming for the task ahead.

How Anxiety Can Help

Performance is better at moderate anxiety levels than at low or high anxiety levels, as you can see in Figure 10-2.

For example, imagine having dinner with your roommate. Your anxiety level is so low that you might doze off in your pizza. Conversationally, you're not at your best. Next, suppose you're having dinner with the President and First Lady. Your anxiety might be so high that you become tongue-tied and so flustered that you begin eating your soup with a fork. Conversationally, you're far from your best. Now, suppose that you're having dinner with your coach, minister, or favorite instructor. You'd probably display a moderate degree of anxiety that would probably result in stimulating dinner conversation and appropriate utensil selection.

One prize example of anxiety's effect is the time students were taking the Scholastic Aptitude Test when a hurricane hit the testing site. Anxiety levels rocketed upward as test-takers worried about their homes, transportation arrangements, and loved ones. Examiners figured they might have to throw out the results, given the anxiety-producing conditions. But what happened was that test scores were significantly above average. The increased anxiety apparently improved performance. This incident suggests that moderate anxiety is good, and that students should invite rather than squelch moderate anxiety levels.

Figure 10–2. *The Relationship Between Anxiety and Performance*

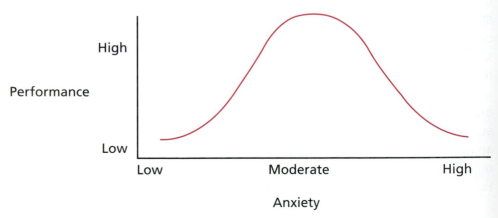

Causes of Test Anxiety

As we've indicated, most test anxiety is caused by unpreparedness. Students who aren't mentally prepared for a test are naturally anxious. Such anxiety can cripple a student already disabled by inadequate test preparation.

Schools often manufacture test anxiety. They do so by instilling needless student competition, penalizing poor performance, and publicizing grades. One author had a teacher who raised test anxiety to new heights. Following a test, the instructor returned tests in descending order, from high score to low score. The instructor called the student's name, publicly announced his test score, and then reseated him accordingly. High scorers sat toward the front; low scorers toward the back. What was meant to motivate only ridiculed. When negative events, like ridicule or failure, are paired with tests, students naturally become anxious when faced with future tests.

When students assume a mastery approach to learning, test anxiety ceases to be an issue. Students who master a domain and satisfy personal curiosity aren't anxious. For example, if your forte is photography, are you anxious when you read a book about photography or later share your photographs with others? Of course not. A mastery approach is one way to handle test anxiety. Other coping methods are described below.

How to Cope with Test Anxiety

Since most test anxiety is the result of unpreparedness, the best solution is to overprepare. Know the information forward, backward, and sideways. Master the information at least three days before the test. Think about the test as "showtime," a time to show off how much you know.

Because your test anxiety can also come from associating tests with bad, or merely negative, experiences, you can lessen your anxiety by associating tests with positive events. The best way to create a positive event is to prepare thoroughly for, and succeed on, the test. Now, positive events, such as a high score, and praise from your teacher and fellow students, plus your personal satisfaction, and increased knowledge, replace your negative associations with tests.

A less direct method for replacing the negative events with positive events happens through practice testing. Prepare practice tests with study group members. Practice taking the tests under authentic conditions. For instance, work under a time limit and without reference materials. Intersperse the tests throughout your review sessions during the ten days preceding the test. Continue the practice tests until you achieve repeated high scores. The success you'll achieve under these simulated conditions will replace the negative associations of past test experiences.

Another indirect method you can use for associating tests with positive experiences occurs through visualization. Imagine mildly anxious events, such as having a test announced in class, to severely anxious events, such as not understanding a test question. Replace your panicked reactions with rational reactions by imagining yourself handling the situation confidently. For instance, when there's a test announcement, imagine yourself jotting down the date on your calendar and arranging a study plan that leads up to that day. For a question that you don't understand, imagine seeking assistance from the instructor, calmly rereading the question a second time, or temporarily skipping the item and answering several other items with ease, then returning to the skipped question and answering it successfully. You've used mental imagery to overcome the fear of other things—spiders, snakes, heights, confined places, maybe?—and now, tests. In each case, you replace irrational anxious reactions with the vision of a rational and positive reaction. By practicing the vision, the vision soon becomes the reality.

How to Defuse Anxiety

When anxiety does occur before or during tests, there are several sure-fire ways to defuse it. Find the way or ways that work best for you.

1. **Exercise.** Nothing works as well as regular exercise in keeping anxiety levels low. One author reports that his brain buzzes like a high-tension wire at the end of the day . . . "I have to do this . . . I have to do that." Following his evening run, the buzzing is nothing more than a faint hum.

2. **Take a deep breath.** Deep breaths are anxiety's circuit breaker. When you feel stressed, take a few long, slow, deep breaths, and you'll find you've cut anxiety's power.

3. **Tense and relax a couple of times or more.** Anxiety tightens muscles. Show anxiety that its stranglehold on you is weak. Tense affected muscles even more, relax, and feel anxiety release its grip.

4. **Escape to a better place.** The test situation is making you nervous. Take a brief escape. Just for a minute, imagine yourself in your favorite safe, calm place. Maybe you're strolling along the water's edge at your favorite beach on a cool fall morning, or watching the sun set on the ocean, or reclining in your easy chair in front of a roaring fire. Go there, sit a spell, and come back refreshed and ready to work.

5. **Maintain your perspective.** Keep things in perspective. A test is not a matter of life or death. Ask yourself, "What's the worst that can happen?" Be positive. Think to yourself, "I'm healthy and happy and this test result won't change that. I'll do the best I can now and do better next time."

Do keep things in perspective. It's only a test not a broken leg, lost job, sick baby, or leaking water heater. And, hey, even those things are manageable.

Use General Test Strategies

In this section, we give you ten general test strategies that are useful for all kinds of tests.

1. **Preview the test.** Don't jump into a test before you check the number of items and their point values. Leaf quickly through the test and determine the number of test items and their associated point values.

Exercise

Try practicing the deep breathing and muscle-tightening anxiety defusers. First, imagine a stressful test situation:

> You arrive late for class and the other students are already hard at work on the test. You glance at the test, expecting to see multiple-choice questions. Instead, you see a single essay. You read it quickly. The question is long, contains many parts, and is confusing. You notice unfamiliar terms. You begin to panic.

Deep Breathing

The purpose of breathing is to get refreshing oxygen into the body. When most people breathe deeply, they expand their chests and lift their shoulders and gulp in great quantities of air. This sort of breathing is inefficient. It's also not relaxing.

Instead, follow these steps for relaxed breathing.

1. Gently blow all the air from your lungs.
2. With your hand across your tummy, inhale gently through your nose as you silently count to four. Feel your tummy expand like a balloon slowly filling with air.
3. Gently exhale most of the air from your lungs. With your hand still gently resting on your tummy, feel your tummy deflate.
4. Slowly repeat the inhaling and exhaling sequence four or five times. Concentrate on the warm relaxing air flowing in and moving throughout your body.

Muscle Tightening

When you're stressed, your body secretes hormones that mobilize your muscles to face a threat. The threat can be real, such as a barking, snapping dog charging at you, or imagined, such as fear or worry about a test.

Turn your muscles off when you don't need them. Do you leave your car running in the parking lot while you're at a movie? Of course not. You turn the engine off and let it rest. When you turn off your muscles when they're not needed you relieve anxiety.

Much of the tension people carry is visible in their faces, necks, and shoulders. Those lines along your forehead and around your eyes are largely the result of tense muscles. Try isolating certain muscles, such as those needed to raise your eyebrows, squint your eyes, clench your teeth, and raise your shoulders.

Deliberately tighten a muscle for a few seconds and then release the tension. Feel the tension drain from the muscle. Feel relaxation sweep over you as you shut the muscle off and let it rest.

Do this when you feel anxious about a test or another matter.

For instance, you might note that there are forty recognition items (multiple-choice, matching, and true/false), each worth two points, and two essay items, each worth ten points.

Quickly check the page numbers as well. Look to see if any are missing. Clerical errors are not uncommon when multiple pages are copied and collated.

2. **Establish a plan**. Once you've established the number of items and their point values, you should sketch out a time plan for answering the test. This prevents you from mismanaging the allotted time and not completing the test. For instance, suppose the test contained forty recognition items (worth eighty points) and two essay items (worth ten points each), and the allotted test time was one hour. You might plan to spend about thirty minutes on the recognition items (an average of forty-five seconds per item), about twenty minutes on the essays (an average of ten minutes per item), and the final ten minutes reviewing your answers.

But suppose point weights were switched, and the forty recognition items were worth a total of forty points, while the two essays were worth sixty points. In a test with point weights like this, you might plan on spending less time on the recognition items (perhaps twenty minutes) and more time on the essays (maybe thirty-five minutes), and leave only five minutes for review.

You'll find it's very helpful to jot down the estimated time allotment for each test section (for example, "twenty minutes") or the time you anticipate beginning each section (for instance, "10:15"). You don't need to recalculate or reconsider these time notations, once you've recorded them alongside the test sections. This minimizes your time worries and focuses your concentration solely on the test.

One last planning tip: If possible, answer recognition items (such as multiple-choice, true/false, and matching) before essay items. Recognition items are generally easier, because they usually provide the correct answer and are answered rapidly. You boost your confidence when you get off to a quick, positive start. Furthermore, recognition items might provide you with clues for answering essay items later.

3. **Read instructions carefully**. Have you ever waited in a line at the supermarket, checkbook in hand, only to find you had to change lines because you failed to read the sign indicating "cash purchases only"? The point is, don't make costly mistakes by not reading test instructions.

Instructors have tremendous latitude in the way they construct tests. They can, for example, twist conventional items. They can make up multiple-choice questions that require more than one correct answer, or true/false items that require you to correct false statements. A matching item might specify that alternatives are reusable. Directions for essay items might specify that you answer only one of the two items. General instructions might indicate a penalty for incorrect responses.

Read all test instructions carefully. If you're not sure how to proceed, then immediately ask the instructor for clarification. Misunderstanding directions can leave you in line for failure.

4. **Answer easy items first.** Think of a test more as a buffet table than a seven-course meal. You don't have to begin with Item 1 and continue with succeeding items until you're finished. You can start wherever you want to, then proceed to another item, and return to any item any time until all are finished.

We recommend starting with a section you're comfortable with (perhaps multiple-choice questions) and then moving onto another section (perhaps matching). In each test section, answer the easy items—the ones you're sure about—first. Don't struggle too long with tough items on the first pass—come back to them again later. Struggling with difficult items at the start dampens your confidence, piques your anxiety, and consumes valuable time you can spend better on accruing points by answering easier items.

For difficult questions, eliminate alternatives that you know are wrong (for example, choices D and E) by marking them with an X; indicate what you believe is the best response (for example, letter A); and finally, mark the item with an asterisk as a signal that the item be reworked later.

5. **Make notes on the test.** This can really help you. However, some instructors don't allow students to write on exams. They prefer to keep exam books clean and reusable. Although this practice is environmentally sound, it is not educationally sound, unless instructors let you make notes on another sheet of paper. Determine your instructor's policy well in advance of the test. Convince instructors who prohibit note-making that such notes are helpful. You can give them the following reasons:

As we've already mentioned, it is helpful to mark incorrect choices with an X and to mark difficult items with an asterisk to ensure that you rework those items later. You can also mark test questions in other ways, such as circling key words in the question and placing a checkmark alongside possible answers.

A second reason for making test notes is to help you interpret questions and formulate answers. Consider the item below from a psychology exam.

A man has the new telephone number, 436–1382. His telephone number last year was 436–7142. When asked his new telephone number, the man responds "436–1342." The man's error is best attributed to _____.

There are several notes you can make that will help you to answer this item. First, organize the information given in the question. The

USE TEST-TAKING STRATEGIES TO GET THROUGH THE TEST EFFICIENTLY

notes appearing in Figure 10-3 do just that. It is evident from Figure 10-3 that the man is recalling part of his old telephone number in place of his new telephone number.

Figure 10–3. *Notes for interpreting a test item*

Old number:	436-71 42
New number:	436-13 82
Misrecalled number:	436-13 42

Next, this occurrence must be classified. Working this test item, you should recall that there are two types of interference that might cause the recall error: proactive and retroactive. Because these two types of interference are so similar, it helps to note their differences on the test paper, as shown in Figure 10-4, before determining which is at work.

Figure 10–4. *Noted Information Helpful in Answering a Test Item*

| Proactive interference: | Learn A | Learn B | A interferes with B |
| Retroactive interference: | Learn A | Learn B | B interferes with A |

Having recalled and noted the information found in Figure 10-4, you now compare this information with the noted example found in Figure 10-3 and determine that the test item was an example of proactive interference. Although it is possible to solve this problem in your head, given the limitations of short-term memory, you benefit greatly by noting these ideas on paper. A great deal of thinking occurs during a test, and there is no greater thinking tool than the pen.

6. **Use clues from other items**. Expert test constructors make certain that clues for answering a test item are not found in other items—but most instructors aren't expert test constructors. Consequently, they occasionally reveal the answers to some items in other items.

   For example, consider the question in the previous section about the man who misremembers his phone number. Now, suppose that a test-taker is uncertain whether the question is an example of proactive or retroactive interference. Does the related essay item below provide a clue?

   Explain why Ebbinghaus's declining memory performance on subsequent lists was an example of proactive interference.

It sure does! The essay item confirms that proactive interference occurs when previous information interferes with learning new information—as was true with the man whose previous phone number interfered with his learning a new one.

   Tests not only *request* a wealth of information, they *provide* a wealth of information. Keep your eyes open for ideas that help you to answer other items.

If you have a question—or fifty questions—during a test, ask them

7. **Ask questions.** Just as you should ask for clarification during lectures by raising questions, do the same during exams. Remember that instructors test you to measure your knowledge. They're trying to get an accurate measurement. They aren't trying to trick you or to have you perform at less than your best. Instructors are therefore willing to answer questions that are intended to clarify the test items.

Now is your chance. If you have a question—or fifty questions!—during the test, ask them. When students approach instructors after exams complaining that they didn't understand a term or a question, instructors can only tell them they should have asked for clarification at that time.

What kinds of questions should be raised during a test? Certainly any questions to do with directions. Given a matching item without instructions, for example, ask whether responses are used more than once, only once, or not at all.

Ask about words you don't know. Don't be embarrassed to admit that you don't know a word's meaning. If the word is not a unit vocabulary word, then the instructor will certainly tell you its meaning.

It is also acceptable to ask how you should interpret a question. Suppose an essay item directs you to compare the political problems faced by Presidents Nixon and Clinton. You might wonder whether problems faced prior to their presidencies can be compared. Further, you might be uncertain whether legal and personal problems qualify as political problems. Don't hesitate to ask your instructors these and other questions.

8. **"Retake" the test.** After working through the entire test once, return to those items you were either unable to answer confidently (those with asterisks), or couldn't answer at all. Having completed the remainder of the exam, you can revisit those items with greater confidence, less anxiety, and perhaps enhanced knowledge from reading or answering other items. Be certain to answer all items, even if you're uncertain of the answer. You receive no credit for leaving an answer blank.

   After completing the difficult items, "retake" as much of the exam as time permits. Don't just check your work by rereading questions and answers. Cover your answers and try to answer each question anew. When you only read something, particularly something you've written, it seems correct even when it's wrong. Consider the two statements below.

   1. Jamie has an extended vocabulary.
   2. Moses brought two of every type of animal on the Ark.

   Sentence one is incorrect because the word *extended* should be replaced by *extensive*. People have *extensive*, not *extended* vocabularies. Sentence two is wrong because it was Noah, not Moses, who led animals onto the Ark. People are not likely to catch their own errors. That's why it's a good idea to have others proofread our work.

   During a test, this is not possible. Therefore, a smart test-taker covers his or her answers and retakes the exam as if taking it for the first time. Errors that might have gone unnoticed are more likely recognized when the test is "retaken."

   Remember, too, that reading and answering other exam questions can activate knowledge in memory that wasn't accessible the first time you answered an item. With this new-found knowledge and the clues you've gathered from other items, you are now better prepared to respond.

9. **Change answers.** Whoever said, "Trust your first response" was *not* talking about test-taking. There is no reason to trust your first inclination. Don't trust your first inclination, trust the *correct* inclination. If you believe that your revised answer is more accurate, then change your answer. Again, you're probably more relaxed and knowledgeable later in the testing process than you were earlier. Research supports the idea of changing answers, because it has determined that the majority of changed answers are correct.

10. **Use all the allotted time.** Use all the time allotted for the test. Students who "retake" the exam once or twice, as suggested, require considerable time. Tests are important and it's best to do a thorough and careful job, rather than run off ten minutes early to grab a soda or commiserate with other students about the test. Our own experience suggests that students can avoid careless errors, such as misreading instructions, leaving items blank, and confusing similar terms, by taking their time.

When the allotted time is insufficient, ask for more time. Many instructors allow you an additional five or ten minutes to complete the exam before the next class begins. If this additional time still isn't sufficient, ask if you might accompany the instructor to her office to complete the exam there.

If you have a history of not completing exams in the allotted time, you should speak to the instructor in advance, explain your problem, and ask for additional time. Many instructors permit students who are anxious, learning disabled, or slow readers to complete the exam outside the scheduled test session. But you won't know and your instructor won't be able to help you unless you ask.

Don't rush when taking tests; "retake" the test and use the entire time

Exercise

Given the following test information, establish a plan for how you might spend your time taking each test.

History Test (thirty-minute time limit)
- ten multiple-choice items (fifty points)
- one essay (fifty points)

Sociology Test (one-hour time limit)
- forty short answer questions (eighty points)
- two essays (twenty points)

Biology Test (fifty-minute time limit)
- ten true/false items (twenty points)
- ten multiple-choice items (thirty points)
- 10 short-answer items (forty points)
- one essay (ten points)

Exercise

Below are three test items. Make notes on or below the items that help you interpret and answer the questions.

1. Soda sells for $3.18 a six-pack at Jack's. This is six cents less per six-pack than soda at Pat's. How much do four six-packs cost at Pat's?

2. Jay took Chemistry I during the first semester and Chemistry II during the second semester. Fay never took Chemistry I but took Chemistry II second semester. To the chemistry teacher's surprise, Fay outperformed Jay in Chemistry II. Jay often confused information from the two chemistry classes. Jay's relatively poor performance in Chemistry II is most likely due to:
   a) decay
   b) retroactive interference
   c) mental lapses
   d) proactive interference

3. Maggie is taller than Archie but shorter than Sammie. Mabel is taller than Maggie but shorter than Sammie. Sammie is taller than Ned. Ned is taller than Archie. Who is third tallest?

Use Specific Item Strategies

Test items are categorized by both their type (fact, concept, and skill) and form (for example, multiple-choice, matching, short-answer, and essay). For instance, an item might be concept and matching, or fact and essay. Although there is some relationship between item type and form—for example, many concept items are multiple-choice and many fact items are short-answer—any item form can be used to test any item type. For this reason, it's a wise idea to partition item strategies by both type and form. First, strategies are presented for item types, then for item forms.

Use Item-Type Strategies

Benefiting from item-type strategies requires that you first identify the types of items on a test. Recall from Chapter 9 that *fact items* request previously learned information; *concept items* require the classification of new examples; *skill items* require the application of rules or procedures to solve new problems.

Below are several test questions. Some stem from material presented throughout this book. Classify each item as fact, concept, or skill.

1. Ted blows bubbles in his soda through a straw. His mother yells at him to stop. Ted stops blowing bubbles. What operant technique is displayed?

2. What type of lips do white rhinos have?

3. When a presented stimulus increases a behavior, what operant technique is functioning?

4. Mrs. Lowgrade gave her ostrich reading group a test and got these scores: 18, 22, 40, 12, and 8. Calculate the group's mean.

5. An agent gets work and notoriety for the client while the agent gains wealth and notoriety. Loosely speaking, what symbiotic relationship is occurring?

6. Two train stations are fifty miles apart. At 1 P.M. on Sunday a train pulls out from each of the stations and the trains start toward one another. Just as the trains pull out from their stations, a hawk flies into the air in front of the first train and flies ahead to the front of the second train. When the hawk reaches the second train, it turns around and flies toward the first train. The hawk continues in this way until the trains meet. Assume that both trains travel at the speed of twenty-five miles per hour and that the hawk flies at a constant speed of a hundred miles per hour. How many miles will the hawk have flown by the time the trains meet?

Items 2 and 3 are fact items. You must recall the type of lips white rhinos have (Item 2) and recognize the definition of positive reinforcement (Item 3). Items 1 and 5 are concept items. You must recognize novel examples of positive punishment (Item 1) and mutualism, a form of symbiosis, (Item 5). Items 4 and 6 are skill items. You must apply the procedures for calculating the mean (Item 4) and calculating distance in a distance, rate, and time problem (Item 6).

Strategies for Answering Fact Items

Fact items require the recall or recognition of learned information. Too often, students mistakenly answer a question other than the one asked.

Thus, your first step in answering fact items is to determine what information is sought or requested. Do this by circling key words in the item. Circle the words that signify the item's request. In Item 2, circle the words *lips* and *white rhino* because the item requests this information.

Next, use the key words as cues to retrieve the requested information from memory. Search your memory for details about white rhinos and lips. Your search is simple if you originally learned the information in an organized form. Ideally, you should recall a matrix representation that includes the topic, white rhino, and the repeatable category, *lips*, as shown in Figure 10-5.

When you have a tough time retrieving the answer, conduct a more thorough and systematic memory search by re-creating a more complete representation that includes related topics, repeatable categories, and details. For example, if you're trying to recall details about the lips of white rhinos, re-create the matrix representation originally constructed during learning. Compare the topics, white and black rhinos, in terms of the repeatable categories lips, food, and habitat, as shown in Figure 10-6.

Because of the many relations across and within topics, Figure 10-6 should aid your recall. You perhaps remember that a rhino's habitat, food, and lips are related. Black rhinos eat twigs with hooked lips perfect for grasping the twigs that are prevalent in jungles. White rhinos have square lips that are ideal for grazing in the grassland prevalent in their habitat.

Figure 10–5. *Portion of Representation Recalled to Answer Fact Items About Rhinos*

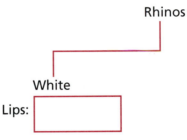

Figure 10–6. *Larger Portion of Representation Recalled to Answer Fact Item About Rhinos*

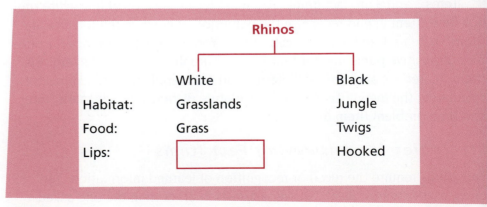

For Item 3, use the same strategies. First, circle the key words *presented stimulus* and *increases behavior*. These are the details associated with the requested operant technique. Next, search your memory for the operant technique that involves a presented stimulus and increased behavior. Follow this with a more systematic search to confirm or produce the operant technique.

Re-create the representation that displays the family of operant techniques, as shown in Figure 10-7. This representation confirms that the definition in Item 3 corresponds to positive reinforcement. It is especially wise to generate the representation in Figure 10-7 if there are several test items pertaining to operant techniques. Referring to the representation reduces the possibility of confusion, increases your accuracy, and speeds your responses.

Figure 10–7. *Representation Used to Answer Fact and Concept Items About Operant Techniques*

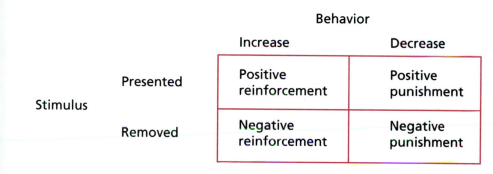

Operant Techniques

		Behavior	
		Increase	Decrease
Stimulus	Presented	Positive reinforcement	Positive punishment
	Removed	Negative reinforcement	Negative punishment

Strategies for Answering Concept Items

Concept items require you to classify novel examples. Circling key words and recreating representations help you answer concept items.

First, circle key words. In concept items, the key words exemplify the concept's attributes (or definition). In Item 1, for example, the key words are *blows bubbles, mother yells,* and *stops blowing bubbles.*

Next, determine what concept attributes are exemplified. In this case, blowing bubbles is a *behavior*. Mother yelling is a *presented stimulus*. And stopping bubble blowing is a *decreased behavior*.

Then re-create representations that help you categorize these attributes. Two such representations are found in Figures 10-7 and 10-8. Figure 10-7 confirms that a presented stimulus resulting in decreased behavior is termed *positive punishment*. Figure 10-8 confirms this information by presenting positive punishment's definition and an example comparable to the one presented in Item 1.

Concept Item 5 is approached the same way. The key words *gets* and *gains*, and *agent* and *client* are circled. You determine that the *client* and agent are, loosely speaking, the organisms, and that *gets* and *gains* indicate that

Figure 10–8. *Representation Used to Answer Concept Item About Positive Punishment*

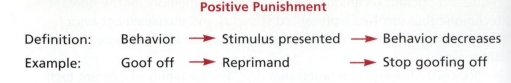

Positive Punishment

Definition: Behavior ⟶ Stimulus presented ⟶ Behavior decreases

Example: Goof off ⟶ Reprimand ⟶ Stop goofing off

both "organisms" benefit from the relationship. Represent this relationship as shown in Figure 10-9. Then compare it with the three types of symbiotic relationships shown in the recreated representation in Figure 10-10. This comparison confirms that the example in Item 5 is one of mutualism.

Figure 10–9. *Representation of Concept Item for Symbiosis*

Agent (+) ⟷ Client (+)

Figure 10–10. *Recreated Symbiosis Representation for Answering Concept Item*

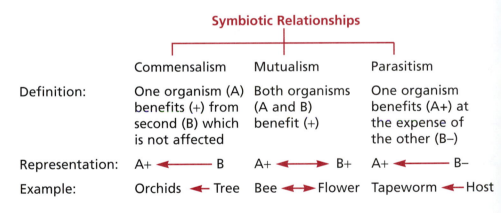

Symbiotic Relationships

	Commensalism	Mutualism	Parasitism
Definition:	One organism (A) benefits (+) from second (B) which is not affected	Both organisms (A and B) benefit (+)	One organism benefits (A+) at the expense of the other (B–)
Representation:	A+ ⟵ B	A+ ⟷ B+	A+ ⟵ B–
Example:	Orchids ⟵ Tree	Bee ⟷ Flower	Tapeworm ⟵ Host

Strategies for Answering Skill Items

Skill items require you to apply rules or procedures to solve a novel problem. As was true with fact and concept items, circling key words and generating representations is helpful for answering skill items. Key words include the request made and the information necessary to respond. In Item 4, for instance, the request is to *calculate the mean*. The information needed is the five test scores. Circle these key words.

Next, recall the formula for calculating the mean and represent it. Recall that the formula is a) sum the scores, and b) divide the sum by the number of scores. Next, calculate the mean below the represented formula, as shown in Figure 10-11. Working beneath the represented formula improves your accuracy.

Figure 10–11. *Representation Used for Calculating the Mean in Skill Item*

Calculating the Mean

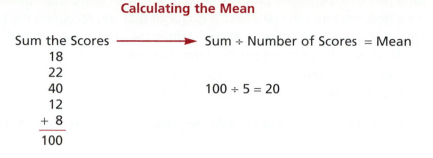

Sum the Scores ———————→ Sum ÷ Number of Scores = Mean

```
  18
  22
  40
  12
+  8
─────
 100
```

$$100 \div 5 = 20$$

Item 6 looks sickeningly difficult. Did you get queasy just reading it? Apply the recommended prescription for answering skill items and you'll see how easy the problem really is. The item requests the total number of miles the hawk flies, so first you circle the key word *miles* in the last sentence. Also circle the relevant information contained in the problem: two trains, fifty miles apart, twenty-five mph for the trains, and a hundred mph for the hawk. At this point, you might sketch a diagram like that in Figure 10-12 to represent the relationships among the variables (that is, hawk, trains, speed, and distance).

Figure 10–12. *Diagram Showing Relationships Among Hawk, Trains, Speed, and Distance for Skill Problem*

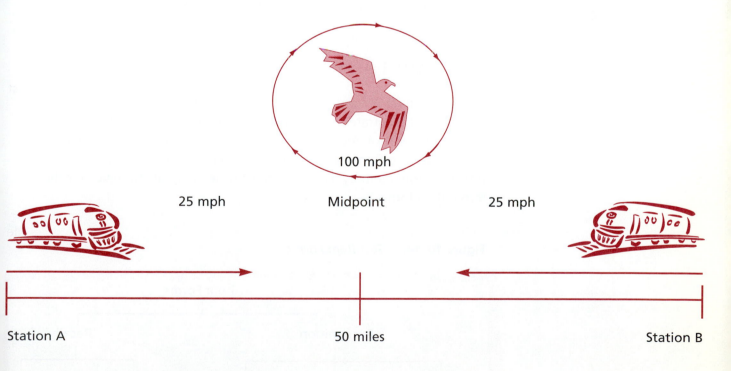

Next, classify the problem. What sort of problem is it? For instance, is it a ratio problem, perimeter problem, area problem, or percentage problem. No, it's a distance/rate/time problem. It is crucial that you recognize the problem type. If you don't, you cannot possibly apply the appropriate procedure.

Next, recall and represent the formula for solving distance/rate/time problems. Then plug in the given information under this formula for the trains and hawk, as shown in Figure 10-13.

Figure 10–13. *Procedure Used for Solving Distance/Rate/Time Problem*

	Distance	=	Rate	×	Time
Train A:	25 miles	=	25 mph	×	
Train B:	25 miles	=	25 mph	×	
Hawk:		=	100 mph	×	

Last, calculate the unknowns. First, determine time. This is simple. If the trains travel twenty-five miles at twenty-five mph, then they traveled one hour. The hawk also traveled one hour, since it flew until the trains met. Knowing the hawk's rate was a hundred mph and its traveling time was one hour, you can calculate its distance by multiplying one hundred mph by one hour, resulting in a distance of one hundred miles.

Note that there are two overriding strategies for answering fact, concept, and skill items: Circling key words and re-creating representations, just as you did when you first learned and studied the information. You can see now that representations are useful for note-taking, review, and test-taking.

Use Item-Form Strategies

Items that differ in form require somewhat different test-taking strategies. Figure 10-14 illustrates the five major forms of test items. Three forms require information recognition; the correct answer is recognized among distractors. Two forms require information recall; the correct answer is retrieved from memory. This section provides helpful strategies for the different item forms.

Figure 10–14. *Test Item Forms*

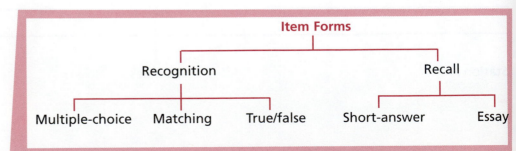

Exercise

For each test question below, identify the type of test question, mark key words in the question, and, on your own sheet of paper, develop representations (or representation frameworks) that might help you answer the questions.

1. Define symbiosis.

2. In mutualism, does one organism benefit from another organism?

3. In commensalism, how many organisms benefit?

4. In parasitism, what happens to the host organism?

5. A plover picks food from a crocodile's mouth. The crocodile gets its teeth cleaned by the plover. What type of symbiotic relationship is this?

   a) commensalism

   b) parasitism

   c) mutualism

6. A passerby rests on a park bench. Loosely speaking what symbiotic relationship exists between the passerby and the bench?

   a) commensalism

   b) parasitism

   c) mutualism

7. Provide a definition and example for the following four terms: producer, primary consumer, secondary consumer, and decomposer.

8. Suppose the toot hoot owl and the lone moan owl occupy the same niche. Suppose, too, that both types of owls enjoy eating the juicy beetles that reside in the area. Predict the two most likely outcomes from this situation. Explain in detail how each result might come about.

Strategies for Answering Multiple-Choice Items

Multiple-choice items are probably the items that appear most frequently on college tests. They consist of a stem (a statement or question) and options or alternatives (choices). Among the options is a correct answer and several distractors (incorrect answers). A labeled item appears below.

Stem   { Which of the following is not a recognition item?

Distractors   { a) Multiple-choice
                b) True/false   } Options or Alternatives
                c) Matching
Correct Answer { d) Short-answer

Below are several strategies for handling multiple-choice items.

1. **Circle key words.** In the previous section about item types, you learned to circle key words that signal the item's request and highlight critical information. The critical information for fact items is details (for example, *presented stimulus* and *increases behavior*); for concept items, attribute examples (for example, *blowing bubbles, mother yelling, child stops blowing bubbles*); and for skill items, relevant data (for example, the distance traveled by the trains).

   In addition, you should **circle negative words that might confuse you**. In the item above, circle the word *not*. If the word not is overlooked, the question is answered incorrectly. Other negative words include *no* and *never*, and those words that include the prefixes *un* (unclear), *dis* (disagree), *a* (atypical), *in* (incongruent), *im* (impartial), *il* (illiterate), *ir* (irrational), *non* (nonsense), and *mis* (misinterpret). Negative words might appear in the stem or alternatives. Circle them in both places.

2. **Convert the item into a recall item.** Cover the alternatives for a multiple-choice item and try to recall or calculate the answer before considering the alternatives. For instance, given the multiple-choice question below, try answering it before considering options A through D.

   > Ernie bought a used car for $10,000. He sold it two years later for 20 percent less than he paid for it. The new owner sold it again two years later for 30 percent less. How much money did the new owner get for the car?
   >
   > A) $5,000
   > B) $5,600
   > C) $8,000
   > D) $10,000

   The test-taker who reads the stem and rushes to consider the alternatives is likely to select the seductive response, A. After all, 20 percent plus 30 percent equals 50 percent and 50 percent of $10,000 is

$5,000. However, A is incorrect, The test-taker is best served by calculating the answer and then determining if that answer is an option.

The same problem occurs if the test-taker rushes to consider the alternatives in the item below.

Punishment is best understood as _____.

A) spanking
B) praising
C) decreased behavior

Again, choice A is seductive and plausible. Most people, in fact, associate punishment with spanking. Technically, however, punishment always involves decreased behavior (choice C). The test-taker who reads the stem and goes to the options without first formulating an answer is apt to select the incorrect alternative, A. Instructors, knowing that fools rush in, often stock alternatives with incorrect responses that look correct. Don't be foolish. Attempt to answer the item before considering alternatives.

3. **Consider *all* the alternatives**. As you can see from the two items just presented, it is best not to respond hastily. Don't select the first option that looks good. In some cases, multiple-choice items require a "best answer," meaning that more than one option might be correct. Consider the item below.

To determine the average income for a city it is best to calculate the _____.

A) mean
B) variance
C) standard deviation
D) median

Answers A and D are both correct. The mean and median are measures of central tendency. However, the best answer is median, because the median is the appropriate measure when there are extreme data. Incomes tend to be extreme, with a few either well below or way above the rest. Therefore, the median provides a more accurate measure. Again, however, the test-taker who fails to consider all the options is likely to select incorrect option A without fully considering correct option D.

4. **Choose "all of the above."** When you recognize one or more options as correct, then "all of the above" is the correct option. Consider the item below.

Positive reinforcement is characterized by

A) a presented stimulus
B) an increased behavior
C) a favorable stimulus
D) all of the above

Although you may not know that answer C is true, if you know that A and B are true, then the correct answer must be D, "all of the above."

5. **Eliminate distractors.** Suppose that you either can't remember or can't calculate the answer before you read the options. Further suppose that after reading all the options, you still can't select the correct answer. What should you do? You should eliminate as many distractors as possible in hopes of deriving the correct answer through the process of elimination. Even if you can't eliminate all the distractors, eliminating even one dramatically improves your odds for guessing the correct answer. For example, eliminating one distractor in a four-alternative multiple-choice item increases your guessing odds from 25 percent (one in four) to 33 percent (one in three).

How do you eliminate choices? Consider the sample item below from a psychology test:

The mnemonic technique ideal for learning foreign language vocabulary is the _____.

- A) rehearsal method
- B) episodic method
- C) Lowci method
- D) image and recite methods
- E) keyword method

You can eliminate choice A, because it was not introduced during the section on mnemonics. It was introduced previously in discussions about short-term memory.

You can eliminate choice B, because it's a new term. You simply do not recognize this term from the course. Test constructors often use terms from past or future lessons when they're developing distractors.

You might be able to eliminate choice C, because it's misspelled (the correct spelling is Loci). Test-makers are often more careful preparing the correct response than alternatives.

And you might be able to eliminate choice D, because it's grammatically inconsistent with the stem. The stem requires a singular response and choice D is plural. Again, the test-maker has not carefully written this option.

When options are misspelled or grammatically inconsistent, they should not be selected unless you're certain they are accurate. Technically, you can argue against being penalized for missing poorly constructed items. If you protest, speak with the instructor privately and explain politely how certain distractors contained errors that led you astray.

6. **When in doubt, employ test-wise strategies.** When you are just plain clueless about the correct answer, consider these test-wise strategies, which you can use as a last resort. Strategies are based on tendencies that instructors display when they're constructing multiple-choice tests.

- **Select the midrange option among numerical choices.** Test constructors tend to cushion correct numerical options with distractors. Consider the item below.

The average number of items held in the short-term memory is ____.

   A) 3
   B) 5
   C) 7
   D) 9

If you're unsure of the answer, you are advised to select midrange options B or C. The correct answer is C, 7.

- **Select an option that contains a form of the word in the stem.** Consider the item below.

   What is encoding specificity?

   A) A type of forgetting
   B) A mnemonic system
   C) When a specific encoding cue aids retrieval
   D) When learning is restricted to a single context

If you're uncertain of the answer, select option C, because it contains terms consistent with those in the stem (that is, *specific* and *encoding*).

- **When two options are similar or opposite, select one of them.** The instructor uses similar options to determine whether you can make the subtle distinction between them. Consider the item below.

   Janna listened to the announcer read the starting lineup for the Yankees. Immediately after she was able to remember only the first four names announced. This exemplifies _____.

   A) proactive interference
   B) retroactive interference
   C) retrieval cue failure
   D) decay

The two similar answers are A and B. Chances are that one of these options is correct.

With opposing responses, it is likely that one is correct, particularly when the opposing responses lower the range of possibilities. Consider the item below.

   Most poisonous snakes live

   A) on land
   B) in water
   C) in rocks
   D) near trees

The correct answer has to be A or B. Unless snakes also live in space, most poisonous ones must live either on land or in water. Even if most do live in rocks, isn't that still on land? Choose A or B if you're not sure, since they are opposites.

- **Select options with relative, rather than absolute, qualifiers.**
  Qualifiers are words like *always*, *sometimes*, *never*, *frequently*, *often*, *invariably*, and *constantly*. Some of these are absolute, because they indicate that something is always so. Words like *always*, *never*, *invariably*, and *constantly* are absolute qualifiers.

  Relative qualifiers indicate that something is occasionally so. Words like *sometimes*, *frequently*, *often*, and *occasionally* are relative qualifiers. Because few things are absolute other than death and dinnertime calls from telemarketers, rarely are absolute qualifiers correct. An option containing a relative qualifier is more likely to be correct. The relative qualifier, in fact, was probably inserted to make the option just right. Consider the item below.

  Which statement is true about time management?
  A) Students must study in the mornings
  B) Students should study about twenty-five hours per week
  C) All students waste time
  D) Time management is the most important study skill

  If in doubt, choose option B, which contains a relative qualifier. The other options contain absolute qualifiers.

- **Choose the longest option.** Test constructors take more care preparing the correct answer than the distractors. The correct answer is usually longer and commonly contains carefully chosen words.

- **Choose C or D.** Instructors tend to make options C or D the correct answer. Perhaps this is done to lure impatient students to seductive distractors that appear as options A and B. When in doubt, choose options C or D.

Strategies for Answering Matching Items

Below is a matching item from an educational psychology test administered to college students.

Match the statements on the left with their associated event of instruction on the right.

___ 1. "Class, I expect you to build a relief map like the one I'm showing you now."	A) Activate prior knowledge
	B) Provide feedback
___ 2. "Class, look here at the solution."	C) Present objective
___ 3. "You missed items requiring borrowing across zero."	D) Gain attention
___ 4. "Remember that nouns are people, places, or things. Keep that in mind as we now address proper nouns."	E) Enhance encoding
___ 5. "Notice the pattern of differences between moths and butterflies."	

Exercise

Eliminate distractors and use test-wise strategies to answer the items below.

1. Oximuc is found in the
   a) stomach
   b) digestive system
   c) brain
   d) nervous system
   e) foot

2. What is a side effect of Espogeltate?
   a) watery eyes
   b) dry eyes
   c) bloating and cold sores
   d) asma

3. Ploxnosis is a process instrumental in
   a) removing brich from a flupe
   b) interchanging snafe for snufe
   c) adding ploxins to troats
   d) filtering spanules

4. What type of drug is Angolstat?
   a) pharmaceutical
   b) illicit
   c) psychedelic
   d) opiate

5. When plish enters into the tradon cavity _____.
   a) Ixnet is usually present
   b) Feglow is never released
   c) Splittle is always oxidized

A matching item is really several multiple-choice items, each of which contains the same options. If you examine the matching item above, you see that it is essentially five multiple-choice stems (1–5), each with the same five options (a–e).

Given the similarity between multiple-choice and matching items, there are several strategies for handling multiple-choice items that are also appropriate for matching items. Below are a few additional strategies aimed specifically at matching items.

1. **Read instructions carefully.** Matching items can contain drastically different instructions. In some, an alternative is used once. In others, an alternative is used more than once or not at all. If the instructions

do not explain how options are used, then ask your instructor before proceeding. Don't assume, for example, that because the sample item contains five stems and five options that each option is used once.

2. **Work from the longer side.** Matching items have left- and right-hand columns. When you're completing matching items, work from the column that contains more words. In the sample matching item above, work from the longer, left-hand column. Read the first statement in the left-hand column and search for its match in the right-hand column. Then read the second statement in the left-hand column and again search for its match in the right-hand column. Working from the longer column saves time. In this case, it's faster to search repeatedly for matches in the shorter right-hand column than in the longer left-hand column.

3. **Answer easy items first; reserve guessing for the end.** In matching items where an option is used once, selecting an incorrect alternative produces two wrong answers. Return to the sample item above. If you choose option D for Item 1, you not only get that item wrong but Item 2 as well, because the correct option for Item 2 is D.

   Because there is "double jeopardy" for selecting an incorrect alternative, it is best to answer easy items first and save guessing for the end. If you can correctly match three of the five stems and alternatives in the sample item above, then you can guess at the last two and still have a 50 percent chance of answering both correctly.

   Suppose you're in that situation where you know that you've matched three items correctly. Two remain for which you do not know the answer. Options A and C remain. What should you do? If you guess that one is A and the other is C, you either get both items correct or both items wrong. In the end, you score either 60 percent (three out of five items correct) or 100 percent (five out of five items correct) on the matching portion.

   Another course of action is to answer the remaining two items the same way, for example, by selecting A for both. Given that you have already answered three items correctly, this strategy guarantees that you're going to answer one of the two remaining items correctly. The result is a score of 80 percent correct (four out of five items). This is a more conservative strategy than guessing differently for each, and perhaps answering only 60 percent correctly (a failing mark).

4. **Consider all the options.** Matching items are tricky, because there are so many options. Read and consider each option for each stem.

5. **Mark used options.** After you've selected an option, mark it to indicate that it's been used. This is essential when an option is used just once. Don't obliterate the option by crossing it out and rendering it unreadable. You might change your mind later and want to refer to it. A simple check mark adequately signals that you've already used an option.

Exercise

Practice the strategies just presented to answer the matching item below.

Matching

Match the five types of representations on the left with their related information on the right. A letter can be used more than once or not at all. Provide the best single response for each item.

A. Sequence   _____ 1. Shows coordinate relations

B. Matrix   _____ 2. Shows superordinate-subordinate relations

C. Diagram   _____ 3. Shows temporal relations

D. Hierarchy   _____ 4. Ideal for comparisons and contrasts

E. Photograph   _____ 5. Useful for making within-topic and across-topic connections

---

Strategies for Answering True/False Items

True/false items are like multiple-choice or matching items, because you select an option. They are generally simpler than other recognition items, because there are only two options: true or false. Below are a few tips or strategies for answering true/false items.

1. **Assume the statement is true.** Begin with the assumption that the statement is true. Only mark it false if you uncover false information. If any part of the statement is false, then the whole statement is false and should be marked accordingly. Are the statements below true or false?

   - The seven dwarfs were named Happy, Bashful, Sleepy, Grumpy, Doc, Sneezy, and Buster.
   - Snow White fell into a deep sleep after drinking a magic potion.

   Both statements are false because they contain some false information. Six of the seven dwarfs are named correctly, but there is no Buster. The statement is false. Snow White did fall into a deep sleep, but not because of a magic potion. She ate the poisoned apple. The statement is therefore false.

   If you have no idea whether a statement is true or false, then mark it true. Instructors generally include more true statements than false. This might be because teachers consciously or unconsciously use tests to reiterate correct ideas. Or it might happen because more work is involved in creating false statements. Creating false statements involves adding, deleting, or changing already true statements or ideas. Choosing the path of least resistance, instructors construct more true items than false items.

2. **Consider absolute and relative terms.** A general rule is that statements that include absolute terms (for example, *always*, *must*, and *never*) are often false, whereas statements that include relative terms (for example, *sometimes*, *often*, *rarely*, and *should*) are often true. As we mentioned previously, few things are absolute.

How would you answer these true/false items?

- Short-term memory capacity never exceeds seven items.
- Mnemonic strategies are the only strategies that aid long-term memory.
- Alzheimer patients usually experience deficits related to encoding.
- Blixtwix is sometimes contained in grinrich.

Without knowing whether the statements are really true or false, respond false, false, true, and true, respectively, given that the first two items contain absolute terms (never and only) and the last two items contain relative terms (usually and sometimes).

3. **Consider other factors.** If you don't know whether a statement is true or false, consider two more factors:

Statements that include explanations are more often false. The explanation is usually provided to convert a true statement to a false one, as in the item below.

White rhinos have square lips to attract mates.

The statement is false. The first part is correct—white rhinos do have square lips. The explanation, however, makes the statement false. Their square lips permit grazing.

Negative statements are most often false. Remember that instructors generally transform true statements to false ones by altering the statement. Another convenient means for doing this is by making the statement negative. In the item below, a true statement is made false by adding the negative term "not."

Black rhinos are not aggressive.

Remember that you only consider these factors if you are stumped and cannot determine a statement's truth.

4. **Don't anticipate patterns.** Some students believe that instructors organize the true/false section of a test in a predetermined pattern (for instance, true, true, false). This belief was illustrated in one *Peanuts* cartoon in which Peppermint Patty explained to another student that true/false tests always follow the same pattern. She explained that instructors start off with a true followed by a false and then two trues to break the pattern. Next come three falses, two more trues, and a false. Patty scored a zero on the test and her astute reaction was "I should have trued when I falsed."

Exercise

Answer the following true/false items, which were taken from a chapter on aging. Use the strategies above to answer those about which you are uncertain.

_____ 1. Families don't bother with their older relatives.

_____ 2. All people become confused or forgetful if they live long enough.

_____ 3. You can become too old to exercise.

_____ 4. Heart disease is a much bigger problem for older men than for older women.

_____ 5. The older you get, the less sleep you need.

_____ 6. Most older people are depressed. Why shouldn't they be?

_____ 7. Older people take more medications than do younger people.

_____ 8. People begin to lose interest in sex around age 55.

_____ 9. Older people may as well accept urinary accidents as a fact of life.

_____ 10. Suicide is mainly a problem for teenagers, not for older people.

_____ 11. Falls and injuries just happen to older people.

_____ 12. Extremes of heat and cold can be especially dangerous for older people.

Strategies for Answering Short-Answer Items

Short-answer items are those that require a brief response ranging from a single word to a short paragraph. No options are provided for selection. Information is recalled from memory. Four sample items appear below.

1. _____ are credited with formulating the cognitive levels of processing theory.

2. An _____ is an insect that can carry many times its own weight.

3. List the first four locations in the body that are used for digestion.

4. What is the main advantage of the matrix over outlines? What evidence supports this?

Notice that the first two items require the completion of a sentence. Usually, a word or two is adequate. The next two items require longer responses. Item three requires a brief list, and item four a brief paragraph.

There are fewer unique strategies associated with short-answer items than with recognition items because short-answer items have less parts—

they contain no alternatives. What follows are a few good strategies or reminders for handling short-answer items.

1. **Use available cues.** While it's true that short-answer items do not provide the answer, they still provide cues for locating the answer. For sample Item 1, search your memory for the category levels of processing or cognitive theories. For Item 2 search your memory for insect knowledge. Perhaps you once generated a matrix representation for comparing several insects along common categories like strength and diet. Try activating that knowledge.

2. **Answer the entire question.** Often, students answer only a portion of a short-answer item. They read the item rapidly and fail to note all directives. For sample Item 4, you must present advantages and provide evidence. Use number or letter symbols to mark an item's multiple requests. After writing your answer, reread the item making sure you've addressed all parts.

3. **Don't leave blanks.** When you leave items blank, your instructor assumes you know nothing and grades you accordingly. When you don't quite know the answer, but you do know something about the topic, then present that information. You're likely to receive partial credit. For instance, suppose that you don't know the cognitive psychologist who formulated the levels of processing theory. You could still explain the theory, tell when it originated, provide research support for it, and discuss its educational implications. Our recommendation is not to fill the space with stuff you don't know about (commonly called "BS"). Our recommendation is to fill the space with related stuff you *do* know about.

4. **Use item clues.** Some items contain clues about an answer. Sample Item 1 clues you that more than one person is credited with the theory formulation. The clue is the verb *are*. Plural verbs agree with plural subjects, and singular verbs agree with singular subjects.

   Item 2 clues you that the insect name begins with a vowel. The clue is the indefinite article *an*. An is used before words with vowel sounds. A is used before words with consonant sounds.

Strategies for Answering Essay Items

Essay items, like short-answer items, are recall items. No options are provided and you have to recall information from memory. Unlike short-answer items, essay items require a lengthy response, which can range from a long paragraph to several pages. Essay items determine how well you recall, organize, and apply information. They also measure how well you think and present ideas.

Many students drop the ball when it comes to answering essay items. The costliest error is not knowing the material. It is impossible to write about something you don't know. Have you ever been confronted with an essay question you were totally unable to answer? Was your test paper as barren as a desert? If so, you can be helped by the note-taking, reading, and review strategies presented in this book.

Most students fumble essay items in other damaging, but less obvious, ways. They neglect to identify the requested behavior, organize ideas, write an introductory statement, write cohesively, and generate conclusions. Below, we use a sample essay item to address each of these mistakes and methods for correcting them.

> Compare and contrast the three types of creativity with respect to outcome, motivation, and time demands.

1. **Identify the requested behavior.** Students occasionally ignore the behavior requested in the essay item. Instead, they treat all essay items as an invitation to say anything and everything about the topic at hand.

   Identify the exact behavior expected by circling the verbs and their objects. For example, in our sample essay, the writer must compare and contrast the three types of creativity. Evaluating them or tracing their development are both unnecessary and inappropriate. A listing of some common behaviors and their translations follow:

   compare and contrast—discuss similarities and differences
   analyze—describe the elements
   evaluate—pass judgment based on evidence
   trace the development—explain the sequence of events
   conclude—provide an explanation or interpretation of the data
   synthesize—describe commonalities among the elements

2. **Create a representation of the content.** Ineffective writers write "off the top of their heads." Effective writers plan, often writing from representations they construct.

   A representation includes the content for the writing assignment organized in an optimal way. An effective representation for the sample essay appears in Figure 10-15. This representation helps the writer compare and contrast the types of creativity by reading across the subcategories of definition, motivation, and time demands.

Figure 10–15. *Representation for Organizing Essay Content*

	Types of Creativity		
	Adaptive	**Innovative**	**Emergent**
Outcome:	Solving a new everyday problem	Creating a new or improved product	Reshaping the direction of a discipline
Motivation:	External	External	Internal
Time Demands:	3–5 yrs.	5–10 yrs.	10 or more yrs.

Two other sample essay items (A and B) appear below. Their corresponding representation frameworks appear in Figures 10-16 and 10-17, respectively.

Sample Item A: Trace the Piagetian stages of development with respect to age of onset, and social and cognitive characteristics.

Sample Item B: Christopher Columbus's voyages to the New World were more characteristic of French and British exploration than those of the Spanish. Explain how this is so with respect to goals, methods, and relations with Native Americans.

Figure 10–16.   *Representation Framework for Sample Item A*

Piagetian Stages

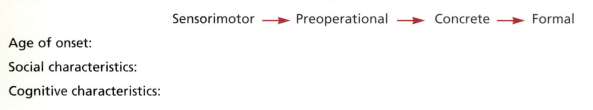

Sensorimotor ⟶ Preoperational ⟶ Concrete ⟶ Formal

Age of onset:

Social characteristics:

Cognitive characteristics:

Figure 10–17.   *Representation Framework for Sample Item B*

Voyages

	Columbus	French	British	Spanish
Goals:				
Methods:				
Relations with Native Americans:				

3. **Write a directive, opening statement.** When writing, don't plunge headlong into your thesis. Instead, begin by restating the question or issue; then provide a framework for your response. Your opening statement provides a "road map" for the reader, and it directs you, the writer. The opening statement for the sample essay about creativity might be as follows:

> The three types of creativity . . . differ with respect to definition, motivation, and time demands. I compare and contrast the three types along each of the dimensions in turn. I conclude with general observations about how the types are similar and different.

4. **Write cohesively.** Creating a complete and organized representation does not guarantee a good essay. The essay must address the question or issue and be organized appropriately.

Return to the representation for the creativity essay in Figure 10-15. There are several ways to misuse this representation. One is to describe each type of creativity in turn. For example, "Adaptive creativity involves solving a new, but everyday, problem; internal motivation; and takes three to five years to develop. Innovative creativity. . . ." This topic-by-topic approach fails to compare and contrast the topics.

A second misuse of the representation involves "writing across the topics" but failing to illustrate their similarities and differences. For example, "The motivation for adaptive creativity is external. The motivation for innovative creativity is external. The motivation for emergent creativity is internal."

A well-organized essay in this case compares and contrasts the types of creativity along each dimension (outcome, motivation, and time demands), as stated in the beginning statement, but also presents the interrelationships among those dimensions. For instance, how time demands and motivation relate to one another for the types of creativity:

> The three types of creativity differ with respect to the **outcomes** produced. Going from adaptive, in which a novel, everyday problem is solved; to innovative, in which a product is invented or improved; to emergent, in which an entire discipline is reshaped, it is evident that the outcome is progressively more sophisticated and worldly.
>
> In line with this progression of outcomes is the corresponding progression of years necessary to create the product. The **time demand** for acquiring adaptive creativity is about three to five years. Innovative creativity requires about five to ten years of preparation, and emergent creativity requires ten or more years. Thus, it can be seen that the more sophisticated or worldly the creative **outcome**, the greater the **time commitment** necessary to create that product.
>
> The **motivation** for the types of creativity stems from either internal or external sources. The motivation source is external for adaptive and innovative creativity, but internal for emergent. The source of **motivation** seems consistent with the **outcome**. Adaptively creative people and innovatively creative people are concerned with solving problems that arise from the environment (an external source), whereas emergently creative people are concerned with their own ideas and thoughts about a discipline (an internal source). Their motivation to master a discipline ultimately leads them to produce ideas that ultimately reshape the thinking within that discipline.

Notice that in the sample essay above the writer wrote in a "zigzag" fashion. Patterns of information observed across one dimension (such as outcome) are discussed relative to information observed across a related dimension (such as time demands).

Notice, too, that the essay is cohesive—it ties ideas together. This sort of writing is much preferred to a linear, point-by-point style of writing.

5. **Generate conclusions.** Although several conclusions were drawn in the body of the essay, it is still appropriate to finish with an integrative summary of ideas that ties all ideas into a neat package. A fitting conclusion to the essay about creativity might be as follows:

> In conclusion, it is evident that the three types of creativity differ with respect to the sophistication and importance of the creative outcome or product. These differences correspond to the time demands for producing the creative product. The more sophisticated and important the product, the greater the time commitment. Most creative products, meanwhile, stem from external sources, such as an everyday problem or the need to build a better mousetrap. Only the most sophisticated and important type of creativity (emergent) depends on an internal striving to reshape the direction of an entire discipline.

To summarize, most writing suffers not from lack of content, but from a lack of direction and organization. The five strategies presented here are crucial for improving an essay's direction, organization, and clarity. But there are a few more things you should know about effective essay writing. The tip list continues:

6. **Write a lot; write something.** As instructors, we are surprised when we provide two blank pages to answer an essay item and students restrict their answer to a single half-page paragraph. Given the space provided, students should recognize that we're looking for a more detailed answer.

Don't hold back. Answer the item as completely as time and your knowledge allow. There are two times in this world when brevity is a poor choice: when answering essay items and when the executioner asks if you have any last words. If time limits your response, then remember to ask for additional time. Before time does run out, make a list of the key points you intended to address along with a note explaining your time limitations. Most instructors make concessions for students short on time.

When you don't know the answer, bend the item slightly and write what you do know about. Perhaps you can't compare the three types of creativity as requested. If you can write about one of them, then do so. If you can write about a creative individual, then do that.

Don't miss the point. The best essay response is complete, organized, and accurate, and answers the question at hand. Our point is that a too-brief answer might penalize you, and no answer might doom you.

7. **Present facts, not feelings.** A good essay is stocked with facts, not feelings. It is inappropriate to confide how you feel about creativity, Piaget, or Columbus unless you're asked to do so. Remember what Sergeant Friday on *Dragnet* used to say as witnesses or suspects rambled on: "Just gimme the facts."

8. **Write neatly.** Instructors hate messy papers. They are difficult to decipher, hard to follow, and take longer to grade. Instructors despise messy papers so much that they sometimes unknowingly assign them lower grades than they would the same paper written more legibly. Is this fair? Not really, but it's a reality that you can control by writing more legibly.

   We recommend that you print if your handwriting is bad. Leave adequate space between words, between lines, and along margins. And never print in all capital letters. CAPITAL LETTERS SLOW PROCESSING AS THE READER STUMBLES OVER EACH LETTER RATHER THAN READ EACH WORD.

9. **Take the reader by the hand.** Help the reader along by using headings, underlining, and transitions. Too often, essay writers are unclear about which question part they are addressing. One author recalls asking educational psychology students to describe the reading process from the standpoint of attention, encoding, and metacognition. A student composed an essay that never named those terms. Although the essay was stocked with many correct ideas, it was impossible to tell which ideas applied to attention, encoding, or metacognition.

   Use headings to signal main topics. An essay written to answer the item about creativity would include these headings: outcomes, time demands, motivation, and conclusion.

   Highlight important ideas by underlining them. Highlight terms that correspond to requests made in the essay item. The educational psychology student just mentioned should have introduced and highlighted the terms *attention, encoding*, and *metacognition*. Highlight other critical ideas in your answer, such as concept names (for example, "The reader must develop *automaticity*") and important details (for example, "The short-term memory holds only about *seven* bits of information").

   Use transitions to gently move the reader from one idea to the next. Transitions help readers link previous ideas with new ones. A helpful transition sentence linking two paragraphs might read: "Although French and British explorers shared common goals (previous idea), their goals were in contrast with Spanish explorers (new idea)." Single words and short phrases, such as those in the following examples, can also offer the reader a helpful nudge: *alternatively, then, first, later, however, invariably, next, on the other hand*, and *to summarize*.

10. **Write forcefully and accurately.** Most instructors don't subtract points for spelling, split infinitives, and dangling participles. Nevertheless, your writing mechanics and style do leave an impression. They might impress the instructor with your brilliance or your ignorance. These impressions might have a spillover effect for measuring your essay's quality. Before the spillover drains away, an instructor might overlook the value of a poorly crafted essay.

Although there are many ingredients in forceful writing, the two most prominent are writing concisely and using the active voice. Consider the sentence "The voyages of Columbus were long and hard on his crew." A more forceful sentence is "Columbus's long voyages tired his crew." Eliminate wordy prepositional phrases (voyages of Columbus) and replace weak verbs (were) with active verbs (tired) whenever possible.

Several final tongue-in-cheek tips for accurate and forceful writing follow:

- Avoid run-on sentences they are hard to read.
- No sentence fragments.
- It behooves us to avoid archaisms.
- Also, avoid awkward or affected alliteration.
- Don't use no double negatives.
- If I've told you once, I've told you a thousand times: Resist hyperbole.
- Avoid commas, that are not necessary.
- Verbs has to agree with their subjects.
- Avoid trendy locutions that sound flaky.
- Writing carefully, dangling participles should not be used.
- Kill all exclamation points!!!
- Never use a long word when a diminutive one will do.
- Proofread carefully to see if you any words out.
- Take the bull by the hand, and don't mix metaphors.
- Don't verb nouns.
- Never, ever use repetitive redundancies.
- Last but not least, avoid clichés like the plague.

How to Analyze Test Errors (Error Analysis)

Consider two true stories. The first involves a student in an educational psychology class who received a score of 100 percent on all semester tests. On the cumulative final exam, the student answered ninety-nine out of a hundred questions correctly. But because the test was administered on the last day of final exams before summer vacation, the student was unable to review the final test. To this day, twenty years later, the student wonders which item was missed.

Exercise

To help organize your ideas before you write, create representation frameworks on your own paper for the essay questions below.

1. Trace the six steps in drug breakdown, describing each in terms of location, time, and negative effects.
2. Compare the three types of cancers in terms of severity, location, treatments, and prognosis.
3. Compare the four types of seizures: Grand Mal, Petit Mal, Psychomotor, and Jacksonian.

On your own paper, rewrite each sentence below. Make each sentence clear, concise, and correct.

1. The data is flawed.
2. We should dialogue about this.
3. Matrices are much much more effective than outlines!!
4. We should not retreat backwards.
5. It's cool to go, to the library.
6. In most situations students who are good use strategies that are effective.
7. He utilized his strength to break away.
8. A matrix is effective. When comparisons or contrasts are made.
9. When only a small boy, my father took me with him to a ball-game.
10. Alway reread what have written.

The second story revolves around retake exams. Your authors often administer these exams to students who hope to improve their original test scores. The retake exams are identical in form, type, and content to the original exams, but contain different items. If students score higher on a retake exam, then that score is counted and the original score is dropped. One semester, an instructor administered an exam on the last day of class and could only provide feedback by posting the test grades and offering to visit with students in his office to talk with them about the test. Amazingly, only one of the twenty-five students met with the instructor to discuss the test. Perhaps more amazingly, five students who had received no feedback about the items missed on the original test showed up a week later to retake the exam.

The students in these two stories are at extremes. The first student really wanted feedback, even though it did not influence the course grade. The student simply wanted to understand the nature of the error. The other students couldn't have cared less about feedback that could raise their performance significantly on the retake exam.

You cannot improve future performance if you do not recognize your errors.

You cannot improve future performance if you do not recognize your errors. As an example, suppose your were asked to draw a line three inches long without the aid of a ruler. Now, suppose you were asked to draw a second and third three-inch line. Does your performance change? Of course not. All your lines look the same. Without feedback such as "It's a little short" or "It's a bit long," you have no reason to change. It is crucial that you recognize test errors so you can correct them and not repeat them.

Below is a graded ten-item test on the measurement topic, central tendency. Suppose you answered five items correctly and earned a score of 50 percent. Don't be satisfied just knowing your score. Analyze your errors and determine *what* went wrong (the type and content of errors). Investigate further and find out *why* things went wrong by determining the error source.

Test on Central Tendency

1. What score occurs most?
X 2. What score divides a set of scores?
3. What is the sum of all scores divided by the number of scores?
4. What measure of central tendency is affected by extreme scores?
5. To find out how students did on the test, Mr. Marsh added all the scores and divided by the number of total scores. What did Mr. Marsh find?
X 6. There are twenty-five students in Ms. Brom's class. She arranged their test scores from highest to lowest. The thirteenth score on the test represented what?
X 7. Looking over the height chart for her volleyball team, the coach said, "It looks like most of you are 5 feet 8 inches. What concept has the coach expressed?

For items 8 through 10, use the following scores: 5, 2, 4, 5, 6, 8, 5

X 8. Calculate the mean.
X 9. Calculate the median.
10. Calculate the mode.

Begin by conducting a quick analysis of the test—both the correct and the incorrect answers—in terms of item type and item content to learn what went wrong. Examine each item and determine whether the item is a fact, concept, or skill item (its item type) and whether it pertains to the mean, median, or mode (its item content). This information appears in Figure 10-18.

From this analysis, it's easy to see *what* went wrong. In terms of item type, you missed mostly concept items (numbers 6 and 7) and skill items (numbers 8 and 9). You only missed one fact item (Item 2). In terms of item content, most errors pertained to the median (items 2, 6, and 9). One item each was missed pertaining to the mode (Item 7) and mean (Item 8).

Now the investigative work begins. You must determine *why* things went wrong. You must determine the error source. The most common error sources are note-taking (from texts or lectures), review, and test-taking. Let's locate the source for the five test errors.

Figure 10–18. *Analysis Showing Item Type and Content. X Indicates Items Missed*

Item Number	Type	Content
1	Fact	Mode
X 2	Fact	Median
3	Fact	Mean
4	Fact	Mean
5	Concept	Mean
X 6	Concept	Median
X 7	Concept	Mode
X 8	Skill	Mean
X 9	Skill	Median
10	Skill	Mode

You missed three items (numbers 2, 6, and 9) pertaining to the median. This was a lecture topic. You check your notebook for the lecture on central tendency and notice there are no notes about the median. You remember coming to class late that day because of a dental appointment. Not having that information in notes was the error source.

You now examine the error source for Item 7. This was a concept item pertaining to the mode. You check your lecture notes and find the definition of mode and a range of examples. Your notes appear to be complete. Next, you examine review notes and see that you did not include examples in a matrix you constructed for comparing the mean, median, and mode. This was a review error.

Last, you analyze your error for Item 8, which is a skill item about the mean. Your lecture notes and review notes are complete. You noted the sequence of steps and worked several practice problems correctly beneath those steps. You return to your test and rework the problem. This time you calculate the mean as being five rather than seven, as indicated on your test. You now recognize that you made a careless error dividing thirty-five by five instead of by seven. This was a test-taking error.

With this information, make changes to bolster your performance on future tests. If a retake exam or cumulative measurement final awaits, then you must acquire fact, concept, and skill knowledge about the median. You must also learn the concept of mode. Methods for learning facts, concepts, and skills are covered in Chapter 9.

For another test in this course or any course, you must improve note-taking. You should not miss lectures. When you do miss a lecture, you should get notes by tape-recording the lecture and borrowing notes from several students.

You must also improve concept review. Reviewing concepts depends on representing definitions and a range of examples for a concept family (see Chapter 9). You should match concept definitions and examples, and compare and contrast definitions and examples across concepts.

Last, you must avoid test-taking mistakes by checking and reworking problems. The first answer should be covered while you're reworking the problem so it doesn't influence your recalculation.

There are two other error sources all students should consider: motivation and time management. For example, a student who performs poorly because of skipped lectures and disregarded reading assignments has a motivational problem. The student must use the DIFS model described in Chapter 2 to increase motivation. A student who wants to learn but cannot find the time between work, sports, and personal commitments should use the time management strategies described in Chapter 3.

Everyone makes mistakes; everyone stumbles. The key is recognizing mistakes and correcting them. Students who do so improve learning and test performance.

Exercise

Below is a ten-item test on grammar. Suppose you had answered the items marked with Xs incorrectly. Conduct an error analysis to learn what you got wrong. Provide some possible reasons for why you missed those items. (The information in parentheses did not appear on the test, but is presented to help in your analysis.)

1. Define a restrictive clause.
2. What is the difference between a restrictive clause and a nonrestrictive clause?

Underline the restrictive clauses in the items below.

X 3. The two things most universally desired are power and admiration—Bertrand Russell.

X 4. He spent long hours caring for the children who were sick with the AIDS virus.

Underline the nonrestrictive clauses in the items below.

5. This intrigued Newton, who sought knowledge in many strange places.—Joseph F. Goodavage

6. He unbuttoned his coat with its shiny silver buttons like a child.

Punctuate the following sentences correctly based upon whether they include restrictive or nonrestrictive clauses.

X 7. An experienced driver does not fear the open road generally speaking. (nonrestrictive)

X 8. An experienced driver generally speaking does not fear the open road. (nonrestrictive)

X 9. Students who use drugs tend to earn lower grades. (restrictive)

X 10. Aunt Maple my Dad's sister is coming for dinner Thursday evening. (nonrestrictive)

Summary

Optimal test performance depends on test preparation and test strategies. Prepare mentally by using good learning strategies. Master the material three days in advance of the test. Prepare physically by readying your body through proper exercise, rest, and nutrition, and by readying the test environment. A good seat and appropriate materials are helpful. Prepare emotionally by controlling anxiety. Anxiety is lessened by replacing negative test associations with positive ones and by using anxiety defusers. The best way to reduce anxiety though is being prepared mentally.

There are general test strategies useful for all tests. The general strategies include: previewing the test, establishing a plan for taking the test, reading instructions carefully, answering easy items before difficult ones, making notes on the test, using clues from one item to answer other items, asking questions of the instructor, "retaking" the test a second time, changing answers when the new answer is preferred, and using the allotted time.

For all types (fact, concept, and skill) and all forms (for example, multiple choice and essay) of test items, it is especially helpful to circle key words in the item and generate representations. Representations help in recalling facts, identifying concepts, and applying skills. They also help organize information for writing essays.

There are various item forms (such as multiple-choice, matching, true/false, short-answer, and essay) and strategies suited for each. For instance, one multiple-choice strategy involves converting the item into a recall item. A true/false strategy involves noting the use of absolute and relative qualifiers.

When the test is finished, it is important that you analyze test errors. Determine the type of item missed, the content missed, and the error source (for instance, note-taking, review, or test-taking). You benefit from mistakes by improving learning and testing activities and ultimately by increasing your knowledge.

Answers to focus questions

1. A good place to sit during an exam is along the far wall (away from the door). Here, there are likely to be fewer distractions. If possible, angle your desk toward the wall to improve concentration.

2. Most students are test-anxious for good reason. They are not mentally prepared for the exam.

3. Moderate levels of anxiety are beneficial. Too low or too high a level of anxiety hinders performance.

4. Besides unpreparedness, test anxiety is caused by negative experiences (such as embarrassment and reprimands) that are associated with testing.

5. Test anxiety is easily defused by exercise, deep breathing, tensing and relaxing muscles, mental escape, and maintaining perspective about the importance of tests.

6. Ten general strategies for test-taking are as follows:
    1. Preview the test
    2. Establish a plan for answering the test
    3. Read instructions carefully
    4. Answer easy items first
    5. Make notes on the test
    6. Employ clues from other items
    7. Ask questions
    8. "Retake" the test
    9. Change answers
    10. Use allotted time

7. "Item form" refers to the structure of the item. Item forms include multiple-choice, true/false, matching, short-answer, and essay. "Item type" refers to the type of learning necessary to answer the item. Item types include fact, concept, and skill.

8. Answers to matching items: 1. a, 2. c, 3. b.

9. The two general strategies recommended for answering fact, concept, and skill items are circling key words and creating representations. Creating representations helps you recall information and understand relationships among ideas.

10. Multiple-choice items should be answered initially as if they were recall items. Cover the alternative answers and try to answer the item without considering the alternatives. This is done because distractors (wrong answers) are often seductive. When you try to recognize the correct response, you might select the seductive alternative instead.

11. Eliminate alternatives that are new, not from this portion of the course, misspelled, and grammatically inconsistent with the stem.

12. When answering matching items, you should read the instructions carefully because they can vary considerably from test to test. Also, work from the longer side to conserve time, and reserve guessing for the end.

13. When answering true/false items, assume the statement is true unless you detect something false. If any portion is false, then mark it false. Be careful of absolute and relative terms. Absolute terms are usually false, whereas relative terms are usually true.

14. When answering short-answer items, answer the entire question and don't leave blanks.

15. When writing an essay, identify the requested behavior, create a representation of the content, write a directive beginning statement, write cohesively, and generate conclusions.

16. Although an essay is generally evaluated by its content, other factors, such as neatness, also count (even when the instructor says they don't). Don't diminish the value of an essay packed with good content by using sloppy handwriting. "Package" your essay by writing neatly and writing well.

17. Through error analysis, you learn what went wrong and why. *What* pertains to the type of error (that is, fact, concept, and skill) and the content missed. *Why* pertains to the error's source (such as note-taking, review, or test-taking).

chapter 11
Real-World Strategy Applications

OVERVIEW

Focus Questions

Introduction

Using DIFS to Get Fit
Desire
Intention
Focus
Sustain

Using Representations to Earn Financial Wealth

Using Strategies to Become a Chess Master
The Will to Learn
The Skills to Learn
Metacognition
Reading and Note-Taking
Representations
Building Connections
Concept and Skill Acquisition
Note-Taking and Error Analysis

Teaching My Child How to Learn
Teaching Reading Comprehension
Teaching Representations
Teaching Studying
Teaching Self-Control

Summary

Answers to Focus Questions

focus questions

1. What does the advertising executive do to turn desire into action?
2. What does the advertising executive do to sustain an exercise program?
3. Can you list the decisions the nurse made about investments that were partly due to representations the nurse developed?
4. How long did it take the barber to become a chess master?
5. How does the barber use reading strategies to become a chess master?
6. How do representations aid the chess master?
7. How does the chess master learn chess patterns?
8. How does error analysis aid the chess master?
9. How should children be taught to learn?
10. How does the parent teach reading strategies to a child who is learning to read?
11. What review strategies did Megan learn while studying for her test on clouds?
12. What did Megan do to illustrate that she learned self-control strategies?

Class Reunion

Carlos: Hi, Marsha! I figured you'd be one of the early ones. What are you doing these days?

Marsha: I'm a clinical psychologist with a private practice. How about you, Carlos?

Carlos: I haven't gone too far. I stayed on at the University and got my PhD in cellular biology. Now, I'm an assistant professor in the Biology Department. Hey, there's George. George, you ol' rascal, are you the one designing those big high-rises sprouting up throughout the city?

George: Actually, I've had a run of bad luck. I started with a big corporation but I didn't stay on. It was too big. I worked for a couple of smaller companies, but things didn't work out. At one place, the boss was a jerk. At the other, the work was too Borrrring.

Marsha: What do you do now, George?

George: I run my own business. I design pet houses. Perhaps you've seen my "Cat Flat" or "Mutt Hut"?

Carlos: Do you ever see Angie or Debbie?

George: Not any more. I married Angie, but we divorced. She was too pushy. Later I married Debbie, but we divorced. She was too laid back. I know things will work out with Cecilia over there. She's a Pisces. Ciao.

Marsha: Look, there's Josh.

Carlos: Wasn't he the guy who always carried a yellow highlighter in his pocket? His shirts had indelible yellow stains.

Marsha: Yeah, rather than sign my yearbook he highlighted his name . . . Oh, hi, Josh.

Josh: (Gazing at Marsha's and Carlos' name tags) Hi . . . Marsha, hi . . . Carlos. Your tags are hard to read. Mind if I highlight them?

Carlos and Marsha: No, not at all.

Marsha: What are you doing these days, Josh?

Josh: I work for the Transportation Department— road crew supervisor. I paint the solid yellow lines on the highway. I hope you won't be passing any of my work soon.

(Josh departs, highlighter in hand, and Sandy saunters over.)

Marsha: Hi, Sandy, how are you? I see you have a name tag streaked with yellow.

Sandy: Yes, it's the—uh—highlight of my evening.

Marsha: What are you doing with your life, Sandy?

Sandy: I'm vice president for *Product Reports*. It was me who introduced the matrix for product comparison.

Carlos: I love your magazine. We won't buy a toothbrush or a blow torch without consulting *Product Reports* first.

Sandy: Great! I can tell you that the beer you're drinking rates high in effervescence and pourability, but keep it under your pop top. The beer matrix isn't due out until the January issue.

Carlos: (Raising his can.) It's our secret.

(Sandy leaves and Roger hurries over.)

Roger: Hey guys, I just wanted to say "Hi" before I leave.

Carlos: Already?

Roger: Yeah, some things never change. I'm taking the police test tomorrow. They give you a book to study with about four hundred laws.

Marsha: So you're heading home to get a good night's rest.

Roger: Are you kidding? I'm heading home to study. I haven't even cracked the book yet. It's going to be an all-nighter. See ya!

Carlos: Some things never do change.

(Donna strolls by)

Marsha: Hi, Donna, I'm Marsha from psychology class. Did you end up going into psychology?

Donna: No, I was afraid to take the Graduate Record Exam. Ever since college I've had a fear of exams.

Marsha: Is that right?

Donna: Yeah. I even shudder at the thought of an eye exam or a blood test.

(Lanny joins in)

Lanny: Hey, gang. Having fun? I need to ask each of you about your most cherished college moment. I'm compiling a yearbook supplement.

Carlos: Hey, I remember you went into journalism, didn't you?

Lanny: I covered sports for *Sport and Adventure* magazine, but I lost my job.

Marsha: What happened?

Lanny: I arrived five minutes late for a championship boxing bout. Some ham-and-egger knocked out the champ in the first round. I missed it. Another time, I accompanied the oldest climber ever to scale Mt. Everest. I spent three weeks with him, but I forgot to bring a pencil. After we got down off the mountain, he tripped over a curb in the parking lot and died. So much for that interview. Oh, that reminds me, I need to get a pencil. Hold those cherished moments.

Carlos: Hey Marsha, isn't that your old friend Tammy, just arriving?

Marsha: Why yes, it is. Yoo hoo, Tammy!

Tammy: Hi, Marsha, sorry I'm late. I was watching *Star Trek: The Next Generation* reruns and lost track of time. I heard you were a psychologist. How nice. Do you still find time for your family?

Marsha: Oh yeah. My husband and I are taking two weeks off to visit our son in New York. He plays trombone for the Philharmonic. How are you?

Tammy: Moving up in the world. I'm now the night manager at the Holiday Hotel. I can't stay long. Work starts in an hour and it's about a ninety-minute drive from here. You know, sometimes I feel like I never left college.

Marsha: Me too.

What will life be like for you at your class reunion? Will you be healthy, wealthy, and wise, or flabby, flat broke, and foolish? In part, the answer depends on your use of strategies. The same strategies that can earn you higher grades in college can earn you greater health, wealth, and knowledge. This chapter illustrates how people in real-world settings improve their lives by applying the strategies taught in this book. These are their stories.

Using DIFS to Get Fit

"I'm an advertising executive, and I'm not one of those weight-conscious people who only weigh themselves when they're stark naked, after a haircut and a bout with intestinal flu. Heck, I'll even weigh myself on a doctor's scale (are those scales set on planets without gravity?) carrying pocket change. Actually, my weight has only increased about ten pounds since college, and according to a statistical formula I vaguely recall from college, those ten pounds could easily be accounted for by measurement error.

"No, it wasn't the scale that tipped me off that I was overweight; it was my clothes. My tailored business suits, which once hung neatly at my sides, now rode up my back, hugged my shoulders, and constricted my waist like a boa. I didn't dare inhale for fear the suits would tighten their grip.

"At first I believed that a little exercise might loosen them, so I chose a sport requiring little exercise: softball. But weekly softball games were not the right prescription. My suits still fit me like surgical gloves, my weight was unchanged, and my poor conditioning left me sore and humbled. I got winded running the bases, strained my rotator cuff warming up before a game, twisted my ankle on the dugout steps, and pulled a calf muscle so badly that I had to walk downstairs backwards for a week. I was a wreck in tight suits.

"Next, I did what any soundly trounced person would do—I quit. I hung up my twisted spikes and my tight suits. The suits were banished to the back of my closet and replaced by bulky sweaters. Eventually, I turned things around, although I'm not sure what prompted the turnaround. Perhaps it was escalating weight, unyielding lethargy, a doctor's recommendation, or viewing old snapshots from fitter days. In any event, I had had enough. I became committed to regaining my fitness through desperate measures: real exercise.

"The **DIFS** (Desire, Intention, Focus, and Sustain) motivation model helped me develop and adhere to an exercise program.

Desire

"I had desire. I sought to regain the fitness level I had maintained through college, before I became an advertising executive. Regaining fitness was my north star—my overriding goal.

"I expressed my goal by generating specific goal statements. These included:

- losing ten pounds
- fitting comfortably into my former clothes
- increasing aerobic fitness and muscle strength

"I went public with these goals to solidify my commitment and gain support. I wrote these goals on cards and posted them on my fridge and on my bathroom mirror to serve as daily reminders. I also displayed an old college picture of me playing lacrosse. I moved my exiled suits to the front of my closet as testimonies of my bygone fitness and what is possible. I told my parents. My Sunday visits to their home began to feature low-fat suppers and steamed rice recipes. I told a few close friends. Some volunteered to exercise with me on weekends. One volunteered to inherit my cache of bulky sweaters. All encouraged me.

The DIFS motivation model can help you develop and adhere to an exercise program

Intention

"After establishing and publicizing my goals, I developed a plan to meet them. My plan was simple and reasonable. Simple, because unlike softball, it was not overly taxing. Reasonable, because it could be incorporated easily into my daily routine. To increase aerobic fitness and lose weight, I would walk. I would walk in a nearby park for twenty to thirty minutes during my lunch hour. Afterwards, I would eat a brown-bag lunch at my desk—no more lunching at expensive restaurants and eating more than necessary! Each morning and evening I would walk the half-mile between my house and the train station. This routine would provide an additional twenty minutes of exercise each day and eliminate excessive parking fees. On weekends, I planned to walk in my neighborhood or ride my bicycle.

"I planned to increase strength by exercising with modest hand weights while watching the evening news. At work, I would bypass the elevator and step up the stairs.

Focus

"Although barriers arose, I remained focused on carrying out my plan. When there were sudden work deadlines, I sometimes worked through lunch and walked in the evening. Business lunches, too, occasionally upset my schedule, leaving me to do some extra walking in the morning or evening. Some of my clients, I discovered, enjoyed exercise and fresh air. We replaced power lunches with power walking.

"Severe weather was a chilling barrier. Frigid temperatures and whipping winds made me want to huddle indoors. Instead, I dressed in layers of polypropylene, wool, and Goretex®; donned a face mask, wool hat, and wool mittens; and withstood winter's roar. Winter walking was invigorating.

"Winter skating was not. A slip on the ice brought back my twisted ankle. I couldn't walk for two weeks. Being on crutches could've been all the excuse I needed to unearth my sedentary lifestyle. Those crutches were my meal ticket to fattening lunches. But I wasn't buying. Instead, I bought an exercise bike with the money I saved eating brown-bag lunches and walking to and from the train. During my recovery period, I rode the bike twice a day. Whatever challenge arose, I rose above it.

Sustain

"I chronicled my exercise program in a journal. I recorded my daily exercise activities and various fitness indicators such as weight and clothes size. Writing in the journal and reviewing my accomplishments helped sustain my effort.

"I met my initial goals of losing ten pounds, reducing my clothes size, and attaining fitness in about eight months. After that, I exercised to maintain my weight and increase my fitness. But my chief reason for continuing was that I enjoyed the exercise process. I enjoyed being outside, moving, and thinking. About a year after beginning my walking program, I started jogging on weekends. Eventually, I joined a group of fun-runners that went out each Saturday morning. I branched into other activities, occasionally playing golf, racquetball, and soccer. Varying exercise activities helped me sustain my exercise commitment.

"Now, six years down the road, I look, feel, and sleep better than before I began exercising. I am more fit than when I was in college. There is no end in the road before me. The suits that I once wanted to wear are worn out. I intend to wear out a lot more."

Exercise

The advertising executive used DIFS to change ineffective health practices. Make a list of things you might want to change now or at some later time in your life. Choose one and explain how the DIFS model can be applied to help you make this change.

Using Representations to Earn Financial Wealth

"I am a thirty-year-old nurse making about $40,000 a year. I own a small home and drive an old but dependable car. I have about $10,000 saved that is available for emergencies. For the present, I'm neither rich nor poor—I'm comfortable. My financial future, however, is bright. When I retire in thirty-five years, I will be a millionaire. I'm not planning on winning the lottery or receiving a huge inheritance. I'm not a broker or a soothsayer. I have no financial training and no crystal ball. I have simply made a few smart financial decisions, guided by representations I developed.

"When I was twenty-one and about to graduate from nursing school, I saw a representation in a magazine that convinced me to open a retirement account immediately. The chart, shown in Figure 11-1, illustrates the value of early savings. The chart shows that Anna invested $2,000 for five consecutive years, resulting in a $10,000 investment. Ben invested $2,000 for twenty-five consecutive

Smart investing now can put you on "Easy Street" later

years, resulting in a $50,000 investment. Anna wisely began investing when she was only twenty-one. Ben began investing when he was forty. Each retired at age sixty-five. Ben's $50,000 investment had grown to $230,000. Not bad. Anna's meager $10,000 investment now equaled a whopping $608,000. (Both investments earned an average yield of 10 percent per year.) I figured that if I invested just $2,000 each year beginning at age twenty-one, at retirement I would accumulate about $1.5 million dollars from my $88,000 investment.

"Having decided to save for retirement, I next decided *how* to save. My parents had money socked away in savings accounts and certificates of deposit (CDs), and recommended I do the same. Before heeding their

Figure 11–1. *Representation Showing the Value of Early Investing*

	Anna	Ben
Age at Initial Investment:	21	40
Investment Plan:	$2,000 each year for 5 years	$2,000 each year for 25 years
Total Invested:	$10,000	$50,000
Retirement Savings (Age 65):	$608,000	$230,000

advice, I browsed through a few financial magazines and learned that there are three primary investment sources: savings accounts and CDs, stocks, and bonds. After reading about these investment sources, I developed the representation shown in Figure 11-2. Doing so helped me plot my investment strategy.

"I learned from Figure 11-2 that savings accounts and CDs, despite my parents' endorsement, are a dead-end road for long-term growth. I chose stocks, because they offered the greatest opportunity for growth. Although they are riskier than bonds in the short run, they outperform bonds in the long run.

"After deciding to invest in stocks, I next considered whether to invest in a single stock, a few stocks, or a mutual fund that invests in several stocks. Again, I looked up information about these options, and developed the stock investments representation shown in Figure 11-3.

Figure 11–2. *Representation for Choosing Investment Type*

	Types of Investments		
	Savings or CDs	Bonds	Stocks
Philosophy:	Safety	Fixed income	Growth
Purpose:	Short-term savings	Yearly income	Long-term growth
Realistic Short-Range Yield:	Very low	Moderate	Variable (low or high)
Realistic Long-Range Yield:	Very low	Moderate	High
Risk:	None	Moderate	High

Figure 11–3. *Representation Showing Stock Investment Options*

	Stock Investment Options		
	Mutual Fund	Few Stocks	Single Stock
Diversification:	Most	Some	None
Risk:	Least	Average	Most
Potential Gain:	High	Higher	Highest
Potential Loss:	Least	Average	Most
Investment Manager:	Fund manager	Self or paid broker	Self or paid broker

"After I'd examined Figure 11-3, I chose to invest in mutual funds. I didn't want to manage my stock investments, because I had neither the time or expertise. Nor did I want to pay a broker. Having a professional manager invest my money was appealing.

"Other factors that favored mutual funds were diversification and reduced risk. A mutual fund that invests in several stocks poses less risk than if I were to invest directly in a single stock or a few stocks. Although a mutual fund has less potential for growth than a single stock, mutual funds still offer wonderful growth potential with fewer risks.

"My next decision determined my choice of the type of mutual fund that I thought was best for me. I learned there are three major types: growth, balanced, and sector. I developed Figure 11-4 to compare them.

Figure 11–4.   *Representation Displaying Types of Mutual Funds*

Types of Mutual Funds

	Balanced	Growth	Sector
Invests in:	Stable and diverse companies, and bonds	Stable and diverse companies	Stable companies in one area
Examples:	Coca Cola General Electric Treasury Bonds	Coca Cola Burger King General Electric	Paper, electricity, or electronics
Objective:	Long-term growth and yearly capital	Long-term growth	Short- or long-term growth
Diversification:	Very high	High	Low
Risk:	Least	Average	Most
Long-Range Potential:	Average gain	High gain	High or low gain

"After analyzing the types of mutual funds, I chose to invest in growth funds. Sector funds lacked diversification and appeared too risky. They could either hit a home run or strike out. Furthermore, a smart investor invests in sector funds before they're 'hot' and while prices are low. I had little faith that I could predict advancing sectors. Furthermore, the sector market is volatile and needs to be watched closely. I preferred a more stable investment.

"The balanced funds were appealing, but because I was young and could ride out fluctuations in growth funds, I chose growth funds because of their historically higher long-term gains.

"The last decision was selecting a specific growth fund. I located a publication that listed the performance of all mutual funds. From that listing I constructed Figure 11-5, which compared last year's top-performing growth funds.

Figure 11–5. *Representation Displaying Top-Performing Growth Funds*

Top-Performing Growth Funds

	A	B	C	D	E
Average Total Return:					
Last year:	19.37	32.61	17.38	24.83	22.77
5 years:	—	—	16.34	20.64	18.34
10 years:	—	—	19.44	14.23	17.92
Risk:	Average	Above Average	Average	Above Average	Average
Performance in Bull Market:	*****	*****	***	*****	****
Performance in Bear Market:	?	?	***	**	***
Minimum Investment:	$1,000	$2,500	$250	$1,000	$250
Load:	3%	3%	None	None	None
Manager Stability:	1 year	1 year	2 years	6 years	10 years

"Using Figure 11-5, I chose Fund E. I preferred it for several reasons. First, its risk was average. I felt uncomfortable selecting the overly risky funds B and D. Second, the fund's minimum investment of $250 was appealing. This meant that I could make eight monthly investments of $250 to reach my $2,000 investment objective. Having to invest $1,000 (Fund A) or $2,500 (Fund B) all at once meant that first I had to save that money. I was afraid I might squander it, rather than save it. Third, I liked Fund E's no-load system. No-load funds have no investment fee. The 3 percent loads charged by Funds A and B would actually reduce my yearly $2,000 investment to $1,940.

"Perhaps most appealing was Fund E's stability. It had been managed by the same person for ten years. I read that the manager was thirty-four years old and planned to continue managing the fund for some time. Another indicator of stability was the fund's solid performance over the past ten years. Other funds (such as A and B) had much shorter track records or were less profitable (Fund D). Fund E's stability over ten years reflected its solid performance in both bull (upward) and bear (downward) markets. The previous seven years were predominantly bull markets, but the three years before that were bear markets. Strong ten-year growth reflected Fund E's performance in both bull and bear markets. Also, its four- and three-star ratings (out of a possible five-star rating) for bull and bear markets, respectively, confirmed its stability in varied market conditions.

"I strongly considered Fund C for the same reasons I chose Fund E. But overall, I saw that Fund E was better because of greater growth last year, slightly better performance in a bear market, and its manager's greater experience and stability.

"Since I drew up this plan and began investing I've made some minor changes. I still invest in Fund E, but I've diversified and invest in other funds, too. Representations, of course, helped me make those decisions. I'm also investing more than $2,000 per year. I've always liked the ring of the word 'multimillionaire.'"

Exercise

The nurse used representations to make important decisions about financial matters. Make a list of decisions you must make now or in the future. Choose one and demonstrate how representations help you reach a decision.

Using Strategies to Become a Chess Master

"I'm a chess master. Only 2 percent of all chess players can say that. It's hard to believe that I'm among the best. I always thought chess players were intellectual giants. I'm no rocket scientist or neurosurgeon doing cutting-edge work at NASA or in medicine. I'm a college graduate doing cutting-edge work on hair. I'm a barber. My master status is also perplexing because I pushed my first pawn at age forty, twilight time for most chess champions.

Mastering the game of chess requires many of the same learning strategies that produce academic success

"The dawn of my chess career broke when my seven-year-old daughter joined her school chess club. She was my first teacher, teaching me the pieces' names and how they move and capture. I followed her to weekend tournaments and watched her and others play. I became enthralled by the strategic assembling of chess armies and the quick tactical strikes of its warriors. Before long, I left the sideline and joined the battle. My first tournament was a massacre. I lost all five games, including one to a kindergartner who checkmated me in four moves.

"Losing didn't make me surrender, it made me learn. I read chess books, joined a weekly chess club, and played in weekend tournaments. Hard work paid off. My chess rating soared from 200 to 1,200. I was competitive at local tournaments (no more embarrassing four-move mates). For all my hard work and progress, though, I only stood at the threshold of what chess world champion Garry Kasparov calls the 'Black and White Jungle' (in reference to a chess board's black and white squares). Standing there, however, I could see the beauty of masterfully played games. I knew that I wanted to create those games the way that others must know they want to create art or music. I set out to tame that jungle, believing that I had both the will and skill to do it.

The Will to Learn

"I had the will to learn chess, and the **DIFS** motivation model (**D**esire, **I**ntention, **F**ocus, and **S**ustain) helped me harness it. My desire was to become a chess master. This meant boosting my 1,200 rating to 2,200.

Rating points are earned for tournament-game victories and deducted for tournament-game defeats. Victories or defeats against players of similar ratings result in small rating changes. Victories or defeats against much lower- or higher-rated players result in greater rating changes.

"My chess master dream could not be realized overnight. My intention was to invest time daily over a ten- to twenty-year period. I planned to study chess at least one hour a day and participate in at least two tournaments per month. I planned to invest time wisely by studying at work when business was slow, and before bed when I normally watched television.

"I maintained focus by varying my chess activities. I studied chess books and magazines, worked chess puzzles, practiced weekly with a local chess club, and took private lessons from a chess master. I also matched wits with my chess computer, faceless foes across the Internet, and with sweaty-palmed opponents at local, regional, and national tournaments. Eventually, I instructed my daughter's chess club and gave private lessons to chess novices.

"The only barrier I faced was occasionally noticing little growth. My chess rating stalled for long periods, and even dipped from time to time. I was not discouraged. I maintained focus by recognizing that jungle travel is slow and sometimes involves backtracking, and by appreciating the journey, however winding the trail might be.

"Chess awards, rating points, and the journey have sustained my efforts. I've won area tournaments and state titles. I passed 2,200 points and earned my Master's Certificate when I was fifty-eight, eighteen years after pushing my first pawn. More than the awards or points, the journey has carried me. I've relished the solitary hours spent studying a complicated chess position and my stimulating interactions with chess teachers, opponents, and students. My daughter's unbroken chess enchantment has been the sunlight filtering through the jungle's canopy. Today, I stand deep in the 'Black and White Jungle' in awe of its beauty, order, and depth. There is much more to explore.

The Skills to Learn

"I can't possibly recount all that I've learned about chess, but I can provide insights about *how* I learned. The same skills or strategies that earned me high grades in college helped me master chess.

Metacognition

"I began studying the games of chess legends like Alexander Alekhine, José Capablanca, Emanuel Lasker, Bobby Fischer, and Garry Kasparov. Although I could not understand and appreciate all their moves, studying their games helped me develop internal guideposts and measuring sticks for masterful chess.

"Thereafter, I was able to check my chess plans and actions relative to experts. For instance, I might ask myself during a match whether I am denying my opponent all opportunities, as Fischer did to Spassky in Game 6 of their 1972 world title match, or whether I can force my opponent's knight to occupy an inferior square as Kasparov did to Karpov in Game 16 of their 1985 championship match. Specific megacognitive checks like these are more helpful than general checks such as 'How am I doing?'

Reading and Note-Taking

"Various strategies helped me acquire a mountain of chess knowledge. Reading and note-taking strategies helped me scale the mountain of more than two hundred books. While reading, I marked key ideas and later noted them in scores of notebooks that I kept. The notebooks were organized around broad themes, such as history, openings, tactics, and strategies; and around narrow themes, such as doubled and isolated pawns, endgames with bishops of opposite colors, and blockading past pawns.

"My reading was guided by comprehension strategies. When reading accounts of chess games, I predicted subsequent moves and questioned a move's purpose. I noted these questions and later asked my teacher the questions. I related text ideas to my own experiences. While reading about trading inactive bishops or minimizing pawn islands, for example, I related these ideas to games I played previously. Building relations helped me understand and apply new ideas.

Representations

"Developing representations was instrumental in acquiring chess knowledge. Figure 11-6 shows the framework for a representation I developed to learn the history of outstanding chess players. This representation is organized by country. Others I created were organized chronologically or by playing style.

Figure 11–6. *Representation Framework of Outstanding Chess Players*

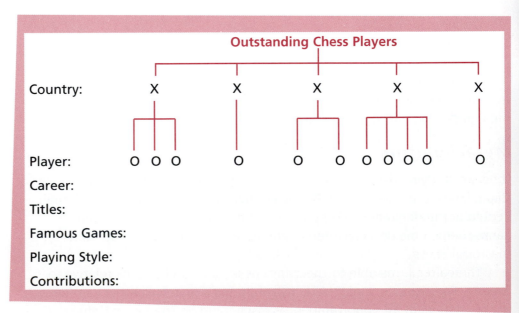

"I relied on representations to learn chess openings. There are roughly fifty standard openings (for example, the 'Queen's Gambit') each with several variations (for example, the 'Queen's Gambit Declined'). Chess masters memorize the first ten or so moves in the standard openings and in dozens of variations. Not knowing these opening lines can result in wasting time considering moves, lost material, or a weakened position.

"Figure 11-7 shows a sample framework I developed for representing chess openings.

Figure 11–7. *Representation Framework of Chess Openings*

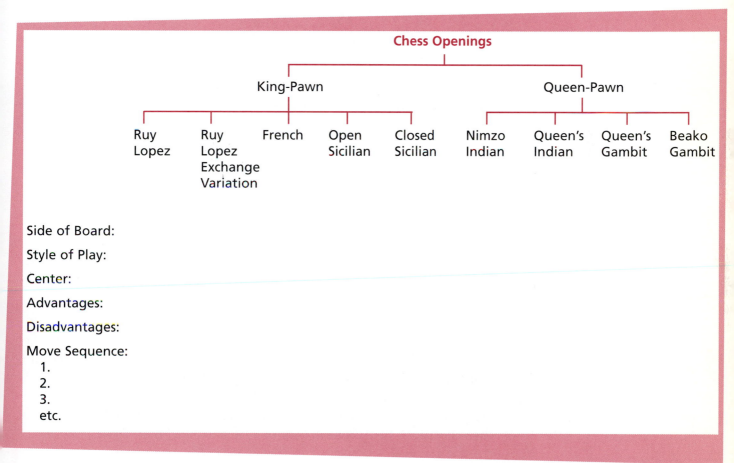

Building Connections

"The completed chess-openings representations helped me memorize move sequences and build connections within and across openings. For example, I noted that king-pawn openings invite play on the king side and encourage a sharp, tactical, style of play, whereas queen-pawn openings invite play on the queen side and encourage slow, positional play. The 'French' opening is plagued by a blocked queen-side bishop making its army susceptible to a king-side attack. Its advantage is a strong end game pawn structure if the king-side attack is withstood. The 'Open Sicilian' results in an open position (pawns not blocking the center) and ample opportunities for tactical strikes, whereas the 'Closed Sicilian' results in a closed center and a steady buildup of forces behind the center.

"Move sequences are also easy to compare by using my chess-openings matrix. For example, comparing the standard 'Ruy Lopez' and the 'Ruy Lopez Exchange Variation,' below, it is evident that their move sequences are identical for White's and Black's first three moves. They differ on move four. In the 'Ruy Lopez,' White moves its bishop (B) to the a4 square and Black moves its knight (N) to the f6 square. In the 'Exchange Variation,' White exchanges its bishop for Black's knight. White's bishop captures (x) Black's c6 knight and Black's d-pawn captures White's c6 bishop.

| | Ruy Lopez | | Ruy Lopez Exchange Variation | |
	White	Black	White	Black
1.	e4	e5	e4	e5
2.	Nf3	Nc6	Nf3	Nc6
3.	Bb5	a6	Bb5	a6
4.	Ba4	Nf6	Bxc6	dxc6

Concept and Skill Acquisition

"Chess is all about making the right moves. Master players make the right moves (most of the time) because they recognize chess patterns and calculate potential move sequences in their mind. The same academic strategies that govern concept learning govern chess-pattern learning, and the same academic strategies that govern skill learning govern calculation-skills learning.

"I've read that chess masters can recognize about fifty thousand chess patterns. For instance, they recognize White's strongly positioned knight on d5 in Figure 11-8. It looms over the board's center and is defended by its pawns on c4 and e4. It blockades Black's d6 and d7 pawns, which cannot move forward. The White knight cannot be budged by any of Black's pawns on the adjacent c and e files. In Figure 11-9, chess masters recognize that Black's c5 bishop and e5 knight can be attacked simultaneously (forked) if White pushes its d-pawn to d4. Only one black piece can escape and White's d-pawn gobbles up the other. Patterns like these are learned by experiencing a wide range of examples. Therefore, I've studied thousands of chess positions [like those in Figures 11-8 and 11-9] that display various chess patterns.

"Calculation is the inner game of chess. Top players often consider multiple moves and their opponent's likely response to each possible move. Moreover, top players look deep into the chess position, often calculating each variation several moves ahead. For instance, looking at the position in Figure 11-10, I notice (pattern recognition) my opponent's vulnerable king on e8. I notice too that my queen could attack it from h5 if my own knight on f3 was moved to make way for my queen. I calculate some potential move sequences to see if I might checkmate the enemy king.

"Calculation is aided by mentally constructing move hierarchies like that shown in Figure 11-11. In this partial move hierarchy, I consider the sacrifice: knight takes pawn at g5 (Nxg5). I calculate several variations. The left-most and middle variations show Black capturing my sacrificed knight (fxg5) and being checkmated (++) four moves later. The right-most varia-

Figure 11–8. *Diagram Showing White's Strongly Positioned Knight on e5*

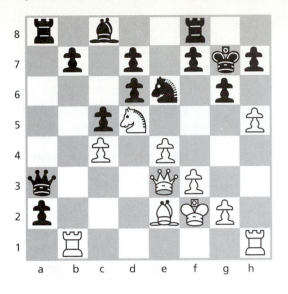

Figure 11–9. *Diagram Showing a Potential Fork by White's d2 Pawn*

Figure 11–10. *Diagram of Chess Position for Calculation*

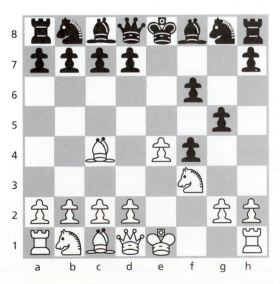

Figure 11–11. *Move Hierarchy for Calculation*

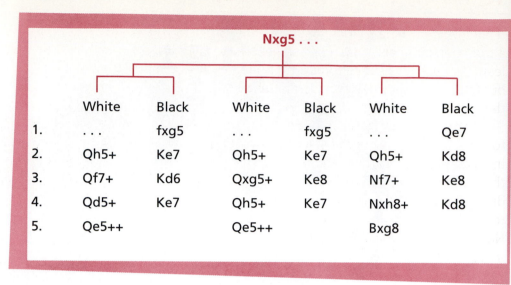

Nxg5 . . .

	White	Black	White	Black	White	Black
1.	. . .	fxg5	. . .	fxg5	. . .	Qe7
2.	Qh5+	Ke7	Qh5+	Ke7	Qh5+	Kd8
3.	Qf7+	Kd6	Qxg5+	Ke8	Nf7+	Ke8
4.	Qd5+	Ke7	Qh5+	Ke7	Nxh8+	Kd8
5.	Qe5++		Qe5++		Bxg8	

tion shows Black moving its queen instead (Qe7). This results in the tragic loss of its pawn (Nxg5), rook (Nxh8), and knight (Bxg8) and a brutal assault on its king.

"I practice developing move hierarchies. Initially, I developed them on paper. Eventually, I was able to construct them and visualize them in my mind.

Note-Taking and Error Analysis

"Two other learning strategies, used in combination, have helped me reach master status: note-taking and error analysis. When I compete in chess tournaments, I record notes representing all the chess moves made. Later, I study these notes with my teacher or with chess colleagues. During these post-game analyses, we recognize missed patterns, dissect both strong and weak moves, and repair faulty calculations. Analyzing chess errors helps me not repeat them in future tournaments.

"Without these learning strategies, I could have never found my way through the 'Black and White Jungle.'"

Exercise

The barber used various strategies to attain chess expertise. List a few things you wish to master. Explain how motivation, time management, reading, note-taking, and review strategies will help you achieve mastery.

Teaching My Child How to Learn

"I am giving my nine-year-old daughter, Megan, a truly wonderful gift. I am teaching her how to learn. Her teachers should present this gift, but they don't. They present information, but they don't teach Megan how to learn it.

"Every day I teach Megan more about how to learn. There is no special lesson for practicing learning such as there is with practicing the piano. Instead, I teach her how to learn during natural learning opportunities as we read a book, plan a trip, or study for a test. Natural opportunities are ripe for strategy instruction.

Teaching Reading Comprehension

"Strategy instruction began when Megan was a preschooler. As I read to her, I modeled read-ing comprehension strategies such as ques-

Reading to children is enjoyable and provides opportunities to teach them reading strategies

tioning, predicting, bringing in background knowledge, organizing, and retelling. Below is a portion of a fable I read to Megan. My modeled strate-gies are in parentheses.

The Mice and the Weasels

For months, the weasels and the mice had been at war. (I'm bring-ing in some background knowledge here. I know that weasels are much bigger than mice. I'm predicting that the weasels have won the battles.) The weasels were bigger and stronger than the mice, they won battle after battle. (Ah, my prediction was correct.) The surviving mice called a meeting. (I have a question. Why did they call this meeting? I predict they will give up.)

"I have a plan," said one mouse. "We have lost all our battles because we do not have any leaders. I vote that we choose four mice to be our generals and lead us into battle." (Wow, my predic-tion was way off, the mice aren't giving up. Some background knowledge I have is that certain generals are great leaders and can make a difference.) To show that they were generals, the four mice were given large helmets with great feathers called plumes in them. They also had large heavy badges dangling on ribbons from their necks. (I have background knowledge that these things are too big and bulky for tiny mice. I predict that these outfits will cause prob-lems for the mice. I'm going to retell the story to this point:

Weasels were defeating mice in wars. The mice decided they needed generals to lead them. They dressed the generals in heavy outfits.)

"Soon, Megan was able to apply the strategies with some prompting. The example below, also from "The Mice and the Weasels," shows how I prompted her:

> Before long, the four generals began to feel very important. (Can you bring in some prior knowledge about how you feel when you are dressed up?) They held many meetings at which they made plans to defeat the weasels. They talked so bravely it made them feel proud and strong. (Can you predict what might happen?)
>   Alas, for all their plans they were still defeated. (Was your prediction correct?) After a fierce battle, the mice turned and fled. (Do you have a question or a prediction? Can you organize and retell the story to this point?)

"Eventually, Megan needed no prompts. She applied comprehension strategies as I read. Today, she is an independent and strategic reader confident she can learn from text.

Teaching Representations

"Another opportunity to teach strategies occurred when Megan was six and was invited to perform a piano recital in Knoxville, Tennessee (eight hundred miles away). Together we developed a representation to help us make travel plans for our five-day stay (see Figure 11-12). Our options included driving to Knoxville, flying to Knoxville, or flying to Nashville and then driving to Knoxville (roughly two hundred miles away). From this experience Megan learned how to develop and use representations for decision-making. We chose "flying to Nashville and then driving to Knoxville," given that it was only slightly more expensive and a lot more convenient than driving all the way to Knoxville, and given that it was far less expensive and slightly less convenient than flying to Knoxville. This natural experience also provided opportunities to teach information gathering strategies (for example, determining airline costs and schedules) and to demonstrate mathematical applications in real-world settings (such as estimating and adding meal costs).

Figure 11–12. *Representation for Making Travel Plans*

| **Alternative Travel Plans** | | |
	Drive	Fly to Nashville	Fly to Knoxville
Airfare:	—	$235	$960
Car Rental:	—	$140	$140
Gas:	$130	$40	$10
Hotel:	$420	$300	$300
Meals:	$400	$300	$300
Parking:	——	$15	$15
Total:	$950	$1030	$1725

Teaching Studying

"Several learning opportunities arise as Megan studies for weekly spelling tests. In terms of time management, I've taught her to invest early, daily, and wisely. Megan begins early, studying her word list on Monday for Friday's exam. She invests daily, studying approximately fifteen minutes per day. Megan wisely empties pockets of unstructured time and spends them studying. When riding the school bus or waiting for school to begin, Megan routinely pulls her spelling list from her backpack and studies.

"I've taught Megan to build internal and external connections while she's studying her spelling. Given the spelling list below, she organizes (internal connections) the words according to spelling rules or other commonalities, and sometimes relates spelling words to words or images outside her list (external connections).

While helping children with school assignments, parents can also teach children strategies

hear	star	defeat
load	president	trapeze
prone	heart	extra
trite	execute	separate
cut	nap	trace

- Words beginning with the "x" sound begin with "ex."
     - execute
     - extra
- A final "e" makes the previous vowel long.
     - separate
     - trapeze
     - trite
     - trace
     - prone
- Without a final "e" the vowel is short.
     - nap
     - cut
     - star
- In words with joining vowels, the first vowel does the talking.
     - hear
     - defeat
     - load

- Some words contain other words. Use mnemonic imagery to associate the word and its embedded word.

  hear (contains ear)—Imagine holding an ear of corn to your ear to hear.

  president (contains side)—Imagine seeing the president on the side of Mt. Rushmore.

  separate (contains para)—Imagine a parachute separating from the skydiver.

  trapeze (contains ape)—Imagine an ape swinging from the trapeze.

  defeat (contains eat)—Imagine eating a hamburger after losing a soccer game.

"Another strategy Megan uses for spelling is self-testing. I've taught Megan to test herself so thoroughly that she is confident of earning a perfect score on Friday's test. Megan simulates test conditions while self-testing by recording the words on a tape recorder in a varied order, and then writing each word as the tape is played.

"She also uses a related strategy, self checking. Rather than immediately using her spelling list to correct her practice tests, Megan first checks them thoroughly without the list. Megan also checks her Friday test before handing it in. She monitors her test for spelling errors, mistakes related to capitalization and apostrophes, and silly goofs, such as omitting a letter or adding the wrong suffix.

"Last, Megan uses error analysis to determine the type and source of spelling errors. She modifies her study or testing techniques to eliminate future errors.

"Now that Megan is a fourth-grader, she is tested frequently in other subjects. Recently, she studied the northeast states and had to learn the states' capitals. I taught her to use a mnemonic technique that verbally or visually associates state names and capitals. Below are a few of the associations that Megan developed.

Boston, Massachusetts—Imagine someone chewing on a Boston Cream Pie during Mass.

Trenton, New Jersey—Imagine someone treading on my new jersey.

Concord, New Hampshire—Imagine the Concorde flying into a new hamper.

Augusta, Maine—Remember that Caesar Augustus was the main man in Rome.

Providence, Rhode Island—Roads were provided for the island.

"Another recent topic was 'clouds.' Together, we developed the matrix representation in Figure 11-13 to study for the test. Studying the matrix, Megan built several connections. She noted that the rain clouds (stratus) formed a low dark ceiling, whereas the fair-weather clouds (cirrus) were high, white, and wispy. Megan noted that the fluffy, white cumulus clouds appeared at all levels and signaled only a slight chance of rain. Looking across the matrix, Megan noted that all average heights included the number five (ranging from 0.5 miles to 5 miles).

"I helped Megan incorporate a mnemonic technique to relate the cloud's name to its properties. For stratus, Megan used the similar-sounding word 'straight.' She remembered that stratus clouds form straight across the sky. 'Circus' was our keyword for cirrus clouds. Megan imagined a circus tightrope walker walking high above the circus crowd. The similar sounding word 'column' helped Megan recall that cumulus clouds can form in a column at all elevation levels.

"Learning about clouds also lent itself to learning about various types of tests. I showed Megan the difference between fact questions and concept questions. Together we developed possible fact questions from our matrix such as 'What do cumulus clouds look like?' 'Which cloud brings rain?' and 'At what height are cirrus clouds found?'

"We also developed and answered concept questions by finding cloud pictures and identifying their types.

Figure 11–13. *Matrix Representation for Clouds*

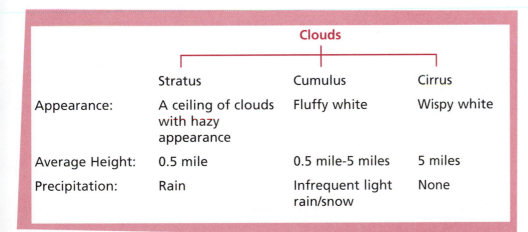

	Stratus	Cumulus	Cirrus
Appearance:	A ceiling of clouds with hazy appearance	Fluffy white	Wispy white
Average Height:	0.5 mile	0.5 mile-5 miles	5 miles
Precipitation:	Rain	Infrequent light rain/snow	None

Teaching Self-Control

"Perhaps the most important thing I've taught Megan is taking responsibility for learning. When Megan forgot to return completed homework assignments to school, I taught her to place her homework in her backpack immediately upon completion. When she announced that she was stupid in math, I pointed out that she is a talented piano player because she practices, and that math skills, too, can only be learned with practice. Math practice has brought Megan success and confidence.

"Another time, Megan was assigned to a cooperative group to answer science questions. One group member dominated and quickly wrote answers without input from other members. When Megan related this incident, I asked who was at fault. She blamed the group member for being pushy and the teacher for not noticing. I pointed out that responsibility must be shared by the group members, who neglected to slow down the "pushy" one and balance group participation. Now, Megan takes steps to ensure that all group members are involved.

"My responsibility lessons are paying dividends. Recently, Megan independently made two simple, but important, requests of her teacher. Megan asked that the partition between her classroom and the adjoining classroom be closed so that distractions were minimized. She also asked for more time at the completion of spelling tests to thoroughly check her answers.

"I'm delighted that Megan is taking control of her learning and is learning to learn. Her future in the classroom and beyond is bright."

Exercise

Your fourth-grader has to do a report on spiders. What opportunities are available to teach learning? Describe three learning strategies you might teach and how you might teach them.

Summary

This chapter illustrated how the strategies crucial for academic success are crucial for life success. Strategies made people healthy, wealthy, and wise. The advertising executive used motivation strategies to become healthy. The nurse just out of college used representation strategies to become wealthy. A barber used a variety of strategies to become wise. And a parent imparted wisdom by teaching a child how to learn.

Strategy application can be cast in another light. In these scenarios, people took control, made smart decisions, and learned. The advertising executive took control of health, appearance, and weight. Certainly there are other things to control, such as tempers, destructive attitudes, and time spent with family. The nurse made smart investment decisions. Certainly other decisions await, such as choosing a graduate school or a job and deciding whether to rent or buy a home. The chess master learned chess. Learning opportunities abound. You can learn about your job, your culture, or rare coins.

Your life awaits you. Be healthy, wealthy, and wise. Take control, make good decisions, and learn. Take what you learn and pass it along.

Answers to focus *questions*

1. The advertising executive turns desire into action by making goal statements, publicizing goals, and then deriving a plan (intentions) for meeting these goals.

2. The advertising executive sustains an exercise program by recording progress in a journal, varying activities, exercising with others, and recognizing the benefits of feeling, sleeping, and looking better. In addition, the executive enjoys the exercise process.

3. Due in part to the representations developed, the nurse chooses to invest in retirement accounts, stock accounts, mutual funds, growth-oriented funds, and a particular growth-oriented fund.

4. The barber studied chess for eighteen years before reaching the level of chess master.

5. The barber uses several reading strategies. The barber 1) predicts upcoming moves and questions puzzling moves, 2) relates new ideas to previous experiences, 3) selects text ideas and organizes them in notebooks, and 4) makes representations for comparison.

6. The chess master uses representations to understand chess history and to compare and memorize chess openings. The chess master visualizes move hierarchies to consider potential moves and opponent responses.

7. The chess master learns patterns, such as forks, by studying many different examples.

8. The chess master records moves during tournament games and later analyzes these moves with the help of colleagues or teachers. This "error" analysis helps the master uncover and repair weaknesses.

9. Children should be taught to learn in the context of natural learning opportunities, such as reading or when studying for a test.

10. Reading strategies are introduced to nonreaders or children by adults or others who model and name strategies during reading practice.

11. While studying for her test on clouds, Megan learned to construct representations, use mnemonics, and review for various types of tests.

12. Megan illustrated self-control by asking her teacher to close a partition to minimize distractions and by requesting more time to use effective self-checking skills following a spelling test.

Index

Abbreviations, in note-taking, 265–266
Ability
    and academic success, 47
    defining, 30
    innate, 6, 7, 80
    personal attributions, 46–47
    in special education, 47
Absence from class, 57–58, 257–258
Academic goals, 63
Academic success
    ability and, 47, 48
    defining, 85
    intention and, 65
    visualizing, 66–69
Alert words
    in chapter headings, 206
    common, 167
    listening for, 171
    signaling diagrams, 167–169, 174
    signaling hierarchies, 57, 109, 171
    signaling sequences, 172, 173
    text's structure drawn from, 207
Analogies, generating, 119
Assignments
    long-term, 89–91
    in study groups, 295
Attention
    focusing your, 104, 105–109, 210–213
    to overviews, 108
    to personally relevant ideas, 107–108
    to physical properties, 106–107
    selective nature of, 105
    to summaries, 108
Attitude, in lectures, 257
Attributions
    environmental, 55–61
    personal, 46–54

Block schedule, 35, 81–85, 94
Bold print, 108
Boredom, 36, 56–57

Changing, 2–38
    commitment to, 26
    learning beliefs, 6–25
    with learning strategies, 31
    obstacles to, 26–31
    reasons for, 31, 32–38
Chapter headings, 206–207, 208

Chapter questions, 213, 214
Chapters, surveying, 202–210, 213
Chapter summaries, 244–246
Chess, 9, 23, 155, 318
    using strategies for, 385–392
Chores, 81, 93
Chronology, 145–146
Classes
    absence from, 57–58, 257–258
    boring, 56–57
    size of, 55
    time of day of, 55
Comparison
    with matrices, 22, 24, 134, 166
    with outlines, 136
    as a reading strategy, 233–234
    with representations, 136–139
Comprehension strategies, 201–202,
        227–242
    creating summaries, 235–237, 239
    evaluating ideas, 234–235
    generating elaborations, 231–235, 239
    generating examples, 232–233
    making comparisons, 233–234
    making predictions, 228–229, 238
    note-taking, 34, 57
    organizing ideas, 230–231, 238
    raising questions, 227–228, 238, 246–249
    for real world application, 388
    sample passage for, 239–242
    self-monitoring, 122, 237–239
    teaching, 393–394
Concepts
    learning, 311–312, 390–391
    questions of, 304, 305, 309–314, 343,
        345–346
    reviewing, 369
Connections
    building, 104, 111–121, 389–390
    contrived, 120–121
    external, 111, 113–117, 118–121, 228,
        303–304
    internal, 111, 113–117, 270, 299–302
Control, taking, 35–38
Cramming, 27, 36–37, 292

Daily scheduling, 88–92
Details, in note-taking, 262–264
Diagrams, 129, 139, 152–157

alert words signaling, 167–169, 174
compared to matrices, 155
dynamic, 152–155
generating while reading, 244
included in matrices, 156
to organize ideas, 230–231
static, 152–155
two functions of, 152
DIFS (Desire, Intention, Focus, Sustain),
        61–72
    in error analysis, 370
    in lectures, 256–257
    in reading, 201–202
    in real world applications, 378–380, 386–387

Eating properly, 329
Elaboration
    as a comprehension strategy, 201,
        231–235, 239
    of notes, 56, 274–277, 280–282
Emphasis, noting, 108
Enjoyment, increasing, 33
Environmental distractions, 59, 107
Error analysis, 366–370, 392, 396
Essays, writing, 22
Essay tests, 22, 360–366
Evaluation, unfair, 59–60
Examples
    generating when reading, 119, 232–233
    in note-taking, 262–264
Excuses, 44–45, 46, 61, 258
    sample, 58
Exercise, 329, 334
    using DIFS, 378–380
External connections, 111, 113–117,
        118–121, 303–304
    in reading, 213, 228

Fact, questions of, 304, 305, 306–308,
        343–345
Feedback, 318, 367
Figures of speech, 21
Final exams. See Review for exams; Tests
Financial considerations
    cost of college education, 85, 86
    investing in education, 86–88
    see also Working students
Focusing attention, 104, 105–109
    in lectures, 256–257, 258
    on objectives, 108–109
    on personally relevant ideas, 107–109
    on physical properties, 106–107
    in reading, 210–213
    while studying, 104

Goals
    academic, 63
    challenging, 62
    future, 48
    identifying enjoyable, 63

increasing your, 61–64, 65–69
long-term, 64
meager, 62
motivation and, 48
for reading, 201
short-term, 65
vague, 64
Goal statements, 64
Grading policies, 60
Graphs, organizing ideas with, 230–231
Group study. See Study groups

Hierarchies, 129, 141–143
    alert words signaling, 171, 172
    constructing, 189
    extending into matrices, 139, 148–149
Highlighted material, noting, 210, 211
Highlighting, 15–16, 33–34

Ideas
    evaluating when reading, 234–235, 239
    following in lectures, 267–268
    organizing when reading, 230–231, 239
    see also Main ideas
Illness, 48–50, 258
Illustrations, 152. See also Diagrams
Information
    grouped, 185–186
    linear, 133, 135
    localized, 137, 138
    memorizing, 20–22
    ordered, 187–188
    organized, 116, 152
    presentation of, 133
    see also Representations
Instructions, test, 336, 355
Integrative approach, 134
Internal connections, 111, 113–117, 270,
        299–302
Interval schedules, 14
Italics, noting, 108

Knowledge
    prior, 118, 119, 120, 213, 303
    skill, 316

Learning
    long-term, 104, 109–111
    by necessity, 24
    piecemeal approach to, 133–134
    principles of, 100–125
    self-monitoring your, 104, 122–125
Learning-disabled students, 47, 341
Learning strategies, 4, 6
    application to the real world, 23–25,
        374–398
    developing effective, 10, 11, 104–109
    general principles, 104
    lack of, 31
    teaching, 7

Lecture notes
    complete, 262–269, 277–282, 299
    effective, 256, 261–277
    elaborate, 274–277, 280–282
    incomplete, 19
    organized, 270–274, 278–279, 300
    studying, 88, 261
    taking good notes, 20, 36
    see also Note-taking
Lecturers
    influencing the, 266–267
    questioning, 281
Lectures
    absence from, 258
    concentrating in, 259, 268
    disorganized, 57
    emotional preparation for, 256–257
    important ideas in, 267–268
    learning from, 256, 257
    materials for, 259–260, 276
    mental preparation for, 256
    physical preparation for, 256
    recognizing the structure of, 177–178, 270
    repeatable categories in, 179
    reviewing for, 260
    tape-recording, 109, 269
    using DIFS in, 256–257
    verbal cues in, 108
    visual displays in, 267
    what to do after, 277–282
    what to do before, 256–261
    what to do during, 261–277
    writing a summary of, 280–281
    see also Lecture notes
Leisure time, 84–85, 93, 96
Linear information, 133, 135
Localization, 137, 138
Long-term assignments, 89–91
Long-term learning, 104, 109–111

Main ideas
    listening for, 109
    in note-taking, 262–264
    in summaries, 236
Marking systems, 16, 218–226, 239–242
Marking the text, 218–226, 239–242
Matching tests, 354–357
Materials
    for lectures, 259–260, 276
    for test-taking, 330
Matrices, 129, 148–152
    based on chapter overview, 209
    big-picture pattern evident with, 14, 116, 138, 139
    compared to diagrams, 155
    for comparison, 22, 24, 134, 166
    constructing, 179–182
    details in, 150–152
    diagrams included in, 156
    extending hierarchies and sequences into, 139, 148–149

    reducing clutter with, 137, 138–139
    repeatable categories in, 150–152, 175–182
    spotting missing details with, 138, 139
    three parts of, 150–152
    topics in, 150–152
Memorizing
    by rehearsing, 114
    for tests, 20–22
Memory
    mnemonic techniques, 121, 306–308, 396
    note-taking as an aid to, 261
    principles of, 100–125
    retrieval from, 114, 118
    strategies for learning-disabled, 47
Metacognition, 387–388
Mnemonic techniques, 121, 306, 307–308, 396
Monitoring. *See* Self-monitoring
Mood
    for lectures, 256–257
    and motivation, 50–51
    for reading, 201–202
    for studying, 50–51
Motivation, 8, 42–72
    ability and, 46–47, 53–54
    absence from class and, 57–58
    boredom and, 56–57
    class size and, 55
    distractions and, 59
    enhancing with DIFS, 61–72, 370, 378–380, 386–387
    environmental attributions and, 55–61
    focus and, 69–70
    goals and, 61–69
    illness and, 48–50
    lack of, 31
    liking the subject and, 52
    mood and, 50–51
    personal attributions as barriers, 46–54
    personal problems and, 54
    time management and, 60–61
    using mental imagery in, 66–69
Multiple-choice tests, 22, 310, 350–354

Notebooks, 259
Note-taking
    as an aid to memory, 261
    complete, 277–282
    effective, 261
    elaborate notes, 56, 274–277, 280–282
    good notes, 20, 36
    levels of, 262
    organized notes, 270–274, 278–279
    paraphrasing, 264
    as a reading strategy, 34, 57
    real world application, 388, 392
    from recorded lectures, 109
    recording main ideas, details and examples, 262–264
    self-monitoring your, 268–269
    on tests, 337

three types of, 172
using abbreviations and notations, 265
see also Lecture notes; Study notes

Objectives
    focusing on, 108–109
    surveying, 211–213
    in texts, 210, 211–213
Organizing
    ideas, 230–231
    information, 116, 152
    using diagrams and graphs, 230–231
Outlines
    comparing to representations, 136–139
    ineffectiveness of, 13–15, 33, 135
    linear information in, 135
Overviews, surveying, 208–210

Paraphrasing, 264
Personal problems, 36, 54
Personal values, and choices, 24
Physical properties, attending to, 106
Piecemeal approach, 133–134
PIE TAP review model, 297–298
Predictions, making, 201, 228–229, 238

Questions
    asking during tests, 339
    asking in lectures, 281–282
    chapter, 211, 213, 214
    compiling after reading, 246–249
    as a comprehension strategy, 201,
        227–228, 238
    to make predictions, 228–229
    test (*see* Test questions)

Reading
    establishing an anchor for, 213–215
    generating a final summary, 244–246
    generating representations, 243–244
    goals for, 235
    marking the text, 16, 218–226, 239–242
    setting the mood for, 201–202
    surveying the chapter, 202–210
    what to do after, 243–249
    what to do before, 201–217
    what to do during, 218–242
    see also Comprehension strategies
Real world applications
    learning strategies in, 23–25, 374–398
    in teaching strategies, 393–398
    using DIFS, 378–380, 386–387
    using representations for financial
        matters, 381–385
    using strategies to become a chess
        master, 385–392
Reciting, 33, 34
Rehearsal, 114
    ineffectiveness of, 109–111
    for long-term learning, 104, 109–111

Repeatable categories, 150–152, 175–182
    embedded in material, 179–182
    identifying, 183–184
    indirectly stated, 218–226
    in lectures, 179
    in matrices, 150–152, 175–182
    recognizing, 177–182
    reordering of, 187, 243–244
Repetition strategies, 10–11, 297
Representations
    advantages of, 135–139
    from alert words, 166–174
    changing, 162–163
    choosing the type of, 166–174
    comparing to outlines, 136–139
    constructing, 57, 160–190, 223
    generating while reading, 243–244
    grouped and nongrouped, 185–186
    as a learning strategy, 14, 35
    from marked text, 223, 224, 225
    multiple, 188–190
    principles of, 182–190, 191
    real world applications, 381–385,
        388–389, 397
    relationships illustrated with, 139–157
    for taking tests, 344–348, 361, 362
    teaching, 394
    types of, 129, 139–157
    see also Diagrams; Hierarchies; Matrices;
        Sequences
Rereading, 33, 34, 104, 297
Retake exams, 367
Review for exams, 286–319
    building external connections, 303–304
    building internal connections, 299–302
    on a daily basis, 292–293
    four-step model for, 297–298
    guidelines for study groups, 293, 295–296
    how to, 297–319
    preparing the study notes for, 298–299
    reasons to, 289
    using TAP, 297, 304–319
    what to, 297
    when to, 292–293
    where to, 290–291
    see also Studying; Test preparation
Review for lectures, 260, 261

Scenarios, surveying, 213
Schedules of Reinforcement, 13, 15, 34–35
Scheduling, 35, 88–92. *See also* Time
        management
Self-Awareness Questionnaire, 27, 28–29
Self-control
    lack of, 30
    teaching, 397–398
Self-monitoring
    comprehension strategies, 237–239
    learning, 104, 122–125
    note-taking, 268–269

progress and performance, 122–125
  skills in, 122–125
  in time management, 94
Self-testing strategy, 37, 104, 396
Semester planner, 89–91
Sequences, 129
  alert words signaling, 172, 173
  chronology in, 145–146
  extending into matrices, 139, 148–149
Short-answer tests, 359–360
Skills, 61
  defined, 46
  keys to acquiring, 318, 390–391
  questions of, 304, 305, 314–319, 343, 346–348
Special education, 47
Spelling, 395–396
Static diagrams, 152–155
Stress reduction strategies, 37
Students, types of, 7
Study groups
  assignments in, 295
  guidelines for, 293, 295–296
  noncontributors in, 296
Studying
  distractions while, 27, 59, 107
  environment for, 290–291
  focusing and, 104
  importance of time spent, 9–10
  in the mood for, 50–51
  motivation and, 50–51
  number of hours per week, 60–61, 80, 87, 88
  optimal time for, 9–10, 59, 293
  teaching, 395–397
  time blocks for, 84, 292
  see also Review for exams; Test preparation
Study lounges, 291, 297
Study notes, 298–299
Subheadings, 206
Subject areas
  recognizing structures of, 176
  use of diagrams in, 156
Summarizing
  as a comprehension strategy, 108, 201, 208, 235–237, 239, 244–246
  in essay tests, 364
  lectures, 280–281

Table of contents, 203–205
Tape-recording, of lectures, 109
TAP (test-appropriate practice), 297, 304–319
Teaching, 8, 393–398
Term papers, 89–91
Test anxiety, 330–334
  causes of, 37, 327, 333
  coping with, 37, 333–334
  and performance, 332
  physiological reaction in, 331–332

Test preparation, 36–37, 326–334
  emotional, 330–334
  inadequate, 123
  memorizing information, 20–22
  mental, 326
  and performance, 53–54
  physical, 328–330
  preparing practice tests, 333
  test anxiety and, 327, 330–334
  three components of, 326
  time line for, 89–91
  tiredness and, 329
  see also Review for exams; Studying
Test questions
  clues and information in, 338, 344
  concept items, 304, 305, 309–314, 343, 345–346
  essay items, 22, 360–366
  fact items, 304, 305, 306–308, 343–345
  key words in, 344–350
  main types of, 225, 304–305, 342–343, 348
  matching items, 354–357
  multiple-choice items, 22, 310, 350–354
  procedures and rules, 314–316, 317
  short-answer items, 359–360
  skill items, 304, 305, 314–319, 343, 346–348
  true/false items, 357
  see also Test strategies
Test results
  attributions and, 59–60, 327
  blaming the instructor, 59–60, 327
  effect of anxiety on, 332
  error analysis, 27, 366–370
  scoring methods, 336
  studying, 27
Tests
  practice, 333
  retake exams, 367
  self-, 37, 104, 396
  types of, 37, 53
Test strategies
  general, 334–366
  item-form, 342, 348–366
  item-type, 342–348, 343–348
  weak, 326
  see also Test questions; Test-taking
Test-taking
  careless errors in, 53–54
  distractions and, 329
  materials for, 330
  personal problems and, 54
  using representations in, 344–348
  see also Test strategies
Text aids, purposes of, 216, 217
Textbooks
  boring, 57
  emphasis in, 106
  reading, 199–201
Texts, determining the structure of, 203, 204, 207

Time, and money, 86
Time lines, 89–91
Time management, 9, 74–96
    for chores, 81, 93
    in college, 80
    control over, 78
    daily scheduling, 79–85, 88–92
    developing a block schedule, 35,
        81–85, 94
    estimating text reading time, 216
    financial considerations of, 85–86
    in high school, 80
    investment principles for, 79–96
    of leisure time, 84–85, 93, 96
    for long-term assignments, 89
    for mastering chess, 387
    for nontraditional students, 85
    not enough time, 60–61
    for other commitments, 81
    overviewing texts for, 215–217
    in preparing for tests, 36–37, 89
    principles to follow in, 79–96
    problems with, 86
    rewards for, 96
    scheduling early classes, 55, 59
    self-monitoring, 94
    semester planning, 89–91
    for study time, 84, 87, 88
    in taking tests, 336, 340–341
    taking tests, 340–341
    term papers, 89–91
    using DIFS, 370
    weekly scheduling, 91–92
    for working students, 81, 85–86
Topographical maps, using diagrams in, 156
True/false tests, 357

Underlining, noting in texts, 108

Values, 24

Weekly planner, 91–92
Will, defined, 46. *See also* Motivation
Working students, 81, 85–86
Writing
    essays, 22
    essay tests, 363–366
    from representations, 22
    summaries, 235–237
    summaries of lectures, 280–281
    using matrices in, 22